# VARIATIONS IN C

# VARIATIONS IN C

**SECOND EDITION**

STEVE SCHUSTACK

PUBLISHED BY
Microsoft Press
A Division of Microsoft Corporation
16011 NE 36th Way, Box 97017
Redmond, Washington 98073-9717

Library of Congress Cataloging in Publication Data
Schustack, Steve, 1952–
    Variations in C : building professional applications with
    Microsoft C / Steve Schustack.—2nd ed.
        p.        cm.
    Includes index.
    ISBN 1-55615-239-6 : $22.95
    1. C (Computer program language)        I. Title.
QA76.73.C15S37        1989
650'.028'55133—dc20                                        89-12615
                                                            CIP

Printed and bound in the United States of America.

1 2 3 4 5 6 7 8 9   MLML   3 2 1 0 9

Distributed to the book trade in the United States by Harper & Row.

Distributed to the book trade in Canada by General Publishing Company, Ltd.

Distributed to the book trade outside the United States and Canada by Penguin Books Ltd.

Penguin Books Ltd., Harmondsworth, Middlesex, England
Penguin Books Australia Ltd., Ringwood, Victoria, Australia
Penguin Books N.Z. Ltd., 182–190 Wairau Road, Auckland 10, New Zealand

British Cataloging in Publication Data available

**Project Editor:** Ron Lamb        **Technical Editor:** Mary Ottaway

*To my mother and father*

# Contents

# Foreword

C is a computer programming language whose name has no more exciting origin than the fact that C is a successor to an earlier language named B. But I like to think that C stands for craftsman—a competent artisan in control of the computer and the tools of programming, confident of his skill at his craft.

Steve Schustack is such a craftsman. He "speaks" C as if it were his native tongue, and he uses the language with the style and precision its originators intended. Not only that, Steve can communicate these qualities to other programmers. His list of successful corporate training programs attests to that.

I was among the many who encouraged Steve to make his knowledge and experience with real-world C available to a wider audience, so I was delighted when I received a draft of the manuscript that was to become *Variations in C*. The book is everything I'd expect from Steve—thorough, lucid, and utterly professional. Also down-to-earth and just plain practical.

But *Variations in C* is not for every programmer. It's definitely not for beginners, and it's really not for amateurs with little interest in machine-level functions. It's for serious programmers who want to produce business applications that will work so efficiently and so transparently that people will be willing to pay for them.

Steve really hasn't written about variations in C at all but about variations in the way people use C. Even a variation as simple as using C on different hardware or with a different compiler has a great deal to do with the programmer. The portability of C programs is as much a property of the way each programmer uses C as of the C language itself. C makes portability possible, but the programmer must bring that possibility to realization. In *Variations in C*, Steve simply teaches the programmer how.

In a very real sense, *Variations in C* is about style. C is known as a "powerful" language, but that power is undifferentiated. It can produce good or bad results. You can write a good program in any language, but it's easier in C than in most. You can write a bad program in any language, too, but it's a lot easier in C than in most. Steve Schustack teaches you how to write good programs. More than that, he teaches you how to stay out of trouble!

I've said that *Variations in C* is not a beginner's book, but I'd like to see beginners have it by their sides as they learn so they can develop elegance and precision in programming style right from the start. It's not an easy book, because applications programming isn't easy, but unlike some difficult books, it rewards those who devote themselves to its subject. If you're willing to take the time to understand each of Steve's carefully chosen examples, your style, and therefore your power in C, will grow steadily.

Programming is complicated, and because each program is a bit different from the previous one, magic formulas aren't possible. So Steve has written a guidebook, not a book of formulas. Many good programming books teach you how to do things in a specific language—only a few of the best teach you why you do them (or shouldn't do them). *Variations in C* is one of the best.

—Gerald Weinberg

# Preface

Because of its efficiency and portability, C has become the language of choice for professional software developers. It is being implemented in new environments almost daily to meet the need for compact, efficient code that requires little or no modification to run on a large variety of systems. I've written this book to enable you, the experienced programmer, to take advantage of this powerful development tool.

I've said that *Variations in C* is for the experienced programmer. However, it does not require knowledge of the C language. I'll teach you that as we go along. And you'll see the programming techniques you're learning used to develop a large, high-quality, interactive order-entry application that can be used as part of a business system.

The chapters in Section I will give you the skills you need to write useful programs with a powerful subset of C. Section II will then help you to extend your knowledge of C data structures and the program constructs used to implement them. All the examples used in these chapters, and indeed throughout the book, are oriented toward the development and maintenance of serious, real-world C applications.

In Section III, you'll meet the application that is central to this book: The Software Vendor Order-Entry Application, with over 1500 lines of source code. Rather than mystify you by including untaught features in the code, I use a few "stub" functions at this stage. These are replaced later in the book, as the relevant new topics are covered. The completed application is a fully functional order-entry program that you can use in your own systems.

Section VI discusses jobs formerly done primarily in assembly language—jobs that you can do more quickly in C and with more maintainable results. The linked-list data structure, dynamic allocation of memory, bit fields, and unions are all discussed in Section VI, where you can easily turn to them or skip them, depending on your needs. Performance-tuning techniques for optimizing the efficiency of your C programs are presented in the form of timing experiments that you can copy and extend.

The last chapter takes a serious look at OS/2 as an alternative that MS-DOS C software developers must consider. Microsoft C 5.1 supports OS/2 program development. Several options for porting applications from MS-DOS to OS/2 are discussed in this chapter.

The example programs used throughout the book are practical ones, and they will be useful to you in coding your own applications. Each example program rigorously follows the style rules for writing readable C code, so you will have little trouble maintaining or modifying the programs to suit your needs.

ANSI and Microsoft Corporation have changed the face of C. As a result, I've had to change my own programming style. I faced choices between the advantages of new syntax and functionality and potential incompatibility with older, perhaps-soon-to-be-obsolete C compilers. This book uses the new features of the ANSI standard C, which Microsoft chose to implement in version 5.1 of their C compiler. Where a new ANSI-motivated feature is presented in this book, the equivalent or nearly equivalent older-style C alternative is also described. The ANSI style is then used in subsequent example programs.

The computer I used for this edition was a Mega Comm Technology Professional 386, a PC/AT compatible with an Intel 80386 chip, 4 MB of RAM, and a 40-MB hard disk. All example programs were developed and tested using MS-DOS version 3.1 and OS/2 version 1.1.

If you have questions or comments about the programs in this book, please write to:

Steve Schustack
P.O. Box 99161
San Diego, CA 92109

I hope you will enjoy the second edition of this book and feel the same thrill I did when I discovered the infinite Variations in C.

# Acknowledgments

Many good people have contributed to the creation of the first and second editions of this book, and once again I take great pleasure in extending my appreciation to all of them. Thanks!

Those readers of the first edition who took the time to write to me to express their appreciation and suggestions belong at the top of my list.

Jerry Weinberg, my teacher and good friend of many years, and his wife Dani are sources of inspiration in my writing, learning, and teaching. Their philosophy and methods have contributed much, both to my career and to this book.

The people at Microsoft Press have earned my gratitude for their help with editing, layout, and production. Their dedication to quality, spirit of cooperation, and many hours of hard work continue to make it a pleasure to work with them. Dean Holmes, acquisitions editor; Ron Lamb, editor; and Mary Ottaway, technical editor, have all given superior support to this book and are dedicated professionals. Thanks to Mike Halvorson and Dave Rygmyr for superior technical assistance above and beyond the call of duty. Thanks also to Suzanne Viescas, Shawn Peck, Alice Copp Smith, Ellen Setteducati, Kathleen Atkins, Patrick Forgette, Cynthia Riskin, Jean Zimmer, Susan McRhoton, Lynda Twede, Debbie Kem, Cathy Thompson, Darcie Furlan, Peggy Herman, Becky Johnson, Russell Steele, Carol Luke, Mark Souder, and Joy Ulskey.

John Socha, author and assembler authority, generously provided the assembler code in Chapter 21. Brook Jarret helped with suggestions for the appendices.

Bill Gladstone of Waterside Productions continues to do great work, as always, as my publishing agent. His efforts laid the groundwork for this book.

Bill Morgan, with Mega Comm Technologies, the San Diego, California–based manufacturer of my fast and reliable MCT PRO-386 OS/2 and MS-DOS compatible computer, has been tremendously helpful with information and support.

# SPECIAL OFFER
## Companion Disk for
## VARIATIONS IN C, 2nd ed.

Tap directly into the power of all the programs and code segments from this book with the Companion Disk for VARIATIONS IN C, 2nd ed., now available from Microsoft Press in either 5.25-inch or 3.5-inch format. The companion disk supplies you with all the function and header files from the book, plus selected illustrative code segments. All C code is in uncompiled source form, and each program's text is stored in a separate ASCII text file, ready for you to edit and compile.

The book's entire order-entry application program—more than 1500 lines of source code—is also included on the companion disk. The completed application is a fully functional order-entry program that you can use in your own system. You can also adapt the program to a different application with little modification. Save yourself valuable typing and error-hunting time. With the Companion Disk for VARIATIONS IN C, you can get started right away.

Send your questions or comments about the files on the disk to Steve Schustack, P.O. Box 99161, San Diego, CA 92109.

The Companion Disk for VARIATIONS IN C, 2nd ed., is available only from Microsoft Press.

### Domestic Ordering Information:

To order, use the special reply card bound in the back of the book. If the card has already been used, please send $29.95, plus sales tax if applicable (CA residents 5% plus local option tax, CT 8%, FL 6%, KY 5%, MA 5%, MN 6%, MO 4.225%, NY 4% plus local option tax, WA state 7.8%), and $5.50 per disk set for domestic postage and handling charges. Mail your order to: Microsoft Press, Attn: Companion Disk Offer, 21919 20th Ave SE, Box 3011, Bothell, WA 98041-3011. Specify 5.25-inch or 3.5-inch format. Payment must be in U.S. funds. You may pay by check or money order (payable to Microsoft Press) or by American Express, VISA, or MasterCard; please include both your credit card number and the expiration date. Allow 2–3 weeks for delivery.

### Foreign Ordering Information (except within the U.K., see below):

Follow procedures for domestic ordering and add $8.00 per disk set for foreign postage and handling.

### U.K. Ordering Information:

Send your order in writing along with £27.95 (includes VAT) to: Microsoft Press, 27 Wrights Lane, London W8 5TZ. You may pay by check or money order (payable to Microsoft Press) or by American Express, VISA, MasterCard, or Diners Club; please include both your credit card number and the expiration date. Specify 5.25-inch or 3.5-inch format.

### Microsoft Press Companion Disk Guarantee

If this disk proves defective, send the defective disk along with your packing slip (or copy) to: Microsoft Press, Consumer Sales, 16011 NE 36th Way, Box 97017, Redmond, WA 98073-9717.

# S E C T I O N

# I

Section I explores C as a programming language. **Chapter 1** introduces C: how it arrived on the scene, its advantages and special features, and the importance of an ANSI C standard. **Chapters 2 through 5** provide a fast-paced introduction to the C language, at a level suitable for experienced programmers: **Chapter 2** deals with data types and the declaration and manipulation of variables; **Chapter 3** discusses C's operators and their use with data in constants and variables; **Chapter 4** presents the control-flow statements used to direct conditional execution and repetition; and, finally, **Chapter 5** analyzes the basic unit of all C programs, the function.

# About C

When you first heard about a new programming language called C, I suspect that you, like many others, may have asked, "Why do we need yet another programming language?" Well, there are actually several answers to that question.

## The Need for C

Systems programmers have long been forced to labor with assembly language in order to produce fast, compact code that doesn't waste the resources of the computer. But assembly-language code is cumbersome to work with, time-consuming to develop, and specific to the hardware and operating system for which it is written.

C was developed as an alternative to assembly language for coding at the system level. C's operators and statements are close to the computer's own machine instructions, yet C's data-handling and program-control constructs make it a high-level language. At last, system programmers have high-level benefits in a language that generates programs compact and fast enough for stringent operating-system efficiency requirements—benefits like more readable and modifiable code, to name but two.

Dennis Ritchie, working at Bell Telephone Laboratories, is credited with creating C around 1972, for use in developing the UNIX operating system. C evolved from a language called B, and B came from a language called BCPL. (C was briefly called NB, short for New B.) Use of C, except at Bell and a few universities, remained minimal until about 1981, when commercial interest in the language began to develop as a result of the promotion of UNIX as a "standard" operating system.

But the popularity of C has far outstripped that of UNIX. In fact, C has opened up a whole new software industry. C compilers have been created for most current operating-system and hardware environments, and new C productivity tools reach the marketplace every month.

## The Philosophy of C

As I've already mentioned, C has been called both a high-level and a low-level language. Its high-level aspects include support for a modular programming style, numerous data types, and a good set of control-flow statements. Its low-level side consists of powerful bit-level and memory-addressing data structures and operators closely tied to the capabilities of the underlying hardware.

C is so versatile and general-purpose that it can be used to control complex machinery, crunch numbers, play video games, or perform business accounting and inventory control. And C is not tied to any particular hardware configuration. In fact, C programs are executing right now in environments with no terminals, no printers, no disks, even no operating system. Can you picture such a system? Well, consider a C program controlling an elevator. The program controls the movement of the elevator and "listens" for inputs from the elevator's control buttons and other sensors. But that's all. Such a C program has little use for library functions that interact with a terminal or access data files!

C provides maximum support for modular programming, which speeds program development and simplifies maintenance since each module can be designed and tested independently. A modular program is one that is constructed from a set of small, independent functions, each of which does a single clearly defined job. High-level functions outline or manage the overall processing in a general way and call low-level functions to perform detailed data manipulations. The high-level functions don't care how the low-level functions do their jobs, just as long as the jobs get done.

Clearly, C's flexibility goes far beyond the norm. Many ways exist for doing almost any job in C. The right tools are there; we just need to learn how to get the most from them.

## C Source Code and Portability

Picture yourself for a moment as the owner of a successful software company. Nice? Well, yes and no. Since most programs are restricted to the machine or operating system (or both) for which they were compiled, you could be faced with a very difficult maintenance task. You will probably have to sell and maintain different versions of your programs for different operating systems and for each specific hardware configuration. Every time a new computer or operating system becomes popular, which happens surprisingly often, your programs will have to be modified if they are to continue to ride the wave of popularity. And when an established client upgrades to a more powerful computer installation, you may face costly software rewrites if you want the customer to continue using your programs.

Not only that, you'll want to continue to improve your programs and increase their capabilities, and the probability of programmer error when adding an enhancement to all those versions of all your programs is high. The cost of fixing problems *after* a sale is also high, both monetarily and professionally.

Well, if your programs are written in C, you've already solved most of these problems. Much of the rewriting of software to accommodate new and changing computer environments has been eliminated by C. (By *environment* here, I mean a specific combination of operating system, computer hardware, and C compiler.) Many (but not all) C programs can be compiled and executed in one environment and later recompiled and executed in a different environment, with exactly the same behavior in both. The principal factor in defining your program's portability is simply the amount of work it will take to port your source code from environment A to environment B. (The term *source code* refers to uncompiled C programs, in human-readable text form. C programs in compiled form are much more limited in their range of portability.)

How did C achieve such a high degree of source-code portability among different environments? Well, for one thing, many features included as part of other languages are not found in C itself. These features are instead supplied by the standard library that comes with your C compiler. This standard library permits you to deal with many variations in environment without any modification to the C language or your source code. You choose the proper compiler for a given environment, and the compiler takes care of the specifics.

## Function libraries

The standard library supplied with your compiler contains useful functions in object form, ready to be linked with and called by functions that you write yourself. These library functions extend, but are not part of, the C language. Standard library functions are available to interact with a user, access file data, manipulate strings of text, perform mathematical calculations, and handle many other routine tasks.

You can also write your own libraries of functions, or you can purchase specialized libraries containing business-oriented file-access methods, programmer-productivity tools, or graphics and screen-control routines, to name only a few. All of these additions extend and customize your C programming tools.

## File handling and device independence

File handling is also accomplished by library functions, rather than by C statements, which means that C programs are not limited to machines that support a specific type of file input and output. C programs can be *device independent*—that is, they can, without modification, accept input from a terminal, a modem, a disk file, or some other special device. The source of input is said to be *transparent* to the program because the program doesn't care where its data come from.

Device independence also applies to program output, which can be redirected to a disk file, a printer, a terminal, a modem, or some other device—again, without program modification. (The conversion of *PRINT* statements to *LPRINT* statements to divert a BASIC program's screen output to a printer is an example of the device dependence of BASIC programs.)

Input- and output-device information for C programs is usually given with the operating-system command that causes a program to execute. We'll discuss this in detail later on.

Of course, C programs are not *totally* device independent. For example, it would make no sense to try to clear the screen of a disk or to input data from a standard printer. Some device dependence is inevitable.

## How C Programs Are Created

As I've already noted, a C program is simply a set of independent functions (known as subroutines in some other languages) that call each other to perform some task. Each function may be written separately and saved in its own file.

But there's more to the story. Development of a C program isn't a one-step process. Like assembly-language code, C source code must be compiled and modules must be linked before a C program can be executed. Let's look at the sequence a little more closely.

- You use a text-editing utility like the MS-DOS *EDLIN* program to build or modify C programs in source form.

- Then you use a C *compiler* to translate C source code to *object code*. C object code consists of binary machine instructions, so you can't edit or list object files.

- Finally, you use an operating-system utility called a *linker* (supplied with your compiler) to link your object modules with one another and with the library functions called by your code. You invoke the linker only after all compilations have been completed. Its output is the executable program, saved in a file, ready for use on computers that use your operating system or one compatible with it.

## Standards for C

At this time, not all C compilers behave in exactly the same way. However, a document that describes a standard implementation of the C programming language has been developed. The goal of the standard is to eliminate ambiguities and extend the capabilities of the C language in order to promote portability, reliability, maintainability, and efficient execution of C programs. It describes in great detail how a generic C compiler should behave, including details of syntax, operators, expressions, statements, data structures, and standard library functions.

The X3J11 Language Subcommittee of ANSI (the American National Standards Institute) prepared a series of proposed C standards in draft form. Each draft was subjected to public review. This book teaches you to program in accord with this widely accepted standard and shows ways in which Microsoft C (version 5.1) diverges from it.

## Peeking Ahead

C programs look strange at first. They are terse, not wordy. They use symbols extensively: for example, { and } in place of the words *BEGIN* and *END* found in some other languages. Nor are C statements very much like English, which means fewer keystrokes for programmers and less valuable disk space devoted to storage on the computer, but less familiar-looking code. And C is a lowercase language. Where uppercase characters *are* used, they are distinct from lowercase characters in C source code, so the names *num*, *Num*, and *NUM* all represent different variables.

C supports many different data types, and the data type of a variable must be declared before the variable can be used. But C also permits many data conversions, making it a "weakly typed" language. This means that C expressions can "legally" combine different data types for such special operations as arithmetic on characters (as in the expression *'a'+1*, whose value is *'b'*).

Another C characteristic that may take some getting used to, depending on which programming language you have used in the past, is the fact that the index of the first element in any C array is always zero, not one. So expect to be "off by one" array element from time to time during your initiation into C.

More about all that later. For now, I hope I've given you enough information about this exciting and powerful programming language to make you want to read more. If you've already written a few C programs, you'll probably want to skim the next few chapters. For the rest of you, let's get down to business and learn how to "speak" C.

# Data Output
# and Input

This chapter will take you from the most basic C program possible to compiled programs that input and output various types of data. We have a lot to cover in between, so let's jump right in.

```
/* The most portable C program. It does nothing everywhere! It is an
 * empty shell, a bread sandwich with nothing inside.
 * Note: The function name main() must always be in lowercase.
 */

main()
    {
    }
```

You may think that was a joke, but it wasn't. Every C program *must* have a *main()* function. In this case *main()* does absolutely nothing and immediately terminates, returning control to the operating system, but it still constitutes a legitimate C program.

The first four lines of the program are a comment. Comments always begin with /* and must end with */. They can legally continue for many lines, but if you forget to close the last line with */, the rest of your program will become just one long comment!

The next line begins the function named *main()*. (Although all C programs are simply collections of functions that you write yourself or call from a library, only *main()* is a required function.) The last two lines hold an opening curly brace ({) and a closing curly brace (}), each indented three spaces. The curly-brace symbols act like the keywords *BEGIN* and *END* in other languages.

The style you'll learn in this book is to indent braces alone on a line so that you can easily locate them and the blocks of code they surround. Program format is of special importance with a language as terse as C. The compiler actually ignores most white space (indenting spaces, tabs, and skipped lines), so we're free to use spacing and indenting in any way we wish to help improve readability. (Use the tab key to ensure consistent indenting.) To see why a structured format is so important in C, look at the following two programs. Both of them are equivalent to the bread-sandwich program.

```
main(
      )     {
   }
```

```
main(){}
```

The first program is nearly incomprehensible. The second would work only in this bread-sandwich situation. Clearly, structure is going to be very important in helping us keep track of what's going on.

The example listings in this book will be indented in increments of three spaces, for reasons of page width. A five- or eight-space tab is perfectly acceptable if your viewing screen and printer output are at least 80 characters wide.

Now that we've dealt with the basics, let's see how to write and compile useful programs—programs that produce some output.

# Programs That Output Text

First we'll write a C program that outputs the names and telephone numbers of three people. We'll store the code in a source file named *phonenum.c*, and then we'll look at the simple series of commands used to compile, link, and execute it.

```
/* phonenum.c:  List of telephone numbers */

main()
    {
    printf("Telephone Numbers\n\n");
    printf("Lee Smith\t\t\t\t(619) 555-1234\n");
    printf("Pat West\t\t\t\t(206) 555-4321\n");
    printf("Chris Young\t\t\t\t(617) 555-4444\n");
    }
```

Here's how the output from our program will look:

```
Telephone Numbers

Lee Smith                       (619) 555-1234
Pat West                        (206) 555-4321
Chris Young                     (617) 555-4444
```

The term *printf()* is the name of a library function used for formatted printing. The character pair \n (read as "backslash n") is the abbreviation for a *newline* character. You may know this character as *line feed*. They are the same: The \n you output with *printf()* moves the cursor to the beginning of a new line. The symbol \t is the abbreviation for a horizontal tab character, which is expanded to eight spaces before it is displayed.

This source code provides another good example of the importance of a structured program format. The body of the *main()* function, which has four statements, could be replaced with a single statement but the sacrifice in readability is tremendous and would make the program difficult to debug and maintain.

## Producing executable code

We'll use the *EDLIN* text editor to create the *phonenum.c* source file that holds the statements from the first version of our sample program.

(Most other text editors and word-processing programs are equally suitable for editing C source code.) Just press the spacebar three times to indent lines 4 through 9. Your *EDLIN* screen will look like this:

```
C>EDLIN PHONENUM.C
New File
*i
        1:*/* phonenum.c:  List of telephone numbers */
        2:*
        3:*main()
        4:*    {
        5:*    printf("Telephone Numbers\n\n");
        6:*    printf("Lee Smith\t\t\t\t(619) 555-1234\n");
        7:*    printf("Pat West\t\t\t\t(206) 555-4321\n");
        8:*    printf("Chris Young\t\t\t\t(617) 555-4444\n");
        9:*    }
       10:*^C ——————— (Control-Break)
*e
C>
```

After you've finished editing, use the *CL* command to compile and link your C source file into an executable program, named *phonenum.exe*. (The *CL* command and file names may be entered in either uppercase or lowercase.)

```
C>CL PHONENUM.C
```

Following a successful compile and link, the executable program is saved in a file with the extension *.exe* (in our example, *phonenum.exe*) and may then be executed by simply typing the file name (without the extension):

```
C>PHONENUM
Telephone Numbers

Lee Smith                       (619) 555-1234
Pat West                        (206) 555-4321
Chris Young                     (617) 555-4444
C>
```

The *CL* command resembles the UNIX and XENIX *CC* commands, but the options (switches) are different.

## Capturing diagnostics and output

The operating system, in conjunction with the compiler, provides two output-redirection commands, > and >>, that permit program output to be diverted from the screen to the file or device whose name follows the redirection symbol. We'll discuss these commands further in Chapter 8, along with two additional redirection commands: < for redirecting input and ¦ for piping the output of one command as input into the next. For now, let's look at some simple examples of output redirection that can help us in developing and debugging C programs:

```
C>CL PHONENUM.C > PHONENUM.ERR
C>PHONENUM > PHONENUM.OUT
C>PHONENUM > LPT1:
```

The first command compiles and links the source code in *phonenum.c* and stores the compiler diagnostic output in *phonenum.err*. The second command executes the compiled program *phonenum* and sends the output to the disk file *phonenum.out*. The last command executes *phonenum* and sends the output to the printer.

If you use redirection to save the compiler's diagnostic output in a file, as in the preceding example, you can view the diagnostics as you correct the mistakes that caused the output. The easiest way to do this is to use your editor to read the saved output (in this case, *phonenum.err*) into your source file and then surround the copy of the diagnostics with /* and */, making it one big comment that you can use to remind you of the changes needed.

A couple of words of warning about output redirection. The > command creates an empty file into which output is directed. If a file by the name specified after the > symbol already exists, its old data are *erased*, so *be very careful* with >. The >> command appends output to the *end* of the file named after the symbol, creating a new file only if the named file does not already exist. Therefore, >> is both safe and handy for collecting the output of a series of programs into a single file.

## Special Characters in String Constants

A series of zero or more characters surrounded by double quotes (for example, "i") is called a *string constant*. You know from our *phonenum* example that messages you want printed can be surrounded by double quotes and passed as string expressions to the library function *printf()*. But what if you want to print a message that *contains* a backslash and some double quotes? Well, the backslash itself can take care of the problem by combining with the character following it to create a special abbreviation. You've already seen the backslash behave in a special way in the \n and \t abbreviations for newline and tab. In this next example, you'll see how two backslashes (\\) can be used to print a single backslash, \" to print a quotation mark, and \\n to print the symbol \n rather than newline. In order to print the program statement

```
printf("C no evil!\n");
```

as output, you could just call the *printf()* function like this:

```
printf("printf(\"C no evil!\\n\");\n");
```

Here's a list of the backslash abbreviations that are permitted in string constants:

| SYMBOL | OUTPUT | SYMBOL | OUTPUT |
|--------|--------|--------|--------|
| \\ | Backslash | \t | Horizontal tab |
| \b | Backspace | \n | Newline (line feed) |
| \r | Carriage return | \' | Single quote |
| \" | Double quote | \v | Vertical tab |
| \f | Form feed | \a | Bell (alert) |

## C A U T I O N

*Be careful not to confuse the slash (/) and backslash (\). The slash is the division operator; the backslash is used before other characters to give them a different meaning, or to continue a line of C source code. (See Chapter 6.)*

To output an ASCII character that cannot be represented as a printable ASCII character and has no abbreviation, you need to specify that character's ASCII value in octal (base 8) or hexadecimal (base 16) notation, using the appropriate backslash code. In octal notation, the backslash is followed by one to three octal digits (0 through 7), as in the following examples.

| OCTAL NOTATION | ASCII NONPRINTABLE EQUIVALENT |
|---|---|
| \0 | Null character |
| \33 | Escape character |
| \033 | Escape character |
| \24 | Paragraph (¶) character |
| \024 | Paragraph (¶) character |
| \5 | Club (♣) character |
| \005 | Club (♣) character |

## C A U T I O N

*Some older C compilers do not recognize hex notation for characters. Octal notation offers a portability advantage over hex for these older compilers.*

The paragraph and club characters are specific to IBM PCs. Other machines handle ASCII characters associated with the octal numbers 24 and 5 differently.

Most programmers do seem to prefer hexadecimal notation over octal. (If you have no preference, I recommend that you use hex.) In hexadecimal notation, the backslash is followed by an *x* and one to three hex digits (0 through 9 and A through F or a through f). Here are the same ASCII characters in hex notation:

| HEXADECIMAL NOTATION | ASCII NONPRINTABLE EQUIVALENT |
|---|---|
| \x0 | Null character |
| \x1b | Escape character |
| \x14 | Paragraph (¶) character |
| \x05 | Club (♣) character |

```
              C  A  U  T  I  O  N
```

*If additional characters immediately follow (no spaces) a one- or two-digit octal number or a hexadecimal number, the compiler will treat the additional characters as part of the notation, resulting in an unexpected character. For example, the string \x05Club is output as \lub because \x05C is the \ character. To avoid printing unexpected characters in such cases, supply three octal or hexadecimal digits. The string \x005Club results in the string ♣Club.*

## Identifiers and Data Types

By far the most important step a programmer can take to make C programs more readable and easier to modify is to use meaningful identifier names. Use of meaningful names for variables and constants helps shorten coding and debugging time by reducing confusion. It helps eliminate the kind of bug you really kick yourself for missing after you've wasted 12 hours hunting for it. One-letter identifier names were forced on us by toy languages; they make programs difficult to understand and therefore should always be avoided. C is a serious working language that allows you room for clarity, so take advantage of it!

*Misleading* identifier names also confuse program readers and writers alike. Misleading names, perhaps more than meaningless names, can lead to bugs that take hours to locate. Resist the temptation to reuse an existing variable for something other than what its name implies. Instead, declare a new variable with its own meaningful and honest name. You'll be glad later that you took the time.

```
              C  A  U  T  I  O  N
```

*Even though it's legal, don't use the underscore as the first character of a name. You risk conflict with a compiler- or linker-generated symbol.*

Identifier names must begin with a letter or an underscore (_), and can include numbers, as well as additional letters and under-scores. Two identifier names must differ within the first eight charac-ters to be recognized as different by most C compilers, although Microsoft C allows 31 significant characters in identifiers. C treats uppercase and lowercase letters in identifier names as distinct. (That is, b and B are not equivalent.)

Reserved words must not be used as identifier names, but they may be part of a longer name. Microsoft and other ANSI-compatible C compilers reserve the following 32 lowercase keywords:

| | | | |
|---|---|---|---|
| *auto* | *double* | *int* | *struct* |
| *break* | *else* | *long* | *switch* |
| *case* | *enum* | *register* | *typedef* |
| *char* | *extern* | *return* | *union* |
| *const* | *float* | *short* | *unsigned* |
| *continue* | *for* | *signed* | *void* |
| *default* | *goto* | *sizeof* | *volatile* |
| *do* | *if* | *static* | *while* |

and Microsoft C reserves these six additional keywords as well:

| | |
|---|---|
| *cdecl* | *huge* |
| *far* | *near* |
| *fortran* | *pascal* |

It is good C programming style to use lowercase letters for vari-able names and uppercase letters for the names of constants (see Chapters 9 and 11), to distinguish between them.

## Data types

The appropriate data type for a variable depends upon the range of values the variable must hold. Data types that can hold a wider range of values take up more memory than narrower-range data types, but they provide greater flexibility for data manipulation. Figure 2-1 on the following page shows C's standard simple data types. The ranges of permissible values may vary among compilers; these are for Microsoft C.

| DATA TYPE | BYTES REQ'D | MINIMUM VALUE | MAXIMUM VALUE |
|---|---|---|---|
| char | 1 | −128 | 127 |
| unsigned char | 1 | 0 | 255 |
| short or int | 2 | −32,768 | 32,767 |
| unsigned short | 2 | 0 | 65,535 |
| long | 4 | −2,147,483,648 | 2,147,483,647 |
| unsigned long | 4 | 0 | 4,294,967,295 |
| float | 4 | −3.402823466E+38 | 3.402823466E+38 |
| double | 8 | −1.7976931348623158E+308 | 1.7976931348623158E+308 |

FIGURE 2-1
*C's standard data types and their ranges*

The *unsigned* modifier means that the value won't be negative. The floating-point type *double* allows approximately 15 significant digits, whereas type *float* allows only seven.

If not handled carefully, C's *int* data type can limit source-code portability. Microsoft C on 16-bit and 32-bit CPUs considers type *int* as equivalent to *short*, as shown in Figure 2-1. Some non-Microsoft C compilers on 32-bit machines treat *int* as equivalent to type *long*. Similarly, *unsigned int* may be equivalent to either *unsigned short* or *unsigned long*. Therefore, it is good style to use *short* or *long*, explicitly, in C *int*-type declarations.

## Numeric constants

But which data type does C assign to numeric expressions whose values never change? Let's turn from variables for a moment and see how we represent constant expressions in C.

A series of digits 0 through 9, possibly preceded by a minus sign, is called an *integer constant*. Commas may not be included in integer constants. Here are some typical examples:

| | |
|---|---|
| 24 | +10596 |
| −4587 | 7 |
| −17 | −30545 |

The range of values an integer constant may take on and the amount of memory consumed to hold that value are the same as for an *int*-type variable: that is, two or four bytes, depending upon the CPU and brand of compiler being used. Integer constants too large to store in an *int* variable automatically become type *long*. The letter *L*, when used as the last digit of an integer constant, makes the constant type *long* even if its present value would fit the *int* type. Here are some examples of long constants:

```
546767
0L
-35L
```

Not all constants in our programs are whole numbers, however; sometimes we need to use fractions. C has provided a special data type called the *floating-point constant* to handle fractional values. Although C has two sizes of floating-point variables (*float* and *double*), it has only one size of floating-point constant: type *double*, eight bytes wide.

You can choose between two floating-point notations: decimal and scientific. Here are some examples of the familiar decimal notation:

```
24.387551
-1.0
-1763.73
```

The less familiar scientific notation (*E notation*) uses powers of base 10 to express very large numbers. An E value consists of a decimal constant multiplied by an integral power of 10 (positive or negative), like this:

| E NOTATION | INTERPRETATION | VALUE |
| --- | --- | --- |
| 1E5 | $1.0 \times 10^5$ | 100,000.0 |
| -1.3495E3 | $-1.3495 \times 10^3$ | -1,349.5 |
| 4E-2 | $4.0 \times 10^{-2}$ | 0.04 |

## Declaring variables

C requires that all variables be *declared* before they are used. A declaration is simply a statement of the data type, followed by one or more variable names separated by commas and ending with a semicolon.

Here are some examples of variable declarations and the sorts of descriptive comments you should get into the habit of including in your programs:

| DECLARATION | COMMENT |
|---|---|
| char product_code; | /* one-digit product code */ |
| long salary; | /* type long necessary for higher salaries */ |
| double tax_rate; | /* double-precision sales tax (use .06 for 6%) */ |

### Declarations with initializers

The value of a variable is not predictable unless it has been *initialized*, or assigned a starting value. Fortunately, C gives you the option of assigning an initial value to a scalar (non-array) variable right in the declaration.

> # C A U T I O N
>
> *Be sure the initializing expression is of the same data type as its variable; otherwise, the compiler will send you an error message.*

The syntax is simply *variable = initializing_expression*. Each initializer applies only to the variable it follows and not to any others in the same declaration. The following example initializes all variables declared except *not_init*:

```
short not_init, number_of_accounts = 50;
short account_months = number_of_accounts * 12;
long total_salary = 0L;
double sales_tax = .06;
```

## Formatted input and output

Values that remain locked within the computer do us little good. We need to find ways to send data to our programs and get information back. Let's take a look at how C handles these activities.

The library functions *scanf()* and *printf()* control formatted input and output, respectively. You've already seen how to call *printf()* to display characters and strings of characters. The values listed in parentheses after the name of the function to be called are the *arguments* to the called function. Basically, arguments are the vehicle by which a function sends values to a subfunction it calls.

The first argument to both *printf()* and *scanf()* is the format string that allows you some control over the size and appearance of output and input data. The format string is made up of one or more format specifiers, literal text, or both. (So far all the arguments we've passed to *printf()* have been only literal text.)

The format specifiers that dictate the types of data to be input by *scanf()* or output by *printf()* consist of a percent sign and a character code for the data type (for example, *%d* for integer). The format specifier may also dictate field width (*%3d* for a 3-digit integer), precision (*%12.5f* for 5-decimal accuracy), and justification (*%-4d* for a 4-digit integer, left justified). Figures 2-2 and 2-3 show some of the more common C numeric format specifiers and their meanings. (See Appendix F for complete listings.) Notice the effect of the *%u* specifier on a negative value and the different behavior of the *%2d* specifier with output and input values too wide for the format.

| DATA | FORMAT SPECIFIER | OUTPUT | FORMAT DESCRIPTION |
|------|------------------|--------|--------------------|
| 234 | *%d* | 234 | Decimal (base 10) integer |
| 191543L | *%ld* | 191543 | Long decimal integer |
| −1 | *%u* | 65535 | Unsigned decimal integer; unexpected output |
| 7 | *%4d* | 7 | 4-digit decimal integer, right justified |
| 1985 | *%2d* ' | 1985 | 2-digit decimal integer; value too wide, but is output completely |
| 8 | *%03d* | 008 | 3-digit decimal integer, zero filled |
| 2 | *%−03d* | 200 | 3-digit decimal integer, left justified, zero filled |
| 2.735 | *%f* | 2.735000 | Floating-point decimal, zero filled to default precision (6) |
| 3.18 | *%5.1f* | 3.1 | 5-digit, floating-point decimal, one decimal place |
| 10000.0 | *%e* | 1.000000e+004 | Scientific notation |

FIGURE 2-2
*Format specifiers for numeric output using* printf( )

| DATA | FORMAT SPECIFIER | INPUT | FORMAT DESCRIPTION |
|------|------------------|-------|--------------------|
| 234 | %d | 234 | Decimal (base 10) integer |
| 191543L | %ld | 191543 | Long decimal integer |
| −1 | %u | 65535 | Unsigned decimal integer; unexpected input |
| 7 | %4d | 7 | 4-digit decimal integer |
| 1985 | %2d | 19 | 2-digit decimal integer; last two digits not input |
| 2.735 | %f | 2.735 | Floating-point decimal |
| 3.18 | %5f | 3.18 | 5-digit floating-point decimal |
| 10000.0 | %e | 1.0e4 | Scientific notation |

FIGURE 2-3
*Equivalent format specifiers for numeric input using* scanf( )

Don't let all this overwhelm you. You'll see plenty of examples as we go along. We'll start with some simple ones.

The following program declares a *short* variable named *number*, assigns the value 7 to it, and prints *number*'s value and then its value multiplied by 2:

```
/* Assign value to short int variable and display it using formatted output. */

main()
    {
    short number;        /* declare name and type of number to display */

    number = 7;                            /* assign integer 7 to number */
    printf("Number is now %d.\n", number);    /* display messages and values */
    printf("%d * 2 = %d\n", number, number * 2);
    }
```

A format string with more than one format specifier will cause the input or output of more than one piece of data. In the preceding example, the first call to *printf()* uses one *%d* format specifier to output *number*'s value. The second call to *printf()* must output two values, so the format string has two *%d* format specifiers. In the output, each of the specifiers is replaced by a number, like this:

```
Number is now 7.
7 * 2 = 14
```

In this next program, you see the input and output of both *long* integer and *double* floating-point data. (The scalar arguments *lng* and *dbl* in *scanf()* require the & *address-of* prefix to let *scanf()* know where in memory to store the converted input. We'll discuss this in detail in Chapter 14.)

```
/* This program will input and output long and double data. */
#include <stdio.h>      /* we'll learn about this later */

main()
  {
  long lng;              /* declare variables and their types */
  double dbl;

  printf("Enter long int and double: ");     /* prompt for numbers */
  scanf("%ld %lf", &lng, &dbl);              /* input numbers */
  printf("You entered %ld %lf.\n", lng, dbl); /* display results */
  }
```

It is important that the specifiers in the format string match the data types of the arguments that follow, or results may become meaningless, at best.

# C O M M E N T

*Because some compilers on 32-bit systems distinguish between* short *and* int *data, you can ensure portability of your code by using* %hd *to input* short *integer values.*

## Portability of variables

We've already noted that not all C data types are implemented identically in all environments, which can lead to unpredictability in program behavior (otherwise known as portability concerns). Let's look at some examples.

Programmers concerned about portability used to ask the question "Will the program need to run on both 16- and 32-bit CPUs?" Now the issue is clouded. The PCs based on the Intel 80386 chip are 32-bit machines, yet *int*-type variables in Microsoft C programs that are compiled and executed on those PCs are still two bytes wide, not four. We have 32-bit machines behaving in some ways like machines with 16-bit architecture.

The DEC (Digital Equipment Corporation) VAX family, SUN Microsystems computers, and Apple Macintosh are all examples of 32-bit machines, on which *int*-type variables are four bytes wide, not two. Where I describe 32-bit behavior, I refer to that class of machines with their C compilers.

Programs that declare *int* and *unsigned int* variables can have portability problems because the range of values these variables may hold differs among environments. Compare the behavior of the following program on 16- and 32-bit systems:

```
main()
    {
    int count;              /* variable count is either 2 or 4 bytes wide */

    count = 32766;          /* assign (maximum value of a short) - 1 */
    printf("%d, %d, %d\n", count + 1, count + 2, count + 3);
    }
```

On a 16-bit CPU computer, the *int* data type is two bytes wide, the same size as a *short,* so the output is:

32767, -32768, -32767

(Notice that the commas in the format string are treated as literal text and are printed between the numbers listed.)

On a 32-bit computer, the *int* data type is four bytes wide, the same size as a *long.* The additional width of *int* on the 32-bit system prevents the integer overflow that we got on the 16-bit system, so the 32-bit output is:

32767, 32768, 32769

The integer overflow on 16-bit systems, caused in this case by the expressions *count+2* and *count+3,* is not considered an error and therefore goes unreported during program execution. (C unfortunately provides minimal run-time protection, trading it off for fast execution. This is a good example of the kinds of problems that can result.)

What would the behavior of this program be on 16- and 32-bit systems if *count* were declared as type *long*? The output would be the same on both machines, so the program becomes portable.

---

## C A U T I O N

*To avoid portability problems, do not use* int *type for counter variables. Use* short *or* long *instead.*

---

The *char* data type can also create portability problems because some C compilers treat it as *signed,* giving it a range of −128 through +127, while other C compilers treat it as *unsigned,* yielding a range of 0 through 255. The easiest solution to this potential problem is to make it a rule to store only ASCII characters or numbers in the range 0 through 127 in a *char* variable.

---

## C O M M E N T

*Type* char *is* signed *(−128 through +127) by default. The* CL *option* /J *causes* char *to be* unsigned *(0 through 255) by default. You can override either default by declaring* char *variables as* unsigned char *or* signed char.

---

The types *unsigned char, unsigned short*, and *unsigned long* are described in the ANSI X3 *C Standard* and are supported by Microsoft C as well as by most other C compilers. (The type *unsigned* is equivalent to *unsigned int* and is supported on all compilers.) It is good style to use the *signed* types over the *unsigned* types, except where *unsigned* offers some special advantage (for example, where no negative values are needed and you want to count to a higher positive value than the *signed* type would permit).

So far, we've limited our discussion of the input and output of numeric data to single values. However, much of our programming will involve *numeric expressions* containing more than one value. Because the techniques for managing these expressions are quite detailed, we'll cover them separately, in the next chapter.

# The Value of Expressions

In the previous chapter, you learned how to input and display values. Now you'll learn how to operate on C data to produce useful results. C provides an unusually rich set of operations for you to use in managing your data, but we'll examine only two of them here: performing arithmetic on numbers and accessing array elements.

## Operators, Operands, and Expressions

*Operators* are the symbols you use to specify the actions to be performed on data. They are the "verbs" of C. The values acted on by the operator or used by the operator to calculate a result are called *operands*. Depending upon the exact operator and the context in which it is used, C operators take from one to three operands. Unary operators take only one operand, binary (or dyadic) operators need two, and C has one ternary conditional operator ( ?:) that takes three operands.

```
       C  O  M  M  E  N  T
```

*It is good programming style to break up overly complex expressions that might be difficult to understand into smaller, more obvious ones by using intermediate variables.*

A variable or constant alone is called an *expression*. We use operators to combine these simple expressions into new and larger expressions. Any legal combination of constants, variables, and expressions joined by operators is also considered an expression. Here are some examples:

| EXPRESSION | TYPE |
| --- | --- |
| *9* | Constant |
| *quantity_ordered* | Variable |
| *(12 * dozens) + units* | Compound expression |

## Precedence and grouping

*Precedence* and *grouping* are terms we use to explain the way expressions involving two or more operators are evaluated. Precedence rules define the priority of an operator in relation to other operators in the same expression. The higher-precedence operation takes place first. The use of parentheses ensures that operations that would otherwise violate the rules of precedence take place in the order we desire. For example, the expressions *2 * 15 + 10 / 5* and *(2 * 15) + (10 / 5)* are equivalent, since the higher precedence of both multiplication and division over addition would make addition the last operation in either case. But the expressions *2 * 15 + 10 / 5* and *2 * (15 + 10) / 5* are not equivalent, since the parentheses cause the addition to be executed first in the latter example, yielding *10* rather than *32*.

Figure 3-1 lists the C operators and their actions in descending order of precedence. We'll look at specific examples as we go along.

| PRECEDENCE LEVEL | OPERATOR | ACTION |
|---|---|---|
| 15 | () [] -> . | Precedence, array subscript, structure pointer, structure member |
| 14 | ! ~ ++ -- -<br>(*type*) * & *sizeof* | Logical not, one's complement, increment, decrement, unary minus, data type, indirection, address-of, size of an object |
| 13 | * / % | Multiplication, division, modulo |
| 12 | + - | Addition, subtraction |
| 11 | << >> | Shift left, shift right |
| 10 | < <= > >= | Less than, less than or equal, greater than, greater than or equal |
| 9 | == != | Relational equal, not equal |
| 8 | & | Bitwise AND |
| 7 | ^ | Bitwise XOR |
| 6 | ¦ | Bitwise OR |
| 5 | && | Logical AND |
| 4 | ¦ ¦ | Logical OR |
| 3 | ?: | Conditional expression |
| 2 | = += -= etc. | Assignment |
| 1 | , | Comma |

FIGURE 3-1

*C operators in descending order of precedence*

Notice that the precedence and meaning of the minus (−) operator depend upon how many operands it has in the expression where it is used. With only one operand (−*num*), we have a unary minus with very high precedence; with two operands (*high* − *low*), the minus means subtraction and has lower precedence.

The grouping (sometimes called *associativity*) of operators controls the order of operations in an expression with two or more of the same operator or with operators of equal precedence. Most operators automatically group left to right. The exceptions are the unary operators, the assignment operators (the last expression in the following example), and the conditional operator, all of which group right to left.

| EXPRESSION | PARENTHESIZED EQUIVALENT |
|---|---|
| *balance – principal – interest* | *((balance – principal) – interest)* |
| *tax_pcnt / 100.0 * balance* | *((tax_pcnt / 100.0) * balance)* |
| *first = last = 0* | *(first = (last = 0))* |

All this seems clear enough, but what happens if your C operators have operands of two different data types? We'll discuss this addition of apples and oranges next.

# Data Type Conversions

How is an expression with an operator and two operands of different data types evaluated? Well, it's not as mysterious as you might have expected. C simply converts a copy of one (or both) of the operands to a common data type before the operation takes place. *Conversion* is automatic in these cases, and the new values are as equivalent as possible to the original ones. The operation you specified with the operator then takes place with the new data types, rather than the originals.

C performs any necessary data-type conversions *before* evaluation of an expression or assignment of a value to a variable. There are some rules that control conversions, but before we discuss them, let's look at how type conversion happens.

## How C converts data types

The combination of data of types *long* and *double* causes two conversions to take place in the assignment statement at the end of this code segment:

```
double rate;
long total, price;

    /* ... */
total = rate * price;  /* two conversions needed: one for * and one for = */
```

Before the multiplication is performed, C converts a copy of *price*'s value to type *double*. It then multiplies *rate* by the converted *price*; the result is, of course, type *double*. But to assign the result to *total*, C must convert that result to the same type as *total*, a *long*. Any fractional portion of the *double* result is simply truncated (discarded without rounding) during the conversion to *long*. Two different kinds of conversion occurred in this example: one to evaluate an expression (*rate * price*) and one to assign the result to a variable (*total*).

The evaluation of expressions containing a mixture of operand data types can be more complex than assignment conversion. For example, let's look at conversions among the integral data types *char*, *short*, *int*, *long*, and their *unsigned* counterparts.

Conversions among the signed and unsigned integral types *char*, *short*, *int*, and *long* may involve either promotion (conversion to a wider data type) or truncation. A change of value may or may not occur during promotion, but truncation always causes one or more of the *most significant bytes* of data to be discarded, which can mean a large change in value if the discarded bytes are non-zero.

## C O M M E N T

*Careful planning of data types to be used in arithmetic operations is very important for the success and efficiency of your program.*

Here is a list of the integral promotion and truncation conversions. (The term *sign bit extended* in the promotion conversion refers to the internal bit manipulation performed by the CPU to maintain the positive or negative sign of the value.)

| FROM TYPE | TO TYPE | NATURE OF CONVERSION |
|---|---|---|
| *char, short, int* | *int, long* | Promotion; sign bit extended to keep negative values negative |
| *int, long* | *char, short, int* | Truncation; high-order bytes discarded, low byte(s) kept |

The modifier *unsigned* with a data type means that the variable being declared will never be negative. This permits *unsigned* variables to have positive values twice as large as their *signed* counterparts. If you assign a negative value to an *unsigned* variable, that variable ends up with a large positive value that has the same internal bit representation as the negative value. Conversely, the assignment of a large *unsigned* value to a variable of a *signed* type may result in that variable being assigned a negative value.

The following program demonstrates the effects of the sign, truncation, and promotion conversions we've just discussed on a *short* integer named *short_var*:

```
/* Convert a short int copy of -3 to other integral types. */

main()
    {
    short short_var = -3;
    unsigned short uns_short_var = short_var;
    char char_var = short_var;                    /* truncate: 2 bytes to 1 */
    unsigned char uns_char_var = short_var;
    long long_var = short_var;                    /* widen: 2 bytes to 4 */
    unsigned long uns_long_var = short_var;

    printf("short_var = %d, uns_short_var = %u\n", short_var, uns_short_var);
    printf("char_var = %d, uns_char_var = %u\n", char_var, uns_char_var);
    printf("long_var = %ld, uns_long_var = %lu\n", long_var, uns_long_var);
    }
```

Here is the output from this program:

```
short_var = -3, uns_short_var = 65533
char_var = -3, uns_char_var = 253
long_var = -3, uns_long_var = 4294967293
```

Let's look more closely at the effects of type conversion on C's two floating-point data types, *double* and *float*. Variables declared as type *double* are double-precision and consume 8 bytes of memory. Type *float* variables are single-precision and occupy only 4 bytes of memory. Promotion of data from *float* to *double* simply adds insignificant zero digits after the last digit of the fractional portion and causes no change in value. Conversion from *double* to *float*, however, truncates some of the least significant digits and narrows the range of possible values considerably.

The Microsoft C compiler converts a *double* value to *int* type by first converting the *double* to *float* and then converting the *float* to *int*. Unfortunately, this intermediate conversion may result in a greater loss of precision than with other C compilers that convert directly.

The conversion of integral data to floating-point data is as simple as adding *.0* after the integer being converted, assuming the floating-point type has enough significant digits to hold the entire integer.

Now that you know *how* various conversions are performed, let's look at the rules for *when* they take place.

## Conversion rules

The rule for conversion in assignment expressions is that a copy of the value on the right-hand side of the assignment operator is converted to the type of the variable on the left-hand side. In the following example, the converted value of *small* is assigned to the variable *big*:

```
short small;
long big;

small = 32;     /* The short value 32 of small is converted to the */
big = small;    /* long value 32L and then assigned to big. */
```

The rules governing data conversions prior to the evaluation of an expression, known as the *usual arithmetic conversions*, are more complex. One or both of two kinds of conversion may take place prior to an expression's evaluation: *Promotion* ensures that operands are wide enough to be operated on; *type balancing* converts the narrower of the widened operands to the same data type as the wider. (Width of a data type simply means the number of bytes of memory a value of that type occupies.) Once both operands are wide enough and of the same type, the operation specified by the operator is executed.

Promotion conversions for expression evaluation in C programs follow these rules:

- All *char* or *short* operands are converted to *int*.

- All *float* operands are converted to *double*.

- All *unsigned char* and *unsigned short* operands are converted to *unsigned int*.

Type-balancing rules for expression evaluation are applied in the following order *after* promotion:

- If one operand is *double*, the other operand is converted to *double* and the result is *double*.

- Otherwise, if one operand is *unsigned long*, the other operand is converted to *unsigned long* and the result is *unsigned long*.

- Otherwise, if one operand is *long*, the other operand is converted to *long* and the result is *long*.

- Otherwise, if one operand is *unsigned int*, the other operand is converted to *unsigned int* and the result is *unsigned int*.

# The Assignment Operators

We talked about assignment earlier in relation to grouping and conversions. Now let's look at this operation in greater detail.

The simple assignment operator of C is the single equal sign (=). It is used to set the value of a variable. (C also has a set of shorthand assignment operators that we'll discuss later in this chapter.) The actual value assigned to the variable on the left side of the assignment operator is not just the value on the right side of the operator; it is the value on the right side *converted* to the data type of the variable on the left side. All assignment operators have equal and very low precedence, and group from right to left.

A powerful and unusual feature of the assignment operators is that they give assignment expressions a type and value that can be used in a larger expression. Multiple assignments and embedded assignments in a statement are permitted precisely *because* assignment expressions have a value, as in the following example:

```
main()
{
long big;                /* 4-byte integer */
short little;            /* 2-byte integer */

big = little = 131073;          /* multiple assignment */
printf("#1: big = %ld, little = %d\n", big, little);
big = (little = 50) * 1000;   /* embedded assignment */
printf("#2: big = %ld, little = %d\n", big, little);
}
```

These lines actually produce the following output:

```
#1: big = 1, little = 1
#2: big = -15536, little = 50
```

Notice that the multiple assignment in the example program causes *big* to be *1*. This is because *131073* is first assigned to *little*, but *little* is type *short* and can hold at most *32767*, so *little* receives only the low-order two bytes of *131073*, which contain *1*. Because assignment groups data from right to left, the value *1* is then assigned to *big*, even though *big* is wide enough to hold the original *long* value of *131073*.

The statement with the embedded assignment needed the parentheses in order to overcome the precedence of multiplication over assignment. Without the parentheses, *little* would be assigned the low-order two bytes of *50000*, and that value would be assigned to *big*.

The parentheses cause 50 to be assigned to the *short* integer *little*. The multiplication of the *short* integers 50 and 1000 overflows, yielding the *short* integer −15536, which is assigned to the *long* integer *big*.

The variable on the left side of an assignment operator *must* be a scalar variable or an element of an array (that is, it must refer to a manipulatable region of storage) and is called an *lvalue* (pronounced "ell-value"). The name of an array alone, without an index expression in square brackets, is not an *lvalue* and therefore cannot have values assigned to it.

## Assignment shorthand operators

Assignment shorthand operators are a more terse and efficient way of expressing some assignment expressions. They are used when the variable being assigned a value also appears in the expression on the right-hand side of the statement.

Shorthand assignment is more efficient than simple assignment and should be used wherever possible. Let's look at a few examples of shorthand assignments that produce the same results as the simple assignments in the right-hand column:

| SHORTHAND ASSIGNMENT | SIMPLE ASSIGNMENT |
|---|---|
| *num += 3;* | *num = num + 3;* |
| *val *= num + 4;* | *val = val * (num + 4);* |
| *ans /= div *= div;* | *ans = ans / (div = div * div);* |

Here is the complete list of assignment shorthand operators, including the bitwise operators, which we'll discuss in greater detail in Chapter 20:

| TYPE | OPERATORS |
|---|---|
| Arithmetic | +=, −=, *=, /=, %= |
| Bitwise | <<=, >>=, &=, ^=, != |

# Sequence Guarantees and the Comma Operator

C makes a rather fine distinction between order of evaluation of the terms of an expression and order of the operations that combine those terms. For example, the next statement calls three functions:

```
ans = func_one(num) + func_two(num) * func_three(num);
```

The *return values* from functions *func_two* and *func_three* are multiplied and then added to the return value from *func_one*. The order of operations on the return values is controlled by the precedence of multiplication over addition, but C makes no sequence guarantee about the order in which the *operands* of the multiplication and addition are evaluated. In other words, you cannot depend on *func_two* being called before *func_three* nor, in fact, on any of these three functions being called in any particular order. To assume an order would be dangerous since other compilers (or a new release of your present compiler) might generate a different order of calls.

Now, if the functions called in an expression are truly independent of one another, the order of calls doesn't matter. But if one function writes to a file another function will read or if two functions share some common data in memory, they are dependent, and the order of calls becomes important.

One way to guarantee sequence in C is to put the function calls in separate statements so that you gain control over the order in which they are called, like this:

```
hold = func_one(num);
ans = func_two(num);
ans *= func_three(num);   /* equivalent to ans = ans * func_three(num) */
ans += hold;              /* equivalent to ans = ans + hold */
```

Another approach is to use the *comma* operator to join two expressions into a single expression. The comma operator guarantees to evaluate the expressions from left to right. The type and value of the result are the type and value of the rightmost expression, the last one to be evaluated. For example, to exchange the values of the variables *curr* and *prev* in a single statement using the comma operator, you could use this code:

```
temp_swap = prev, prev = curr, curr = temp_swap;
```

```
              C   A   U   T   I   O   N
```

*Don't overwork the comma operator. It can make for very hard-to-read source code.*

## The Increment and Decrement Operators

Assignment expressions are not the only expressions that can change the value of a variable. Two other operators also have that ability.

The *increment* operator adds 1 to the value of a variable. Increment is written as a pair of pluses (++) before or after the variable name, with no spaces between. It is a unary operator, meaning that it acts on only a single operand. The action of the increment operator depends upon whether it is applied to its operand as a prefix or as a postfix:

```
++posit;      /* increment operator as a prefix */
posit++;      /* increment operator as a postfix */
```

Both statements achieve the same result: The new value of the variable *posit* is equal to its old value plus 1. But if you use increment as a prefix, the variable is incremented before its value is used in the surrounding expression. If you use it as a postfix, the increment occurs after the variable being incremented is used and before the next sequence-guarantee point. Here are a couple of examples:

```
count = 1;
flag = count++;  /* equivalent to flag = 1, count = 2; */
flag = ++count;  /* equivalent to count = 3, flag = 3; */
```

The *decrement* operator is used to subtract 1 from its operand. The syntax and behavior of the decrement operator, a pair of minuses (−−), are the same as for the increment operator.

Increment and decrement both assign values to their operands, which means that their operands must be *lvalues* or your compiler will reward you with an error message:

```
--(qty * 3);    /* will produce error message: */
                /* error C2105: '--' needs lvalue */
```

Use of the variable being incremented or decremented a second time in the same expression, before a sequence guarantee, creates ambiguous code that will behave differently in different environments, so don't do it! For example, the following two statements could set *junk* to 1 or 3, depending upon whether or not *bad* is incremented before the second *bad* is multiplied by 2.

```
bad = 0;
junk = ++bad + 2 * bad;
```

## One-Dimensional Arrays

An *array* is a variable that holds one or more values in ordered sequence. These values are called *elements*, and they must all have the same data type. To declare a variable as an array, you supply an integer-constant array dimension in square brackets (*[]*) after the name of the variable. You cannot declare an array's dimension with an expression containing a variable; only constant expressions are permitted. Arrays can be multidimensional and of any type (we'll discuss those later in this chapter), but for now we'll stick with simple one-dimensional arrays.

Let's look at a 30-element array of *short* integers named *orders* and an 81-byte *char* array named *buf*. They're represented diagrammatically like this:

```
short orders[30];
```

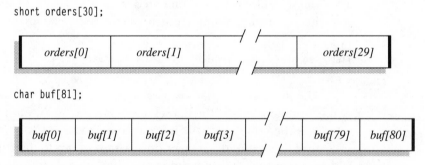

```
char buf[81];
```

You'll notice that the *index* (the subscript in the square brackets) of the first element of the array is always 0, not 1. (Arrays are referred to as *zero-origin*.) Thus, the index of the last element of an array is one less than the declared dimension of the array.

If you forget that the index of the first element of an array is zero, you may fall victim to a class of errors called "off by one." Not using the zeroth element of an array is harmless (and can sometimes even yield more efficient code because it eliminates repeated addition and subtraction of 1 to compensate for the zero origin). However, if you try to use an element beyond the declared dimension of the array, you risk a nasty bug—one that will not be reported to you by the compiler or even be evident during execution. Since your programs are not blocked from accessing nonexistent array elements, no error message is produced, but other types of program errors usually result. Checking for indexes that exceed array bounds is an option provided by many languages, but it is not present in C at this time for efficiency reasons. Because of this, you should be certain that you always access arrays properly.

The subscript operator ([]) is used to access a single element of an array. All array accesses in C must be element by element; no C operator will examine or change more than a single element of an array at a time in any statement. You should usually set up a loop when you need to operate on all elements of an array. (However, you can call library functions like *strcpy()* and *strncpy()* to copy arrays using a single statement.)

As you can see from the following examples, you can use the subscript operator for array accessing on either side of an assignment operator, and you can use any kind of integral expression as the index. Keep in mind that the zeroth element is first and that the index of the last element is the array dimension minus one.

```
curr_order_count = orders[order_num];
orders[order_num] = 0;
first_char = buf[0];
last_char = buf[80];
```

This next array assignment statement is a candidate for the *= shorthand operator:

```
ar[5 * x - y * y] = ar[5 * x - y * y] * 4;
```

The subscript $[5 * x - y * y]$ is evaluated twice here, but the following shorthand assignment evaluates the array subscript only once, with exactly the same results:

```
ar[5 * x - y * y] *= 4;
```

The increment and decrement operators are also very useful in array operations. This next example demonstrates how the position of the increment operator affects evaluation of the index:

```
pos = 1;
ar[pos++] = 11;    /* equivalent to ar[1] = 11, pos = 2; */
ar[++pos] = 33;    /* equivalent to pos = 3, ar[3] = 33; */
```

## Buffers and strings

The dimension of an array is used to reserve storage for the values of its elements. Often your code will use only some of the elements from the beginning of an array, so you'll need a way to keep track of how many data elements have actually been used. There are two groups of utility functions in the standard library to help you with this task for character arrays. Let's look at each of them separately.

You can designate a special element value, such as zero, to mark the end of the data elements in an array. The one-dimensional character array called a string uses a null character ( '\0' ) to mark the end of its data. (Of course, this means that the string itself can never contain a null character.)

The other option is to use the character-array buffer, which will hold as many of any character (including the null) as you like. However, you must store the length of your buffer in a separate variable, whose data type is usually *short* or *long*. The length of the buffer should never exceed the dimension of the array.

C gives the programmer control over which of these options is used with character arrays. Buffer-oriented library functions are quicker because they don't have to keep checking for null characters. But if you use buffers for faster data access, you increase memory requirements, because you must store a length for each buffer. If you use strings, you have a more standard, portable set of library functions to work with, and there is no need to clutter up your program with a bunch of string-length variables, but program execution may be a little slower.

As I've already mentioned, by C convention the null character is used to mark the end of the contents of a string: That is, a string is a *null-terminated array* of characters. (The value of the null character is numerically zero.) The following example builds a null-terminated string named *text* and uses the %s format to display it.

```
main()
{
char text[3];              /* declare 3-element char array */

text[0] = 'h';             /* single quotes make a char constant */
text[1] = 'i';             /* 2nd character has element index 1 */
text[2] = '\0';            /* null character ends text string */
printf("%s\n", text);      /* show each character before the null */
}
```

This program outputs just one word:

```
hi
```

Since C has no operators that can act on whole strings, the compiler provides library functions instead. (All Microsoft C standard library string functions have names that begin with *str*.) All library string functions expect, and depend upon, the presence of a null character to mark the end of each string. The string *hi* in the preceding example could have been copied to the string variable text and then changed to *higher* by using the library string copy and concatenation function calls:

```
char text[81];
```

```
/* ... */
strcpy(text, "hi");        /* copy 'h', 'i', '\0' to text */
strcat(text, "gher");      /* add 'g', 'h', 'e', 'r' to text */
                           /* now text equals "higher" */
```

Obviously, this is quicker and easier than assigning each element in text, as we did in the first example.

Library *buffer* functions treat the null character like any other character. (The buffer-oriented library functions have names that begin with *mem*.) However, they require that buffer lengths be passed as additional arguments. For example, this call to the library buffer function *memcpy* copies 6 bytes from the 7-byte string *higher* to *buf*:

```
memcpy(buf, "higher", 6);
```

## Breaking Long Strings and Statements

You can break a long statement in C code between words and continue the statement on the following line, provided the break is not in the middle of a quoted string. You can break source text at any point, including the middle of a string, by ending the line to be continued with a backslash (\) and continuing on the following line.

The compiler treats two quoted strings separated only by blank lines, tabs, or spaces as a single string. For example, these two string copy operations are equivalent:

```
strcpy(speech, "My fellow C programmers, we are gathered here tonight \
to launch the long-awaited new standard for the C programming language.");

strcpy(speech, "My fellow C programmers, we are gathered here tonight "
"to launch the long-awaited new standard for the C programming language.");
```

Now that you've learned some basic techniques for creating variables and managing data in C, we can turn to the statements that control the flow of execution in C programs. Because there is quite a bit to discuss, we'll devote a separate chapter to the subject.

# The Flow of Control

Statements are normally executed in the order they are entered in the program, unless a control-flow statement causes execution to jump to a different location. Machine languages have only a few simple control-flow commands, but higher-level languages like C have more variety, to facilitate modular block-structured programming. Let's look at C's control-flow commands individually.

## The *if* Statement

The *if* statement uses the value of a conditional expression to determine whether to execute another statement or to choose which of two statements to execute. Here are the two forms of *if* syntax:

```
if (condition_expression)      /* is expression non-zero? */
    statement_1;               /* then execute statement_1 */

if (condition_expression)      /* is expression non-zero? */
    statement_1;               /* then execute statement_1 */
else                           /* otherwise execute else's statement_2 */
    statement_2;
```

In the first example, *statement_1* is executed if *condition_expression* is non-zero; otherwise, the program moves on to the next executable line of code. In the second example, *statement_1* is executed if the value of *condition_expression* is non-zero; otherwise, the optional *statement_2* is executed.

Before we talk further about *if* statements, let's look at how condition expressions are evaluated.

## Comparing two values

C has six relational operators (see Chapter 3, Figure 3-1) that return the result of a comparison test on their two operands:

| SYMBOL | MEANING | SYMBOL | MEANING |
|--------|---------|--------|---------|
| == | Equal | >= | Greater than or equal |
| != | Not equal | < | Less than |
| <= | Less than or equal | > | Greater than |

If the condition tested for is true, the value of the relational expression is the integer 1; otherwise, the value is 0: *1* means true; *0* means false. Here are a few examples of relational expressions and their values:

| EXPRESSION | VALUE OF EXPRESSION | EXPRESSION | VALUE OF EXPRESSION |
|------------|---------------------|------------|---------------------|
| *3 == 5* | *0* | *1.32 <= 1.31* | *0* |
| *2 != −3* | *1* | *'A' < 'Z'* | *1* |

The relational operators are useful only for comparing scalar (non-array) values or single elements of an array. Two of the standard library's string functions, which we'll discuss in a moment, can be called to compare arrays of characters.

## Logical operators and expressions

C's three logical operators are used to combine true and false values, such as those from relational expressions. The result of any logical operation will be either *1* for true or *0* for false. C's logical operators are shown in the following table.

| OPERATOR | NAME | EXAMPLE | RESULT |
|----------|------|---------|--------|
| && | Logical *AND* | p && q | 1 if both *p* and *q* are non-zero, else *0* |
| ¦¦ | Logical *OR* | p¦¦q | 1 if either *p* or *q* is non-zero, else *0* |
| ! | Logical *NOT* | !p | 0 if *p* is non-zero, else *1* |

The *&&* and ¦¦ operators also possess two special features:

- Left-to-right sequence guarantee and sequence point

- Short circuit: Second operand not evaluated unless needed

Left-to-right sequence guarantee means that the left operand is always evaluated before the right operand. The order of evaluation can be important with operands that call functions or have side effects applied to them. (Side effects are changes an operator causes to the value of a variable. The *assignment, increment,* and *decrement* operators produce side effects.) Most operators don't have a sequence guarantee. For example, the following statement adds the return values from functions *func_1* and *func_2*; however, we can't rely upon which function might be called first.

```
sum = func_1(num) + func_2(num);        /* no sequence guarantee *
```

The fact that the *&&* and ¦¦ operators are sequence points simply means that all outstanding side effects will be applied to the first operand before the second is evaluated. In other words, the side effects are completed *before* the operation is executed. Let's look at an example. The next code segment tests for a newline character at the end of the string *text* and increments *full_lines* if the character is found:

```
if (text[pos++] == '\n' && text[pos] == '\0')
    ++full_lines;           .
```

The *&&* sequence point guarantees that the *pos++* increment in the first expression will happen before *text[pos]* is compared with the *'\0'* in the second expression.

The *&&* and ¦¦ operators have an interesting and useful conditional aspect, as you can see from the following segment:

```
if (elem_count < array_dim && array[elem_count] > 0)
    ++positives;
```

If the first expression, *elem_count < array_dim*, is false *(0)*, then the second expression, *array[elem_count] > 0*, is not evaluated! This is the short-circuit feature. It's practical and efficient, because if the value of the first expression in a logical *AND* condition is *0*, the result of the entire expression must be *0*, regardless of the value of the second expression. The ¦ ¦ (logical *OR*) operator short-circuits if its first operand is *non*-zero, because the result of the entire expression will have to be *1*, regardless of the value of the second operand.

## Comparing two strings

The number and power of string functions have benefited from the influence of ANSI definitions of standard library functions. Nowhere is this more evident than with functions that manipulate and test the contents of strings:

| FUNCTION | ACTION |
|---|---|
| *strcmp(s1, s2)* | Compares two strings and returns *0* if strings *s1* and *s2* are equal; *> 0* if *s1 > s2*; and *< 0* if *s1 < s2*. |
| *strncmp(s1, s2, n)* | Compares up to *n* characters of two strings and returns same values as *strcmp( )*. |
| *stricmp(s1, s2)* | Compares two strings without regard to case and returns same values as *strcmp( )*. |
| *strnicmp(s1, s2, n)* | Compares up to *n* characters of two strings without regard to case and returns same values as *strcmp( )*. |
| *strstr(s1, s2)* | Returns address of first occurrence of *s2* in *s1*, or *NULL* (zero) if *s2* is not found in *s1*. |

In the following example, the strings *curr_name* and *prev_name* are compared; if they are equal, a message is printed.

```
char curr_name[40], prev_name[40];

    /* ... */
if (0 == strcmp(curr_name, prev_name))
    printf("Current and previous equal.\n");
```

In the next example, the third, fourth, and fifth characters of the string *part_id* are compared with *"BAA"* to see whether they are higher in the ASCII coding sequence. If they are greater than or equal to *"BAA"*, a message is printed.

```
char part_id[20];          /* part number */

if (strncmp(&part_id[2], "BAA", 3) >= 0)
   printf("3rd, 4th, and 5th characters in part_id >= BAA.\n");
```

Notice the unary *address-of* operator (&) used before *part_id[2]* in the *if* statement. The library string functions *strcmp()* and *strncmp()* (among others) expect two arrays of characters to be passed. But passing an array argument does not transfer the entire array to the called function; it transfers only the memory address of the first byte of the array. Used as an argument to a function or within another expression, the name of an array is therefore equivalent to the address of its zeroth element. (More on this in Chapter 15.) For example, the address of the first character of a string named *part_id* could be expressed in two ways:

```
&part_id[0]          /* avoid this method */
part_id              /* this is the preferred method */
```

To pass the address of the third character of *part_id* as an argument, you would use:

```
&part_id[2]      /* remember: part_id[0] is the first character */
```

The combination of relational operators and library functions should give you plenty of comparison tools to work with, but if they still aren't enough to do what you have in mind, you can always write your own specialized functions.

## Compound statements as blocks

To control execution of a set of statements using an *if* or other control-flow statement, you must surround the set with a pair of curly braces (*{}*). We call such a set of one or more statements surrounded by curly braces a *compound statement*. A compound statement is, for purposes of syntax, considered a single statement. No semicolon is needed to end a compound statement, since the closing curly brace (*}*) does that job, as in this next example:

```
if (condition)          /* is condition non-zero? */
   {
   statement_1;          /* yes. execute statements 1 and 2 */
   statement_2;
   }
```

*(continued)*

*continued*

```
else
    {
    statement_3;              /* no. execute statements 3 and 4 */
    statement_4;
    }
```

The value of this syntax will become apparent in this next section, where we look at controlled statements that are themselves control-flow statements.

## Nesting and chaining

One of the powerful aspects of C syntax is that it allows for statements within statements. The *if* and optional *else*, together with the statements they control, actually form a single statement. But either of the statements controlled by *if...else* may also be an *if...else* statement. When an *if...else* statement is controlled by a surrounding *if...else* statement, like the one here, it is known as a *nested if* statement:

```
if (expression_1)
    {                         /* Style rule: */
    if (expression_2)         /*    Surround nested if with {} to */
        statement_1;          /*    prevent accidental mismatch of */
    else                      /*    an else with the wrong if. */
        statement_2;
    }
else
    statement_3;
```

If *expression_1* is zero, *statement_3* is executed and not *statement_1* or *statement_2*. If *expression_1* is non-zero and *expression_2* is non-zero, *statement_1* is executed and not *statement_2* or *statement_3*. If *expression_1* is non-zero and *expression_2* is zero, *statement_2* is executed and not *statement_1* or *statement_3*.

The *else if* construct is used to choose one of a set of actions based on conditions that are tested in a given order (hence the term *chaining*). The *else if* is not actually a new statement; it's merely a construct that bends the indenting rules in order to resemble the *case* statement found in some other programming languages. (The *switch* statement, discussed later in this chapter, is C's *case* construct.)

```
/* Case_like if statement */          /* Equivalent else_if construct */

if (expression_1)                     if (expression_1)
   statement_1;                          statement_1;
else                                  else if (expression_2)
   {                                     statement_2;
   if (expression_2)                  else if (expression_3)
     statement_2;                        statement_3;
   else                               else
      {                                  statement_4;
      if (expression_3)
        statement_3;
      else
        statement_4;
      }
   }
```

# Loop Statements

The *if* statements we've been discussing are used to conditionally execute one or more statements just once. But what if you want one or more statements to be conditionally executed over and over, as long as a condition expression remains non-zero? Let's take a look at how C handles such *loops*.

## The *while* statement

*Loop statements* are used to execute a statement repeatedly as long as a condition expression, known as the *loop test,* is non-zero. The statement that is executed repeatedly is called the *loop body*. The loop body can be a simple or compound statement or the null statement, about which you will learn more shortly. Here is the syntax of the *while* loop statement:

```
/* The while statement: If the condition_expression test is */
/* non-zero, then execute body_statement and repeat. */

while (condition_expression)
   body_statement;
```

The *while* statement tests the condition at the top of the loop before executing the body of the loop. If the *while* test is non-zero, the body is executed once and the test is repeated. If the test is non-zero again, the body is executed once more and the test is repeated. This process continues until the test expression evaluates as zero, in which case the loop terminates and the statement following the end of the loop is executed.

We've seen how the function *scanf()* can be used to input long integers (Chapter 2), but so far we've ignored the return from *scanf()*, which is the count of the pieces of data successfully input according to the format specifiers in the format string. Now let's see how we can make use of that return value in a program that acts like an adding machine: It accepts as input as many long integers as you care to supply, and outputs their total value. When you input a 'q', *scanf()* returns a 0 because a letter cannot be read as a long integer—the type required by the format specifier.

```
/* Adding machine: This program will input and add long integers. */
#include <stdio.h>

main()
    {
    long number, total = 0;

    printf("Enter numbers to add, or q to quit.\n#: ");
    while (1 == scanf("%ld", &number))
        {
        total += number;
        printf("#: ");
        }
    printf("Total: %ld\n", total);
    }
```

The interaction produced if you use this program to add *123* and *987* looks like this:

```
Enter numbers to add, or q to quit.
#: 123
#: 987
#: q
Total: 1110
```

The *while* loop makes its test (in this case, on the value *scanf()* returns) before each execution of the loop body. But suppose you want to make the test *after* execution of the body. Let's see how you can do this.

# The *do* statement

The *do...while* loop test is made *after* the body is executed, at the bottom of the loop, so a *do...while* loop will always execute at least once. Here is the syntax of the *do...while* loop:

```
/* The do...while loop: Execute loop body. If the */
/* condition_expression is non-zero, then repeat. */

do
    body_statement;
while (condition_expression);      /* caution: don't forget
                                      the semicolon here */
```

Let's see how we can modify our adding-machine program to use the *do* statement.

```
/* Adding machine, using do...while */
#include <stdio.h>

main()
    {
    long number, total = 0;
    int more = 1;              /* initialize true/false flag */

    printf("Enter numbers to add, or q to quit.\n");
    do
        {
        printf("#: ");
        if (1 == scanf("%ld", &number));
            total += number;
        else
            more = 0;
        }
    while (more);
    printf("Total: %ld\n", total);
    }
```

(Note that the *do...while* loop test, (*more*), could also have been written as (*more == 1*) or (*more != 0*), with no change in the program's behavior.)

Both the *while* and the *do...while* loops are simple combinations of a loop test and a loop body. However, there is one other type of loop, the *for* loop, that has additional components.

## The *for* statement

The *for* loop is used to count from a starting value to an ending value, or until some condition becomes false. To accomplish this, the *for* loop has two features not found in the *while* loop: an *initializing expression* and a *step expression*.

```
for (init_expression; test_expression; step_expression)
    body_statement;
```

The *for* initializing expression is evaluated once and only once, as the first action of the loop. The loop test is made at the top of the loop after the initializing expression is evaluated. If the test is non-zero, the loop body is executed and then the step expression is evaluated. (Even though initialization has already been performed, if the test fails before the first pass through the *for* loop, the body is not executed and control passes out of the loop.)

The second and all subsequent iterations of the *for* loop repeat the pattern: test, body, step. The loop terminates when the test is zero. Like the *while* loop, the *for* loop guarantees that the condition was non-zero immediately before each execution of the loop body. This next example shows a *for* loop that counts from 1 to 3 and in the body of the loop prints the value of *loop_counter*:

```
main()
{
short loop_counter;    /* declare counter */

/* Count from 1 to 3. */
for (loop_counter = 1; loop_counter <= 3; ++loop_counter)
    printf("%d\n", loop_counter);
printf("After loop, %d\n", loop_counter);
}
```

Notice that because *loop_counter*'s value after the loop is executed three times is the first value that caused the loop test to fail, *four* lines are output by the program above:

```
1
2
3
After loop, 4
```

Which loop statement is right for a given job? Well, the choice is really fairly straightforward. The *for* loop is always preferable if the loop requires initialization, a step expression, or both. However, if neither is needed, use a *while* loop, unless the test must be made after the body of the loop, in which case use a *do...while* loop.

## The Null statement

The following code segment strips leading spaces off the character string named *text*. Notice that the body of the first *for* loop is a *null statement*, created by the semicolon indented alone on the line following the *for* expressions—that is, the semicolon creates an empty statement that serves as the loop body. This construct is useful when all the conditional work is done by the test and step portions of the loop.

```
/* Loop until a nonspace character (may be null) is found. */

for (last_space = 0; text[last_space] == ' '; ++last_space)
    ;                                    /* null statement for loop body */

/* strlen() returns the index of text's null character. */
len_text = strlen(text);                 /* get string length of text */

/* Loop: move characters back to replace leading spaces. Notice the use
 *    of the comma operator to perform two initializations and two step
 *    expressions in each loop.
 */
for (from_pos = last_space, to_pos = 0;  /* loop initializer */
    from_pos <= len_text;                /* loop test */
    ++from_pos, ++to_pos)                /* loop step */
        text[to_pos] = text[from_pos];   /* loop body */
text[to_pos] = '\0';                     /* new end of string for text */
```

Actually, all three expressions that follow the keyword *for* are optional, but if they are omitted, the semicolons are still required as placeholders. For example, the next program has a *for* loop with no initializing expression. It inputs a number to start from and then counts down to zero.

```
main()
    {
    short count_down;

    printf("Enter number to count down from: ");
    scanf("%hd", &count_down);
    for (; count_down >= 0; --count_down)          /* no initializer */
        printf("%d\n", count_down);
    }
```

If you were to enter *4* at the prompt, the output from this segment would look like this:

```
Enter number to count down from: 4
4
3
2
1
0
```

# The *switch* Statement

The *switch* statement is used to transfer program control to a labeled *case* statement within the compound statement that follows it. The C *switch* statement behaves much like the *case* statements other languages use: It lets you choose among an arbitrary number of actions on the basis of the value of an integer expression that is matched against the *case label constants*. (No two case label constants may have the same value in a *switch*.) If no label is equal to the *switch* expression, program control is transferred to the *default:* label, if one has been supplied. Otherwise, control passes to the next executable C statement after the body of *switch*.

The *switch* statement is executed starting from the matching label and continuing until control is explicitly transferred out of *switch* by the *break* statement, which causes the program to jump to the first statement after the body of *switch*. Without an intervening *break* statement, control simply flows into the *case* statement following the one that matched successfully.

```c
/* Prompt for command; then call appropriate function to do it. */

main()
    {
    short command;
    int rtn;

    do              /* loop until quit command given */
        {
        printf("CUSTOMER DATA MANAGEMENT MENU\n\n");
        printf("1. List\n2. Add\n3. Change\n4. Quit\n\t#: ");
        rtn = scanf("%hd", &command);
        if (rtn == 0)
            command = 0;    /* unknown command */
```

*(continued)*

*continued*

```
        else if (rtn != 1) /* end of file reached */
            command = 4;    /* quit */
        switch (command)
            {               /* begin switch statement body */
            case 1:         /* list */
                list_cust(); /* call list_cust function */
                break;       /* don't allow add_cust call after list */
            case 2:         /* add */
                add_cust()
                break;
            case 3:         /* change */
                change_cust();
                break;
            case 4:         /* quit */
                break;       /* do nothing in this case */
            default:        /* bad command; ring bell */
                printf("Unknown command: %d\7\n", command);
                break;       /* here to prevent problems if new cases */
                             /*    are added later */
            }               /* end switch statement body */
        }                   /* end do...while loop body */
    while (command != 4);   /* repeat if not quitting time */
    }                       /* end of main() function */
```

To compile this program successfully, the functions *list_cust*, *add_cust*, and *change_cust* must also have been written. (The writing and calling of other functions is covered in Chapter 5.)

The *switch* statement is more efficient than the equivalent *else if* construct, but the *else if* construct is more flexible and cannot always be replaced by a *switch*. For example, if tests must be made in a specific order or if two expressions containing variables must be compared, *else if* is required.

# Common Control-Flow Blunders

The syntax of control-flow statements is easy to learn, but the bugs described in this section are just as easy to create. We're going to look at several examples of incorrect code. *Please don't imitate them* in programs you write. Simply learn to recognize and avoid them. Each code segment has at least one mistake in it. The text following the segment explains what is wrong, but try to figure it out for yourself before you read the explanation: You'll find you learn more that way.

The following code segment produces only the single line of output *Loop counter = 6.* Why?

```
for (loop_counter = 1; loop_counter <= 5; ++loop_counter);
    printf("Loop counter = %d\n");
```

Only one line is output because the call to *printf()* is not inside the body of the loop. The loop body is the null statement created by the misplaced semicolon at the end of the first line of code. That semicolon is the mistake.

How many times will the following loop body be executed? What criticisms (if any) can you make about this piece of code?

```
short a[100];
short p;
long t;

for (t = p = 0; p <= 100; ++p)
    t += a[p];
```

This loop executes 101 times, which causes the statement

```
t += a[100];
```

to be executed once, since the last time the loop body is executed, the variable *p*d equals 100. Unfortunately, *a[99]* is the last element of the array *a*. Off by one! In addition, the total is meaningless because the variable names used in this segment are too short and lack meaning, making the code difficult to understand, and the elements of the array have never been assigned values. (Since the total is never displayed, maybe that's not really a problem in this particular case.)

The next segment of code will not compile. It will cause a fatal error. Why?

```
if (curr_val > max_val)
    max_val = curr_val;
    total += curr_val;
else if (curr_val < min_val)
    small_tot += min_val;
```

Here the *if* was intended to control the two statements that follow it. The curly braces that should surround the pair of statements to make them a compound statement are missing. This blunder creates what we call a *dangling else*, which will make the compiler very unhappy. The code should correctly read as follows.

```
if (curr_val > max_val)
   {
   max_val = curr_val;
   total += curr_val;
   }
else if (curr_val < min_val)
   small_tot += min_val;
```

This next goof is a subtle one, and it has caught most C programmers at least once, just as it's going to catch you someday.

```
if (array_index = last_element)
   printf("At last element.\n");
```

The mistake is that the single = assignment operator was used where the double == equality operator was intended. As the segment stands, *array_index* is assigned the value of *last_element*, and as long as that value is non-zero, the *if* condition will be considered true and *printf()* will be called.

C compilers ignore indenting: They skip over comments and white space as if they weren't there. So incorrect indenting can fool *you* but not the compiler, as in the next example. This segment of code will subtract *qty_on_order* from *qty_on_hand* whenever the stock of the item is less than the quantity on order and the item isn't back-ordered, rather than only when *qty_on_hand* is greater than or equal to *qty_on_order*:

```
/* line 1 */      if (qty_on_hand < qty_on_order)
/* line 2 */          if (qty_back_ordered > 0)
/* line 3 */             printf("HELP!!!");
/* line 4 */      else
/* line 5 */          qty_on_hand -= qty_on_order;
```

Faulty indenting makes the *else* on line 4 appear to match the *if* on line 1. But the rule is that, when an *else* is used, it matches the closest preceding *if* statement that does not have a corresponding *else*. In this case, the *if* without an *else* is on line 2. A style rule that requires use of braces around all nested *if* statements can prevent this problem.

```
if (qty_on_hand < qty_on_order)
   {                /* protect nested if */
   if (qty_back_ordered > 0)
      printf("HELP!!!");
   }                /* mark end of nested if */
else
   qty_on_hand -= qty_on_order;
```

This next piece of code prints *Got one!* no matter what the value of *num*. Can you see why?

```
if (num == 1 || 18 || 37)
    printf("Got one!\n");
```

The *if* test in this example is equivalent to *((num ==1) || 18 || 37)*. Obviously, something is wrong with the use of the logical *OR* (||) operator. The correct code reads:

```
if (num == 1 || num == 18 || num == 37)
    printf("Got one!\n");
```

# Statements to Handle with Care

We know that the flow of control through a function should generally be from top to bottom, down the page of a listing, and that C's *if*, *switch*, and *loop* statements provide neat mechanisms for altering this flow of control without letting the flow get too out of hand. But C also has three less benign statements that alter control flow: *break*, *continue*, and *goto*. Abuse of these three statements leads to programs that are difficult to read, write, or modify, so be very cautious with them.

The *goto* statement is Enemy #1 and should simply never be used. A few *goto* statements sprinkled around can turn a readable program into a bowl of spaghetti. Those *goto* statements that jump to earlier lines create hidden loops: Replace them with one of C's *loop* statements. And *goto* statements that jump to later lines can generally be replaced by *if* or *switch* statements. If, after all I've said, you still want to learn more about the syntax of *goto*, *goto* your manual...!

The *continue* statement is Enemy #2. It is used to jump to the end of the loop body and begin the next iteration. This amounts to conditionally executing the rest of the loop body after the *continue* statement. The readable way to accomplish conditional execution of a set of statements at the end of a loop body is to make them into a compound statement (using {}) and then control the block with an *if* statement.

```
/* Avoid using continue. */
while (more_to_do)
    {
    /* ...statements */
    if (expression)
        continue;
    /* ...statements */
    }
```

```
/* Use an if statement instead. */
while (more_to_do)
    {
    /* ...statements */
    if (!expression)
        {
        /* ...statements */
        }
    }
```

Enemy #3 is two-faced. You've seen the friendly side of *break* used when coding a *switch* statement: It causes the program to jump to the statement following the end of the innermost surrounding *while*, *for*, *do...while*, or *switch* statement. But sometimes *break* isn't the best way to accomplish what you want. Look at this example:

```
/* Avoid using break. */           /* Use an if statement instead. */
while (more_to_do)                  while (more_to_do)
    {                                   {
    /* ...statements */                 /* ...statements */
    if (expression)                     if (!expression)      /* use ! */
        break;                              {
    /* ...statements */                     /* ...statements */
    }                                       }
                                        else
                                            more_to_do = NO;
                                        }
```

Does the use of *break* on the left side look more readable at first glance? It certainly may. However, if each set of statements contains 15 lines, *break* becomes hidden, and the fact that the second group of statements is executed only if *expression* is non-zero is hard to see.

Now that you have a thorough understanding of C statements and data handling, let's start pulling it all together into functions. In the next chapter, we'll talk about the structure and management of functions and the techniques for joining functions to form complete programs.

# Functions:
# The Backbone of C

A function is an independent set of statements executed to perform a specific task. All C programs are built from functions: a *main()* function, the functions that *main()* calls, and the functions that these functions call. As we discussed in Chapter 1, the philosophy underlying all C programming is that you can speed program development and reduce maintenance by building large programs from smaller, self-contained functions, each of which does a single job well.

Your program can include functions you write, compiler library functions that your code calls, and library functions that other library functions call. It's important to plan your functions as useful building blocks. Make their purposes simple and clear so that you can concentrate on how to combine them to do a job and not need to worry about the details of how each performs its specific task.

The greatest impact of the ANSI C Standard is on the appearance of functions and on how functions interface with each other. Back in the olden days of C, the style for functions was fairly wide open. You could interface incorrectly with them by passing too many values, too few values, or ones with incorrect data types. If you were lucky, the errors were obvious and easy to detect.

ANSI has made C functions more civilized through improved argument-type checking, and at no cost to program execution. Microsoft C facilitates this checking by offering a way of automatically generating function declarations from your program (with the */Zg* option of *CL*). The combination is unbeatable and has changed our lives as C programmers!

You will face decisions about whether to use the new style of writing functions or to stick with the old style (which is on its way to becoming obsolete). The old style has only one advantage: portability. It is supported by all C compilers. Both styles are presented in this chapter, but in the remainder of this book, all functions are coded in accordance with the new (ANSI) style.

This chapter is about the control-flow and data-management aspects of a function's personality, and (briefly) about the compilation and linking processes that take functions from source form to executable program.

## Functions and Control Flow

To call a function, use its name followed by a pair of parentheses, as in this call to the Microsoft library function *abort()*, which terminates program execution:

```
abort();
```

You can call a function from as many other functions as you like. You can follow the function call by a semicolon, making it an executable statement, or you can make the call a part of a larger expression that expects the called function to return some value. Let's look first at functions that don't return a value so that you can become familiar with the syntax and appearance of functions in general.

When a function is called, control transfers to the beginning of the function's body, and statements are executed one by one from that point until the program encounters a *return* statement or the closing brace of the called function. Control then returns to the calling function, which resumes execution with the next command after the subfunction call. The following program contains a simple example of a *main()* function with a single subfunction named *subf()*.

```
main()
   {
   printf("Begin main.\n");
   subf();                        /* call function subf() */
   printf("End main.\n");
   }

subf()                           /* define function subf() */
   {
   printf("Function subf() called.\n");
   }
```

and here is the output the program produces by calling the library function *printf()*:

```
Begin main.
Function subf() called.
End main.
```

Function bodies cannot be nested. The closing brace of one function *must* precede the beginning brace of the function that follows it. For example, in the preceding program, the body of *subf()* was not defined until after *main()* was closed with a *}*.

The order of functions in a source file makes no difference to C, but it can make a difference to the programmer hunting through a printed listing to find a particular function. One practical approach to organizing functions in your source file is to put the high-level functions first, followed by the low-level functions. Or you may prefer to arrange the functions alphabetically by name, especially if there are many of them. A comment section at the start of your program with the names of all functions contained in the source file is also helpful.

## Functions and Data

There are several paths through which data can flow between functions in C programs:

- The calling function can pass copies of argument values to the called function.

- The called function can return a single value to the calling function.

- Functions can share a single copy of variables that have been properly declared.

65

Variables declared within a function are known only within that function, so you can use the variable names from one function again in another function without any fear of conflict between variables with the same name. (Some exceptions do exist, such as the variables of shared data-storage classes mentioned earlier, but we'll look at those in Chapter 7.)

## Passing arguments to functions

The arguments passed from a calling function supply data and option information to the called function. The parentheses after the function name contain these arguments, which consist simply of a list of expressions separated by commas. The following statement calls *printf()* and passes it four arguments:

```
printf("%d * %d = %d\n", var, num, var * num);
```

Copies of the values of the arguments are passed to the parameter variables declared in the code within the function being called. The value of the first argument is passed to the first parameter, that of the second argument to the second parameter, and so on.

Most functions expect a specific number of arguments, each of a specific type. In response to ANSI's C Standard, several C compilers now use the source code's function declarations to verify that the correct numbers and types of arguments are being passed in function calls. This feature is a great help in catching argument-passing bugs before they can create problems during program execution.

## Calling functions that return data

A function that returns a value is called by using its name, followed by parentheses, within a larger expression. (You'll recall that we use the function name followed by parentheses and a semicolon to call functions that do *not* return a value. Some languages refer to functions that *do not* return a value as subroutines and those that *do* return a value as functions, but in C *both* are called functions.)

Every function except *main()* has the option of executing a *return* statement followed by an expression. The return expression's value is sent back to the calling function by the same reference that called the subfunction: That is, only one call is needed to accomplish both data transfers.

Recall the library function *strcmp()* that was introduced in Chapter 4. The returned integer is 0 if the two strings passed to *strcmp()* are equal in length and value; otherwise, a positive or negative integer is returned. The value returned from *strcmp()* may be used in an expression, such as an assignment to a variable, or as a condition in an *if* statement, or both:

```
comp = strcmp(month, "Jan");        /* assignment expression */

if (0 == strcmp(name, "Steve"))     /* condition in an "if" statement */

/* both assignment expression and condition */
if (0 == (comp = strcmp(entry, text)))
```

The library function *strlen()* takes a single string as an argument and returns an integer equal to the length of that string. The following statement makes two calls to *strlen()*, each of which returns an *int*, and assigns the sum of the two lengths plus 2 to the variable *full_length*:

```
full_length = strlen(begin) + strlen(middle) + 2;
```

Not all functions return data to their callers. Some don't need to be passed any data either. The function *main()* is an example of that kind of function. Let's look at *main()* more closely.

## Using maximum compiler diagnostics

The very first C program we looked at did nothing:

```
main()
  {
  }
```

If you compile this "bread sandwich" with the maximum warning level, by giving the *CL* command the */W3* option (type *CL /W3 BREAD.C*), these warning-level messages result:

```
bread.c(2) : warning C4103: 'main' : function definition used as prototype
bread.c(3) : warning C4035: 'main' : no return value
```

You designate the return type of a function by supplying a data type before the name of the function. If you insert the keyword *void* before *main()*, as shown on the following page, the compiler will no longer expect a return value, so it does not give the second warning message.

```
void main()
    {
    }
```

If you explicitly tell the compiler that no arguments need to be passed to *main()*, and no value is returned, no warnings are given.

```
void main(void)
    {
    }
```

The default warning level for *CL* compilations is 1. The default can be changed by adding this line to your AUTOEXEC.BAT file so that you can have the strictest checking, without supplying */W3* in each *CL* command:

```
SET CL=/W3
```

Most functions don't operate in a void. They need arguments and will return values to their callers.

## New- and old-style function definitions

A function consists of a *definition* and a *body*. The definition, which appears before the first brace ( *{* ), describes how a function interfaces with other functions through parameters and a return value. The body of the function, which appears in the outermost pair of braces ( *{}* ), contains statements that specify the operations that are performed when the function is called.

---

# C O M M E N T

*Good style dictates that* all *parameters, including* int-*type ones, be explicitly declared.*

---

The old style of function definition requires that the names of all parameters passed to the function be listed between the parentheses after the name of the function. All parameters of a type other than *int* must be declared between the closing parenthesis and the opening brace of the function body. Good style dictates that *all* parameters, including *int*-type ones, be explicitly declared. You can code the function *avg_3_ints()*, which returns an integer that is the average of three *int*s passed in, using the old style of function definition, like this:

```
/* avg_3_ints returns an int, the average of the 3 integers passed. */

int avg_3_ints(parm_one, parm_two, parm_three)
int parm_one;          /* first int parameter */
int parm_two;          /* second int parameter */
int parm_three;        /* third int parameter */

   {
   return ((parm_one + parm_two + parm_three) / 3);   /* return the average */
   }
```

(Notice the space after the reserved word *return*. We'll discuss this style rule in Chapter 9.) You must mention each parameter twice, once in the parameter list and again in the declarations that precede the opening brace. The new style of function definition is superior in that it mentions each parameter, with a data type, only once, right in the parameter list:

```
/* avg_3_ints returns an int, the average of the 3 integers passed. */

int avg_3_ints(
   int parm_one,       /* first int parameter */
   int parm_two,       /* second int parameter */
   int parm_three)     /* third int parameter */

   {
   return ((parm_one + parm_two + parm_three) / 3);   /* return the average */
   }
```

Use of the new function-definition style is not always adequate to completely satisfy the type-checking requirements of the highest warning level of Microsoft C. Prototype declarations of functions may be needed, and I strongly recommend that you use them to gain as much type checking as possible.

## Function-prototype declarations

To check the types of arguments and the return values, the compiler must encounter a declaration (or definition) for each function prior to its being called. If you fail to meet this requirement and use warning level 3, the compiler will issue a warning message.

---

### C A U T I O N

*Many C compilers cannot check the number or types of arguments. Some of these compilers ignore parameter declarations within function-prototype declarations, so the function declarations will compile and will not create a portability problem. The worst cases are the compilers that consider parameter declarations in a function-prototype declaration to be illegal. To make your program portable to those compilers, you can use the #if preprocessor command to conditionally compile the parameter declarations. (See Chapter 6.)*

---

There are two styles of function-prototype declaration. You can mention parameter names with their types or simply list the parameter types:

```
int avg_3_ints(int, int, int);
int avg_3_ints(int parm_one, int parm_two, int parm_three);
```

Place prototype declarations at the start of source files, before any function definitions or bodies. The declarations are made available to all functions that reside in the same source file as the declarations.

---

### C A U T I O N

*Note to old-style coders: Function declarations are mandatory for calls to functions that return any type other than* int. *To omit them invites a garbage return. Old-style C compilers may reject parameter-type declarations, so declare functions without including the parameters (e.g.* int avg_3_ints();).

---

Files called *headers* may be included in your source file to obtain prototype declarations for related groups of library functions. (Chapter 6 describes the C preprocessor's *#include* command and header files in more detail.) A header file called *stdio.h* contains prototype declarations for standard input/output functions, such as *printf()* and *scanf()*. The complete three-integer averaging program obtains three integers from the user and displays their average:

```
/* Obtain an int return value: the average of three integers. Use the
 * return value from avg_3_ints() in main() as an argument to printf().
 */

#include <stdio.h>      /* needed for prototype declarations */
                        /*  of scanf() and printf() */

/* Function prototype declaration. */
int avg_3_ints(int parm_one, int parm_two, int parm_3);

void main(void)         /* nothing passed into or returned from main() */
   {
   int first, second, third;

   printf("Enter 3 integers:  ");
   if (3 == scanf("%d %d %d", &first, &second, &third))
      printf("Average of %d and %d and %d = %d\n", first, second, third,
             avg_3_ints(first, second, third));
   }

/* Note:  Code from here on could be placed in another source file and
 * compiled separately. No prototype declarations would be needed in that
 * file, since no functions are called from this point on.
 */

/* avg_3_ints returns an int, the average of the 3 integers passed. */

int avg_3_ints(int parm_one, int parm_two, int parm_three) /* new style */
   {
   return ((parm_one + parm_two + parm_three) / 3);  /* return the average */
   }
```

Function declarations do not always need to describe all parameters. Let's take a look at one that doesn't:

```
long func_two(double, ...);
```

The declaration of *func_two()*'s parameter types ends with three periods, which means that the first parameter is type *double* but that no type checking is to be performed for any subsequent arguments. This would be useful if *func_two()* took a variable number of arguments.

## Generating function-prototype declarations

The */Zg* option gives the *CL* command a whole new meaning. Instead of compiling C programs to produce object files, you can use the command *CL /Zg program.c* to output function-prototype declarations for every function in *program.c*. The declarations can be captured in a file using output redirection, like this:

```
CL /Zg program.c > program.h
```

Chapter 6 will take this discussion further, as part of its coverage of prototype declarations in header files.

# Joining Functions to Form Programs

As I mentioned at the beginning of this chapter, you build C programs by combining functions that perform specific tasks. These functions need not even reside in the same source file. The factors you'll need to consider when deciding how to organize functions into source files are discussed in detail in Section II.

For now, let's suppose that our program consists of two source files, *avg3main.c* and *avg3ints.c*, each containing one or more functions. These two files are created with a text editor and compiled separately using the */c* option. The */c* option of the *CL* command specifies that the program should be compiled but not linked.

---

# C O M M E N T

*Functions stored in separate source files are easier to locate and maintain. This is good style for larger programs with many functions.*

---

Then the object files generated by the compiler are joined by the linker. The sequence shown in Figure 5-1 demonstrates the use of the compiler commands and the *EDLIN* editor to compile, execute, modify, and recompile our program. Notice that *avg3main.c* was not recompiled, because it was not modified.

| COMMAND | PURPOSE |
|---|---|
| C>CL /c AVG3MAIN.C | Compile *avg3main.c.* |
| C>CL /c AVG3INTS.C | Compile *avg3ints.c.* |
| C>LINK AVG3MAIN + AVG3INTS | Link object modules. |
| C>AVG3MAIN | Execute program. |
| C>EDLIN AVG3INTS.C | Modify *avg3ints.c* based on results. |
| C>CL AVG3MAIN.OBJ AVG3INTS.C | Recompile *avg3ints.c* and link. |
| C>AVG3MAIN | Execute modified program. |

FIGURE 5-1
*Typical C compilation/modification sequence*

The linker searches all available libraries for functions that you call but do not supply in object form. If it can't find the called function either in the object files you specify or in the libraries it was told to search, it will return a fatal-error message stating that an undefined symbol named *_function name* was found.

A library is simply a special file that holds a collection of functions in compiled (object) form. It is a good place to collect utility functions shared by the members of a team working on the same application or basic functions that will be used companywide in a variety of applications. The *LIB* command allows you to construct new libraries as needed or add new functions to existing libraries. (Chapter 10 shows how to build a library using *LIB*.)

You now know enough C to write lots of basic C applications code, but there are still some technical points we need to cover before you'll be ready to develop an effective interactive business application. I'll present these in Section II.

S E C T I O N

Section II discusses C programs as data: ways programs can store and access data both within and outside themselves. **Chapter 6** teaches you how to use the compiler's preprocessor commands to help make your programs more portable and easier to maintain. **Chapter 7** looks at the storage classes a variable may have and their effects on its lifetime, scope, and behavior. **Chapter 8** deals with accessing data outside your program—data in the command line and in environment variables controlled by the operating system—and with filter programs that can be chained together using pipes. **Chapter 9** summarizes coding styles and standards for C programs.

# The C Preprocessor

The C preprocessor is a program with its own command language. It is used to expand C programs into full code before compilation. The preprocessor allows programmers to write C source code that is readable, portable, easily modified, and terse. We'll see how in a minute.

The C preprocessor is actually a text-processing program, separate from the C language. The compiler invokes the preprocessor as its first pass through your source code. The preprocessor takes text files (either source programs or straight text) as its input and produces an expanded text file as its output. It has commands that allow the programmer to include outside files, substitute text, expand macros, and conditionally exclude lines of text.

## Preprocessor Syntax

Preprocessor syntax is well standardized among the numerous C compilers. Microsoft's C compiler also incorporates some ANSI enhancements that increase the readability and usefulness of its preprocessor commands by making them more closely resemble C control-flow statements.

All preprocessor commands begin with a pound sign (#), followed directly by a name in lowercase. Only one command can appear on a line. (As with C statements, the backslash indicates statements that are continued on the following line.)

## Preprocessor Debugging

To debug your source code or view the effects of preprocessing, you need to halt compilation after the preprocessing pass and capture the results of the pass.

Let's suppose you want to examine the preprocessor's effect on the file *ordentry.c*. You would use the following form of the compilation command to instruct the preprocessor to save its output in the file *ordentry.i*:

```
CL /P /C ORDENTRY.C
```

The */P* option instructs the compiler to save the results of preprocessing in a file with the same base name as the source file, with the *.i* extension instead of *.c*. The */C* option causes the compiler to preserve program comments in the output as an aid to debugging. (They are normally stripped out.)

---

# C A U T I O N

*The options of the* CL *command are case-sensitive. The* /C *switch means "Preserve comments," and* /c *means "Compile, but don't link."*

---

## The *#define* Command

The *#define* command causes all uses of an identifier in the C source code to be replaced by text defined in the preprocessor command. The syntax is *#define IDENTIFIER definition_text*. The definition text can be an expression, a part of a statement, or one or more complete statements.

It is always preferable to use defined constants in C source code, in place of ordinary constants or variables whose values never change. The use of symbols defined with the *#define* command can increase readability, portability, and ease of maintenance. You don't need to include the expanded code when you use a defined symbol in place of the code, and you can change the value of all occurrences of the defined symbol in the entire program with just one change at the preprocessor level. In addition, carefully chosen identifier names add to the clarity of your code by reflecting the purpose of each defined constant.

The *#define* command is followed by the name of the identifier being defined and the text that is to replace it. This is direct text-for-text replacement; no expression evaluation takes place. Note that the preprocessor does not replace defined symbols in your program that are found within quotes or in character constants, or those included as part of a longer name. For clarity, good C programming style dictates the use of uppercase for defined symbols and lowercase for variable names. The command below defines *NMONTHS* to be the number *36*:

```
#define NMONTHS 36
```

(Read as "pound define NMONTHS as 36.") This definition replaces all subsequent uses of the symbol *NMONTHS* in the input program with *36*. The following examples will make this clearer. If these lines are input to the preprocessor,

```
#define NMONTHS 36
#define L_CUST_NAME 30
    /* ... */
long sales_history[NMONTHS];
char cust_name[L_CUST_NAME + 1];
    /* ... */
for (month = 0; month < NMONTHS; ++month)
    total_sales += sales_history[month];
```

this output will be generated by the preprocessor:

```
long sales_history[36];
char cust_name[30 + 1];
for (month = 0; month < 36; ++month)
    total_sales += sales_history[month];
```

## C O M M E N T

*Notice the numeral 1 added to the length of the string* cust_name. *This is to make room for the terminal null character so that the full 30 characters can be used for the customer name.*

The use of defined symbols makes this code easy to read, and only the line *#define NMONTHS 36* needs to be modified to change the number of months of sales history totaled everywhere in the input program. The loop in the example will continue to execute for all months specified, without further modification.

This next example clearly demonstrates the value of defined constants in creating source code that is self-documenting:

```
#define MAX_CREDIT 249999

if (order_amt > MAX_CREDIT)        /* more readable */
    /* ... */

if (order_amt > 249999)            /* less readable and less clear */
    /* ... */
```

Obviously, this is a help to you in writing the program now, but it will be an even greater help to the programmer maintaining the system months or years down the line.

## Definitions with defined symbols

The preprocessor makes a single pass through its input file, but individual lines are repeated until all defined symbols are fully expanded. This may take several passes through the line, since a definition may itself contain other defined symbols. For example, if both *MIDSCREEN* and *SCRNLEN* are defined, with *MIDSCREEN* defined as half of *SCRNLEN*'s value, it will take the preprocessor at least two passes to expand every statement that uses *MIDSCREEN*.

```
#define SCRNLEN 24               /* note use of defined symbol SCRNLEN */
#define MIDSCREEN (SCRNLEN / 2)  /*   in definition of MIDSCREEN       */
```

## Definitions to avoid

Some types of definitions look just fine but can get you into real trouble. So here are a few DON'Ts:

■ Avoid circular definitions in which the symbol being defined appears in its own definition. In the following example, the symbol *INFINITY* expands endlessly and at the very least will tie the preprocessor in knots.

```
#define INFINITY (INFINITY + 1)
var = INFINITY;
```

Is expanded indefinitely to become:

```
var =  ...(((INFINITY + 1) + 1) + 1)...
```

- Omit definitions that don't add clarity. They force the reader to look elsewhere to learn the meaning of the symbol. For example, the following definition doesn't tell us a thing:

```
#define TWELVE 12          /* Yes, I know. */
```

- Along the same lines, avoid confusing definitions. You may know that the following definition means that all 12-month contracts carry 14 percent interest, but anyone else reading your code would be very confused indeed:

```
#define TWELVE 14          /* That's news to me. */
```

- Avoid using definitions that make a program no longer look like C. For instance, you have the ability to define *BEGIN* as { and define *END* as } and then use *BEGIN* and *END* in place of { and }. This is perfectly legal, but another C programmer would find it both confusing and pointless.

    Some C compilers, including Microsoft's, give a diagnostic message if you define a symbol that is already defined. You can get around this by using the preprocessor's *#ifndef* command (if not defined) to test for the existence of a prior definition:

```
#ifndef YES
    #define YES 1
    #define NO 0
#endif
```

## Macro definitions

A macro is a *#define* command that substitutes arguments into the definition text. It is used like a function to make one command execute many commands by passing outside arguments to internal parameters. But the preprocessor expands a macro in place to actually become the code the macro represents. The overhead of calling and returning from a function is saved, but the trade-off lies in the additional code generated by the preprocessor each time a macro is invoked in the source program.

The full macro syntax is *#define MAC_NAME(parameter-list) definition-_text.* In the following example, the macro *AVG3* replaces the function *avg_3_ints()* from the previous chapter to compute the average of three values *regardless of their data types,* a feat impossible with a function:

```
#define AVG3(a, b, c) (((a) + (b) + (c)) / 3)
```

This invocation of *AVG3* combines constants and variables of several data types:

```
result = AVG3(3.89, 23L * num, var);
```

When *AVG3* is expanded by the preprocessor, it will look like this:

```
result = (((3.89) + (23L * num) + (var)) / 3);
```

Macro definitions must be only a single line long; however, that line can be continued by ending it with a backslash (\). No spaces are allowed between the name of the macro and the opening parenthesis that follows. For both style and safety, enclose the entire definition and every macro parameter in the definition text within a pair of parentheses. This will help you avoid the precedence problems that can occur when the macro is invoked as part of a larger expression. Use *only* uppercase for macro names to avoid confusing them with functions, which use lowercase names.

## Macros and functions

In C, a macro has some important differences from a function that performs the same job:

- A macro is generic and will accept different data types for arguments, unlike a function, which is less flexible. For instance, the *AVG3* macro can take arguments that are *char, short, long, float,* or *double.*

- A macro executes faster than its equivalent function because function-call and return processing is not required. (Chapter 21 compares function and macro execution times.)

- A macro is more difficult to debug than a function. In fact, it should be written first as a function, debugged, and then converted to a macro.

- A macro can contain many statements, but if you use a 10-statement macro 100 times, you will add 1000 statements to your program. If you call a 10-statement function 100 times, your program gains only 110 statements.

- A macro, unlike a function, must be passed exactly the number of arguments it expects. Beware of side effects on macro arguments, and don't call a function as an argument in order to use the function's return value. The reason is simple: The side effect or function may execute twice and create problems.

## Types of macros

Macros fall into three categories, based on the nature of their expansion: expression macros, statement macros, and block macros. The type of macro determines the context in which it may appear. For instance, an expression macro may be called many times in a statement, but a statement macro cannot be used as part of an expression because statements have no value. Where you have a choice, use expression macros rather than statement macros, because expression macros have a value and can be used like functions that return a value.

Here's an example of the kind of situation where a block macro is very useful:

```
#define ADD_SAFE(a, b, sum, errfn) \
    { \
    (sum) = (a) + (b); \
    if (((a) > 0 && (b) > 0 && (sum) < 0) || \
        ((a) < 0 && (b) < 0 && (sum) > 0)) \
        errfn((a), (b)); \
    }
```

The *ADD_SAFE* macro provides a safer form of integer addition than the + operator because *ADD_SAFE* checks for overflow, whereas ordinary addition does not. If overflow is detected, the program calls the *errfn()* function, whose name you pass as an argument.

If a macro expands into one or more statements, as in the preceding example, it is wise to enclose it in a pair of curly braces. This

forces the macro to be a single (although perhaps compound) statement and thus prevents the nesting problems that may arise if the
macro is invoked as the body of a loop or as the target of an *if*
statement.

The use of macros and ordinary *#define* commands can save repeated typing of frequently used code segments or expressions, as you
can see from this next example using the *AVG3* macro defined earlier:

```
#define PRN(name, val) printf("The value of %s is %d.\n", (name), (val))

PRN("income average", AVG3(income, year_one_income, year_two_income));
```

Wouldn't it be nice if there were a way to code a macro that took
only one argument (a variable) and displayed the name of the variable
and its value? Now there is, using the powerful new stringizing
operator.

## The stringizing operator (#)

The pound sign (#) is the stringizing operator when it is applied to a
reference to a macro's parameter in the definition of the expansion
text. When you use this operator, the argument passed to the macro is
treated as if it were a quoted string inside the macro expansion.

You cannot code a completely generic macro that can output the
name and value of any variable in a C program. But the stringizing
operator makes possible the next best thing, *NUM_PUT*, which can display the name and value of any short or long integer. The following
definition of the macro *NUM_PUT* uses the stringizing operator with
the *name* (*#name*) as a string argument to *printf*:

```
#define NUM_PUT(name) printf("Integer %s = %ld\n", #name, (long)(name))
```

The *NUM_PUT* macro will work equally well on a variable and an
arithmetic expression:

```
short age = 12;
NUM_PUT(age);
NUM_PUT(3 * age - 4);
```

And this output is produced:

```
Integer age = 12
Integer 3 * age - 4 = 32
```

Recall from Chapter 3 that two string constants separated only
by spaces will be joined to form a single string. This fact can be useful with the stringizing operator. The name of the variable being

displayed and a format specifier can be merged right into the *printf()* format string:

```
#define SHOW(name, fmt) printf(#name ":\t(fmt %s): " #fmt "\n", \
    #fmt, (name))
```

```
SHOW(counter, %09d);
```

To produce this output:

```
counter:        (fmt %09d): 000000001
```

  The stringizing operator has a cousin, which is also new, although perhaps you won't find it quite as useful.

## The token-pasting operator (##)

The token-pasting operator is used within a macro definition to join two tokens to form a single one. Token pasting is helpful for operating on variables whose names share some distinct pattern. The two pound signs must appear between two strings of text, one of which is typically a macro parameter. This short program uses both the stringizing and token-pasting operators in the *MSG_SHOW* macro on the second line:

```
#include <stdio.h>
#define MSG_SHOW(num) printf("Message " #num ":  %s\n", message_##num);

void main(void)
    {
    char *message_1 = "Time flies like an arrow.";
    char *message_2 = "Fruit flies like a banana.";

    MSG_SHOW(1);
    MSG_SHOW(2);
    }
```

to produce this output:

```
Message 1:  Time flies like an arrow.
Message 2:  Fruit flies like a banana.
```

  The *#define* command is a flexible means of performing text substitution. The preprocessor's *#if* command also comes in many forms.

## The *#if* compilation command

Conditional compilation commands can be used to control C source and preprocessor commands. The conditional commands cause selected source lines to be compiled or skipped over, depending upon the value or existence of a symbol or macro defined with the *#define* command.

The *#if* command controls the lines of C source and preprocessor command text between itself and the associated *#endif* command, like this:

```
#if restricted_constant_expression
    /* ...text to be conditionally compiled... */
#endif
```

If the *restricted_constant_expression* after #if is non-zero, the lines after the *#if* command are preserved for compilation; otherwise, they are ignored, and the preprocessor continues with the line following the *#endif*.

A *restricted constant expression* is a special type of constant expression. It may contain any constants (except *enum* constants), combined by operators (except *sizeof, cast, comma,* and *assignment*) to form an expression that is evaluated at compilation. The restricted constant expression may also contain the expression *defined(IDENTIFIER)*, which is evaluated as true if *IDENTIFIER* has been defined as a constant or macro. For example, these three lines will cause the statement *draw (10, 20, 30, 40);* to be compiled only if the symbol *GRAPHICS* is already defined:

```
#if defined(GRAPHICS)
    draw(10, 20, 30, 40);
#endif
```

I've already mentioned that you can disable, rather than delete, lines of C code and preprocessor commands that have been entered in a program but are not yet fully functional so that they will be ignored while you debug another section of the code. Unfortunately, the comment delimiters /* and */ will not comment out code that itself contains comments, because the first */ the preprocessor encounters will be regarded as the end of the comment and everything after it will be treated as potentially executable code. But *#if* offers an easy solution to the problem: Simply use *#if 0* to ensure that the surrounded lines will not be compiled.

```
#if 0
    /* ...lines the compiler will forever ignore... */
#endif
```

Among the preprocessor commands that would need to be ignored in certain situations are *CL*'s memory-related keywords *near*, *far*, and *huge*. These keywords are valuable because their use in declarations allows C programs to take advantage of all installed memory on a PC, rather than just the 64 KB of program and 64 KB of data allowed by many earlier compilers. However, they are *not* standard and therefore may have to be removed in order to use certain C compilers that run on 32-bit systems, especially systems with virtual-memory capability. You can use the following command sequence to globally disable these keywords, replacing them with empty strings (provided the name *BIGMEMORY* is already defined):

```
#if defined(BIGMEMORY)
    #define near
    #define far
    #define huge
#endif
```

## Chaining and nesting

You may frequently find yourself in a situation where several alternatives must be considered before a routine is executed. This can be handled by chaining or nesting *#if* statements to cover all required conditions.

The following example of chaining preserves one of the four sets of C command lines (source or preprocessor) and skips over the other three:

```
#if restricted_constant_expression
    /* ...lines of C source or preprocessor commands... */
#elif restricted_constant_expression
    /* ...lines of C source or preprocessor commands... */
#elif restricted_constant_expression
    /* ...lines of C source or preprocessor commands... */
#else
    /* ...lines of C source or preprocessor commands... */
#endif
```

The lines preserved are the ones following the first #*if* or #*elif* whose restricted constant expression is non-zero (and therefore true). The preprocessor's #*elif* command behaves like C's *else if* construct. Should all tests fail, the lines after the optional #*else* at the end are picked for output.

Each #*if* in a nest or chain construct must be paired with an #*endif*, #*elif*, or #*else* to mark the end of its range of control. Like C's *else if* construct, the #*elif* is optional and may be repeated as many times as you like. If used, the optional #*else* must follow the last #*elif* command and must itself be followed by #*endif*.

The following code for an application designed to run in three different environments is a good example of nesting syntax:

```
/* Prepare to display a message for the user to read. */

#if defined(GRAPHICS)
    #if defined(HIGHRES) /* If this display is high resolution, */
        grmove(88, 90);   /* move high-resolution cursor. */
    #else                 /* If not, it must be medium resolution, so */
        grmove(44, 90);   /* move medium resolution cursor. */
    #endif                /* Note: grmove not a standard library function. */
#elif defined(CRT)        /* If not GRAPHICS, is it a CRT text screen? */
    CUR_MV(8, 30);        /* If so, then move text screen cursor. */
#else                     /* This must be a hardcopy terminal */
    printf("\n\n");       /* (no cursor), so skip two lines. */
#endif
```

## Embedded test drivers and debugging code

It is important to save embedded test drivers and debugging code. Test-driver code demonstrates correct calls to the function being tested, as well as the proper return value, given the arguments being passed. You should retain the driver in the source file with the function it verifies, and when you add new function capabilities, you should also add the appropriate new tests to the driver.

The easiest way to save test drivers and debugging code is to conditionally compile them. The following example compiles *linelen()*'s test driver if the symbol *DBGMAIN* is defined. You can define *DBGMAIN* (or any identifier) either by using the */D* switch plus the identifier name (with no space between) in the *CL* compile command, as we do here, or by using a separate #*define* command.

```
/* TO COMPILE FOR DEBUG OUTPUT AND TESTING:  CL /DDEBUG /DDBGMAIN LINELEN.C
****************************************************************************
* linelen() is the line-length function. It returns the number of
* characters before '\n' in the line, or -1 if '\0' is found before '\n'.
****************************************************************************
*/

#include <stdio.h>

int linelen(char
    line[])                 /* the string to be processed */
    {
    short len;

    for (len = 0; line[len] != '\0' && line[len] != '\n'; ++len)
#if defined(DEBUG)
        printf("\nDEBUG: line[%d] = %c (hex: %x)\n",
            len, line[len], line[len]);         /* DEBUG output */
#else
        ;                                       /* no DEBUG; a null loop body */
#endif
    return (line[len] == '\n' ? len : -1); /* returns -1 if '\0' before '\n' */
    }

#if defined(DBGMAIN)
    #define TESTFOR(cond, msg) if (!(cond)) \
    printf("\7\n***TEST FAILED: %s\n", (msg))

    /*********************************************
    * Test driver to test the linelen() function.
    *********************************************
    */

    void main(void)
        {
        TESTFOR(linelen("12\n") == 2, "linelen #1");
        TESTFOR(linelen("\n") == 0, "linelen #2");
        TESTFOR(linelen("") == -1, "linelen #3");
        printf("linelen tests complete\n");
        }
#endif
```

In the previous example, the tests were compiled with the constants *DBGMAIN* and *DEBUG* defined (*DEBUG* controls the debugging output from the *printf()* function), producing this output:

```
DEBUG: line[0] = 1 (hex: 31)
DEBUG: line[1] = 2 (hex: 32)
linelen tests complete
```

## New ANSI command syntax

The *#ifdef* (if defined) and *#ifndef* (if not defined) commands with which you may be familiar have been rendered semiobsolete by the new ANSI *#if defined(ID)* syntax you saw in some of the preceding examples. Both the old and the new forms of the *if defined* command are followed by the names of identifiers, and both will compile the code after them if *ID* is defined as a macro or a symbol:

```
#if defined(ID)    ←——————→    #ifdef ID
```

One advantage of *#if defined(ID)* is that it permits the use of the new *#elif* command to make an *else if* construct. Before this ANSI modification, the processing of alternatives always involved sometimes-messy sets of nested *#if* commands. A second benefit of the new syntax is the ability to combine tests using logical operators. This is demonstrated in the following program, which uses the old and the new preprocessor syntax.

```
/* Compare old and new preprocessor definition testing. */
#include <stdio.h>

void main(void)
    {
    /* Use old preprocessor commands to see if NOSUCH defined. */
#ifdef NOSUCH
    printf("#ifdef NOSUCH is true\n");
#else
    printf("#ifdef NOSUCH is false\n");
#endif

#ifndef NOSUCH
    printf("ifndef NOSUCH is true\n");
#endif

    /* Use new preprocessor commands to see if NOSUCH is defined. */
#if defined(NOSUCH)
    printf("#if defined(NOSUCH) is true\n");
#else
    printf("#if defined(NOSUCH) is false\n");
#endif
```

*(continued)*

*continued*

```
#if !defined(NOSUCH)
    printf("#if !defined(NOSUCH) is true\n");
#endif

    /* Logical operators can be used to combine tests. */
#if ((!defined(NOSUCH) && defined(SOMESUCH) || !defined(NODEF))
    printf("logical combination is true\n");
#endif
    }
```

The following output results from running the program because the symbols *NOSUCH*, *SOMESUCH*, and *NODEF* were not defined:

```
#ifdef NOSUCH is false
#ifndef NOSUCH is true
#if defined(NOSUCH) is false
#if !defined(NOSUCH) is true
logical combination is true
```

## Undefining variables

Some preprocessors require that a symbol be undefined before it can be defined with a new value. The *#undef* command accomplishes this by removing the existing definition of the symbol. The following command sequence checks to see whether *ENDSTEPS* is already defined, undefines it if necessary, and then redefines it with the new value 5:

```
#if defined(ENDSTEPS)
    #undef ENDSTEPS
#endif
#define ENDSTEPS 5
```

# Header Files

Definitions included in a special source file called a header file can be used by C functions in many different source files. This means that you won't have to duplicate common definitions in every file in an application. Some header files, such as *stdio.h* and *stdlib.h*, come with your compiler, in conjunction with the standard library. (For good style, header-file names should end with the *.h* extension.) Others may be associated with a corporate or project library. Or you may want to develop your own. More on all that later. First, let's learn how to use these files to simplify C programming.

## The *#include* command

The preprocessor's *#include* command makes the contents of a header file available to C source files by simply replacing each *#include* command in a source program with the contents of the header file that it names.

For good style, *#include* commands should be placed at the beginning of the C source file, after the initial comments describing the source file but before the first function.

There are two forms of syntax for the *#include* command. Your choice depends upon where the included file is to be searched for. (If the path is complete and unambiguous, no search is needed and the forms are equivalent.)

| COMMAND | ACTION |
|---------|--------|
| *#include "pathname"* | Searches current directory first, then standard places if needed |
| *#include <pathname>* | Searches standard places only |

Use the < > form for header files that are to be used systemwide; they may be included from many directories to compile a wide variety of applications. Use the " " form for files that are intended only for a specific program or for personal use.

To create a path for the default directories or the "standard search places" for header files, use the MS-DOS *SET* command to set the environment variable *INCLUDE*. (You can use this command from the command line or in your *autoexec.bat* file.) For example, the following command makes *\INCLUDE* on drive C the directory where the compiler looks for header files:

```
SET INCLUDE = C:\INCLUDE
```

---

# C A U T I O N

*An included file may itself contain other #include commands. Although such nesting of header files is legal, it has risks, since the danger of invisible changes in a hidden header file cannot be ignored.*

---

To add to this setting, use the *CL* command's */I pathname* switch, which causes the compiler to search the designated pathname before the standard places. The */I* switch can be given more than once to have additional directories searched. The following *CL* command makes the compiler search *A:\SPECDIR* for header files before searching C:\INCLUDE:

```
CL SPEC.C /I A:\SPECDIR
```

The *CL* */X* switch (exclude) prevents the compiler from searching the standard places at all and is usually used in conjunction with the */I* switch.

## Headers and library functions

Let's take a minute to clarify the difference between header files and library files, since some people confuse the two. A header file is a text file that contains C source and preprocessor commands to be compiled when the header file is included with the *#include* command in a C source file. A library file is an object file that contains a collection of already-compiled modules for frequently used functions. Libraries are searched by the linker for functions you call but did not write. Remember: Libraries are used by the linker; header files are used by the preprocessor.

To add to the confusion, most libraries also have associated header files to hold *#define* commands, declarations of library-function parameter and return types, and related information needed by functions in the library. Let's look briefly at one of these.

### The *stdio.h* header file

The most frequently used library header file is *stdio.h*. It contains declarations and definitions needed for calls to standard I/O functions, such as single-character input and output using the macros *getchar()* and *putchar()*.

The *getchar()* macro returns the next character that is input as an integer. This macro returns the defined symbol *EOF*, whose value is −1, if the end of the file was reached. The *putchar()* macro prints whatever character is passed to it. Let's look at an example to see how this works.

```
/* Program to copy input to output, one character at a time. */
#include <stdio.h>      /* needed for getchar(), putchar(), EOF */

void main(void)
  {
  int char_input;      /* character that was input, or EOF */

  /* Copy all input characters to output, one by one. */
  while ((char_input = getchar()) != EOF)
     putchar(char_input);
  }
```

This little program copies each input character to output until the end-of-file marker is reached. For more information on the *putchar()* and *getchar()* functions, see the ''Input Using Standard Library Functions'' section in Chapter 13. You may wonder why *char_input* is type *int*, not type *char*. The reason is that the symbol *EOF* is defined in *stdio.h* as $-1$, an integer which an *unsigned char* variable can never be equal to. A *signed char* variable will work fine instead of *int*, but an *unsigned char* will cause the program to loop endlessly. The */J* switch of *CL* causes *char* to be *unsigned*, so even though the declaration may read *char*, and *char* by (Microsoft) default is *signed*, it is risky. Type *int* is safe.

The standard input/output header file, *stdio.h*, is but one of the many standard header files supplied with your compiler. Figure 6-1 gives a list of header files found in the directories *\INCLUDE* and *\INCLUDE\SYS*.

| HEADER FILE | PURPOSE |
| --- | --- |
| *\include\ASSERT.H* | Definition of the assert macro |
| *\include\BIOS.H* | Declarations and supporting definitions for bios interface functions |
| *\include\CONIO.H* | Console and port I/O declarations |
| *\include\CTYPE.H* | Character conversion macros and character type macros |
| *\include\DIRECT.H* | Function declarations for directory creation/ handling |

FIGURE 6-1                                                    *(continued)*
*Table of Microsoft standard header files*

Figure 6-1. *continued*

| HEADER FILE | PURPOSE |
| --- | --- |
| \include\DOS.H | Declarations and definitions for MS-DOS interface routines |
| \include\ERRNO.H | Systemwide error numbers (set by system calls) |
| \include\FCNTL.H | File control options used by *open()* and *sopen()* |
| \include\FLOAT.H | Constants for floating-point values and function declarations for floating-point math functions |
| \include\GRAPH.H | Declarations and supporting definitions for graphics library functions |
| \include\IO.H | Declarations for low-level file handling and I/O functions |
| \include\LIMITS.H | Implementation-dependent values |
| \include\MALLOC.H | Declarations and supporting definitions for memory-allocation functions |
| \include\MATH.H | Declarations and supporting definitions for math library functions |
| \include\MEMORY.H | Declarations for buffer (memory) manipulation routines |
| \include\PROCESS.H | Declarations and definitions for process control functions |
| \include\SEARCH.H | Declarations for searching/sorting routines |
| \include\SETJMP.H | Declarations and supporting definitions for *setjmp()*/*longjmp()* routines |
| \include\SHARE.H | Definitions for file-sharing modes for *sopen()* |
| \include\SIGNAL.H | Declarations and definitions for signal routines |
| \include\STDARG.H | Definitions for ANSI-style macros for variable argument functions |
| \include\STDDEF.H | Definitions for common constants, types, variables |
| \include\STDIO.H | Declarations and supporting definitions for standard I/O routines |
| \include\STDLIB.H | Declarations and supporting definitions for commonly used library functions |
| \include\STRING.H | Declarations for string-manipulation functions |
| \include\TIME.H | Declarations and supporting definitions for time routines |
| \include\VARARGS.H | Definitions of XENIX-style macros for variable argument functions |
| \include\sys\LOCKING.H | Flags for *locking()* function |
| \include\sys\STAT.H | Declarations and supporting definitions for *stat()* and *fstat()* |

*(continued)*

Figure 6-1. *continued*

| HEADER FILE | PURPOSE |
|---|---|
| \*include*\*sys*\*TIMEB.H* | Declaration and supporting definitions for *ftime()* |
| \*include*\*sys*\*TYPES.H* | Types returned by system-level calls for file and time information |
| \*include*\*sys*\*UTIME.H* | Declaration and supporting definitions for *utime()* |

## Custom header files for applications

We've just talked about header files for use in functions that call standard library functions. These header files provide you with a great deal of programming power, but you will still need to create your own header files for the specific applications you develop. For instance, the header files *ansiscrn.h, syntypes.h, projutil.h,* and *ordentry.h* that I will refer to in later chapters do not come with your compiler. They are files I've created for use in application development. (You'll find the complete listings of these header files in Chapter 10.)

My header files all contain similar kinds of information. So why do I have four of them, instead of just one large one? That's easy: The contents of the files are grouped according to the scope of their usefulness.

| FILE NAME | CONTENTS |
|---|---|
| *syntypes.h* | General-purpose synonym data types |
| *ansiscrn.h* | General-purpose screen- and cursor-manipulation macros and definitions for use with the ANSI.SYS terminal driver |
| *projutil.h* | Project utility declarations and definitions used by programs that call functions in the project utility library |
| *ordentry.h* | Application-specific declarations and definitions used only for order-entry programs |

The *syntypes.h* and *ansiscrn.h* header files are appropriate for use in any C source file, regardless of the application. The *projutil.h* header should be included in source files that have calls to the project-utility-library functions listed in Chapter 10. The *ordentry.h* header is needed only to compile source files that have no general use beyond the order-entry application, and it serves as a model for other application-specific header files.

What does and does not belong in your header files? Once again, this is really a question of good programming style. Header files should contain preprocessor commands, declarations of function parameter and return types, and some things we haven't discussed yet: structure definitions, *typedef* type-synonym statements, and external non-defining declarations.

Header files should *not* contain non-declarational executable C statements, except in the form of preprocessor macros. (Therefore, header files should not generate object code when compiled.) Nor, it follows, should they use *#include* statements that include entire outside functions. Instead, compile the outside functions separately and then use the linker to join them once they are in object form. That way, if you have to modify one function, you won't need to recompile any unmodified functions along with it.

## Pragmas for the practical, *#error*, and predefined macros

The *#pragma* commands supplied with various C compilers are not standardized. Their purposes are entirely up to the maker of the compiler. Microsoft's pragmas control output listing, embedded comments in object code, local optimization, and source listing.

The program optimization pragmas (not shown here) can improve program performance. The following examples of the *comment* pragma have no effect on the execution of a program. They can be used to add comment text to object and executable files:

```
/* Identify the version of the compiler in object file. */
#pragma comment(compiler)

/* Show compile timestamp in the object file. */
#pragma comment(user, "Last Compile: " __DATE__ ", Time: " __TIME__)"
```

The $\_\_DATE\_\_$ and $\_\_TIME\_\_$ symbols in the previous *comment* pragma (and in the first *message* pragma that follows) are predefined macros that expand to strings giving the date and time of compilation. The *message* pragma outputs the text passed to it when compilation terminates. The *message* pragmas that follow are conditionally compiled, depending on the memory model used during the compilation.

The compiler defines the symbols *M_I86SM*, *M_I86CM*, *M_I86MM*, *M_I86LM*, and *M_I86HM* as zero or one, depending on the memory model being used. Customized error messages that use the same format as those from the compiler can be output using the *#error* directive.

```
/* Show the programmer the compilation timestamp at end of compile. */
#pragma message("Compile Date: " __DATE__ ", Time: " __TIME__)"

/* Show the programmer the memory model used at end of compile. */
#if M_I86SM
#pragma message("Small Model")
#elif M_I86CM
#pragma message("Compact Model")
#elif M_I86MM
#pragma message("Medium Model")
#elif M_I86LM
#pragma message("Large Model")
#endif
#if M_I86HM
#pragma message("Huge Model")
#endif

#error This is a test of the #error directive.

#include <stdio.h>

void main(void)
        {
        }
```

When you compile the program, the *message* pragmas and *#error* directive cause the preprocessor to output the following:

```
Compile Date: Mar 12 1989, Time: 21:01:27
Small Model
pragma.c(19) : error C2188: #error :  This is a test of the #error directive.
```

The preprocessor's many directives form a language of their own. Now let's get back to C.

# CHAPTER 7

# To Share or Not to Share

One of the first decisions you'll need to make when you design a program is whether you want data in some variables to be available to more than one function. This requires an understanding of the way C handles such data.

When a variable is assigned a value in a BASIC program, the variable remains in existence from then on and may be used by any subsequent portion of the program. In fact, the lifetime of all BASIC variables extends beyond execution of the BASIC program—that is, after the program has finished running, you can print the values of your variables as they were when the program ended (very handy for debugging).

FORTRAN, on the other hand, uses separately compiled routines, with each routine's variables isolated from those in other routines, regardless of name. The programmer must specifically define areas in memory called common blocks to hold data to be shared by *all* routines in a program. This is clearly an improvement over BASIC, since it permits the programmer to limit the number of places in a program that can access a given variable.

C, like FORTRAN, has storage classes that allow variables to be shared by several functions. However, C gives even greater control over data by letting the programmer declare variables to be shared by *some, but not all* functions in a program.

---

# C A U T I O N

*Don't use shared data as a lazy way of avoiding passing arguments and declaring parameters.*

---

Since C has provided this added control, use it wisely: Don't make data more widely shared than necessary. If you make all variables global, C will be no more powerful in this respect than good old BASIC. And if a variable can be accessed even where it is not used, you will still have to examine that part of the program for bugs if the variable's value becomes incorrect. So rather than make your C variables global, use arguments to functions to pass data, thereby restricting the data path to the calling and called functions.

## Storage Class of a Variable

Storage class is a characteristic of all C variables. A variable's storage class is controlled by both the placement of its declaration in the program and the use of one, and only one, of the storage-class keywords shown in Figure 7-1.

| KEYWORD | DESCRIPTION |
|---|---|
| *auto* | Internal to function or block where declared |
| *register* | Like *auto*, but faster memory access |
| *extern* | Globally shared by all functions |
| *static* | Internal to function or block, or shared by some functions |

FIGURE 7-1
*C's storage classes and their scopes*

The syntax for declaring a variable includes its storage class, data type, name, and optional initializer, followed by a semicolon:

```
static double rate = 0.15;
```

You will see that the storage-class terms *GLOBAL*, *SEMIGLOBAL*, and *IMPORT* are defined in the *syntypes.h* header file from our order-entry application (Chapter 10):

| COMMAND | MEANING |
| --- | --- |
| #*define GLOBAL* | Define a global variable |
| #*define SEMIGLOBAL static* | Define a semiglobal variable |
| #*define IMPORT extern* | Refer to a semiglobal or global variable defined elsewhere |

These are not C terms. They are terms I have defined to make the storage class of a variable clearer than it would be from the normal reserved storage-class keywords. (The definition of *GLOBAL* in the preceding table is not an error. It defines *GLOBAL* as an empty string— that is, the term *GLOBAL* is deleted wherever it is used. This has the same effect as defining all *GLOBAL* variables as *extern*.) We'll discuss these special classes in detail later in the chapter.

## Scope of a Variable

The scope of a variable is the set of statements (functions or blocks) in which the variable's name can be used to obtain its value. For example, an *auto* variable declared within a block can be accessed only by statements within that block. (All variables you have seen declared so far have had the default storage class *auto*.) The storage for an *auto* variable declared in a *block* is allocated when the block is entered and released when the block is exited. The next time the block is entered, the variable will not "remember" its old value, because a different location may be allocated to it. This is exactly the same as the behavior of an *auto* variable declared at the start of a *function*. (If you refer to a variable outside its scope, you will get a compilation error.)

```
                  C O M M E N T ·
```

*It is good programming style to use the most restricted scope possible for each of your variables.*

## Resolution of name conflicts

A name conflict can arise if two variables have the same name and overlapping scopes. The variable that the program will reference where a name conflict occurs is the one with the more restrictive scope. For example, if a block-scope variable appears in a function with a function-scope variable of the same name, the program will reference the block-scope variable during execution of the block.

You'll see a potential name conflict for the variable *overlap* in the next example. The *overlap* variable is declared as type *char* in the *main()* function, except within the block, where it is declared as an array with 100 elements of type *short*. The *overlap* variable the program references in the block is the array of type *short*, because the block scope is narrower than the function scope:

```
main()
    {
    char overlap = 'A';

    /* ... */
    overlap = 'Z';
        {                       /* begin block and begin scope overlap */
        short overlap[100];

        overlap[0] = 9;

        /* ... */
        printf("1: overlap[0] = %d\n", overlap[0]);
        }                          /* end block and end scope overlap */
    printf("2: overlap = %c\n", overlap);
    }
```

The output from the program will look like this:

```
1: overlap[0] = 9
2: overlap = Z
```

```
C  O  M  M  E  N  T
```

*Well-written programs never use the same name for two different items
of data.*

This rule for scope-of-variable conflicts applies to data in all the
storage classes we're about to look at. We'll begin with the most restrictive class (*auto*) and work our way out to the least restrictive (*GLOBAL*).

# The *auto* Storage Class

The keyword *auto* is used to declare a variable as having *automatic*
storage class. Automatic variables are temporary variables internal to a
specific function or to a block within a function. They are temporary
because their lifetime begins when the function or block is entered
and ends when that function is exited or the end of the block is
reached.

Because *auto* is the most frequently used storage class, it is the
default class for variables declared within the body of a C function or
block, as well as for a function's parameters. It is seldom specifically
declared. For example, these two declarations inside a function or
block are equivalent:

```
short item_num;
auto short item_num;
```

The memory reserved to hold the value of a variable for its
lifetime is said to be *allocated* to that variable. Use of the *auto* storage
class conserves memory because only the *auto* variables in active functions need to have memory allocated to them. That is, if a second-level
function is executing, only its own *auto* variables and those of the
main function occupy memory; *auto* variables declared in other functions do not have memory allocated to them at this stage in the program's execution.

## Initializing an *auto* variable

All *auto* variables are allocated and may be initialized upon each entry
to the declaring function or block. The value of an *auto* variable not
explicitly initialized is undefined. This means that whatever value

happens to already be stored in that memory location remains, which may produce problems during program execution.

Expressions used to initialize *auto* variables can include calls to functions that return values, as in this next example:

```
short max_len = strlen(ltoa(max_val, buf, 10));
short min_len = strlen(ltoa(min_val, buf, 10));
```

The initializers used here demonstrate the flexibility of *auto* variables: *max_len* and *min_len* are initialized to the number of digits in the *long* integers *max_val* and *min_val*, respectively, by converting the values of *max_val* and *min_val* to string form with the library function *ltoa* (*ltoa* converts *long* to ASCII) and then using the library function *strlen()* to return the length of the string.

Initializing variables unnecessarily is a waste of execution time and a source of confusion to the program reader. For example, in the segment

```
short cnt = 0;

for (cnt = 1; cnt <= max_cnt; ++cnt)
```

*cnt = 0* is useless because the zero is never used.

C forbids initialization of an *automatic array*. This rule follows naturally from the fact that C will not assign a value to more than a single element during assignment or initialization. For example, *char msg[8] = "illegal";* is an illegal statement within a function and won't compile. To assign values to the elements of an *auto* array, you must assign the values one at a time (in an initialization loop, for instance).

## The *static* Storage Class

We've seen that lifetime is an important characteristic of a storage class. For *auto*, life begins when you enter the declaring function or block and ends when you leave it. But what if you want some variables to be available a little longer? Well, the *static* storage class has a much longer lifetime—in fact, the lifetime is the entire time the program is executing.

Once again we're faced with a trade-off, this time between longer lifetime and increased memory requirements. All *static* variables have memory allocated to them as long as the program is running, which means that there must be enough memory available to hold *all* the *static* data at one time.

The life of a *static* variable begins with initialization, which takes place only once during execution of the program and ends when the program terminates. Its value is stored in the same location throughout the duration of the program.

The scope of a *static* identifier is the function or block in which it was declared. However, unlike *auto* data, *static* values are remembered when the scope is left and reentered, provided program execution isn't terminated.

## Initializing *static* scalars and arrays

Initialization of *static* data takes place once and only once, before execution of the *main()* function begins. All *static* variables not assigned a specific value, including *static* arrays, are initialized by default to zero.

---

# C O M M E N T

*It is good style to explicitly initialize all static arrays and scalars.*

---

Variables with *static* storage class can be initialized by constant expressions only; you cannot call functions or refer to other variables to initialize *static* scalars or arrays.

To explicitly initialize a *static* array, you can supply a comma-separated list of constant expressions in curly braces, like this:

```
static short leap_yrs[5] = {1980, 1984, 1988, 1992, 1996};
```

Arrays of character data (strings) are initialized with text inside double quotes. A double-quoted string constant is equivalent to a constant array with one more element than the number of characters inside the double quotes. This additional element is the null character ('\0'), which marks the end of the array. Both of these next two declarations initialize a four-character array named *country* with the text *"USA"*:

```
static char country[4] = "USA";
static char country[4] = {'U', 'S', 'A', '\0'};
```

It is an error to supply *more* initializers than there are array elements, but if *fewer* initializers are supplied than the number of elements the array was declared to have, the compiler automatically initializes the remaining elements to zero:

```
/* Fills array with: 87346, 96437, 0L, 0L, 0L. */
/* Note: Our company is only 2 years old. */

static long last_five_years_sales[5] = {87346, 96437};
```

Someone reading a C program might easily miss the fact that some of the variables are initialized to zero if those initializers don't appear in the declaration. To initialize to zero with good style, be explicit:

```
static long expense_category_totals[12] = {0};
```

## How to Not Count Characters

We all hate to count characters in the text of a message we want to output, so here's a way to avoid it, at least some of the time. You can use empty brackets (*[]*) in the declaration of a *static* array, with the dimension omitted; the array's dimension will then be taken to be the number of initializers provided. In the following declaration, the dimension of *msg[]* is automatically set to 24:

```
static char msg[] = "C counts my characters.";   /* empty [] */
```

## The *SEMIGLOBAL* Storage Class

The particular types of data we have looked at so far are called *internal* because the scope is restricted to the body of a function or a block within a function. But C also has storage classes that are less restrictive. The first of these *external* classes we'll look at is called *external static*. This class permits data to be shared among a few specified functions that are part of a single source file.

As I mentioned earlier, to make managing and debugging external static data in our order-entry application easier, I've defined two more descriptive symbols to replace these reserved terms (see *syntypes.h*, Chapter 10). The first, *SEMIGLOBAL*, is used to declare a variable as having *external static* storage class (as opposed to *internal*) and is placed *outside* any function body. The second, *IMPORT*, is used *within* a function to tell the program to look outside the function for the variable's definition. The two terms are used together (see also *GLOBAL*), as you'll see later in this chapter.

```
#define SEMIGLOBAL static      /* used to define a semiglobal variable */
#define IMPORT extern           /* used to refer to a semiglobal or global
                                /*   variable defined elsewhere */
```

Here are some examples of the types of *SEMIGLOBAL* declarations used in the C order-entry application:

```
SEMIGLOBAL char company[L_COMPANY + 1] = "";
SEMIGLOBAL char is_resale[L_IS_RESALE + 1] = "n";
SEMIGLOBAL short ship_weights[MAX_ITEMS] = {0};
SEMIGLOBAL short tot_weight = 0;
SEMIGLOBAL char scrn_title[] = "*** ENTER NEW ORDER ***";
```

The declarations in this example are known as *defining declarations* because they cause storage to be allocated to hold the values of the shared data they declare. Defining declarations always appear outside the body of any function and, for good style, should have initializers. The scope of any variable declared outside a function is all of the source file that follows the defining declaration.

This ability to share data is a legitimate reason for grouping certain functions together in a single source file, where they will all be compiled together. (Their *internal* variables will still remain independent of each other.) Otherwise, each function should be stored in a separately compiled source file.

# The *GLOBAL* Storage Class

Most programming languages provide a global (fully shared) storage class of data known simply as *external* or *common* data. In C, this class is called *extern*. Data classified as *extern* are accessible to all functions in the entire program, so you would use this storage class for data needed by many functions in more than one source file.

You'll recall that in *syntypes.h*, I've simply used an empty string to define the term *GLOBAL* for use with *extern* data. Since defining declarations are placed outside any function, this has the effect of causing the storage class to default to *extern*.

A word of caution, however: Tracing the source of shared-data bugs is difficult in applications with large amounts of global data. With so many places to look, debugging can become prohibitively time-consuming. If possible, group functions that need to share data into one source file and use the *SEMIGLOBAL*, rather than the *GLOBAL*, storage class.

The defining declaration of a *GLOBAL* identifier can be accompanied by an initializer. As a matter of good style, every *extern* identifier should have one and only one defining declaration in the entire set of source files that will be compiled and linked to form a program. Here is the defining declaration for *bell_ok*, the only item of *GLOBAL* data in our order-entry application. Notice its position before the *main()* function in the source file.

```
/* Declare data shared among functions in all source files (GLOBAL). */

GLOBAL bflag bell_ok = YES;       /* OK to ring bell */

main()
    {
```

(The term *bflag* in this definition is equivalent to type *char*. The declaration of the type *bflag* as a synonym type of *char* is in *syntypes.h* in Chapter 10. A *bflag* variable is a 1-byte flag designated to hold true/false data in the form 1 or 0. The constant *YES* equals 1; *NO* equals 0.)

## Importing Outside Variables

It is good style to use the symbol *IMPORT* to specifically import any outside (*GLOBAL* or *SEMIGLOBAL*) shared data that a function accesses. We've already defined the symbol *IMPORT* to be the keyword *extern*, so declarations that begin with *IMPORT* clearly designate their variables as shared quantities, to be imported from outside this function. Most compilers require that every variable imported into a function by using *IMPORT* have a defining declaration on the outside. (The Microsoft compiler is an exception: It will create a defining declaration if none is found.)

The following declarations, called *referencing declarations,* are used to access the shared data in the order-entry example from inside a hypothetical function called *imp_sale()*:

```
void imp_sale()
    {
    IMPORT bflag bell_ok;          /* import a GLOBAL */
    IMPORT char company[];         /* import five SEMIGLOBALs */
    IMPORT char is_resale[];
    IMPORT short ship_weights[];
    IMPORT short tot_weight;
    IMPORT char scrn_title[];

    short step;
    short ipart;
```

Let's examine this code segment in more detail. I've included a bit more than just the *IMPORT* declarations to show you where the *IMPORT* symbols are placed: They should be the first declarations after the opening brace of the function and are followed by the internal declarations, if any. Notice that imported array declarations, like *static* array declarations, can use empty brackets (*[]*) rather than a specific dimension constant.

---

# C O M M E N T

*Even where they are not required, good style dictates that you always use referencing declarations, since they document part of a function's external interface—that is, the way the function interacts with its environment.*

---

Referencing declarations are required in each function that needs to access external data, *unless* the function follows the defining declaration in the same source file. Referencing declarations appear inside the function, begin with the symbol *IMPORT* or the keyword *extern*, and do not have initializers. Use of empty brackets (*[]*) for the first dimension is again both permitted and recommended in the referencing declarations of external arrays.

```
void err_warn(
    char first[], char second[])  /* two parts of diagnostic message */

    {
    IMPORT bflag bell_ok;          /* referencing declaration */
    short first_len = strlen(first);
    short second_len = strlen(second);
```

External referencing declarations are also permitted outside a function to make an external identifier visible to all functions in the source file. This saves repeated typing, but at the cost of readability. This type of declaration is commonly (and acceptably) hidden away in one of the header files used to declare the parameter and return types of all functions in a library. The order-entry application's project utility header file, *projutil.h*, is a good example of this approach. This file contains, among other things, the referencing declarations for our project utility library functions. When the header file is included (using #*include*) at the beginning of a source file, outside any function, all its return-type and parameter-type declarations become available throughout the source file. (This also allows the compiler to check calls to these functions.)

```
/* If IMPORT is not already defined, do it now. */
#ifndef IMPORT
    #define IMPORT extern
#endif

    /* ... */
/* Declare project utility function return and argument types.
 * If your C compiler does not support the declaration of argument types,
 * supply empty () after function name, rather than the types listed here.
 * These declarations make it possible to call any of these functions from
 * anywhere within the source file after this header file (projutil.h)
 * is included. The call will be checked for the proper number and types
 * of arguments and use of return values.
 */

IMPORT void beg_scrn(char[], char[], char[], char[]);
IMPORT stepcode prompt(char[], char[], short, short, flag, short, short);
IMPORT stepcode nprompt(long *, char[], long, long, flag, short, short);
IMPORT void tput(short, short, char[]);
IMPORT void ntput(short, short, long, short);
IMPORT flag match(char[], char[]);
IMPORT void err_warn(char[], char[]);
IMPORT void err_exit(char[], char[]);
IMPORT void strrjust(char[], short);
IMPORT void logentry(char[]);
```

# Cartridge and Other ROM-based Software

The following warning applies to only a small group of programmers: those who write C programs that will be ROM-based (for instance, cartridge software).

---

## C A U T I O N

*With ROM-based software,* static *and* external *data won't be initialized.*

---

Ordinarily, when you ask the operating system to use a program, a copy of that program is loaded from disk into RAM and then executed. ROM-based software, however, executes directly from ROM; no loading takes place. You'll recall that the *static* and *extern* initializers are applied at load time; in this case we have no loading, hence no initialization. Therefore, initial *static* and *extern* values for a ROM-based application *must* be assigned explicitly in a non-declaration statement.

## The *register* Storage Class

I've left the discussion of *register* storage until last because it's seldom used in interactive applications. Why so? Well, the explanation is really fairly straightforward. Shorter, faster machine-level instructions are used on data in registers, which reduces code size and improves the efficiency of the CPU in most environments. But the delays encountered in interactive processing are usually caused by the slowness of I/O, not by the CPU, so registers don't help much in these programs.

When *register* storage *is* used, what kinds of data should be placed in registers? Primarily, frequently accessed variables such as loop counters. Parameters may also be declared to have *register* storage class. For portability, use registers only with *char*, *short*, and *int data*, never with *long*, *float*, or *double*.

Microsoft's C compiler supports the *register* storage class, although many others do not at this time. Two registers are available per function or block, and additional register requests are legal. Registers are the same size as an *int* variable: either 2 or 4 bytes, depending upon the CPU chip and compiler.

How many *register* declarations are permitted in a function or block? As many as you like, because the compiler is free to ignore them. Requests for *register* storage are just that: "requests." You are not promised a register, and if denied a register, the declared variable automatically reverts to the *auto* storage class, with no change in results. And although C can use registers, it is unable to access a *specific* register that a system programmer might want to examine or set. In C, the compiler chooses which registers it will use. The only way around this is to write an assembly-language function to set the register.

In all other respects, the behavior of the *register* storage class is identical with that of the *auto* storage class—that is, initialization, scope, and lifetime are the same.

To declare a variable with *register* storage class, simply begin the declaration with the keyword *register*:

```
register short loop_counter;    /* variable loop_counter resides */
                                /*   in a register */
```

# Summary of Storage Classes

A variable is *allocated* when memory is obtained to hold its value and *freed* when that memory is returned to the system's control for other use. The *lifetime* of a variable is the period between these two events. There are two possible lifetimes for a variable:

| FORM | ACTION |
| --- | --- |
| EACH | Allocates storage on entry to declaring block or function; frees storage on leaving block or function (value is lost). |
| ONCE | Allocates storage once, before execution; allocated storage location used for full life of the program. |

A variable can be *initialized* when memory is allocated to it. Two forms of variable initialization are possible in C:

| FORM | ACTION |
| --- | --- |
| EACH | Initializes on each entry to declaring function or block; scalars initialized to expressions; arrays not initialized. |
| ONCE | Initializes only once, before the program begins execution; scalars and arrays initialized to constants only. |

The *scope* of a variable is the set of statements where the name of the variable may be used to obtain a value. Reference to a variable outside its scope is an error. C supports three levels of variable-name scope:

| LEVEL | DESCRIPTION |
| --- | --- |
| INTERNAL | Name is known only in declaring function or block. |
| SEMIGLOBAL | Name is shared among functions following the declaration in the same source file. |
| GLOBAL | Name is shared among all functions in a program that import the name *or* that follow the defining declaration of the name in the same source file. |

Storage classes do not exist for all possible combinations of initialization, allocation, and scope characteristics. Figure 7-2 lists the acceptable storage classes.

| STORAGE CLASS | INITIALIZATION | ALLOCATION | SCOPE |
|---|---|---|---|
| *auto* | EACH | EACH | INTERNAL |
| *register* | EACH | EACH | INTERNAL |
| *static* (internal) | ONCE | ONCE | INTERNAL |
| *static* (external) | ONCE | ONCE | SEMIGLOBAL |
| *extern* | ONCE | ONCE | GLOBAL |

FIGURE 7-2
*Acceptable combinations of initialization, allocation, and scope*

The types of shared data used by an application influence how the functions in that application should be organized into source files. We'll look at the development of source-file structure in Chapters 9 and 10, but first we need to learn how to access data *outside* C programs by using the operating-system command line and C's run-time support.

# Data Outside the Program

So far, we've spent quite a bit of time discussing how C handles the storage and sharing of data in the various components of a source program. But your C program can also access data from external sources: command-line and operating-system environment variables, and data stored in other files. Let's talk about each of these outside sources separately.

## Environment Variables

Environment variables are strings created with the MS-DOS SET command or the library function *putenv()*. Environment data created with the *SET* command last throughout your session at the computer (or until specifically changed), because the data are owned by the operating system, not the program. When you create or change an environment variable with *putenv()*, the data last only as long as the program that contained the call to *putenv()*. Each program works only with a copy of the MS-DOS environment, so any creation or change of a variable is temporary. To obtain the value of an environment variable, call the library function *getenv()*, like this:

```
putenv("UNAME = GREG");  /* assign GREG to environment variable UNAME */
                         /* MS-DOS equivalent: SET UNAME GREG */
printf("UNAME = %s\n", getenv("UNAME")); /* display contents of UNAME */
```

(The UNIX and XENIX operating systems also have environment variables, but instead of calling *putenv()* to set variables in these systems, you access the environment data table directly.)

## The Program Command Line

The command line (the line of text that commands the operating system to execute your program) is a source of high-level data for some programs. For instance, you can pass argument or option data to the *main()* function from the command line, and since the command-line interface to *main()* is implemented on nearly all C compilers, portability isn't an issue.

The syntax of the MS-DOS *DIR* command is a good illustration of the use of command-line interfaces. In fact, *DIR* could easily have been written in C:

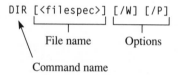

```
DIR [<filespec>] [/W] [/P]
```
File name   Options

Command name

Three types of information can be included on a command line:

- The name of the file that holds the executable program. This must be the first word on the command line. (MS-DOS lets you omit the *.exe* file name extension.)

- Command-line arguments. These optional strings of text are passed to your *main()* using the *array of pointers* data structure. (See Chapter 15.)

- Standard input/output redirections. These come last on the command line and are also optional.

## Command-line arguments

In a sense, command-line arguments are a unique storage class made up of read-only data. Text in the command line is separated into words, which are then grouped into a list to pass to *main()*, which is free to ignore these arguments if they aren't appropriate to the environment.

What kind of data are passed to *main()* in this manner? Well, command-line arguments are typically limited to file names or option strings (sometimes known as *flags* or *switches*), which often appear cryptic. Menus are a friendlier alternative to the command line: They *show* you the options you otherwise are forced to memorize. But menus execute more slowly and take longer to read than the command-line interface, so you will have to decide which is best for your program.

## Standard input/output redirection

The last entries on the command line are the standard file-redirection commands we discussed briefly in Chapter 2. Standard input data are normally obtained by waiting for the user to type at the keyboard. Standard output normally appears on the screen. The redirection commands permit a program to input data from another source, such as a disk or modem, and output data to a different destination, such as a printer or disk file. This ability to redirect program input and output without changing the program itself gives C a device-independent edge over many other languages.

C's standard library output functions will send output to any device. What device that is depends on file-redirection instructions to a small piece of object code called the *C run-time header*, which is responsible for calling your *main()* function as a subfunction. The C run-time header opens three standard files for *main()*:

| NAME | DESCRIPTION |
| --- | --- |
| *stdin* | Standard input file, normally from the keyboard |
| *stdout* | Standard output file, normally to the screen |
| *stderr* | Standard error (output) file, normally to the screen |

An interactive program reads from the standard input file to obtain data from the user and writes to the standard output (or standard error) file to display a message. If you redirect the standard output of a program to a disk file, the redirected output will be saved in that file but won't appear on the screen. The fact that the user will not see this redirected output as it is produced accounts for the standard error file: Data written to *stderr* will appear on the screen, even if *stdout* is redirected elsewhere, so that the user can see any error messages.

An interactive program becomes non-interactive when its standard *input* is redirected to a disk file. In that case, each time your program needs to input a line of text, it reads a line from the disk file. The advantage to this kind of redirection is that responses can be stored in advance and output can be saved for later viewing.

## Filter programs

Programs that get data from standard input, process the data, and then write the results to standard output are called *filter programs*. Command-line redirection permits filter programs to be used in a variety of ways.

Let's use a practical example to demonstrate how the redirection commands work. A filter program that creates line-numbered listings can be very useful to C programmers, since the compiler's diagnostic messages use line numbers to refer to objectionable lines in the source code. Here's a short program, *listing.c*, that will produce such a numbered listing:

```
/*************************************************************************
 * Output a line-numbered program listing of the program read from
 * standard input to standard output.
 *************************************************************************
 */

#include <stdio.h>

void main(void)
    {
    char line[512];        /* holds one source line */
    short line_number;     /* holds line count */

    /* List next line of input until EOF reached, */
    /*    at which time gets() returns zero. */
    for (line_number = 1; gets(line); ++line_number)
       printf("%3d %s\n", line_number, line);
    printf("\n\n\n");        /* skip some lines at end */
    }
```

The interactive use of this listing program, without any redirections, looks a little odd. When you execute the program, each line you type is echoed back to you on the screen with a line number as a prefix, and you must press ^Z (^D with some operating systems) alone on a line to signal the end of the standard input file. (Calls to *gets()* after the end of standard input return a zero, which causes the *for* loop to terminate.) Here is a sample of the results of interactive use of our listing program without any I/O redirection:

```
C>LISTING
first line of input
  1 first line of input
last line of input
  2 last line of input
^Z


C>
```

Seems rather pointless, doesn't it? (Actually, it's an easy way to give *listing* a quick test.) The program becomes more useful, however, when file redirections are applied. The source code for our listing program is saved in the file *listing.c*. Now suppose we use the < symbol to redirect standard input to be read from the file *listing.c*:

```
C>LISTING < LISTING.C
```

This command produces our listing program from *listing.c* in the following format:

```
 1 /*********************************************************************
 2  * Output a line-numbered program listing of the program read from
 3  * standard input to standard output.
 4  *********************************************************************
 5  */
 6
 7 #include <stdio.h>
 8
 9 void main(void)
10    {
11    char line[512];       /* holds one source line */
12    short line_number;    /* holds line count */
13
14    /* List next line of input until EOF reached, */
15    /*   at which time gets() returns zero. */
16    for (line_number = 1; gets(line); ++line_number)
17       printf("%3d %s\n", line_number, line);
18    printf("\n\n\n");      /* skip some lines at end */
19    }
```

The > sign redirects the program's standard output to the file or device named after the symbol. For example, this next command produces a numbered listing of the data in *listing.c* and stores the output in a file named *listing.lst* :

```
C>LISTING < LISTING.C > LISTING.LST
```

(Here's a trick to help you remember which symbol applies to input and which to output. Think of > and < as arrowheads that point toward or away from the command. The > points away from the command, so it controls the command's output. The < points toward the command, so it controls the command's input.)

The >> redirection command redirects standard output to the *end* of the file named after the symbol. There is no risk of losing data using >>, because new lines are simply appended after the last line of the existing file. (With both > and >>, the operating system automatically creates an empty file if the file to hold the output does not already exist.) To number the lines of a series of files with the *listing* program and save the output from all of them in a single file named *c.lst*, you could use the following commands:

```
C>LISTING < BEG_SCRN.C > C.LST
C>LISTING < ERR_EXIT.C >> C.LST
C>LISTING < ERR_WARN.C >> C.LST
```

The >> guarantees that the second and third files will not overwrite the first when they are output.

---

# C A U T I O N

*Use > with great caution, because its first action is to delete all data in the file named after the symbol. Nothing will ruin your day faster than wiping out a valuable data file because you confused > with <!*

---

## Pipes that join commands

No, this isn't a plumbing class, but data *should* flow like water, so the analogy is instructive. The pipe redirection command is a broken vertical bar ( ¦ ) placed between two commands. It causes the standard output of the first command (on the left side) to be redirected and used as the input for the second command. For example, the following

MS-DOS command causes the output from the *DIR* command to be piped into *listing*:

```
DIR *.C ¦ LISTING
```

The output from *listing* appears on your screen as a line-numbered directory of all files with the *.c* extension.

Pipes under the OS/2, UNIX, and XENIX operating systems execute both commands in parallel, passing the output from the first command to the second command immediately, as it is produced, whereas MS-DOS creates a temporary file for the output of the first command and then uses that file as standard input to the second command.

## Standard Files in Interactive Applications

The names of our three standard files—input, output, and error—carry definite implications about how those files are intended to be used. But some programs, such as the order-entry application in Section III, use these files in ways that do not exactly follow the sense of their names. Let's see why this is so.

Interactive programs produce two kinds of output: prompt messages that ask for data to be entered by the user (output on the screen) and data received from the user to be saved for additional processing later. The problem is where to output the user entries validated by the program. If all the program's output is written to the *stdout* file, the validated user data will be mingled with screen-control characters and prompt messages.

One way to keep these two types of output separated is to write the validated data to disk, using a file other than the standard ones. We'll see how to do that in Section V. For now, simply be aware that the disadvantage of this method is that you can no longer use standard file-redirection commands on those data.

A second and more satisfactory solution uses the standard error file (*stderr*) to output prompt messages, diagnostic messages, and screen-control commands (clear screen, move cursor, and the like), leaving the standard output file (*stdout*) free for one purpose only: storage of the validated data resulting from program processing. This approach allows us to redirect application data without simultaneously redirecting display text.

To send output to the standard error file in this way, you will first need to include <*stdio.h*> at the start of your source file so that *stderr* will be available to every function in your file. Then use one of the following library functions to send output to *stderr*:

| FUNCTION | EXAMPLE |
|---|---|
| fprintf(stderr, format_string, arg_1, arg_2, ...); | fprintf(stderr, "Enter a number from %d to %d:", low, high); |
| fputs(data_string, stderr); | fputs("Enter customer name: ", stderr); |
| fputc(data_char, stderr); | fputc('\7', stderr) |

The first function in the example, *fprintf()*, behaves just like *printf()*, except that one new argument, the file variable *stderr*, must precede the rest. (We'll look at file variables more extensively in Section V.) The second function, *fputs()*, resembles the function *puts()* used to output a string to standard output. Unlike *puts()*, however, *fputs()* does not output a newline ('\n') after the string. The third function, *fputc()*, is used to output a single character to a file, which in the example is *stderr*.

Well, that about winds up our quick tour of C basics. You now know enough C to begin analyzing the code for the order-entry application program, so let's quickly review the conventions for C coding style (Chapter 9) and then move on to the advanced topics I've been promising.

# Coding Style
# and Standards

Before we actually begin working with the order-entry system that forms the heart of this book, we need to spend a few minutes discussing the style rules and standards that are so important in creating readable, maintainable C software.

## The Road to Readability

Well-written, clearly structured code is always a pleasure to read. Poorly written code can be a headache, or worse. The following rules have become conventions in C programming; blessed are they who adhere to them consistently.

- Surround operators that take two operands with spaces.

- Do not put a space between a unary operator and its operand.

- Do not put a space between a function name and its opening parenthesis.

- Put one space after reserved keywords.

- Indent blocks uniformly, using the tab key rather than the spacebar.

- Put braces alone on a line, indented in alignment with the block they create.

- Code only one statement per line.

- Skip a line after the last declaration.

When you plan the structural components of your program, keep in mind the following suggestions:

| COMPONENT | STRUCTURE |
| --- | --- |
| Identifier names | Be consistent: Use the same name for the same purpose throughout the program. |
| | Be meaningful: Choose a variable name that explains the meaning of the value, and avoid short names that only a cryptographer could decipher. |
| | Be accurate: Make sure the variable name is always truthful about the nature of the value. |
| Functions | Make them tools that do only one job, but do it very well. Limit function bodies to one page (about 60 lines). |
| Comments | Begin each source file and each function with a comment stating its purpose. |
| | Document all external interfaces with comments. |
| | Explain complex or tricky code segments with step-by-step comments. |
| | Include explanatory comments with each declaration, as needed. |
| *goto* statements | Don't use them. |

# Source-File and Function Formats

Once you've designed the flow of data between functions, you need to decide how those functions should be organized to make the flow not just possible, but also easy to understand. The following example shows a typical organization for C source files. It is logical and readable, and helps make program development and maintenance easier.

```
/* BEGIN SOURCE FILE:   FILENAME.C */
/**********************************************************************
 * Comments describing functions and data in source file.
 **********************************************************************
 */

#include commands
#define commands

Structure and union tag declarations (described later)
Type synonym statements using typedef
GLOBAL (external) defining declarations (with initializers)
SEMIGLOBAL (external static) defining declarations (with initializers)

Functions
    Source files that contain no functions and hold only GLOBAL defining
    declarations are permitted.
```

As we've seen, C source files most often contain only just a single function. This is preferred style. Place more than one function in a source file only when those functions share some *SEMIGLOBAL* (*external static*) data. Here is the recommended style for the layout of each function in a source file:

```
/**********************************************************************
 * Comments describing the function, its uses, and interfaces.
 **********************************************************************
 */

return_type function_name(parameter list)
    {
    IMPORT (extern) referencing declarations
    internal declarations

    function body statements
    }
```

## Compiler-generated Header Files

The */Zg* option of *CL* is a feature I love to rave about: Most of the coding errors that went unreported because of the lack of or weakness of type checking by the compiler can now be caught. Nowhere is accuracy of data type a greater issue than in passing arguments to functions. If you follow the instructions in this chapter for the */Zg* option and compiler warning level, you can be assured that all function calls have been strictly checked for number and type of arguments.

The */Zg* switch used on the *CL* command line instructs the compiler to generate a list of prototype declarations for every function in each of the source files passed to it. The compiler outputs the list of function declarations to standard output—so you can redirect the list to a file, using the output redirection symbol (>):

```
CL /Zg FILE.C > FILE.H
```

```
CL /Zg *.C > FUNC_DCL.H
```

The first *CL* command in the example processes a single source file, *file.c*, and creates the header file, *file.h*. I say "processes" rather than "compiles" because the compiler omits compilation and linking when the */Zg* switch is used. Where application or library source files for one program are organized into separate files in one directory, using a command like the second *CL* command in the example makes good sense.

The */Zg* option works best for catching errors when used in conjunction with a strict level of error checking.

## Compiler Warning Level

The compiler warning level is controlled by the */W* switch of the *CL* command. The */W* is followed by a number from 0 to 3, although new levels may be added in the future. The higher the level, the stricter the checking. I always use the strictest level and encourage you to do the same. You are always free to ignore warnings if you choose, and your coding style may improve as you clean up bad habits with the help of diagnostic messages.

The default warning level for *CL* compilations is 1. You can change the default by adding this line to your *autoexec.bat* file so that you can request the strictest checking, without supplying */W3* for each *CL* command:

```
SET CL=/W3
```

Some software companies make it a rule that all programs must compile without any warnings or errors whatsoever. Other shops make exceptions for certain specific warning messages that they feel are too fussy or could be avoided only by adding extraneous code. It is up to you to decide whether to allow certain warnings or errors.

The style rules presented in this chapter aren't simply arbitrary. They're designed to make your life as a C programmer easier—just how much easier you'll see in the next chapter, where we begin analyzing the order-entry source listings.

# S E C T I O N

# III

Section III focuses on the actual development of our product: the order-entry application program. The user interface is the heart of this highly interactive business application. **Chapter 10** contains the application design and the source code for the program, with detailed comments explaining each function. **Chapter 11** discusses the code used to manage the prompt screens that make up the user interface. **Chapter 12** covers screen output, with emphasis on library and order-entry display functions, and **Chapter 13** deals with strict but "friendly" control of user input.

# The Order-Entry Application Program

In this chapter, we will discuss the design for the Software-Vendor Order-Entry Application and then look at the complete source listings. This program is real: It does let you enter orders for software or, in fact, any other product. The source files compile without any diagnostics at the maximum warning level (level 3; see the *CL* command's /W option).

We'll discuss each of the application's functions and data structures in detail in the chapters in this section following the listings. The functions and data structures are also used throughout this book as examples of C programming. For now, let's concentrate on the system design and the organization of the files.

## Application Design

Let me set the scene for the design and development of the order-entry application, which we are going to use in our own business, not market as part of our product line.

As software entrepreneurs, we are already aware of the deficiencies of running a business manually, with old-fashioned paper-and-pencil records, so naturally we want to automate right from the start. And as experienced software engineers, we know the value of early user involvement and feedback in the design process. So, before we begin to design the application, we interview everyone who will be using the system to obtain as much information as possible about their requirements and work styles. We come up with a list something like this:

| USER | NEED(S) |
| --- | --- |
| System manager | Access control for system security |
| | Maximum input controls, to minimize user problems |
| | Error log to aid in system maintenance |
| Sales personnel | Usable by employees with no data-entry experience |
| | Clear and uniform prompts, efficient defaults, and recognizable numeric displays |
| | Input control and diagnostic messages |
| | Ease of correction within fields, between fields, and between screens |
| Warehouse personnel | Easy-to-read list of items and quantities to be shipped |
| | Complete shipping information, including address, carrier, and shipping charges |
| Accounting personnel | Complete billing address and telephone contact |
| | Resale information |
| | Appropriate tax rate, if not for resale |
| | Customer's payment terms and credit limit |
| Company accountant | Record of sales, by item, for profit/loss analysis |
| | Detailed resale records, for sales-tax reporting |
| | Totals by month/quarter, for IRS reporting |
| | Transaction log, for audit trail |
| Sales manager | Record of sales by product, for planning |
| | Demographic information (location, type and size of business, etc.), for marketing strategies |
| | Customer addresses and telephone numbers, for advertising |
| | Knowledge of how customers heard about company |
| | Record of each salesperson's performance |

When we are satisfied that we have a clear and detailed understanding of the requirements of all these different individuals, we actually begin designing the system.

We then call a second meeting with the users to review the first cut of the design and decide upon any necessary modifications. We prepare a set of sample data screens, as they will be seen by the salespeople taking orders (see Figure 10-1 on the following page), and submit them for approval.

After our users have accepted the screen formats, we begin designing our program structure. We agree that the logical approach is to write a separate function to manage each input screen, one to manage the final order output, and a main routine to control the interactions among them. The tree diagram in Figure 10-1 shows the top-level design we decide upon for our program.

Now we pseudocode each of the functions and plug them back into our tree to be sure all necessary interactions are provided for. We repeat this procedure for all levels of the application. The requirements of the top-level functions dictate the specifications for the lower-level functions, rather than the reverse. (These lower-level functions fall into two categories: those specific to the order-entry application and those general-purpose utility functions that can be called in other applications we write in the future.)

Finally, we write, compile, test, and debug our program, get final approval from our users, and install the system. We're ready to do business!

## Organization of Listings

Figure 10-2 on the page after next shows how the application source-file listings are organized. The source file *ordbuild.c* contains more than one function because the functions share data; *err_warn.c* contains two functions that act as a team; and *stubs.c* contains all the incomplete functions. All other source files hold only a single function each. (See Chapter 9 on style.) The functions in *stubs.c* are only partially developed at this stage because we haven't yet discussed some of the material that needs to go into them. These stubs are still useful for debugging the rest of the application, however, and will be replaced later by fully operational versions.

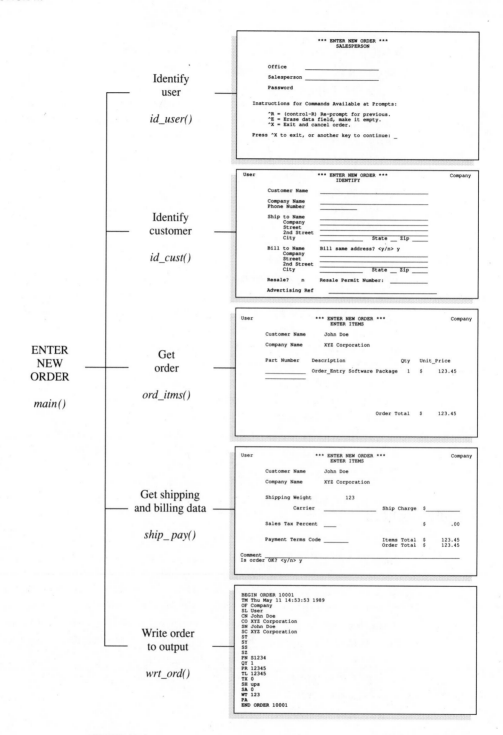

FIGURE 10-1

*Top-level structure of the order-entry application*

| SOURCE FILE | FUNCTION | LEVEL | PURPOSE |
|---|---|---|---|
| *syntypes.h* | | header | Holds company-wide definitions, synonym types, macros |
| *ansiscrn.h* | | header | Holds screen- and cursor-control command definitions |
| *ordentry.h* | | header | Holds order data-field definitions |
| *ordentry.c* | | high | Declares *GLOBAL* data and controls entire application |
| *ordbuild.c* | | middle | Declares *SEMIGLOBAL* data; holds middle-level functions |
| | *id_user()* | middle | Identifies user/salesperson |
| | *id_cust()* | middle | Identifies customer |
| | *ord_itms()* | middle | Inputs items to order |
| | *ship_pay()* | middle | Inputs shipping and payment data |
| | *wrt_ord()* | middle | Writes the order to *stdout* |
| *get_addr.c* | *get_addr()* | low | Prompts for an address |
| *pnt_id_c.c* | *pnt_id_cust()* | low | Paints customer ID screen |
| *pnt_ship.c* | *pnt_ship_pay()* | low | Paints shipping and payment screen |
| *stubs.c* | *inv_find()* | low | Finds a part in inventory |
| | *pw_find()* | low | Finds a user's password |
| | *order_num()* | low | Creates next order number |
| | *logentry()* | low | Saves a message in the log file |
| *projutil.h* | | header | Holds declarations and symbols used with the project utility library |
| *prompt.c* | *prompt()* | lib | Inputs a string from user; verifies match, checks length |
| *nprompt.c* | *nprompt()* | lib | Inputs a *long* integer from user; validates range |
| *fprompt.c* | *fprompt()* | lib | Inputs a double-precision floating-point number from user; validates range |
| *tput.c* | *tput()* | lib | Displays a string at specified row and column |
| *ntput.c* | *ntput()* | lib | Displays a *long* integer, right justified, at specified row and column |
| *ftput.c* | *ftput()* | lib | Displays a double-precision floating-point number, right justified on the decimal point, at specified row and column |
| *beg_scrn.c* | *beg_scrn()* | lib | Clears screen and prints screen headings |

FIGURE 10-2  *(continued)*

*Organization of order-entry source listings*

FIGURE 10-2. *continued*

| SOURCE FILE | FUNCTION | LEVEL | PURPOSE |
|---|---|---|---|
| *match.c* | *match()* | lib | Verifies that a string matches a pattern string |
| *strrjust.c* | *strrjust()* | lib | Right justifies a string, filling with blanks |
| *err_warn.c* | *err_warn()* | lib | Displays a two-string diagnostic warning message and returns |
| | *err_exit()* | lib | Displays a serious diagnostic message and exits application |

## Project utility library functions

The source files with level *lib* hold general-purpose utility functions that are not specific to our order-entry application. You will find them useful for writing many of your own applications. (Programs that call any of these functions should include the header file *projutil.h*, which contains the declarations and definitions used in conjunction with the project utility functions.)

General-purpose functions like these can be compiled to object form and combined in a single file called a library. Building such libraries of commonly used utility functions makes it easy to link them with other functions you write. (With Microsoft C, use the *LIB* command to build and maintain libraries for use with the *CL* or *LINK* command.)

## Header files

Most header files, such as *projutil.h*, are written to be used in conjunction with a specific set of related functions. The related function declarations should also be included in these header files to permit the compiler to check your function calls for the proper number and types of arguments, as well as to handle the return values correctly. (You will find it much easier to call the associated functions if you supply meaningful and descriptive names for constants passed as arguments.)

Header files can also be organized with groups of people in mind rather than groups of related functions: for example, you as the lone author, programmers on the same project, or all programmers throughout the company. The *syntypes.h* file is an example of this last type. If you include *syntypes.h* at the start of a program, you can avoid coding *#define* commands for long lists of single-purpose definitions that you use frequently.

## Printing program listings

You can create line-numbered source listings for the order-entry program by using the listing-filter program we developed in Chapter 8. The commands to prepare the individual listings look like this:

```
LISTING < ORDENTRY.C > PRN:
LISTING < ORDBUILD.C > PRN:
```

The file named after the < redirection for standard input is the file to be listed. The > *PRN:* redirects the standard output to the printer.

An alternative way of making these line-numbered listings is to use the >> output-redirection command to gather all listing output into a single file (for example, *ordentry.lst*) before printing:

```
LISTING < ORDENTRY.C > ORDENTRY.LST
LISTING < ORDBUILD.C >> ORDENTRY.LST
COPY ORDENTRY.LST PRN:
```

(The spaces around the redirection symbols in the preceding examples are optional.)

# Building the Order-Entry Program and Project Utility Library

If you have not purchased the companion disk for this book, you begin this job of building the order-entry program by typing the program source, exactly as it appears in this chapter. The batch job *cc_order.bat* compiles all source files and captures compiler messages in the file C.LST, although there shouldn't be any compiler messages.

You can type in *stubs.c* or the final versions of the stub functions (*inv_find()*, *pw_find()*, *order_num()*, and *logentry()*) from later chapters. The decision you make regarding stub functions will affect the instructions for compiling the program, building the project utility library, and linking the program. The stub functions do not require data files, but their fleshed-out counterparts from later chapters do.

Edit the following batch job in a file *CC_ORDER.BAT*, and then type *CC_ORDER* to compile the order-entry C code.

```
REM CC_ORDER.BAT: COMPILE ALL ORDER-ENTRY SOURCE FILES
CL /W3 /c ordentry.c > c.lst
CL /W3 /c nprompt.c >> c.lst
CL /W3 /c ordbuild.c >> c.lst
CL /W3 /c get_addr.c >> c.lst
CL /W3 /c pnt_id_c.c >> c.lst
CL /W3 /c pnt_ship.c >> c.lst
CL /W3 /c prompt.c >> c.lst
CL /W3 /c fprompt.c >> c.lst
CL /W3 /c tput.c >> c.lst
CL /W3 /c ntput.c >> c.lst
CL /W3 /c ftput.c >> c.lst
CL /W3 /c beg_scrn.c >> c.lst
CL /W3 /c match.c >> c.lst
CL /W3 /c strrjust.c >> c.lst
CL /W3 /c err_warn.c >> c.lst
REM ***
REM *** The next 4 CL compiles are in place of a single compile of stubs.c:
REM ***        CL /c stubs.c >> c.lst
REM *** No data files are needed with the stub version of order-entry.
REM *** pw_find.c, logentry.c, and ordernum.c are finalized in Chapter 17,
REM *** where their data files, passfile.dat, logfile.dat, and ordernum.dat, are
REM *** also described.  passfile.dat should be constructed with a text editor.
REM *** Create the order number file like this:  ECHO 10000 > ordernum.dat.
REM *** The final version of inv_find.c is in Chapter 19. The inventory file,
REM *** invntory.dat, is maintained using the program invmaint.c, listed in
REM *** Chapter 18.
REM ***
CL /W3 /c pw_find.c >> c.lst
CL /W3 /c inv_find.c >> c.lst
CL /W3 /c logentry.c >> c.lst
CL /W3 /c ordernum.c >> c.lst
TYPE c.lst
```

The output file *c.lst* should contain nothing but the names of the compiled source files, one per line. Errors or warnings are an indication that you made a typing mistake.

The next step in the program-building process is to gather up the object files for the project utility library functions and create the project utility library (to be used when linking). Edit *projlib.bat*, and then execute it by typing *PROJLIB*.

```
REM PROJLIB.BAT: CREATE THE PROJECT UTILITY LIBRARY PROJUTIL.LIB
LIB projutil+beg_scrn;
LIB projutil+err_warn;
LIB projutil+fprompt;
LIB projutil+ftput;
REM *** If you are using STUBS.C, not its replacements, logentry.obj
REM *** will not exist and the LIB on the next line will fail.
LIB projutil+logentry;
LIB projutil+match;
LIB projutil+nprompt;
LIB projutil+ntput;
LIB projutil+prompt;
LIB projutil+strrjust;
LIB projutil+tput;
```

The instructions needed to link the order-entry program, *ordentry.exe*, depend on whether you have compiled the stub functions in *stubs.c* or the final versions of the stub functions found in later chapters. Supply the following inputs, after typing *LINK*, to create the non-stub version of *ordentry.exe*:

```
LINK
Object Modules [.OBJ]: ordentry+get_addr+ordbuild+
Object Modules [.OBJ]: pnt_id_c+pnt_ship+
Object Modules [.OBJ]: inv_find+pw_find+ordernum
Run File [ORDENTRY.EXE]:
List File [NUL.MAP]:
Libraries [.LIB]: projutil
```

If you are linking by using the stub versions of some functions, but not the final ones, replace the third input, which is *inv_find+pw_find+ordernum*, with *stubs*.

# Compiler Error Messages

As I said earlier, all of the order-entry source files compile without errors at the maximum warning level. Therefore, if you do receive any error messages from the compiler, it's most likely the result of a typing error. Unfortunately, however, the error messages that the compiler generates don't always spell out exactly what the error is. For instance, if you make a typing error on one line, the compiler might not detect and report an error until the next line. And even then, its report could be misleading.

Let's look at a few intentional errors to get a feel for the kinds of error messages that are generated and why:

```
 1 /*********************************************************
 2  * tput() displays a string at a specified row and column.
 3  *********************************************************/
 4  */
 5
 6 #include <stdio.h>
 7 #include "ansiscrn.h"
 8 #include "projutil.h"
 9
10 void tput(
11     short row,              /* cursor row */
12     short col,              /* cursor column */
13     char text[])            /* text to display */
14
15     {
16     CUR_MV(row, col);
17     fputs(text, stderr);
18     }
```

All of the errors are errors of omission. I have deleted the high-lighted characters one at a time and recompiled *tput()* after each dele-tion to generate the individual error messages. For example, when I deleted the *)* on line 13, I received this message:

```
tput.c(15) : error C2059: syntax error : '{'
```

In this case, the compiler has determined that the function definition was incomplete, due to a missing *)* after the declarations of the para-meters. So it complained about the *{* that began the body of the func-tion. The mistake was not on line 15, as the error message indicated, but two lines earlier. Obviously, just because the compiler reports an error on a certain line, that doesn't mean the problem is in that line! It's not always this tricky.

After we insert the missing *)* into the code, a quick re-compile of *tput.c* displays these messages:

```
tput.c(16) : error C2065: 'row' : undefined
tput.c(17) : error C2146: syntax error : missing ';' before
identifier 'fputs'
tput.c(19) : error C2060: syntax error : EOF
```

In this case, the first message makes the problem clear: The compiler cannot find a declaration for *row*.

A quick scan of the source code makes this typing error on line 11 practically jump out at us.

What about the second error that refers to line 17? Hmmm.... Remember, the compiler recognizes the semicolon as the end of a statement and basically ignores a newline character in the source code. So the compiler is actually trying to make sense of the line:

```
CUR_MV(row, col) fputs(text, stderr);
```

It doesn't know what to do with the function name *fputs* in the middle of this line, and it tells us so. Whether the missing semicolon is placed at the end of line 16 or the beginning of line 17 makes no difference to the compiler. It looks much better at the end of line 16 to us humans.

I've left off the closing brace by deleting it from the last line. During compilation, I received this error message:

```
tput.c(19) : error C2060: syntax error : EOF
```

Now something really seems funny here. The compiler is telling me that I have an error in line 19, but there is no line 19 in this source listing. Ah, but there is, as far as the compiler is concerned. It contains the end-of-file (*EOF*) marker. Since the compiler expects a closing brace before the invisible *EOF*, it tells me I have a syntax error. Once again, the problem is a bit puzzling at first glance, but it is actually quite simple to correct.

Another point: A single mistyped statement could generate a large number of error messages. For instance, if you misspell an identifier in a function declaration, the misspelling will generate an error message wherever the function is called. If you get a flood of errors, try fixing only the first one, and the rest may disappear with it.

# The Header Files

The order-entry application uses four header files, each containing definitions, declarations, and the like, grouped according to their scope of use.

## Company-wide header: *syntypes.h*

This file combines definitions used frequently by all the programmers. Synonym types can be used to make code more readable by describing how data will be used. Definitions for shared data storage classes reside here. Some useful definitions for calls to commonly used standard library functions are missing from standard header files and can be found here.

## SYNTYPES.H

```
/* HEADER FILE: SYNTYPES.H
 ***********************************************************************
 * Symbols related to definition and use of shared data. Declarations of
 *   data with storage class static or external should begin with these
 *   shared-data modifiers:
 *     GLOBAL begins defining declarations for external data; data are
 *       shared by all functions that IMPORT the data.
 *     SEMIGLOBAL begins defining declarations for static external data;
 *       data are shared by functions in the same source file that IMPORT
 *       the data.
 *     IMPORT begins non-defining declarations of GLOBAL and SEMIGLOBAL
 *       data. A defining declaration allocates new, initialized storage.
 *       Non-defining declarations refer to data defined elsewhere, to
 *       allow examination or modification of those data.
 ***********************************************************************
 */

#define GLOBAL
#define SEMIGLOBAL static
#define IMPORT extern

/* Data types that are synonyms of other types. */
typedef unsigned char unchar;           /* unsigned characters */
typedef unsigned short unshort;         /* unsigned short integers */
typedef unsigned long unlong;           /* unsigned long integers */
typedef char byte;                      /* byte: 1-byte number (0 to 127) */
typedef char bflag;                     /* bflag: 1-byte true/false flag */
typedef int flag;                       /* flag: int-sized true/false flag */

/* Constants for true or false data, to be used in conjunction */
/*   with synonym types flag (int) and bflag (char). */
#ifndef YES             /* if not already defined, define YES, NO */
#define YES 1
#define NO 0
#endif

/*************************************************
 * Symbols related to standard library functions.
 *************************************************
 */

/* Status of SUCCEED or FAIL passed to exit(); aborts program. */
#ifndef SUCCEED
```

*(continued)*

SYNTYPES.H *continued*

```
#define SUCCEED 0
#define FAIL 1
#endif

/* File handles (descriptor numbers) for standard files to be */
/*   used with the low-level I/O functions read() and write(). */
#ifndef STDIN
#define STDIN 0
#define STDOUT 1
#define STDERR 2
#endif
```

# Company-wide header: *ansiscrn.h*

These macros and definitions output escape sequences for text-oriented screen and cursor control. To use them, you must boot your machine with the *ansi.sys* terminal driver; otherwise, they output garbage. To install the needed driver, edit your *config.sys* file (or create it if it doesn't exist) in the root (\) directory, insert the line *DEVICE = ANSI.SYS*, and reboot.

The macro expansions in this file call *fprintf(stderr, …)* to output to the standard error file, *stderr*, rather than calling its more familiar standard output counterpart, *printf()*. If you redirect standard output to a file, output of screen-control commands will not be redirected with the output. This point about redirection is important for the order-entry application because the application writes only order-detail information to standard output.

## ANSISCRN.H

```
/* HEADER FILE: ANSISCRN.H
 ****************************************************************************
 * Screen and Cursor-Control Commands.
 * NOTE: Definitions below require the ANSI.SYS terminal driver.  To install
 * ANSI.SYS, include this line in your CONFIG.SYS file:  DEVICE = ANSI.SYS
 ****************************************************************************
 * CUR_MV(r, c)  Move cursor to row r (1-25), column c (1-80).
 * CUR_UP(n)     Move cursor up n lines (ignored if at top).
 * CUR_DN(n)     Move cursor down n lines (ignored if at bottom).
 * CUR_RT(n)     Move cursor right n spaces (ignored at right margin).
 * CUR_LT(n)     Move cursor left n spaces (ignored at left margin).
 * CUR_SKIP      Send newline.
```

*(continued)*

ANSISCRN.H *continued*

```
* CUR_SAVE      Save cursor position.
* CUR_REST      Restore cursor position, to last CUR_SAVE position.
* CLR_SCRN      Clear screen and move cursor to home.
* CLR_LINE      Erase from cursor to end of line.
* CLR_EOS(r, c) Erase from row r, col c to screen end, leave cursor at r,c.
* BELL          Ring bell once by sending control-G.
***********************************************************************
*/

#define CUR_MV(row, col) fprintf(stderr, "\33[%d;%dH", row, col)
#define CUR_UP(num) fprintf(stderr, "\33[%dA", num)
#define CUR_DN(num) fprintf(stderr, "\33[%dB", num)
#define CUR_RT(num) fprintf(stderr, "\33[%dC", num)
#define CUR_LT(num) fprintf(stderr, "\33[%dD", num)
#define CUR_SKIP fprintf(stderr, "\n")
#define CUR_SAVE fprintf(stderr, "\33[s")
#define CUR_REST fprintf(stderr, "\33[u")
#define CLR_SCRN fprintf(stderr, "\33[2J")
#define CLR_LINE fprintf(stderr, "\33[K")
#define CLR_EOS(r, c) {byte i_; CUR_MV(r,c); \
   for (i_=r; i_<=25; ++i_) CLR_LINE, CUR_DN(1); CUR_MV(r,c); }
#define BELL fprintf(stderr, "\a")
```

## Project utility header: *projutil.h*

This file defines synonym data types and declares function argument
and return types for the project utility library functions. The file is
used by programmers in our project group.

### PROJUTIL.H

```
/* HEADER FILE: PROJUTIL.H
***********************************************************************
* projutil.h: project utility library function header file. #include this
*   file near the start of source files containing functions that will call
*   any of the project utility functions listed below.
***********************************************************************


***********************************************************************
* Project Utility Function Summary:
*
*    prompt()     Input a string, check match, check length.
*    nprompt()    Prompt for a long int, echo right justified.
*    fprompt()    Prompt for a double, echo right justified.
```

*(continued)*

PROJUTIL.H *continued*

```
*       tput()          Print a string at specific screen row and column.
*       ntput()         Print a long integer right justified on screen.
*       ftput()         Print a double right justified on screen.
*       beg_scrn()      Clear screen; print four headings at screen top.
*       match()         Compare a data string against a match string.
*       strrjust()      Right justify a string, padding with blanks.
*       err_warn()      Print a warning message, input Escape.
*       err_exit()      Call err_warn(), then terminate program.
*       logentry()      Append message text to log file.
*
* To learn more about these functions, read their source code.
***************************************************************************
*/

/* Type stepcode is a synonym data type defined below. The typedef statement
*   makes stepcode equivalent to type char. Type stepcode declares return
*   values from the functions prompt(), nprompt(), and fprompt().
*/
typedef char stepcode;

/* Argument constants and control symbols for prompt(). */
#define PRMTBSIZ 161        /* prompt buffer size */
#define MAND 1              /* for fifth argument: mandatory input */
#define OPT 0               /* for fifth argument: optional input */
#define C_MASK '_'          /* character to repeat for prompt field */

/* User command characters for prompt(). */
#define C_NULL '\x05'       /* ERASE ENTRY: '\x05' is control-E */
#define C_BACK '\x12'       /* BACK UP: '\x12' is control-R */
                            /* move back to previous prompt */
#define C_CANC '\x18'       /* CANCEL: '\x18' is control-X */
                            /* cancel order and program */

/* These are the possible return values from prompt() that a variable with */
/*   synonym type stepcode may take. */
#define STEPOK 0            /* data were entered; may be null if OPT */
#define STEPBACK 1          /* C_BACK was entered; back up a prompt */
#define STEPCANC 2          /* C_CANC was entered; cancel transaction */

/* Note this statement:
*   enum stepcode {STEPOK, STEPBACK, STEPCANC};
* This enumeration does almost the same job as the typedef synonym type
*   stepcode and the symbols STEPOK, STEPBACK, and STEPCANC. The
*   difference is that a variable of synonym type stepcode is not an
*   enumeration type and so may be a function return value.
*   At some future time, Microsoft may decide to permit functions to
*   return enumeration types.
*/
```

*(continued)*

PROJUTIL.H *continued*

```
/***********************************************************************
 * Declare project utility function return and argument types: If your
 *   (non-Microsoft) C compiler does not support the declaration of
 *   argument types, supply empty () after the function's name.
 * These declarations make it possible to call any of these functions from
 *   anywhere within the source file after this header file is included.
 *   The call will be checked for the proper number and types of arguments
 *   and proper use of the return value.
 ***********************************************************************
 */
extern  void beg_scrn(char *left, char *center, char *right, char *below);
extern  void err_warn(char *first, char *second);
extern  void err_exit(char *first, char *second);
extern  char fprompt(double *d_num, char *match_str, double min_dval,
    double max_dval, short width, short precision, int mand, short row,
    short col);
extern  void ftput(short row, short col, double double_val,
    short dec_place, char *buf, short field_len);
extern  void logentry(char *msg);
extern  int match(char *data_str, char *match_str);
extern  char nprompt(long *p_num, char *match_str, long min_val,
    long max_val, int mand, short row, short col);
extern  void ntput(short row, short col, long long_val, char *buf,
    short field_len);
extern  char prompt(char *data, char *match_str, short min_len,
    short max_len, int mand, short row, short col);
extern  void strrjust(char *str, short fld_len);
extern  void tput(short row, short col, char *text);
```

## Order-entry header: *ordentry.h*

This file holds definitions of type synonyms and of symbols that define the sizes or limits of data fields in an order. It is specific to the order-entry application. (In a database-management system, this kind of information would be stored in the data-dictionary files.) Redefinition of a field or addition of a new field in the order-entry application may make it necessary to recompile source files that use this header file.

## ORDENTRY.H

```
/* HEADER FILE: ORDENTRY.H
 ************************************************************
 * ordentry.h: header file for the order-entry application.
 ************************************************************
 */

/* Type money is defined as a synonym of type long for amounts */
/*   of money in cents ranging between + and - $21,474,836.47. */
typedef long money;

/* Order data maximum field widths defined for data input by prompt(). */
#define L_USER 25
#define L_PASSWORD 8
#define L_OFFICE 25
#define L_CUST_NAME 30
#define L_COMPANY 30
#define L_PHONE 14
#define L_SHIP_NAME 40
#define L_SHIP_CMPY 40
#define L_SHIP_STRT 40
#define L_SHIP_STRT2 40
#define L_SHIP_CITY 15
#define L_SHIP_STATE 2
#define L_SHIP_ZIP 5
#define L_BILL_SAME 1
#define L_BILL_NAME 40
#define L_BILL_CMPY 40
#define L_BILL_STRT 40
#define L_BILL_STRT2 40
#define L_BILL_CITY 15
#define L_BILL_STATE 2
#define L_BILL_ZIP 5
#define L_IS_RESALE 1
#define L_RESALE_ID 17
#define L_ADV_REF 40
#define L_PARTS 15
#define L_PART_DESC 30
#define L_PRICES 11
#define L_TAX_AMT 11
#define L_SHIP_CAR 19
#define L_PAY_TERMS 10
#define L_COMMENT 69

/* Maximum number of items on an order. */
#define MAX_ITEMS 10
```

*(continued)*

ORDENTRY.H  *continued*

```
/* Maximum numeric values input by nprompt() and fprompt(). */
#define H_QUANTITY 999L
#define H_SHIP_AMT 30000.0
#define H_TAX_PCNT 99.9

/* Function prototype declarations. */
extern  char get_addr(char step_rtn, short row, char *name,
    char *company, char *street, char *street2, char *city,
    char *state, char *zip);
extern  int inv_find(char *part, char *part_desc, long *p_price,
    short *p_ship_wt);
extern  char id_user(void );
extern  char id_cust(char step_rtn);
extern  char ord_itms(char step_rtn);
extern  char ship_pay(char step_rtn);
extern  char wrt_ord(void );
extern  void main(void );
extern  long order_num(void );
extern  void pnt_id_cust(void );
extern  void pnt_ship_pay(void );
extern  int pw_find(char *office, char *user, char *password);
```

# The Top Level: *main()*

The source file *ordentry.c* is the location of the *main()* function that directs the entire order-entry process.

## ORDENTRY.C

```
/* SOURCE FILE: ORDENTRY.C
 ***************************************************************************
 * The main() function for the Software Vendor Order-Entry Program. Each
 *   case commands a significant step in order entry, such as prompting for
 *   a screen of data or sending order data to a file.
 * The action after the completion of a step will be one of the following:
 *   Cancel the order.
 *   Back up to the previous step.
 *   Go on to the next step.
 * The action is controlled by the user's use of special command characters
 *   that are described further in the header file projutil.h.
 ***************************************************************************
 */
```

*(continued)*

ORDENTRY.C *continued*

```c
#include "syntypes.h"
#include "projutil.h"   /* needed for prompt() symbols STEPOK, STEPBACK, and */
                        /*   STEPCANC, and synonym type stepcode */
#include "ordentry.h"

/* Declare data shared among functions in all source files (GLOBAL). */
GLOBAL bflag bell_ok = YES;     /* it's OK to ring bell */

void main(void)
   {
   stepcode step_rtn;       /* step_rtn is the return value from a step. It is
                             * passed to the next step. It may equal:
                             *    STEPOK    Step complete; go on to next step.
                             *    STEPBACK  Back up to closest previous step.
                             *    STEPCANC  Cancel order entry (quit).
                             */

   enum prompts {ID_USER, ID_CUST, ORD_ITMS, SHIP_PAY, WRT_ORD,
      ENDSTEPS} step;

   for (step = 0, step_rtn = STEPOK; step != ENDSTEPS &&
      step_rtn != STEPCANC; )
      {
      switch (step)
         {
         case ID_USER:        /* identify user (salesperson) */
            step_rtn = id_user();
            break;
         case ID_CUST:        /* identify customer */
            step_rtn = id_cust(step_rtn);
            break;
         case ORD_ITMS:       /* input order detail items */
            step_rtn = ord_itms(step_rtn);
            break;
         case SHIP_PAY:       /* input shipping info, tax, pay terms */
            step_rtn = ship_pay(step_rtn);
            break;
         case WRT_ORD:        /* write order; update files */
            step_rtn = wrt_ord();
            break;
         }

      /* Determine next step based on return from last one. */
      if (step_rtn == STEPOK)          /* was last step successful? */
         ++step;                       /* yes; go on to next step */
      else if (step_rtn == STEPBACK && step > 0)
         --step;                       /* no; back up to previous step */
      }
   }
```

# The Middle Level: *ordbuild.c*

The source file *ordbuild.c* contains the second-level functions, called directly from *main()*, that control data input and output. These functions make extensive use of *SEMIGLOBAL* data (*external static* storage class) to share the fields in an order. This file is as long as your longest application source file should ever be: about 500 lines.

## ORDBUILD.C

```
/* SOURCE FILE: ORDBUILD.C
 **************************************************************************
 * Functions for order-entry prompt screens and for saving data. These are
 *   the middle-level functions that call the low-level display and prompt
 *   functions to input screens of order data. They are in one source file
 *   to permit order data in memory to be shared by them, but not by other
 *   functions linked into the order-entry program.
 **************************************************************************
 */

#include <stdio.h>
#include <conio.h>
#include <string.h>
#include <stdlib.h>
#include <time.h>
#include "syntypes.h"
#include "projutil.h"
#include "ordentry.h"
#include "ansiscrn.h"

/* Semiglobal data shared by functions in this source file only. */
/* Data items are fields of an order. */
SEMIGLOBAL char user[L_USER + 1] = "";
SEMIGLOBAL char office[L_OFFICE + 1] = "";
SEMIGLOBAL char cust_name[L_CUST_NAME + 1] = "";
SEMIGLOBAL char company[L_COMPANY + 1] = "";
SEMIGLOBAL char phone[L_PHONE + 1] = "";
SEMIGLOBAL char ship_name[L_SHIP_NAME + 1] = "";
SEMIGLOBAL char ship_cmpy[L_SHIP_CMPY + 1] = "";
SEMIGLOBAL char ship_strt[L_SHIP_STRT + 1] = "";
SEMIGLOBAL char ship_strt2[L_SHIP_STRT2 + 1] = "";
SEMIGLOBAL char ship_city[L_SHIP_CITY + 1] = "";
SEMIGLOBAL char ship_state[L_SHIP_STATE + 1] = "";
SEMIGLOBAL char ship_zip[L_SHIP_ZIP + 1] = "";
SEMIGLOBAL char bill_same[L_BILL_SAME + 1] = "y";
SEMIGLOBAL char bill_name[L_BILL_NAME + 1] = "";
SEMIGLOBAL char bill_cmpy[L_BILL_CMPY + 1] = "";
SEMIGLOBAL char bill_strt[L_BILL_STRT + 1] = "";
```

*(continued)*

ORDBUILD.C *continued*

```
SEMIGLOBAL char bill_strt2[L_BILL_STRT2 + 1] = "";
SEMIGLOBAL char bill_city[L_BILL_CITY + 1] = "";
SEMIGLOBAL char bill_state[L_BILL_STATE + 1] = "";
SEMIGLOBAL char bill_zip[L_BILL_ZIP + 1] = "";
SEMIGLOBAL char is_resale[L_IS_RESALE + 1] = "n";
SEMIGLOBAL char resale_id[L_RESALE_ID + 1] = "";
SEMIGLOBAL char adv_ref[L_ADV_REF + 1] = "";

/* Variables "parts" and "part_descs" are 2-dimensional character arrays. */
SEMIGLOBAL char parts[MAX_ITEMS][L_PARTS + 1] = {""};
SEMIGLOBAL char part_descs[MAX_ITEMS][L_PART_DESC + 1] = {""};

SEMIGLOBAL long quantities[MAX_ITEMS] = {0};
SEMIGLOBAL short ship_weights[MAX_ITEMS] = {0};
SEMIGLOBAL short tot_weight = 0;
SEMIGLOBAL money prices[MAX_ITEMS] = {0};
SEMIGLOBAL money part_total = 0;
SEMIGLOBAL char ship_car[L_SHIP_CAR + 1] = "";
SEMIGLOBAL money ship_amt = 0;
SEMIGLOBAL double inp_ship_amt = 0.0;
SEMIGLOBAL double tax_pcnt = 0.0;
SEMIGLOBAL money tax_amt = 0;
SEMIGLOBAL char pay_terms[L_PAY_TERMS + 1] = "";
SEMIGLOBAL char comment[L_COMMENT + 1] = "";
SEMIGLOBAL byte last_part = 0;          /* index of last part on order */

/* Shared data not part of an order. */
SEMIGLOBAL char scrn_title[] = "*** ENTER NEW ORDER ***";

/***************************************************************************
 * id_user() identifies the user (salesperson or data-entry clerk). The user
 *  enters office code, name, and password. The password is then verified.
 ***************************************************************************
 */

stepcode id_user(void)
   {
   IMPORT char user[];
   IMPORT char office[];
   IMPORT char scrn_title[];
   char password[L_PASSWORD + 1];
   stepcode step_rtn;
   short ichar;

   /* Paint screen: Show headings for data to prompt for. */
   beg_scrn("", scrn_title, "", "SALESPERSON");
   tput(10, 20, "Office");
   tput(12, 20, "Salesperson");
```

*(continued)*

ORDBUILD.C *continued*

```
    tput(14, 20, "Password");
    do                         /* loop until data entered or order canceled */
        {

        /* Input name of office seller is working in. */
        step_rtn = prompt(office, "L", 3, L_OFFICE, MAND, 10, 32);
        if (step_rtn == STEPBACK)
            err_warn("Office must be supplied:", "");

        }
    while (step_rtn == STEPBACK);
    if (step_rtn != STEPCANC)   /* prompt for user */
        do                      /* loop until data entered or order canceled */
            {
            user[0] = '\0';         /* DON'T show last user id */
            step_rtn = prompt(user, "L", 2, L_USER, MAND, 12, 32);
            if (step_rtn == STEPBACK)
                err_warn("I must know who you are:", "");
            }
        while (step_rtn == STEPBACK);
    if (step_rtn != STEPCANC)   /* input password without echo */
        {
        CUR_MV(14, 32);
        for (ichar = 0; ichar < L_PASSWORD &&
            (password[ichar] = (char)getch()) >= ' '; ++ichar)
            ;
        if (password[ichar] >= ' ')
            ++ichar;
        password[ichar] = '\0';
        if (!pw_find(office, user, password))
            {
            err_warn("Access denied:", user);
            step_rtn = STEPCANC;
            }
        else                    /* display instructions */
            {
            tput(17, 17, "Instructions for Commands Available at Prompts:");
            tput(19, 20, "^R = (control-R) Re-prompt for previous.");
            tput(20, 20, "^E = Erase data field, make it empty.");
            tput(21, 20, "^X = Exit and cancel order.");
            tput(23, 17, "Press ^X to exit, or another key to continue: _\b");
            if (getch() == C_CANC)
                step_rtn = STEPCANC;
            }
        }
    return (step_rtn);
    }
```

*(continued)*

ORDBUILD.C *continued*

```
/***************************************************************************
 * id_cust() prompts for customer identification information: customer name,
 *   company, phone, shipping/billing addresses, resale number, and
 *   advertising reference.
 ***************************************************************************
 */

stepcode id_cust(
    stepcode step_rtn)      /* if screen is backed into, step_rtn == STEPBACK; */
                            /*   otherwise step_rtn == STEPOK */
    {
    /* Shared data accessed in this function. */
    IMPORT char office[], user[], cust_name[], company[], ship_name[],
        ship_cmpy[], ship_strt[], ship_strt2[], ship_city[], ship_state[],
        ship_zip[], bill_name[], bill_cmpy[], bill_strt[], bill_strt2[],
        bill_city[], bill_state[], bill_zip[], adv_ref[], is_resale[],
        resale_id[], scrn_title[];

    /* Names of case labels for data-field prompts. */
    enum prompts {NAME, COMPANY, PHONE, SHIP_ADDR, BILL_ADDR,
        RESALE, ADV_REF, ENDSTEPS} step;   /* step is a prompts type variable */

    /* Begin new screen. */
    beg_scrn(user, scrn_title, office, "IDENTIFY");
    pnt_id_cust();              /* paint the screen */
    tput(4, 30, cust_name);
    tput(6, 30, company);

    /* Begin at last prompt if screen backed into. */
    step = (step_rtn == STEPOK) ? 0 : ENDSTEPS - 1;

    /* Loop: Input each field of this screen. */
    for (step_rtn = STEPOK; step_rtn != STEPCANC &&
        (step < ENDSTEPS) && (step >= 0); )
        {
        switch (step)          /* select next field to prompt for */
            {
            case NAME:              /* get customer name */
                step_rtn = prompt(cust_name, "L", 3, L_CUST_NAME, MAND, 4, 30);
                break;
            case COMPANY:           /* get company name */
                step_rtn = prompt(company, "L", 3, L_COMPANY, OPT, 6, 30);
                break;
            case PHONE:             /* get customer phone number */
                step_rtn = prompt(phone, "P", 7, L_PHONE, OPT, 7, 30);
                break;
            case SHIP_ADDR:         /* get address to ship to */
                if (ship_name[0] == '\0')  /* no address input yet? */
```

*(continued)*

ORDBUILD.C *continued*

```
                {                          /* then set default name and company */
                strcpy(ship_name, cust_name);
                strcpy(ship_cmpy, company);
                }

            /* Prompt for address data. Call get_addr(). */
            step_rtn = get_addr(step_rtn, 9, ship_name, ship_cmpy, ship_strt,
                ship_strt2, ship_city, ship_state, ship_zip);
            break;
        case BILL_ADDR:                    /* get address to send bill to */
            tput(15, 30, "Bill same address? <y/n>    ");
            step_rtn = prompt(bill_same, "Q", 1, L_BILL_SAME, MAND, 15, 56);
            CUR_MV(15, 30);                /* move cursor and    */
            CLR_LINE;                      /* erase question */
            if (step_rtn == STEPOK && strchr("NnO", bill_same[0]))
                step_rtn = get_addr(step_rtn, 15, bill_name, bill_cmpy,
                    bill_strt, bill_strt2, bill_city, bill_state, bill_zip);
            else if (step_rtn == STEPOK)
                bill_name[0] == '\0';      /* bill same address */
            break;
        case RESALE:                /* is purchase for resale? */
            step_rtn = prompt(is_resale, "Q", 1, L_IS_RESALE, MAND, 21, 25);
            if (step_rtn == STEPOK && strchr("Yy1", is_resale[0]))
                step_rtn = prompt(resale_id, "L", 3, L_RESALE_ID, OPT, 21, 53);
            break;
        case ADV_REF:               /* how did customer hear about product? */
            step_rtn = prompt(adv_ref, "L", 1, L_ADV_REF, OPT, 23, 30);
            break;
        }

    /* Determine next step based on return from last one. */
    if (step_rtn == STEPOK)     /* last was successful? */
        ++step;                 /* yes; go on to next step */
    else if (step_rtn == STEPBACK)
        -- step;                /* no; back up to last step */
    }
    return (step_rtn);
    }

/******************************************************************************
 * ord_itms() prompts repeatedly for part numbers and quantities of each
 *    item ordered by customer. Displays price and shipping weight of each.
 ******************************************************************************
 */

stepcode ord_itms(
    stepcode step_rtn)
```

*(continued)*

ORDBUILD.C *continued*

```
{
IMPORT char user[], office[], scrn_title[];
IMPORT char parts[][L_PARTS + 1];
IMPORT char part_descs[][L_PART_DESC + 1];
IMPORT long quantities[];
IMPORT short ship_weights[];
IMPORT money prices[];
IMPORT byte last_part;
IMPORT money part_total;
char dbuf[14];                   /* output buffer for ftput() and ntput() */
byte ipart, part_cnt;
byte row;                                /* line number on screen */
bflag part_found, more_items = YES;   /* part_found not initialized */
enum {PART_NUM, QUANTITY, ENDSTEPS} step;

/* Paint screen. */
beg_scrn(user, scrn_title, office, "ENTER ITEMS");
tput(4, 10, "Customer Name");
tput(4, 30, cust_name);
tput(6, 10, "Company Name");
tput(6, 30, company);
tput(9, 10, "Part Number      Description");
tput(9, 59, "Qty  Unit-Price");
tput(22, 51, "Order Total");
step = ipart = 0;              /* initializer for loop */
for (step_rtn = STEPOK; step_rtn != STEPCANC &&
     ipart < MAX_ITEMS && ipart >= 0 && more_items; )
    {
    row = ipart + 11;          /* row to prompt on */
    switch (step)
        {
        case PART_NUM:              /* get next part number */
            do                      /* while part entered and not found */
                {
                step_rtn = prompt(parts[ipart], "L", 1, L_PARTS, OPT, row, 10);

                /* Got a part number and it checks out? */
                part_found = (bflag)((step_rtn == STEPOK) &&
                    inv_find(parts[ipart], part_descs[ipart],
                    &prices[ipart], &ship_weights[ipart]));

                /* Check for end of order. */
                if (step_rtn == STEPOK && parts[ipart][0] == '\0')
                    more_items = NO;
```

*(continued)*

ORDBUILD.C  *continued*

```
                /* If part not found, then tell user. */
                else if (!part_found && step_rtn == STEPOK)
                    err_warn("No such part:", parts[ipart]);
                else if (part_found)    /* show description and price of part */
                    {
                    tput(row, 27, part_descs[ipart]);
                    tput(row, 64, "$");
                    ftput(row, 65, (double) prices[ipart] / 100.0, 2,
                        dbuf, L_PRICES);

                    /* Default quantity is 1. */
                    if (!quantities[ipart])
                        quantities[ipart] = 1;
                    }

                /* Indent avoids confusion of do...while with the for loop. */
                } while (step_rtn == STEPOK && !part_found && more_items);
            break;
        case QUANTITY:                      /* get quantity for part ordered */
            step_rtn = nprompt(&quantities[ipart],
                "#", OL, H_QUANTITY, MAND, row, 59);
            break;
        }
    if (step_rtn == STEPOK)                  /* update total on screen */
        {

        /* Update the number of parts on this order. */
        if (ipart < MAX_ITEMS && quantities[ipart] > 0 && parts[ipart][0])
            last_part = ipart;

        /* Sum the prices times quantities of parts ordered. */
        for (part_total = part_cnt = 0; part_cnt <= last_part; ++part_cnt)
            part_total += prices[part_cnt] * quantities[part_cnt];
        tput(22, 64, "$");
        ftput(22, 65, (double) part_total / 100.0, 2, dbuf, L_PRICES);
        }

    /* Determine next part to prompt for and next step. */
    if (step == PART_NUM)      /* just got a part number */
        {
        step = QUANTITY;        /* next get a quantity */
        if (step_rtn == STEPBACK)
            --ipart;
        }
    else                        /* just got a quantity */
        {
        step = PART_NUM;        /* next get a part number */
```

*(continued)*

ORDBUILD.C *continued*

```
        if (step_rtn == STEPOK)
         ++ipart;
         }
      }
   return (step_rtn);
   }


/***********************************************************************
 * ship_pay() prompts for shipping carrier, shipping charges, sales-tax
 *   rate, and payment terms. Input these data after items are entered.
 ***********************************************************************
 */

stepcode ship_pay(
   stepcode step_rtn)        /* if screen is backed into, step_rtn == STEPBACK; */
                             /*    otherwise step_rtn == STEPOK */
   {
   IMPORT char office[], user[], cust_name[], company[],
      ship_car[], pay_terms[], comment[], scrn_title[];
   IMPORT money part_total, tax_amt, ship_amt;
   IMPORT double inp_ship_amt, tax_pcnt;
   IMPORT char is_resale[];                    /* yes means no sales tax */
   IMPORT byte last_part;
   IMPORT long quantities[];
   IMPORT short ship_weights[];
   IMPORT short tot_weight;
   char dbuf[14];
   byte ipart;
   enum prompts {SHIP_CAR, SHIP_AMT, TAX, PAY_TERMS, COMMENT, ENDSTEPS};
   enum prompts step;

   /* Verify that something has been ordered; else return STEPBACK. */
   if (quantities[0] == 0 !! parts[0][0] == '\0')
      {
      err_warn("Nothing ordered:", "");  /* give diagnostic */
      return (STEPBACK);                 /* back up to previous screen */
      }

   /* Begin new screen. */
   beg_scrn(user, scrn_title, office, "SHIP, TAX, PAY");
   pnt_ship_pay();                        /* paint screen */
   tput(4, 30, cust_name);
   tput(6, 30, company);

   /* Sum ship weights and show total (weights in ounces). */
   for (ipart = 0, tot_weight = 0; ipart <= last_part; ++ipart)
      tot_weight += (short)(ship_weights[ipart] * quantities[ipart]);
```

*(continued)*

ORDBUILD.C *continued*

```
    ntput(9, 30, (long) tot_weight, dbuf, 10);    /* show total weight */

    /* Begin at last prompt if screen backed into. */
    step = (step_rtn == STEPOK) ? 0 : ENDSTEPS - 1;
    for (step_rtn = STEPOK; step_rtn != STEPCANC &&
        (step < ENDSTEPS) && step >= 0; )
        {
        switch (step)
            {
            case SHIP_CAR:          /* get shipping carrier */
                step_rtn = prompt(ship_car, "L", 1, L_SHIP_CAR, OPT, 11, 30);
                break;
            case SHIP_AMT:                  /* get shipping charges, if */
                if (ship_car[0] != '\0')     /*  a carrier was entered */
                    step_rtn = fprompt(&inp_ship_amt, "F", 0.20,
                        H_SHIP_AMT, 11, 2, OPT, 11, 65);
                    ship_amt = (money) (inp_ship_amt * 100.0 + 0.5);
                break;
            case TAX:               /* get sales-tax percentage */

                /* If sale is for resale, then don't add sales tax. */
                if (strchr("Yy1", is_resale[0]))
                    tax_pcnt = 0.0;
                else                /* prompt for local tax rate, if any */
                    step_rtn = fprompt(&tax_pcnt, "F", 0.0,
                        H_TAX_PCNT, 4, 2, OPT, 14, 30);
                tax_amt = (money)((tax_pcnt * (double)part_total) / 100.0);
                tput(14, 64, "$");
                ftput(14, 65, (double) tax_amt / 100.0, 2, dbuf, L_TAX_AMT);
                ftput(18, 65, (double) part_total / 100.0, 2, dbuf, L_PRICES);
                ftput(20, 65, (double) (part_total + tax_amt + ship_amt) / 100.0,
                    2, dbuf, L_PRICES);
                break;
            case PAY_TERMS:         /* get payment terms code */
                step_rtn = prompt(pay_terms, "L", 1, L_PAY_TERMS, MAND, 17, 30);
                break;
            case COMMENT:           /* get order comment (if any) */
                step_rtn = prompt(comment, "L", 1, L_COMMENT, OPT, 22, 11);
                break;
            }

        /* Determine next step based on return from last one. */
        if (step_rtn == STEPOK)             /* last was successful? */
            ++step;                         /* yes; go on to next step */
        else if (step_rtn == STEPBACK)
            --step;                         /* no; back up to last step */
        }
    return (step_rtn);
    }
```

*(continued)*

ORDBUILD.C  *continued*

```
/*****************************************************************************
 * wrt_ord() writes an order to standard output after asking if all is OK.
 * The order number is assigned from a counter.
 *****************************************************************************
 */
/*  File data to be output are written to the standard output file (stdout).
 *    This permits data to be redirected at the command line. For example:
 *      ORDENTRY > SS891225.ORD        Creates new file;
 *                                     note date encoded in name.
 *      ORDENTRY >> NEWORDS.DAT        Appends data to file.
 *      ORDENTRY ! ORDSAVE ! ORDPRINT  Serves as source for a pipeline.
 *
 *  This standard file use scheme gives flexibility in the way the program
 *    may be used. Text and control characters are output to the standard
 *    error file (stderr), so they won't appear in the redirected output.
 */

stepcode wrt_ord(void)
    {

    /* IMPORT all the fields of the order. */
    IMPORT char office[], user[], cust_name[], company[], ship_name[],
        ship_cmpy[], ship_strt[], ship_strt2[], ship_city[], ship_state[],
        ship_zip[], bill_name[], bill_cmpy[], bill_strt[], bill_strt2[],
        bill_city[], bill_state[], bill_zip[], adv_ref[], resale_id[];
    IMPORT char is_resale[];                 /* yes means no sales tax */
    IMPORT char parts[][L_PARTS + 1];
    IMPORT long quantities[];
    IMPORT money prices[];
    IMPORT byte last_part;
    IMPORT short tot_weight;
    IMPORT char ship_car[], pay_terms[], comment[];
    IMPORT money part_total, tax_amt, ship_amt;
    long order_id;                   /* order number, from order_num() */
    long long_time;                  /* time of day, from time() */
    byte ipart;
    char is_ok[2];                   /* are data OK? message buffer */
    char log_buf[80];                /* buffer for logentry() string */
    stepcode step_rtn;

    /* Ask if order is OK. */
    tput(23, 2, "Is order OK? <y/n>  _ ");
    strcpy(is_ok, "y");                       /* default is yes */
    step_rtn = prompt(is_ok, "Q", 1, 1, MAND, 23, 22);
    if (step_rtn != STEPOK)
        return (step_rtn);
    else if (0 != strchr("NnO", is_ok[0]))
        return (STEPBACK);
```

*(continued)*

ORDBUILD.C *continued*

```
/* Write order data to standard output. Each line begins with
 *    two uppercase characters or numbers that indicate the
 *    meaning of that data item.
 */
order_id = order_num();
sprintf(log_buf, "ORD %ld, SL %s, TL %ld", order_id, user, part_total);
logentry(log_buf);                  /* record order in log file as an audit */
                                    /*    trail for sales and commissions */
printf("\nBEGIN ORDER %ld\n", order_id);
time(&long_time);                   /* get time of day as a long */
printf("TM %s", ctime(&long_time)); /* save time of day */

printf("OF %s\nSL %s\nCN %s\nCO %s\n", office, user, cust_name, company);
printf("SN %s\nSC %s\nST %s\n", ship_name, ship_cmpy, ship_strt);
if (ship_strt2[0] != '\0')
   printf("S2 %s\n", ship_strt2);
printf("SY %s\nSS %s\nSZ %s\n", ship_city, ship_state, ship_zip);
if (bill_name[0] != '\0')    /* save billing address if different */
   {
   printf("BN %s\nBC %s\nBT %s\n", bill_name, bill_cmpy, bill_strt);
   if (bill_strt2[0] != '\0')
      printf("B2 %s\n", bill_strt2);
   printf("BY %s\nBS %s\nBZ %s\n", bill_city, bill_state, bill_zip);
   }
if (strchr("Yy1", is_resale[0]))      /* is order for resale? */
   printf("RS %s\n", resale_id);      /* yes; save resale_id */

/* List each part, quantity, and price. */
for (ipart = 0; ipart <= last_part && quantities[ipart]; ++ipart)
   printf("PN %s\nQY %ld\nPR %ld\n", parts[ipart],
      quantities[ipart], prices[ipart]);
printf("TL %ld\nTX %ld\nSH %s\nSA %ld\nWT %d\n", part_total,
   tax_amt, ship_car, ship_amt, tot_weight);
if (adv_ref[0] != '\0')
   printf("AD %s\n", adv_ref);
printf("PA %s\n", pay_terms);
if (comment[0] != '\0')
   printf("CM %s\n", comment);
printf("END ORDER %ld\n", order_id);
return (STEPOK);
}
```

# The Low Level

The four source files listed in this section hold the low-level application-specific functions that actually do the work managed by the middle-level functions.

## get_addr()

The *get_addr()* function prompts the user for the fields that make up a street address. It eliminates the need for duplicate address-prompting code in *id_cust()* (see *ordbuild.c*), which must prompt for both shipping and billing addresses.

### GET_ADDR.C

```
/* SOURCE FILE: GET_ADDR.C
 ************************************************************************
 * get_addr() prompts for address data for order-entry programs. All data
 *   are returned to the caller by arguments 3-9 (yes, 9 is rather high).
 ************************************************************************
 */

#include "projutil.h"
#include "ordentry.h"

stepcode get_addr(
    stepcode step_rtn,    /* step_rtn is passed in and returned */
    short row,            /* screen row to begin prompting */
    char name[], char company[], char street[], char street2[], char city[],
    char state[], char zip[])

    {
    enum prompts {NAME, COMPANY, STREET, STREET2, CITY, STATE, ZIP, ENDSTEPS};
    enum prompts step;

    /* Begin at last prompt if screen backed into. */
    step = (step_rtn == STEPOK) ? 0 : ENDSTEPS - 1;
    for (step_rtn = STEPOK; step_rtn != STEPCANC &&
        (step != ENDSTEPS) && (step >= 0); )
        {
        switch (step)
            {
            case NAME:       /* get name */
                step_rtn = prompt(name, "L", 3, L_SHIP_NAME, MAND, row, 30);
                break;
            case COMPANY:    /* get company name */
                step_rtn = prompt(company, "L", 3, L_SHIP_CMPY, OPT, row + 1, 30);
                break;
            case STREET:     /* get first line of street address */
                step_rtn = prompt(street, "L", 3, L_SHIP_STRT, MAND, row + 2, 30);
                break;
            case STREET2:    /* get second line of street address */
                step_rtn = prompt(street2, "L", 3, L_SHIP_STRT2, OPT, row + 3, 30);
                break;
```

*(continued)*

GET_ADDR.C *continued*

```
        case CITY:        /* get city */
            step_rtn = prompt(city, "L", 2, L_SHIP_CITY, MAND, row + 4, 30);
            break;
        case STATE:       /* get state's two-letter abbreviation */
            step_rtn = prompt(state, "A", L_SHIP_STATE,
                L_SHIP_STATE, MAND, row + 4, 56);
            break;
        case ZIP:         /* get zip code */
            step_rtn = prompt(zip, "#", L_SHIP_ZIP,
                L_SHIP_ZIP, MAND, row + 4, 65);
            break;
        }

    /* Determine next step based on return from last one. */
    if (step_rtn == STEPOK)    /* was last successful? */
        ++step;                     /* yes; go on to next step */
    else if (step_rtn == STEPBACK)
        --step;                     /* no; back up to last step */
    }
    return (step_rtn);
}
```

## pnt_id_cust()

This "artistic" function paints the field names used to prompt the user for customer identification in an attractive and efficient format on the screen. Painting a screen is friendlier than simply displaying the field names one by one as they are prompted for: It lets the user see exactly what data will be needed for the entire section before any individual inputs must be made, and therefore enhances productivity.

### PNT_ID_C.C

```
/* SOURCE FILE: PNT_ID_C.C
 *****************************************************************
 * pnt_id_cust() paints screen for order entry: identify customer. This
 *    function is called exclusively by id_cust() in ordbuild.c.
 *****************************************************************
 */
```

*(continued)*

PNT_ID_C.C *continued*

```c
#include "projutil.h"

void pnt_id_cust(void)
   {
   tput(4, 10, "Customer Name");
   tput(6, 10, "Company Name");
   tput(7, 10, "Phone Number");

   tput(9, 10, "Ship to Name");
   tput(10, 18, "Company");
   tput(11, 18, "Street");
   tput(12, 18, "2nd Street");
   tput(13, 18, "City");
   tput(13, 49, "State");
   tput(13, 60, "Zip");

   tput(15, 10, "Bill to Name");
   tput(16, 18, "Company");
   tput(17, 18, "Street");
   tput(18, 18, "2nd Street");
   tput(19, 18, "City");
   tput(19, 49, "State");
   tput(19, 60, "Zip");

   tput(21, 10, "Resale?");
   tput(21, 30, "Resale Permit Number");
   tput(23, 10, "Advertising Ref");
   }
```

# pnt_ship_pay()

Like *pnt_id_cust()*, *pnt_ship_pay()* paints field names on a formatted prompt screen, this time to prompt for shipping and billing information.

## PNT_SHIP.C

```c
/* SOURCE FILE: PNT_SHIP.C
 ***************************************************************************
 * pnt_ship_pay() paints the screen for order entry: ship, tax, pay. This
 *   function is called exclusively by ship_pay() in ordbuild.c.
 ***************************************************************************
 */
```

*(continued)*

PNT_SHIP.C *continued*

```
#include "projutil.h"

void pnt_ship_pay(void)
   {
   tput(4, 10, "Customer Name");
   tput(6, 10, "Company Name");
   tput(9, 10, "Shipping Weight");
   tput(11, 19, "Carrier");
   tput(11, 51, "Ship Charge");
   tput(11, 64, "$");
   tput(14, 10, "Sales Tax Percent");
   tput(17, 10, "Payment Terms Code");
   tput(18, 51, "Item Total");
   tput(18, 64, "$");
   tput(20, 51, "Order Total");
   tput(20, 64, "$");
   tput(22, 2, "Comment");
   }
```

## Stub functions: *stubs.c*

Top-down structured program development dictates designing and coding high-level functions before the lower-level ones that they call. The first versions of these lower-level functions can be dummies that merely simulate the final versions but still provide realistic enough behavior to allow you to test and debug the calling functions. These lower-level dummies, commonly called *stubs*, are replaced later with fully operational versions. We'll do this in Chapter 17 for the *pw_find()*, *ordernum()*, and *logentry()* functions and in Chapter 19 for *inv_find()* as we discuss the new techniques they require.

### STUBS.C

```
/* SOURCE FILE: STUBS.C
   **************************************************************************
   * Stubs are function prototypes called to test their callers.
   *    Here are inv_find(), pw_find(), order_num(), and logentry().
   **************************************************************************
   */

#include <stdio.h>
#include <string.h>
#include "syntypes.h"
#include "ordentry.h"
```

*(continued)*

STUBS.C *continued*

```
/***********************************************************************
 * inv_find() looks up a part's data in inventory and returns YES if the
 *   part is found, NO if it is not found. Part description, price, and
 *   weight are passed back.
 ***********************************************************************
 */

flag inv_find(
    char part[],            /* part number to look up (pass in) */
    char part_desc[],       /* description of part (returned) */
    money *p_price,         /* pointer to unit price of part (returned) */
    short *p_ship_wt)       /* pointer to shipping weight in ounces (returned) */

    {
    /* Return typical data to test inv_find()'s callers. */
    strcpy(part_desc, "Order-Entry Software Package");
    *p_price = 12345L;
    *p_ship_wt = 123;
    return (part[0] == 'S');        /* YES if 'S' first, else NO */
    }

/***********************************************************************
 * pw_find() looks up a user's name and password and returns YES if the user
 *   is found, NO if not. If the user is found, office ID is also checked.
 *   User data contain indication of whether to ring bell.
 ***********************************************************************
 */

flag pw_find(
    char office[],          /* description of user's office (returned) */
    char user[],            /* name, initials, or abbreviation of user to find */
    char password[])        /* password to look up */

    {
    IMPORT bflag bell_ok;
    if (user[1] == 'S')    /* OK to ring the bell? */
        bell_ok = NO;      /* no; silence the bell */
    return (user[0] == 'S' && password[0] == 'S');
    }

/***********************************************************************
 * order_num() returns the order number to use for the next order. The order
 *   number is a counter that increases by one with each order.
 ***********************************************************************
 */
```

*(continued)*

STUBS.C *continued*

```
long order_num(void)
    {
    return (10001L);
    }


/*************************************************************************
 * logentry() appends message text to the end of the log file, typically for
 *   audit, error detection, and security purposes.
 *************************************************************************
 */

void logentry(char msg[])
    {
    }
```

# The Project Utility Functions

The project utility functions, which are general-purpose enough
for use in many other applications, implement our program's communication with the user. They prompt for data, control input, validate
input, and provide error messages. They are the "workhorses" of our
application.

## prompt()

The *prompt()* function prompts the user for string input, in a friendly
but tightly controlled manner. The input can be either mandatory or
optional, and you can supply a default value if you want. This function
is called to perform all user data inputs in the order-entry application;
therefore, the user prompts are uniform and the user can learn the
system more quickly.

## PROMPT.C

```
/* SOURCE FILE: PROMPT.C
 *************************************************************************
 * prompt() inputs text from standard input to the string "data".
 *   The program matches input against an optional match-string argument
 *   and checks minimum and maximum input lengths. If the Boolean (flag)
 *   argument mand is true, the program will not allow "data" to remain null;
 *   the user must make an entry. The parameter "data" is both passed to
```

*(continued)*

PROMPT.C *continued*

```
 *    prompt() and returned to the calling function. The value passed in is
 *    treated as a default to be used if input is null. Data are input one
 *    character at a time, without automatic echo.
 * Return value: The outcome of prompt has synonym data type stepcode, which
 *    is used to indicate:
 *      STEPOK    Step complete; go on to next step.
 *      STEPBACK  Back up to closest previous step.
 *      STEPCANC  Cancel order entry (quit).
 *    C_BACK, C_NULL, and C_CANC are defined in projutil.h. The user can
 *      request to back up by entering C_BACK, to cancel by entering C_CANC,
 *      or to erase data by entering C_NULL as any character in the reply.
 ***************************************************************************
 */

#include <stdio.h>
#include <string.h>
#include <conio.h>
#include "syntypes.h"
#include "ansiscrn.h"
#include "projutil.h"

stepcode prompt(
    char data[],            /* default passed in, input data returned */
    char match_str[],       /* match string to verify data against */
    short min_len,          /* minimum input data length */
    short max_len,          /* maximum input data length */
    flag mand,              /* if yes, data cannot be null on return */
    short row,              /* cursor row to begin input */
    short col)              /* cursor column to begin input */

    {
    IMPORT bflag bell_ok;   /* global permission to ring bell */
    char buf[PRMTBSIZ];     /* prompt input buffer */
    short ichar;            /* input character counter */
    stepcode rtn = STEPOK;  /* return code */
    bflag more;             /* expect more input? */

    /* Display prompt mask or default value, if any.
     * Copy default to buffer. Fill rest of buffer with prompt mask
     *   characters, to maximum length of field prompted for.
     */
    strcpy(buf, data);
    for (ichar = strlen(buf); ichar < max_len; ++ichar)
        buf[ichar] = C_MASK;
    buf[ichar] = '\0';
    tput(row, col, buf);
    CUR_MV(row, col);
```

*(continued)*

PROMPT.C *continued*

```
/* Input each character. */
strcpy(buf, data);              /* copy default value to buffer */
for (ichar = 0, more = YES; ichar < max_len && more; )
   {
   buf[ichar] = (char)getch();          /* input a character (no auto echo) */
   buf[ichar + 1] = '\0';
   switch (buf[ichar])
      {
      case C_CANC:              /* cancel command */
         rtn = STEPCANC, more = NO;
         break;
      case C_BACK:              /* back up to previous prompt */
         rtn = STEPBACK, more = NO;
         break;
      case C_NULL:              /* force data to null, restart prompt */

         /* Fill buffer with mask characters to maximum length of field. */
         for (ichar = 0; ichar < max_len; ++ichar)
            buf[ichar] = C_MASK;
         buf[ichar] = '\0';
         tput(row, col, buf); /* show prompt mask in buf */
         ichar = 0;            /* restart at first character */
         buf[ichar] = data[ichar] = '\0';    /* erase data */
         CUR_MV(row, col);    /* move cursor to beginning of mask */
         break;
      case '\r':               /* end of line */
      case '\n':               /* alternate end of line */
         if (ichar == 0 && data[0] != '\0')

            /* Pass default back to caller. */
            strcpy(buf, data), more = NO;
         else if (ichar == 0 && data[0] == '\0' && mand)
            {              /* mandatory entry, no default supplied */
            err_warn("Data must be entered:", "");
            CUR_MV(row, col);
            }

         /* Too few characters? Check, unless this is first */
         /*   character of reply and reply is optional. */
         else if (ichar < min_len && !(ichar == 0 && !mand))
            {
            err_warn("Too few characters:", "");
            CUR_MV(row, col + ichar);          /* restore cursor */
            }
         else
            buf[ichar] = '\0', more = NO;      /* end of input */
         break;
```

*(continued)*

PROMPT.C *continued*

```
            case '\b':              /* backspace (BS) entered */
               buf[ichar] = '\0';   /* delete backspace */
               if (ichar > 0)
                  {
                  buf[--ichar] = '\0';       /* wipe character before BS */
                  fputc('\b', stderr);       /* fix display to match */
                  fputc(C_MASK, stderr);
                  fputc(C_MASK, stderr);
                  fprintf(stderr, "\b\b");
                  }
               break;
            default:                /* check match and length; echo character */

               /* Echo if character is legal; else ring bell. */
               buf[ichar + 1] = '\0';   /* save character and increment ichar */
               if (match(buf, match_str))
                  putc(buf[ichar++], stderr);       /* echo good character */
               else if (bell_ok)    /* bad character entered; ring bell */
                  putc('\7', stderr);
               if (ichar > max_len)
                  more = NO;
               break;
            }
         }

   /* Copy buf to data and erase rest of prompt mask (if any). */
   if (rtn == STEPOK)
      strcpy(data, buf);
   ichar = strlen(data);
   CUR_MV(row, col + ichar);
   for (; ichar < max_len; ++ichar)
      fputc(' ', stderr);          /* erase end of mask, using spaces */
   return (rtn);
   }
```

## *nprompt()* and *fprompt()*

The *nprompt()* and *fprompt()* functions are the numeric counterparts of the string-input function, *prompt()*. The *nprompt()* function asks the user for a long integer value, which is input first as a string through a call to *prompt()* and then is converted to binary format using the library function *atol()*. The *fprompt()* function asks for a double-precision floating-point value and uses the library function *atof()* for the conversion.

## NPROMPT.C

```
/* SOURCE FILE: NPROMPT.C
 ****************************************************************************
 * nprompt() inputs a long integer from standard input. The program matches
 *   input against an optional match-string argument and checks minimum and
 *   maximum input values. If the Boolean (flag) argument mand is true,
 *   then the program will not permit data to remain zero; data must be
 *   entered. The parameter *p_num is both passed to nprompt() and returned
 *   to the calling function. The value passed in is treated as a default to
 *   be used if input is null.
 * Return value: The outcome of nprompt() has synonym data type stepcode,
 *   which is used to indicate:
 *     STEPOK    Step complete; valid number obtained.
 *     STEPBACK  Back up to the previous step.
 *     STEPCANC  Cancel order entry (quit).
 *   The user can request to back up by entering C_BACK, to cancel by
 *   entering C_CANC, or to set *p_num to zero by entering C_NULL as any
 *   character in the reply.
 ****************************************************************************
 */

#include <stdio.h>
#include <stdlib.h>
#include <string.h>
#include "syntypes.h"
#include "projutil.h"

stepcode nprompt(
    long *p_num,          /* default passed in, input data returned */
    char match_str[],     /* match string to verify data against */
    long min_val,         /* minimum input value */
    long max_val,         /* maximum input value */
    flag mand,            /* if yes, data cannot be zero on return */
    short row,            /* cursor row to begin input */
    short col)            /* cursor column to begin input */

    {
    char buf[14];         /* prompt input buffer */
    bflag more = YES;     /* prompt again? */
    long in_num;          /* ASCII input number converted to binary */
    short max_len = strlen(ltoa(max_val, buf, 10));
    short min_len = strlen(ltoa(min_val, buf, 10));
    stepcode rtn;         /* return code */
```

*(continued)*

```
    /* Supply as default if p_num points to a non-zero long. */
    if (*p_num)            /* non-zero value passed in? */
       {
       ntput(row, col, *p_num, buf, max_len);      /* display default */
       }
    else                   /* no default */
       buf[0] = '\0';

    /* Loop: Prompt for number in string form, until value */
    /*   entered is in range, or cancel or back up is requested. */
    do
       {
       rtn = prompt(buf, match_str, min_len, max_len, mand, row, col);
       if (rtn != STEPOK)
          more = NO;        /* done prompting (back up or cancel) */
       else                 /* check whether input mandatory and reply in range */
          {
          in_num = atol(buf);      /* convert ASCII input to long integer */

          /* If mandatory and number is zero, this is an error. */
          if (mand && in_num == 0)
             err_warn("Non-zero data mandatory:", "");

          /* Otherwise, verify in_num is inside specified range, provided */
          /*   prompt is mandatory or number entered is non-zero. */
          else if ((in_num < min_val || in_num > max_val) &&
             (mand || in_num != 0))
             {
             sprintf(buf, "%ld to %ld", min_val, max_val);
             err_warn("Enter a number from:", buf);
             buf[0] = '\0';
             }
          else              /* got a good value; done prompting */
             more = NO;
          }
       }
    while (more);
       if (rtn == STEPOK)            /* then echo, right justified */
       {
       *p_num = in_num;             /* pass value back to caller */

       /* Echo number right justified in screen field. */
       ntput(row, col, in_num, buf, max_len);
       }
    return (rtn);
    }
```

## FPROMPT.C

```
/* SOURCE FILE: FPROMPT.C
 ****************************************************************************
 * fprompt() inputs a double-precision floating-point number from standard
 *  input. It behaves the same as nprompt(), except that the arguments
 *  width and precision must be passed to fprompt() to indicate the width
 *  of the field and the number of digits to prompt for on the right of the
 *  decimal point.
 ****************************************************************************
 */

#include <stdio.h>
#include <string.h>
#include <stdlib.h>
#include "syntypes.h"
#include "ansiscrn.h"
#include "projutil.h"

stepcode fprompt(
    double *d_num,         /* default passed in, input data returned */
    char match_str[],      /* pattern describing input format */
    double min_dval,       /* minimum input value */
    double max_dval,       /* maximum input value */
    short width,           /* input field width */
    short precision,       /* number of decimal places */
    flag mand,             /* if yes, data cannot be zero on return */
    short row,             /* cursor row to begin input */
    short col)             /* cursor column to begin input */

    {
    char buf[80];          /* prompt input buffer */
    bflag more = YES;
    double in_dnum;        /* ASCII input number converted to double */
    short min_len = 1;
    stepcode rtn;

    /* Supply the double d_num points to as the default if it is non-zero. */
    if (*d_num == 0.0)     /* zero value passed in? */
        buf[0] = '\0';     /* no default */
    else
        ftput(row, col, *d_num, precision, buf, width);    /* display default */

    do
        {
        rtn = prompt(buf, match_str, min_len, width, mand, row, col);
        if (rtn != STEPOK)
            more = NO;
```

*(continued)*

FPROMPT.C *continued*

```
        else
            {
            in_dnum = atof(buf);     /* convert ASCII to double */
            if (mand && in_dnum == 0.0)
                err_warn("Non-zero data mandatory:", "");
            else if ((in_dnum < min_dval !! in_dnum > max_dval) &&
                (mand !! in_dnum != 0.0))
                {

                /* Create string to pass to err_warn(). */
                sprintf(buf, "%.*f to %.*f", precision, min_dval,
                    precision, max_dval);
                err_warn("Enter a number from:", buf);
                buf[0] = '\0';
                CUR_MV(row, col);
                }
            else
                more = NO;
            }
        }
    while (more);

    if (rtn == STEPOK)              /* then echo, right justified  */
        {
        *d_num = in_dnum;           /* pass value back to caller  */
        ftput(row, col, *d_num, precision, buf, width);
        }
    return (rtn);
    }
```

# tput()

The low-level terminal output function *tput()* displays a string of text at a specific cursor row and column.

## TPUT.C

```
/* SOURCE FILE: TPUT.C
 ***************************************************************************
 * tput() displays a string at a specified row and column.
 ***************************************************************************
 */

#include <stdio.h>
#include "ansiscrn.h"
#include "projutil.h"
```

*(continued)*

TPUT.C *continued*

```
void tput(
    short row,          /* cursor row */
    short col,          /* cursor column */
    char text[])        /* text to display */

    {
    CUR_MV(row, col);
    fputs(text, stderr);
    }
```

## *ntput()* and *ftput()*

The order-entry program uses the functions *ntput()* and *ftput()* as alternatives to *printf()* for the output of a *long* or *double* value (respectively), right justified in a designated field, at a specific cursor row and column on the user's screen.

## NTPUT.C

```
/* SOURCE FILE: NTPUT.C
 ***********************************************************************
 * ntput() converts a long integer to ASCII and displays it right justified
 *   in field of specified width. The left side is padded with blanks.
 ***********************************************************************
 */

#include <stdlib.h>
#include "projutil.h"

void ntput(
    short row,          /* row to output text on */
    short col,          /* column to output text in */
    long long_val,      /* value to be displayed */
    char buf[],         /* output buffer */
    short field_len)    /* length of field to right justify in */

    {
    ltoa(long_val, buf, 10);    /* convert long to ASCII string */
    strrjust(buf, field_len);   /* right justify field */
    tput(row, col, buf);        /* display on screen for user */
    }
```

## FTPUT.C

```
/* SOURCE FILE: FTPUT.C
 ***********************************************************************
 * ftput() converts a double-precision floating-point number to ASCII and
 *   displays it right justified in field of specified width, with
 *   specified decimal places.
 ***********************************************************************
 */

#include <string.h>
#include <stdlib.h>
#include "projutil.h"

void ftput(
    short row,              /* cursor row to display value on */
    short col,              /* cursor column to display value in */
    double double_val,      /* value to be displayed */
    short dec_place,        /* number of decimal places to display */
    char buf[],             /* output buffer for formatting data */
    short field_len)        /* length of field */

    {
    int dec;                /* decimal point position (from fcvt()) */
    int sign;               /* flag (0/1): is minus sign needed?  (from fcvt()) */

    /* Copy contents of temporary string buffer to buf. */
    strcpy(buf, fcvt(double_val, dec_place, &dec, &sign));
    if (sign)                       /* double_val is negative */
        {

        /* memmove needed to copy into overlapping data area. */
        memmove(buf + 1, buf, 1 + strlen(buf));
        buf[0] = '-';               /* insert minus sign prefix */
        }
    if (dec >= 0)                   /* insert decimal point between digits */
        {
        memmove(buf + dec + sign + 1, buf + dec + sign,
            strlen(buf) + 1 - dec - sign);
        buf[dec + sign] = '.';      /* insert the decimal point */
        }
    else                /* dec is negative, so leading zeros are needed */
        {
        memmove(buf + sign + 1 - dec, buf + sign,
            strlen(buf) + 1 - sign);
        for (; dec; ++dec)          /* count from dec up to zero */
            buf[sign - dec] = '0';  /* insert a leading zero */
        buf[sign] = '.';            /* insert the decimal point */
        }
```

*(continued)*

FTPUT.C *continued*

```
strrjust(buf, field_len);
tput(row, col, buf);
}
```

# beg_scrn()

The *beg_scrn()* function sets up a new screen by clearing the existing screen and displaying such headings as the user's name, the application name, and the screen title. This information is helpful to the user and also enhances system security. The enhancement to system security is a subtle point. If a salesperson has another person's name at the top of the screen, a manager can tell that the wrong account is being used and that the system's security has been violated.

## BEG_SCRN.C

```
/* SOURCE FILE: BEG_SCRN.C
**************************************************************************
* beg_scrn() clears the screen and displays screen heading strings. Four
*   headings may be shown: left, center, right, below. The first three
*   headings appear on the top line; the last is centered on the next line.
**************************************************************************
*/

#include <stdio.h>        /* for stderr for screen control */
#include <string.h>
#include "projutil.h"
#include "ansiscrn.h"
#define SCRNWDTH 80        /* screen width in columns */

void beg_scrn(
    char left[],          /* heading text for top left of screen */
    char center[],        /* heading text for top center of screen */
    char right[],         /* heading text for top right of screen */
    char below[])         /* heading text for center of second line of screen */

    {
    CLR_SCRN;
    tput(1, 1, left);
    tput(1, (SCRNWDTH - strlen(center)) / 2, center);  /* center top heading */
    tput(1, 1 + SCRNWDTH - strlen(right), right);
    tput(2, (SCRNWDTH - strlen(below)) / 2, below); /* center line 2 heading */
    }
```

## *match()*

The *match()* function is called by *prompt()* to compare a string typed by the user with a match pattern that specifies all possible acceptable inputs. This enables us to limit user input to specific kinds of data and also helps the user catch typing errors.

### MATCH.C

```
/* SOURCE FILE: MATCH.C
 *************************************************************************
 * match() verifies a data string, character by character, against a match
 *   string. If the match string is shorter than the data string, the
 *   last match-string character is used to verify the data string.
 *   The match string may be composed of these match characters:
 *
 *     A    A-Z                             (uppercase letters)
 *     #    0-9 only                        (numbers)
 *     S    0-9 or + or -                   (signs or numbers)
 *     F    0-9 or .                        (floating-point numbers)
 *     L    a-z, A-Z, 0-9, or ;:.,/?*-$#()'! (names, addresses)
 *          and non-leading spaces
 *     U    A-Z, 0-9, or ;:.,/?*-$#()'!     (uppercase names, addresses)
 *          and non-leading spaces
 *     P    0-9 or - or () or space         (phone numbers)
 *     Q    one of "Yy1Nn0"                 (question reply)
 *     X    any printable character         (text)
 *
 *   Any other character in the match string is ignored. Spaces are matched
 *   by L, U, and P. Empty match string matches any data.
 * Return value: YES = data string matches; NO = no match.
 *************************************************************************
 */

#include <ctype.h>          /* for isxxx() character-type macro definitions */
#include <string.h>
#include "syntypes.h"
#include "projutil.h"

flag match(
    char data_str[],        /* source string to be verified */
    char match_str[])       /* match pattern text */

    {
    short ichar;            /* input character counter */
    char c_data;            /* character of data string */
    char c_match;           /* character of match string */
```

*(continued)*

MATCH.C *continued*

```
/* Initialize a variable to a function return. */
short len_match = strlen(match_str);
bflag matches = YES;

for (ichar = 0; data_str[ichar] != '\0' && matches; ++ichar)
   {

   /* Determine match character. */
   if (ichar < len_match)        /* use next match character */
      c_match = match_str[ichar];
   else if (len_match == 0)      /* empty match_str */
      c_match = '\0';
   else                          /* use last character of match string */
      c_match = match_str[len_match - 1];
   c_data = data_str[ichar];
   switch (c_match)              /* check match with data */
      {
      case 'A':                  /* A-Z */
         if (!isupper(c_data))
            matches = NO;
         break;
      case '#':                  /* 0-9 only */
         if (!isdigit(c_data))
            matches = NO;
         break;
      case 'S':                  /* 0-9 or + or - only */
         if (!isdigit(c_data) && !strchr("+-", c_data))
            matches = NO;
         break;
      case 'L':                  /* a-z, A-Z, 0-9, or ;:.,/?*-$#()'! or space */
         if (!isalnum(c_data) && !strchr(";:.,/?*-$#()'! ",
            c_data))
            matches = NO;
         if (ichar == 0 && c_data == ' ')     /* no leading blanks */
            matches = NO;
         break;
      case 'U':                  /* A-Z, 0-9, or ;:.,/?*-$#()'! or space */
         if (!isupper(c_data) && !isdigit(c_data) &&
            !strchr(";:.,/?*-$#()'! ", c_data))
            matches = NO;
         if (ichar == 0 && c_data == ' ')     /* no leading blanks */
            matches = NO;
         break;
```

*(continued)*

MATCH.C *continued*

```
        case 'P':               /* 0-9 or - or () or space */
            if (!isdigit(c_data) && !strchr("-() ", c_data))
                matches = NO;
            break;
        case 'F':               /* 0-9 or . */
            if (!isdigit(c_data) && !strchr(".", c_data))
                matches = NO;
            break;
        case 'Q':               /* Yy1Nn0 as reply to yes/no question */
            if (!strchr("Yy1Nn0", c_data))
                matches = NO;
            break;
        case 'X':               /* must be printable (' 'through '~') */
            if (!isprint(c_data))
                matches = NO;
            break;
        }
    }
    return (matches);
}
```

# *strrjust()*

The standard library lacks a function for right justifying text in a string of fixed length, so we need the project utility function *strrjust()* to accomplish this. The code for this function demonstrates conditionally compiled debugging techniques, using its own test-driver *main()* function that verifies the correctness of *strrjust()* and documents examples of its use. You can leave all the debug code here in the source file without any execution overhead, provided the symbol *DBGMAIN* is not defined (thus the term *conditionally compiled*).

## STRRJUST.C

```
/* SOURCE FILE: STRRJUST.C
 ***************************************************************************
 * strrjust() takes a string and a length and right justifies the string in
 *   a field of that length. If the string is longer than the field, no
 *   action is taken.
 ***************************************************************************
 */
```

*(continued)*

```c
#include <stdio.h>
#include <string.h>
#include "projutil.h"

void strrjust(
    char str[],    /* text to be right justified (padded on left with spaces) */
    short fld_len) /* length of field to format text in */

    {
    short end_char, ichar, move;

    /* Find index of last non-space in str and back up from there */
    /*   toward beginning; then fill left end of str with blanks. */
    for (end_char = strlen(str) - 1;
        str[end_char] == ' ' && end_char > 0; --end_char)
        ;
    move = fld_len - end_char - 1;          /* number of positions */
    if (move > 0 && end_char >= 0)          /* need to move anything? */
        {
        for (ichar = end_char; ichar >= 0; --ichar) /* copy characters */
            str[ichar + move] = str[ichar];

        /* Fill left end with blanks. */
        for (ichar = move - 1; ichar >= 0; --ichar)
            str[ichar] = ' ';
        str[fld_len] = '\0';                 /* null terminator */
        }
    }
#if defined(DBGMAIN)
#define TEST(cond, msg) printf((cond) ? "" :\
    "!!! TEST FAILED !!! %s\7\n", (msg))

/* Test driver main() for strrjust(). */
main()
    {
    char str[81];

    strcpy(str, "abc");
    strrjust(str, 5);
    TEST(0 == strcmp(str, "  abc"), "strjust #1");
    strcpy(str, "ABCDE");
    strrjust(str, 5);
    TEST(0 == strcmp(str, "ABCDE"), "strjust #2");
    strcpy(str, "");
    strrjust(str, 5);
    TEST(0 == strcmp(str, ""), "strjust #3");
    printf("strrjust tests complete\n");
    }
#endif
```

## *err_warn()* and *err_exit()*

The functions *err_warn()* and *err_exit()* are a team. We employ them to output diagnostic messages to the user. Use *err_warn()* for warnings about errors that can be corrected and *err_exit()* for fatal errors after which you want your program to terminate.

## ERR_WARN.C

```
/* SOURCE FILE: ERR_WARN.C
 ************************************************************************
 * err_warn() displays a two-string diagnostic message on line 24, waits
 *    for the user to press ESC, and then erases the diagnostic message.
 ************************************************************************
 */

#include <stdio.h>
#include <string.h>
#include <stdlib.h>
#include <conio.h>
#include "syntypes.h"
#include "ansiscrn.h"
#include "projutil.h"
#define ESC '\x1b'

void err_warn(
   char first[],                /* first part of diagnostic message */
   char second[])               /* part two of diagnostic message */

   {
   IMPORT bflag bell_ok;
   short first_len = strlen(first);
   short second_len = strlen(second);

   CUR_MV(24, 1);
   CLR_LINE;
   tput(24, 1, first);
   tput(24, 2 + first_len, second);
   tput(24, 3 + first_len + second_len,
      "_ (press ESC)\b\b\b\b\b\b\b\b\b\b\b");
   if (bell_ok)
      BELL;
   while (getch() != ESC)        /* loop until ESC entered */
      if (bell_ok)
         BELL;
   CUR_MV(24, 1);
   CLR_LINE;
   }
```

*(continued)*

ERR_WARN.C *continued*

```
/**************************************************************************
 * err_exit() displays a diagnostic message through err_warn() and calls
 *   exit() to terminate execution. The two-part message is displayed on
 *   line 24. When the user presses ESC, the message is erased.
 **************************************************************************
 */

void err_exit(
    char first[],                   /* first part of diagnostic message */
    char second[])                  /* part two of diagnostic message */

    {
    char log_buf[512];

    strcpy(log_buf, first);
    strcat(log_buf, " ");
    strcat(log_buf, second);
    logentry(log_buf);              /* record the message in the log */
    err_warn(first, second);        /* display the message */
    exit(FAIL);                     /* terminate program: FAIL status */
    }
```

This concludes the source-code listings for the Software-Vendor Order-Entry Application. We'll spend the next few chapters discussing each function in detail.

# Top- and Middle-Level Functions

Now that you have all the source listings in front of you, let's look at each part of the order-entry application in detail. The bulk of the code deals with the input of data about a customer and about the products being ordered. In the spirit of structured programming, we'll begin at a high level and work our way down to the low-level "workhorse" functions.

## The User Interface

The user interface—the manner in which a program and its users communicate commands and data to one another—is at the heart of this highly interactive business application. It is the face our program shows to the human world.

The technology of the user interface has come a long way in a short time. The earliest user/computer communication devices, such as teletypes, had keyboards and hard-copy output, but they were slow and cumbersome. Then came the CRT, with features such as a directly addressable cursor, graphics symbols, and protected and highlighted fields. Today's interface options include light pens, touch screens, mice, track balls, and bit-mapped graphics displays. All of these innovations can decrease training time and increase user productivity.

The physical interface employed by our order-entry application consists of a simple monochrome CRT display and a standard PC keyboard. The CRT needs to be capable only of text display, cursor movement, screen erasure, and erasure from the cursor to the end of the line.

But the user interface is more than simply hardware. It is also the invisible element—the software—that makes the application easy, efficient, and pleasant to use. Productivity is one way of measuring the quality of this side of an interface. Productivity in this case is defined as the number of transactions a user enters per hour, less the number of errors and the amount of effort involved in finding and correcting those errors. The users of our order-entry program are salespeople, not programmers, and they appreciate the ability to correct mistakes in an order quickly and easily, while they are entering it, rather than later. And they are more productive users if they do not need to retype the entire order merely to correct a mistake in one line. Good defaults and abbreviations for frequently entered text also help the user by reducing keystrokes and chance of error.

The order-entry application program incorporates most of these user-interface features, so we'll discuss them in detail as we work our way through the source code.

## Top-Level Program Structure

The file *ordentry.c* holds the top-level function of the order-entry program, *main()*. This function controls the flow among prompt screens, each of which is implemented as a separate middle-level function called from *main()*. The screen called up for display can be the screen following the current screen or the one before it, depending on the outcome of some of the entries in the current screen. (The structure of the *main()* function for our order-entry application was shown in Figure 10-1.)

The prompt-screen functions constitute the middle level of the order-entry application. They reside in the source file *ordbuild.c*. Each function "paints" the screen with field titles and messages that are used to prompt the user for data. The middle-level functions contain many calls to low-level functions and are written to avoid device and environment dependencies. (The code to handle such dependencies is hidden away in the low-level functions that they call.)

Before I began to code the *main()* function, I had to make some decisions about how we would handle our data. Let's look at those decisions more closely before we begin analyzing the code itself.

## Identifiers used in *main()*

There are only a few variables used in *main()*, and they are included in the first few lines of code. The defining declaration of *bell_ok* allocates memory to hold *bell_ok*'s value and sets the value initially to *YES* to permit the bell to sound. Although *main()* itself doesn't use *bell_ok*, I chose to place the defining declaration at the start of the *main()* source file because *bell_ok* is *GLOBAL*. (In fact, the declaration can be in any single source file we choose, as long as it is outside the body of any function.)

```
#include "syntypes.h"
#include "projutil.h"    /* needed for prompt() symbols STEPOK, STEPBACK, and */
                         /*    STEPCANC, and synonym type stepcode */
#include "ordentry.h"

/* Declare data shared among functions in all source files (GLOBAL). */
GLOBAL bflag bell_ok = YES;    /* it's OK to ring bell */

void main(void)
    {
    stepcode step_rtn;        /* step_rtn is the return value from a step. It is
                               * passed to the next step. It may equal:
                               *    STEPOK     Step complete; go on to next step.
                               *    STEPBACK   Back up to closest previous step.
                               *    STEPCANC   Cancel order entry (quit).
                               */

    enum prompts {ID_USER, ID_CUST, ORD_ITMS, SHIP_PAY, WRT_ORD,
        ENDSTEPS} step;
```

The *main()* function has only two variables, *step_rtn* and *step*. The data type of the *step_rtn* variable is unfamiliar: *stepcode*. The declaration of the *enum prompts*-type variable named *step* must also look strange to you. So let's examine these two data types now.

## Synonym data types

Sometimes the standard type declarations don't give us as much information about our data as we would like. C offers us the opportunity to correct this problem by creating *synonym* data types.

Programmer-defined synonym data types are absolutely equivalent to the underlying types they are declared to represent, so why use them? Readability, of course: They supply extra information for the reader of the program—information that clarifies the purpose or uses of the declared variables. Consider the synonym type *flag*, defined in our *syntypes.h* header file. Type *flag* is equivalent to type *int*, but since the word *flag* implies a Boolean true/false range of values, it gives a clearer, more accurate impression of the purpose of the variable. In this next example, *more_data*'s purpose would be more difficult to fathom with an *int* declaration:

```
#include "syntypes.h"        /* needed for flag and YES */

    /* ... */
flag more_data = YES;        /* any data left? */
while (more_data)            /* loop for each item of data */
```

You can define more than one synonym type in a single *typedef* statement, as in this next example, where *byte* and *unchar* are both made synonyms of type *unsigned char*:

```
typedef unsigned char byte, unchar;
```

### The *stepcode* type

The type *stepcode* is designated as a synonym of type *char* by this *typedef* statement in the *projutil.h* header file:

```
typedef char stepcode;
```

The *stepcode* type is used in *main()*'s declarations because it gives the reader more information than type *char*. (Type *char* merely designates a 1-byte value, an ASCII character or a small integer.) A stepcode value is a number returned by a step in the prompting process to describe the outcome of the prompt. The three possible return values defined in *projutil.h* are:

```
#define STEPOK 0        /* data were entered; may be null if OPT */
#define STEPBACK 1      /* C_BACK was entered; back up a prompt */
#define STEPCANC 2      /* C_CANC was entered; cancel transaction */
```

Although a *stepcode* declaration gives the reader more information than a *char* declaration, the program itself will behave the same in either case.

## The *enum* type

The last declaration in *main()* that we need to discuss is the order-entry enumeration data type called *prompts*.

```
enum prompts {ID_USER, ID_CUST, ORD_ITMS, SHIP_PAY, WRT_ORD,
  ENDSTEPS} step;
```

C's enumeration facility permits the declaration of a variable whose value must always be one of the constants in the declaration's enumeration list. In our programs, the enumeration type *prompts* creates a list of constants from 0 through 5 for use as case labels in a *switch* statement. The value of *ID_USER* is *0*, that of *ID_CUST* is *1*, and so on. The names in the enumeration list must be in the same order as that in which they are normally executed. The *switch* statement uses this list to control the call to the next step in the order-entry process, which may in fact be the previous step again, or a subsequent one, depending on the *stepcode* return from the current step. (Uppercase is used for these named constants, as for defined symbols, to avoid mistaking them for variables.)

The name following the keyword *enum* (in this case, *prompts*) is called a *tag* and is the name of the enumeration type being defined. The *prompts* enumeration type is used to declare variables whose values are restricted to the list of enumerated constants specified in the type definition.

The variable *step* is declared as an instance of an enumeration type *prompts* variable. The use of the tag is optional and is really required only if additional declaration statements of other variables of that same enumeration type will follow. The tag does add readability, so I recommend always using one. Here are additional examples of enumeration declarations from different functions in the source file *ordbuild.c*:

```
enum {PART_NUM, QUANTITY, ENDSTEPS} step;          /* no tag used here */
enum prompts {SHIP_CAR, SHIP_AMT, TAX, PAY_TERMS, COMMENT, ENDSTEPS};
enum prompts step;         /* tag defined in previous line and used here */
```

```
  ┌────────────────────────────────────────────────────────┐
  │                                                        │
  │           C   A   U   T   I   O   N                    │
  │                                                        │
  ├────────────────────────────────────────────────────────┤
```

*Some C compilers do not support the enumeration type, and restrictions on its use vary. Microsoft C does support* enum-*type variables and does allow arithmetic operations on them, but it does not permit a function to have an enumeration type as its return type.*

To assign a value other than *0* to the first *enum*-list identifier, or other than *1* plus the previous identifier's value to subsequent identifiers, use the = assignment operator and a constant expression after the identifier *within the list.* The value of the constant expression must be type *int* and can be negative. The next name in the *enum* list after this assignment will be 1 higher, unless it too is assigned a different value. For example, the assignment you see embedded in the enumeration below causes the value of the constant *CAMEL* to be *100*, not *3*, and the value of *MULE* to be *101*:

```
enum shipper {POST, AIR, RAIL, CAMEL = 100, MULE};
enum shipper ship_via; /* declare ship_via as enumeration type shipper */
```

## The flow of control at the top

One of the interface requirements for our program is that the system permit the user to correct data in an earlier part of an order easily, without having to reenter all the data that follow the corrected field. To code for this capability without using the troublesome *goto* statement, we can use a switch statement that chooses the steps to perform. Let's look at how our *main()* handles this.

```
enum prompts {ID_USER, ID_CUST, ORD_ITMS, SHIP_PAY, WRT_ORD,
    ENDSTEPS} step;

for (step = 0, step_rtn = STEPOK; step != ENDSTEPS &&
    step_rtn != STEPCANC; )
    {
    switch (step)
        {
        case ID_USER:        /* identify user (salesperson) */
            step_rtn = id_user();
            break;
```

*(continued)*

186

*continued*

```
    case ID_CUST:        /* identify customer */
        step_rtn = id_cust(step_rtn);
        break;
    case ORD_ITMS:       /* input order detail items */
        step_rtn = ord_itms(step_rtn);
        break;
    case SHIP_PAY:       /* input shipping info, tax, pay terms */
        step_rtn = ship_pay(step_rtn);
        break;
    case WRT_ORD:        /* write order; update files */
        step_rtn = wrt_ord();
        break;
    }

/* Determine next step based on return from last one. */
if (step_rtn == STEPOK)          /* was last step successful? */
    ++step;                      /* yes; go on to next step */
else if (step_rtn == STEPBACK && step > 0)
    --step;                      /* no; back up to previous step */
}
```

The body of the *main()* function is a loop. Each time the program passes through the loop, one step of the order-entry process is executed. A variable of enumeration type *prompts* named *step* is set and then used to select the next step to perform. The value of *step* is always one of the *enum*-type *prompts* values, so setting it to 0 in the initialization of the *for* loop is equivalent to setting it to ID_USER. The *if...else* at the bottom of the loop picks the step from the *prompts* enumeration to be executed next. The value of *step* is incremented after a step is completed successfully or decremented if the user requests the program to back up to the previous step. Thus the *switch* statement gives a clean way for control to flow backward or forward, without the use of *goto*. This control structure makes it easy to add, remove, or reorder steps at a later time.

# Middle-Level Program Structure

The source files *ordbuild.c* and *get_addr.c* hold the middle level of our order-entry application, the prompt screens. The middle level supplies the specifics of the prompt for each of the data fields and calls the low-level functions that actually input and output the data. Text is output at specific cursor locations on the screen, and inputs are made in a specific sequence and checked for validity.

The control-flow style used in *main()* is copied in some of these middle-level order-entry functions to permit the user to move backward as well as forward through the individual fields of a screen, as well as between screens. For instance, if the user is being asked to input the first field of the third screen but instead gives the "back up" command (by typing *control-R*), the next prompt will be for the final field on the second screen.

The primary difference between top- and middle-level steps is the amount of work they do. A step in the *main()* function is all the interactions involved in inputting a whole prompt screen of order data. But in middle-level functions, a step is usually only the input of a single field of data. Figure 11-1 shows the functions included in the two middle-level source files.

| FILE | FUNCTION NAME | PURPOSE |
|------|---------------|---------|
| *ordbuild.c* | *id_user()* | Identify the user/salesperson |
| | *id_cust()* | Identify the customer |
| | *ord_itms()* | Input order items |
| | *ship_pay()* | Arrange shipment and payment terms |
| | *wrt_ord()* | Write order to standard output |
| *get_addr.c* | *get_addr()* | Input an address for shipping or billing |

FIGURE 11-1
*Middle-level order-entry functions*

## The *id_user()* function

The *id_user()* function is responsible for application security. It is called every time an order is entered to ensure that the user is a bona fide company salesperson and not a hacker trying to break into the system.

```
/***************************************************************************
 * id_user() identifies the user (salesperson or data-entry clerk). The user
 *   enters office code, name, and password. The password is then verified.
 ***************************************************************************
 */

stepcode id_user(void)
    {
    IMPORT char user[];
    IMPORT char office[];
    IMPORT char scrn_title[];
    char password[L_PASSWORD + 1];
    stepcode step_rtn;
    short ichar;

    /* Paint screen: Show headings for data to prompt for. */
    beg_scrn("", scrn_title, "", "SALESPERSON");
    tput(10, 20, "Office");
    tput(12, 20, "Salesperson");
    tput(14, 20, "Password");
    do                          /* loop until data entered or order canceled */
        {

        /* Input name of office seller is working in. */
        step_rtn = prompt(office, "L", 3, L_OFFICE, MAND, 10, 32);
        if (step_rtn == STEPBACK)
            err_warn("Office must be supplied:", "");
        }
    while (step_rtn == STEPBACK);
    if (step_rtn != STEPCANC)   /* prompt for user */
        do                      /* loop until data entered or order canceled */
            {
            user[0] = '\0';         /* DON'T show last user id */
            step_rtn = prompt(user, "L", 2, L_USER, MAND, 12, 32);
            if (step_rtn == STEPBACK)
                err_warn("I must know who you are:", "");
            }
        while (step_rtn == STEPBACK);
    if (step_rtn != STEPCANC)   /* input password without echo */
        {
        CUR_MV(14, 32);
        for (ichar = 0; ichar < L_PASSWORD &&
            (password[ichar] = (char)getch()) >= ' '; ++ichar)
            ;
        if (password[ichar] >= ' ')
            ++ichar;
        password[ichar] = '\0';
        if (!pw_find(office, user, password))
            {
```

*(continued)*

*id_user() continued*

```
            err_warn("Access denied:", user);
            step_rtn = STEPCANC;
            }
        else                        /* display instructions */
            {
            tput(17, 17, "Instructions for Commands Available at Prompts:");
            tput(19, 20, "^R = (control-R) Re-prompt for previous.");
            tput(20, 20, "^E = Erase data field, make it empty.");
            tput(21, 20, "^X = Exit and cancel order.");
            tput(23, 17, "Press ^X to exit, or another key to continue: _\b");
            if (getch() == C_CANC)
              step_rtn = STEPCANC;
            }
        }
    return (step_rtn);
    }
```

We use a simpler style of prompting in *id_user()* than we did in the *main()* function: The user can move only forward through these prompt steps. If the user is unable to enter a valid name and password, *id_user()* displays the diagnostic message "Access denied: *user_name _* (press ESC)" and returns the *stepcode STEPCANC*. The *main()* function then receives the instruction to cancel and does so.

The processing in *id_user()* consists of the entry and subsequent validation of the user's name and password. If the user is known to the system, the program displays brief instructions for entering orders. Otherwise, the program terminates itself.

Figure 11-2 lists the functions called by *id_user()*. All but *pw_find()* are useful general-purpose functions, so we'll talk about each in detail.

| FUNCTION | ACTION |
|---|---|
| *beg_scrn()* | Begins a new screen, clears, and shows headings |
| *tput()* | Displays a string at a specified cursor location |
| *prompt()* | Inputs a string and validates match |
| *err_warn()* | Displays diagnostic message for user |
| *pw_find()* | Looks up user's name and password |
| *getch()* | Inputs a character without echo (in Microsoft's C library) |

FIGURE 11-2
*The low-level functions called by* id_user()

### beg_scrn()

The function *beg_scrn()* expects our string arguments to be used to create the heading for a new screen. The first three arguments are displayed on the screen's top line, in the left, center, and right positions. The fourth argument is displayed on the second line of the screen, centered.

```
/* SOURCE FILE: BEG_SCRN.C
 **************************************************************************
 * beg_scrn() clears the screen and displays screen heading strings. Four
 *   headings may be shown: left, center, right, below. The first three
 *   headings appear on the top line; the last is centered on the next line.
 **************************************************************************
 */

#include <stdio.h>        /* for stderr for screen control */
#include <string.h>
#include "projutil.h"
#include "ansiscrn.h"
#define SCRNWDTH 80        /* screen width in columns */

void beg_scrn(
    char left[],           /* heading text for top left of screen */
    char center[],         /* heading text for top center of screen */
    char right[],          /* heading text for top right of screen */
    char below[])          /* heading text for center of second line of screen */

    {
    CLR_SCRN;
    tput(1, 1, left);
    tput(1, (SCRNWDTH - strlen(center)) / 2, center);  /* center top heading */
    tput(1, 1 + SCRNWDTH - strlen(right), right);
    tput(2, (SCRNWDTH - strlen(below)) / 2, below); /* center line 2 heading */
    }
```

The call to *beg_scrn()* in *id_user()* supplies no left or right headings for the top line:

```
beg_scrn("", scrn_title, "", "SALESPERSON");
```

The subsequent three lines of *id_user()* call the terminal-output function *tput()* (see Chapter 12) to display the prompt headings *Office*, *Salesperson*, and *Password* in column 20 of lines 10, 12, and 14 on the screen.

## *prompt()*

The next function, *prompt()*, is the heart of our application's user interface.

```
/* SOURCE FILE: PROMPT.C
 ************************************************************************
 * prompt() inputs text from standard input to the string "data".
 *    The program matches input against an optional match-string argument
 *    and checks minimum and maximum input lengths. If the Boolean (flag)
 *    argument mand is true, the program will not allow "data" to remain null;
 *    the user must make an entry. The parameter "data" is both passed to
 *    prompt() and returned to the calling function. The value passed in is
 *    treated as a default to be used if input is null. Data are input one
 *    character at a time, without automatic echo.
 * Return value: The outcome of prompt has synonym data type stepcode, which
 *    is used to indicate:
 *      STEPOK    Step complete; go on to next step.
 *      STEPBACK  Back up to closest previous step.
 *      STEPCANC  Cancel order entry (quit).
 *    C_BACK, C_NULL, and C_CANC are defined in projutil.h. The user can
 *       request to back up by entering C_BACK, to cancel by entering C_CANC,
 *       or to erase data by entering C_NULL as any character in the reply.
 ************************************************************************
 */

#include <stdio.h>
#include <string.h>
#include <conio.h>
#include "syntypes.h"
#include "ansiscrn.h"
#include "projutil.h"

stepcode prompt(
    char data[],            /* default passed in, input data returned */
    char match_str[],       /* match string to verify data against */
    short min_len,          /* minimum input data length */
    short max_len,          /* maximum input data length */
    flag mand,              /* if yes, data cannot be null on return */
    short row,              /* cursor row to begin input */
    short col)              /* cursor column to begin input */

    {
    IMPORT bflag bell_ok;   /* global permission to ring bell */
    char buf[PRMTBSIZ];     /* prompt input buffer */
    short ichar;            /* input character counter */
    stepcode rtn = STEPOK;  /* return code */
    bflag more;             /* expect more input? */
```

*(continued)*

192

PROMPT.C *continued*

```
/* Display prompt mask or default value, if any.
 * Copy default to buffer. Fill rest of buffer with prompt mask
 *    characters, to maximum length of field prompted for.
 */
strcpy(buf, data);
for (ichar = strlen(buf); ichar < max_len; ++ichar)
   buf[ichar] = C_MASK;
buf[ichar] = '\0';
tput(row, col, buf);
CUR_MV(row, col);

/* Input each character. */
strcpy(buf, data);              /* copy default value to buffer */
for (ichar = 0, more = YES; ichar < max_len && more; )
   {
   buf[ichar] = (char)getch();       /* input a character (no auto echo) */
   buf[ichar + 1] = '\0';
   switch (buf[ichar])
      {
      case C_CANC:              /* cancel command */
         rtn = STEPCANC, more = NO;
         break;
      case C_BACK:              /* back up to previous prompt */
         rtn = STEPBACK, more = NO;
         break;
      case C_NULL:              /* force data to null, restart prompt */

         /* Fill buffer with mask characters to maximum length of field. */
         for (ichar = 0; ichar < max_len; ++ichar)
            buf[ichar] = C_MASK;
         buf[ichar] = '\0';
         tput(row, col, buf); /* show prompt mask in buf */
         ichar = 0;             /* restart at first character */
         buf[ichar] = data[ichar] = '\0';     /* erase data */
         CUR_MV(row, col);   /* move cursor to beginning of mask */
         break;
      case '\r':              /* end of line */
      case '\n':              /* alternate end of line */
         if (ichar == 0 && data[0] != '\0')

            /* Pass default back to caller. */
            strcpy(buf, data), more = NO;
         else if (ichar == 0 && data[0] == '\0' && mand)
            {                     /* mandatory entry, no default supplied */
            err_warn("Data must be entered:", "");
            CUR_MV(row, col);
            }
```

*(continued)*

```
              /* Too few characters? Check, unless this is first */
              /*   character of reply and reply is optional. */
              else if (ichar < min_len && !(ichar == 0 && !mand))
                  {
                  err_warn("Too few characters:", "");
                  CUR_MV(row, col + ichar);           /* restore cursor */
                  }
              else
                  buf[ichar] = '\0', more = NO;       /* end of input */
              break;
          case '\b':                 /* backspace (BS) entered */
              buf[ichar] = '\0';     /* delete backspace */
              if (ichar > 0)
                  {
                  buf[--ichar] = '\0';        /* wipe character before BS */
                  fputc('\b', stderr);        /* fix display to match */
                  fputc(C_MASK, stderr);
                  fputc(C_MASK, stderr);
                  fprintf(stderr, "\b\b");
                  }
              break;
          default:                   /* check match and length; echo character */

              /* Echo if character is legal; else ring bell. */
              buf[ichar + 1] = '\0';    /* save character and increment ichar */
              if (match(buf, match_str))
                  putc(buf[ichar++], stderr);        /* echo good character */
              else if (bell_ok)    /* bad character entered; ring bell */
                  putc('\7', stderr);
              if (ichar > max_len)
                  more = NO;
              break;
          }
      }

/* Copy buf to data and erase rest of prompt mask (if any). */
if (rtn == STEPOK)
    strcpy(data, buf);
ichar = strlen(data);
CUR_MV(row, col + ichar);
for (; ichar < max_len; ++ichar)
    fputc(' ', stderr);            /* erase end of mask, using spaces */
return (rtn);
}
```

We call *prompt()* twice in *id_user()*, first for input of the office name and then for input of the user's name:

```
step_rtn = prompt(office, "L", 3, L_OFFICE, MAND, 10, 32);
   */ ... */
step_rtn = prompt(user, "L", 2, L_USER, MAND, 12, 32);
```

The *prompt()* function requires seven arguments: *reply_string, match_string, minimum_length, maximum_length, mandatory_flag, cursor_row,* and *cursor_column.* In both calls, the symbol *MAND* (defined in *projutil.h* as *1*) is passed so that input at the prompt is mandatory. (The technique of specifying an option by passing a defined constant such as *MAND,* rather than an ordinary constant such as *1,* makes your code much easier to understand.) The string *"L",* an option for a *case* statement in *match.c* that permits the user to type letters, numbers, punctuation, and non-leading spaces, is passed for pattern matching of the input text. See Chapter 13 for a detailed discussion of the *match()* function.

Notice that once again both prompts are placed in the same column on the screen—this time column 32. Since the human eye moves down columns more easily than across lines of a screen, alignment of titles and fields into columns is an important technique in designing the user interface. In our system, all prompt titles are in column 20 and all input fields are in column 32, courtesy of our *tput()* function.

## *err_warn()* and *err_exit()*

The project utility function *err_warn()* issues diagnostic messages to the user. A call to *err_exit()* does the same job and then terminates the program by calling the C library function *exit()*.

```
/* SOURCE FILE: ERR_WARN.C
 *************************************************************************
 * err_warn() displays a two-string diagnostic message on line 24, waits
 *    for the user to press ESC, and then erases the diagnostic message.
 *************************************************************************
 */

#include <stdio.h>
#include <string.h>
#include <stdlib.h>
#include <conio.h>
#include "syntypes.h"
```

*(continued)*

ERR_WARN.C *continued*

```
#include "ansiscrn.h"
#include "projutil.h"
#define ESC '\x1b'

void err_warn(
   char first[],                 /* first part of diagnostic message */
   char second[])                /* part two of diagnostic message */

   {
   IMPORT bflag bell_ok;
   short first_len = strlen(first);
   short second_len = strlen(second);

   CUR_MV(24, 1);
   CLR_LINE;
   tput(24, 1, first);
   tput(24, 2 + first_len, second);
   tput(24, 3 + first_len + second_len,
      "_ (press ESC)\b\b\b\b\b\b\b\b\b\b\b");
   if (bell_ok)
      BELL;
   while (getch() != ESC)        /* loop until ESC entered */
      if (bell_ok)
         BELL;
   CUR_MV(24, 1);
   CLR_LINE;
   }


/***************************************************************************
 * err_exit() displays a diagnostic message through err_warn() and calls
 *    exit() to terminate execution. The two-part message is displayed on
 *    line 24. When the user presses ESC, the message is erased.
 ***************************************************************************
 */

void err_exit(
   char first[],                 /* first part of diagnostic message */
   char second[])                /* part two of diagnostic message */

   {
   char log_buf[512];

   strcpy(log_buf, first);
   strcat(log_buf, " ");
   strcat(log_buf, second);
   logentry(log_buf);            /* record the message in the log */
   err_warn(first, second);      /* display the message */
   exit(FAIL);                   /* terminate program: FAIL status */
   }
```

Like most diagnostic displays, *err_warn()* messages have two parts: a fixed string and a variable string. For example, "Illegal account number" is a typical fixed part, and the actual incorrect account number is a typical variable part. Or "Can't open file" might be the fixed string and the name of the invalid file the variable string. Both calls to *err_warn()* in *id_user()* pass a null string for the variable string—that is, only the fixed diagnostic message is displayed.

## getch()

The next function *id_user()* calls is *getch()*, which is used to read the password input by the user. This Microsoft C library function is called to input a single character from the system console (normally the keyboard). The input character is not automatically echoed, so the user doesn't see what he or she types for *getch()*: The screen display is completely under the control of our program. For example, the user could type an *A* and our program could print * as an echo, if we wanted to acknowledge the input but keep it secret, as with a password.

The *id_user()* function calls *getch()* repeatedly until *L_PASSWORD* reaches its maximum length or until the user enters a character with an ASCII value numerically lower than a space (32). Each character input is saved as the next element in the character array *password*:

```
for (ichar = 0; ichar < L_PASSWORD &&
   (password[ichar] = (char)getch()) >= ' '; ++ichar)
   ;
```

The *(char)* cast operator in this statement converts the value returned from *getch()* from an integer to a character. This conversion is used to obtain a value that has the same type as the members of the *password* array. If it weren't used, the compiler would issue a warning about conversion taking place.

## pw_find()

The last *id_user()* subfunction is *pw_find()*, the password finder. Three strings are passed to *pw_find()*: the office name, the user name, and the password entered by the user.

```
/**********************************************************************
 * pw_find() looks up a user's name and password and returns YES if the user
 *   is found, NO if not. If the user is found, office ID is also checked.
 *   User data contain indication of whether to ring bell.
 **********************************************************************
 */

flag pw_find(
    char office[],        /* description of user's office (returned) */
    char user[],          /* name, initials, or abbreviation of user to find */
    char password[])      /* password to look up */

    {
    IMPORT bflag bell_ok;
    if (user[1] == 'S')   /* OK to ring the bell? */
        bell_ok = NO;     /* no; silence the bell */
    return (user[0] == 'S' && password[0] == 'S');
    }
```

Right now, this function is a stub that returns 1 (signifying that the user and password are accepted) only if the first letter of both the user's name and the password is *S*. This function will be replaced by a fully operational version after we learn more about accessing files.

## The *id_cust()* function

The *id_cust()* function is called by *main()* to prompt the user for customer-identification information. This information includes such data as the customer's name, company, phone number, and shipping and billing addresses. In addition, we'd like to ask the customer how he or she heard about the company and its products, for advertising purposes. If the user is purchasing our products to resell them, we need to know that, too, for price and tax purposes.

```
/**********************************************************************
 * id_cust() prompts for customer identification information: customer name,
 *   company, phone, shipping/billing addresses, resale number, and
 *   advertising reference.
 **********************************************************************
 */
```

*(continued)*

*id_cust()* *continued*

```
stepcode id_cust(
   stepcode step_rtn)        /* if screen is backed into, step_rtn == STEPBACK; */
                             /*    otherwise step_rtn == STEPOK */
   {
   /* Shared data accessed in this function. */
   IMPORT char office[], user[], cust_name[], company[], ship_name[],
      ship_cmpy[], ship_strt[], ship_strt2[], ship_city[], ship_state[],
      ship_zip[], bill_name[], bill_cmpy[], bill_strt[], bill_strt2[],
      bill_city[], bill_state[], bill_zip[], adv_ref[], is_resale[],
      resale_id[], scrn_title[];

   /* Names of case labels for data-field prompts. */
   enum prompts {NAME, COMPANY, PHONE, SHIP_ADDR, BILL_ADDR,
      RESALE, ADV_REF, ENDSTEPS} step;   /* step is a prompts type variable */

   /* Begin new screen. */
   beg_scrn(user, scrn_title, office, "IDENTIFY");
   pnt_id_cust();                /* paint the screen */
   tput(4, 30, cust_name);
   tput(6, 30, company);

   /* Begin at last prompt if screen backed into. */
   step = (step_rtn == STEPOK) ? 0 : ENDSTEPS - 1;

   /* Loop: Input each field of this screen. */
   for (step_rtn = STEPOK; step_rtn != STEPCANC &&
      (step < ENDSTEPS) && (step >= 0); )
      {
      switch (step)          /* select next field to prompt for */
         {
         case NAME:          /* get customer name */
            step_rtn = prompt(cust_name, "L", 3, L_CUST_NAME, MAND, 4, 30);
            break;
         case COMPANY:       /* get company name */
            step_rtn = prompt(company, "L", 3, L_COMPANY, OPT, 6, 30);
            break;
         case PHONE:         /* get customer phone number */
            step_rtn = prompt(phone, "P", 7, L_PHONE, OPT, 7, 30);
            break;
         case SHIP_ADDR:     /* get address to ship to */
            if (ship_name[0] == '\0')  /* no address input yet? */
               {                       /* then set default name and company */
               strcpy(ship_name, cust_name);
               strcpy(ship_cmpy, company);
               }
```

*(continued)*

*id_cust()* *continued*

```
              /* Prompt for address data. Call get_addr(). */
              step_rtn = get_addr(step_rtn, 9, ship_name, ship_cmpy, ship_strt,
                 ship_strt2, ship_city, ship_state, ship_zip);
              break;
          case BILL_ADDR:                    /* get address to send bill to */
              tput(15, 30, "Bill same address? <y/n>     ");
              step_rtn = prompt(bill_same, "Q", 1, L_BILL_SAME, MAND, 15, 56);
              CUR_MV(15, 30);                /* move cursor and    */
              CLR_LINE;                      /* erase question */
              if (step_rtn == STEPOK && strchr("NnO", bill_same[0]))
                  step_rtn = get_addr(step_rtn, 15, bill_name, bill_cmpy,
                     bill_strt, bill_strt2, bill_city, bill_state, bill_zip);
              else if (step_rtn == STEPOK)
                  bill_name[0] == '\0';      /* bill same address */
              break;
          case RESALE:              /* is purchase for resale? */
              step_rtn = prompt(is_resale, "Q", 1, L_IS_RESALE, MAND, 21, 25);
              if (step_rtn == STEPOK && strchr("Yy1", is_resale[0]))
                  step_rtn = prompt(resale_id, "L", 3, L_RESALE_ID, OPT, 21, 53);
              break;
          case ADV_REF:             /* how did customer hear about product? */
              step_rtn = prompt(adv_ref, "L", 1, L_ADV_REF, OPT, 23, 30);
              break;
          }

      /* Determine next step based on return from last one. */
      if (step_rtn == STEPOK)     /* last was successful? */
          ++step;                 /* yes; go on to next step */
      else if (step_rtn == STEPBACK)
          --step;                 /* no; back up to last step */
      }
  return (step_rtn);
  }
```

The customer-identification screen has many fields, so the *id_cust()* function could become quite long. To avoid this, we simply create a separate function called *pnt_id_cust()* to hold the numerous calls to *tput()* that paint the screen (see Chapter 12) and then call *pnt_id_cust()* from *id_cust()*.

8.0  [01]

```
/* SOURCE FILE: PNT_ID_C.C
 ****************************************************************************
 * pnt_id_cust() paints screen for order entry: identify customer. This
 *   function is called exclusively by id_cust() in ordbuild.c.
 ****************************************************************************
 */

#include "projutil.h"

void pnt_id_cust(void)
    {
    tput(4, 10, "Customer Name");
    tput(6, 10, "Company Name");
    tput(7, 10, "Phone Number");

    tput(9, 10, "Ship to Name");
    tput(10, 18, "Company");
    tput(11, 18, "Street");
    tput(12, 18, "2nd Street");
    tput(13, 18, "City");
    tput(13, 49, "State");
    tput(13, 60, "Zip");

    tput(15, 10, "Bill to Name");
    tput(16, 18, "Company");
    tput(17, 18, "Street");
    tput(18, 18, "2nd Street");
    tput(19, 18, "City");
    tput(19, 49, "State");
    tput(19, 60, "Zip");

    tput(21, 10, "Resale?");
    tput(21, 30, "Resale Permit Number");
    tput(23, 10, "Advertising Ref");
    }
```

Two noteworthy features of *id_cust()* are its single parameter *step_rtn* and the use of C's ternary conditional ( *?:* ) operator:

```
/* Begin at last prompt if screen backed into. */
step = (step_rtn == STEPOK) ? 0 : ENDSTEPS - 1;
```

This statement sets the initial prompt step to be either the first field or the final field of this screen. If the user enters the *id_cust()* function from *id_user()* (the most typical way), *STEPOK* will be passed to the parameter *step_rtn*, making *step* the value *0* and thus setting the prompt step to *NAME*. If the user backs into *id_cust()* from *ord_itms()* (the next screen), *STEPBACK* will be passed to *step_rtn*, and *step* will begin at *ENDSTEPS - 1*, which equals *ADV_REF*, the last prompt step.

## *get_addr()*

All but two of the cases in *id_cust()* call for the input of a single field. The exceptions are *BILL_ADDR* and *SHIP_ADDR*, which call the function *get_addr()* to input billing and shipping addresses beginning at the row passed by the calling function.

```
/* SOURCE FILE: GET_ADDR.C
*************************************************************************
* get_addr() prompts for address data for order-entry programs. All data
*   are returned to the caller by arguments 3-9 (yes, 9 is rather high).
*************************************************************************
*/

#include "projutil.h"
#include "ordentry.h"

stepcode get_addr(
    stepcode step_rtn,     /* step_rtn is passed in and returned */
    short row,             /* screen row to begin prompting */
    char name[], char company[], char street[], char street2[], char city[],
    char state[], char zip[])

    {
    enum prompts {NAME, COMPANY, STREET, STREET2, CITY, STATE, ZIP, ENDSTEPS};
    enum prompts step;

    /* Begin at last prompt if screen backed into. */
    step = (step_rtn == STEPOK) ? 0 : ENDSTEPS - 1;
    for (step_rtn = STEPOK; step_rtn != STEPCANC &&
        (step != ENDSTEPS) && (step >= 0); )
        {
        switch (step)
            {
            case NAME:      /* get name */
                step_rtn = prompt(name, "L", 3, L_SHIP_NAME, MAND, row, 30);
                break;
            case COMPANY:   /* get company name */
                step_rtn = prompt(company, "L", 3, L_SHIP_CMPY, OPT, row + 1, 30);
                break;
            case STREET:    /* get first line of street address */
                step_rtn = prompt(street, "L", 3, L_SHIP_STRT, MAND, row + 2, 30);
                break;
            case STREET2:   /* get second line of street address */
                step_rtn = prompt(street2, "L", 3, L_SHIP_STRT2, OPT, row + 3, 30);
                break;
```

*(continued)*

GET_ADDR.C *continued*

```
            case CITY:       /* get city */
                step_rtn = prompt(city, "L", 2, L_SHIP_CITY, MAND, row + 4, 30);
                break;
            case STATE:       /* get state's two-letter abbreviation */
                step_rtn = prompt(state, "A", L_SHIP_STATE,
                    L_SHIP_STATE, MAND, row + 4, 56);
                break;
            case ZIP:         /* get zip code */
                step_rtn = prompt(zip, "#", L_SHIP_ZIP,
                    L_SHIP_ZIP, MAND, row + 4, 65);
                break;
        }

    /* Determine next step based on return from last one. */
    if (step_rtn == STEPOK)      /* was last successful? */
        ++step;                  /* yes; go on to next step */
    else if (step_rtn == STEPBACK)
        --step;                  /* no; back up to last step */
    }
    return (step_rtn);
}
```

## The *ord_itms()* function

Now that we've identified the salesperson and the customer, it's time
to find out which and how many of our products the customer is ordering. The function *ord_itms()* is called by *main()* to prompt repeatedly for part numbers and quantities for each item the customer wants
to order. The function behaves like a simplified spreadsheet in that it
updates the display of the total price of the order with each input of a
part number or quantity. Changes to part numbers or quantities
already entered will also cause the function to update the total.

```
/***************************************************************************
 * ord_itms() prompts repeatedly for part numbers and quantities of each
 *   item ordered by customer. Displays price and shipping weight of each.
 ***************************************************************************
 */

stepcode ord_itms(
    stepcode step_rtn)
```

*(continued)*

*ord_itms()* continued

```
{
IMPORT char user[], office[], scrn_title[];
IMPORT char parts[][L_PARTS + 1];
IMPORT char part_descs[][L_PART_DESC + 1];
IMPORT long quantities[];
IMPORT short ship_weights[];
IMPORT money prices[];
IMPORT byte last_part;
IMPORT money part_total;
char dbuf[14];                   /* output buffer for ftput() and ntput() */
byte ipart, part_cnt;
byte row;                                 /* line number on screen */
bflag part_found, more_items = YES;   /* part_found not initialized */
enum {PART_NUM, QUANTITY, ENDSTEPS} step;

/* Paint screen. */
beg_scrn(user, scrn_title, office, "ENTER ITEMS");
tput(4, 10, "Customer Name");
tput(4, 30, cust_name);
tput(6, 10, "Company Name");
tput(6, 30, company);
tput(9, 10, "Part Number      Description");
tput(9, 59, "Qty  Unit-Price");
tput(22, 51, "Order Total");
step = ipart = 0;              /* initializer for loop */
for (step_rtn = STEPOK; step_rtn != STEPCANC &&
    ipart < MAX_ITEMS && ipart >= 0 && more_items; )
    {
    row = ipart + 11;          /* row to prompt on */
    switch (step)
        {
        case PART_NUM:         /* get next part number */
            do                 /* while part entered and not found */
                {
                step_rtn = prompt(parts[ipart], "L", 1, L_PARTS, OPT, row, 10);

                /* Got a part number and it checks out? */
                part_found = (bflag)((step_rtn == STEPOK) &&
                    inv_find(parts[ipart], part_descs[ipart],
                    &prices[ipart], &ship_weights[ipart]));

                /* Check for end of order. */
                if (step_rtn == STEPOK && parts[ipart][0] == '\0')
                    more_items = NO;
```

*(continued)*

*ord_itms()* *continued*

```
                    /* If part not found, then tell user. */
                    else if (!part_found && step_rtn == STEPOK)
                        err_warn("No such part:", parts[ipart]);
                    else if (part_found)   /* show description and price of part */
                        {
                        tput(row, 27, part_descs[ipart]);
                        tput(row, 64, "$");
                        ftput(row, 65, (double) prices[ipart] / 100.0, 2,
                            dbuf, L_PRICES);

                        /* Default quantity is 1. */
                        if (!quantities[ipart])
                            quantities[ipart] = 1;
                        }

                    /* Indent avoids confusion of do...while with the for loop. */
                    } while (step_rtn == STEPOK && !part_found && more_items);
                break;
            case QUANTITY:                      /* get quantity for part ordered */
                step_rtn = nprompt(&quantities[ipart],
                    "#", OL, H_QUANTITY, MAND, row, 59);
                break;
            }
        if (step_rtn == STEPOK)              /* update total on screen */
            {

            /* Update the number of parts on this order. */
            if (ipart < MAX_ITEMS && quantities[ipart] > 0 && parts[ipart][0])
                last_part = ipart;

            /* Sum the prices times quantities of parts ordered. */
            for (part_total = part_cnt = 0; part_cnt <=last_part; ++part_cnt)
                part_total += prices[part_cnt] * quantities[part_cnt];
            tput(22, 64, "$");
            ftput(22, 65, (double) part_total / 100.0, 2, dbuf, L_PRICES);
            }

        /* Determine next part to prompt for and next step. */
        if (step == PART_NUM)      /* just got a part number */
            {
            step = QUANTITY;         /* next get a quantity */
            if (step_rtn == STEPBACK)
                --ipart;
            }
```

*(continued)*

*ord_itms()* continued

```
    else                    /* just got a quantity */
        {
        step = PART_NUM;        /* next get a part number */
        if (step_rtn == STEPOK)
        ++ipart;
        }
    }
return (step_rtn);
}
```

The style of control flow used in *ord_itms()* is a *for* loop containing two prompt steps managed by a *switch* statement. The prompts are for a part number and the quantity to order. Each part number the user inputs is validated by the function *inv_find()* found in the *stubs.c* file. If the number is valid, *inv_find()* passes back the part's description, unit price, and shipping weight. The two numbers (price and weight) are passed back through arguments, by using the & (*address-of*) operator in the call to the *inv_find()* function:

```
part_found = (bflag)((step_rtn == STEPOK) &&
    inv_find(parts[ipart], part_descs[ipart],
    &prices[ipart], &ship_weights[ipart]));
```

We use a *cast operator* here to force conversion of the value of the logical expression that follows from type *int* to type *bflag*. If we didn't force conversion, we would get a compiler warning message stating that a data conversion took place so that an integer could be assigned to *part_found*, a variable of type *bflag*.

The unary *cast* operator, which consists of a data type or synonym type within parentheses immediately preceding another expression, makes a new copy of an expression's value with a data type that is different from the original expression. (In some cases, such as an assignment, casts are optional because the value on the right will automatically be converted to the type of the value on the left.) Let's look at an example of the use of *cast*.

If you wanted to obtain the square root of a *long* integer named *area*, you would probably use the library function *sqrt()*, which expects a type *double* argument. But your value is a *long*. What to do? One solution would be to pass a new variable named *dbl_area* that is type *double*:

```
dbl_area = area;
side = sqrt(dbl_area);
```

```
C A U T I O N
```

*The unary* cast *operator has high precedence. For safety, enclose in parentheses any non-trivial expressions you want to apply to casts.*

But a shorter, more readable approach would be to use a *cast* operator. To find the square root of the *long* integer *area*, you could cast its value to type *double* and then pass the copy of its value to *sqrt()*:

```
side = sqrt((double) area);
```

## inv_find()

There is more to the call to *inv_find()* than first meets the eye. The function takes four arguments, and the first two arguments are *strings*. A quick look gives the impression that only a single character of the *parts* and *part_descs* arrays is passed to *inv_find()*, but that is not the case: Both *parts* and *part_descs* are declared as two-dimensional arrays. The part-number string in row *ipart* of the *parts* array will be passed to *inv_find()*, and *inv_find()* will fill the *ipart* row of the *part_descs* array with the description of the part that corresponds to the part number. (Arrays of more than one dimension will be covered in Chapter 15.)

```
/***************************************************************************
 * inv_find() looks up a part's data in inventory and returns YES if the
 *   part is found, NO if it is not found. Part description, price, and
 *   weight are passed back.
 ***************************************************************************
 */

flag inv_find(
    char part[],            /* part number to look up (pass in) */
    char part_desc[],       /* description of part (returned) */
    money *p_price,         /* pointer to unit price of part (returned) */
    short *p_ship_wt)       /* pointer to shipping weight in ounces (returned) */

    {

    /* Return typical data to test inv_find()'s callers. */
    strcpy(part_desc, "Order-Entry Software Package");
    *p_price = 12345L;
    *p_ship_wt = 123;
    return (part[0] == 'S');      /* YES if 'S' first, else NO */
    }
```

The *inv_find()* stub will be replaced by a fully operational version later in the book.

## ntput(), ftput(), and nprompt()

Three other order-entry functions are called either directly or indirectly by *ord_itms()*, *ntput()*, *ftput()*, and *nprompt()*. These functions are numeric versions of the string output and input functions *tput()* and *prompt()* from our project utility library. (The *ntput()* function is not called by *ord_itms()*; however, it is called by *nprompt()*, so we'll discuss it here.)

```
/* SOURCE FILE: NTPUT.C
 ************************************************************************
 * ntput() converts a long integer to ASCII and displays it right justified
 *    in field of specified width. The left side is padded with blanks.
 ************************************************************************
 */

#include <stdlib.h>
#include "projutil.h"

void ntput(
    short row,              /* row to output text on */
    short col,              /* column to output text in */
    long long_val,          /* value to be displayed */
    char buf[],             /* output buffer */
    short field_len)        /* length of field to right justify in */

    {
    ltoa(long_val, buf, 10);        /* convert long to ASCII string */
    strrjust(buf, field_len);       /* right justify field */
    tput(row, col, buf);            /* display on screen for user */
    }
```

We call *ntput()* to display a long integer, right justified, with blank padding on the left. The *ntput()* function expects five arguments: the screen row (1 through 25), the screen column (1 through 80), the *long* integer to display, a pointer to a string it will use to store the ASCII representation of the value, and the field width to use for justification and display. Here's an example (found in *nprompt.c*):

```
ntput(row, col, *p_num, buf, max_len);
```

The *ftput()* function is the double-precision floating-point equivalent of *ntput()*.

```
/* SOURCE FILE: FTPUT.C
 **************************************************************************
 * ftput() converts a double-precision floating-point number to ASCII and
 *   displays it right justified in field of specified width, with
 *   specified decimal places.
 **************************************************************************
 */

#include <string.h>
#include <stdlib.h>
#include "projutil.h"

void ftput(
    short row,              /* cursor row to display value on */
    short col,              /* cursor column to display value in */
    double double_val,      /* value to be displayed */
    short dec_place,        /* number of decimal places to display */
    char buf[],             /* output buffer for formatting data */
    short field_len)        /* length of field */

    {
    int dec;                /* decimal point position (from fcvt()) */
    int sign;               /* flag (0/1): is minus sign needed?  (from fcvt()) */

    /* Copy contents of temporary string buffer to buf. */
    strcpy(buf, fcvt(double_val, dec_place, &dec, &sign));
    if (sign)                       /* double_val is negative */
        {

        /* memmove needed to copy into overlapping data area. */
        memmove(buf + 1, buf, 1 + strlen(buf));
        buf[0] = '-';               /* insert minus sign prefix */
        }
    if (dec >= 0)                   /* insert decimal point between digits */
        {
        memmove(buf + dec + sign + 1, buf + dec + sign,
            strlen(buf) + 1 - dec - sign);
        buf[dec + sign] = '.';      /* insert the decimal point */
        }
    else                /* dec is negative, so leading zeros are needed */
        {
        memmove(buf + sign + 1 - dec, buf + sign,
            strlen(buf) + 1 - sign);
        for (; dec; ++dec)          /* count from dec up to zero */
            buf[sign - dec] = '0';  /* insert a leading zero */
        buf[sign] = '.';            /* insert the decimal point */
        }
    strrjust(buf, field_len);
    tput(row, col, buf);
    }
```

In order to display the decimal point of a floating-point number in the correct position, *ftput()* requires one additional argument: a *short* value for the number of digits to appear to the right of the decimal point, as shown in the following:

```
ftput(row, col, f_money, 2, s_money, L_PRICES);
```

If the *double* value you pass to *ftput()* does not have enough precision, *ftput()* will pad the field with zeros on the right.

We call the *nprompt()* function to prompt for a *long* integer, much as we call *prompt()* to input a string. In this program, *ord_itms()* calls *nprompt()* to get the quantity for the part being ordered. (The related function for floating-point numbers, *fprompt()*, isn't called by *ord_itms()*, so we'll discuss it a little later.)

```
/* SOURCE FILE: NPROMPT.C */
/***************************************************************************
 * nprompt() inputs a long integer from standard input. The program matches
 *   input against an optional match-string argument and checks minimum and
 *   maximum input values. If the Boolean (flag) argument mand is true,
 *   then the program will not permit data to remain zero; data must be
 *   entered. The parameter *p_num is both passed to nprompt() and returned
 *   to the calling function. The value passed in is treated as a default to
 *   be used if input is null.
 * Return value: The outcome of nprompt() has synonym data type stepcode,
 *   which is used to indicate:
 *     STEPOK     Step complete; valid number obtained.
 *     STEPBACK   Back up to the previous step.
 *     STEPCANC   Cancel order entry (quit).
 *   The user can request to back up by entering C_BACK, to cancel by
 *   entering C_CANC, or to set *p_num to zero by entering C_NULL as any
 *   character in the reply.
 ***************************************************************************/

#include <stdio.h>
#include <stdlib.h>
#include <string.h>
#include "syntypes.h"
#include "projutil.h"

stepcode nprompt(
    long *p_num,          /* default passed in, input data returned */
    char match_str[],     /* match string to verify data against */
    long min_val,         /* minimum input value */
    long max_val,         /* maximum input value */
    flag mand,            /* if yes, data cannot be zero on return */
```

*(continued)*

NPROMPT.C *continued*

```
short row,           /* cursor row to begin input */
short col)           /* cursor column to begin input */


{
char buf[14];        /* prompt input buffer */
bflag more = YES;    /* prompt again? */
long in_num;         /* ASCII input number converted to binary */
short max_len = strlen(ltoa(max_val, buf, 10));
short min_len = strlen(ltoa(min_val, buf, 10));
stepcode rtn;        /* return code */

/* Supply as default if p_num points to a non-zero long. */
if (*p_num)          /* non-zero value passed in? */
   {
   ntput(row, col, *p_num, buf, max_len);     /* display default */
   }
else                 /* no default */
   buf[0] = '\0';

/* Loop: Prompt for number in string form, until value */
/*   entered is in range, or cancel or back up is requested. */
do
   {
   rtn = prompt(buf, match_str, min_len, max_len, mand, row, col);
   if (rtn != STEPOK)
      more = NO;      /* done prompting (back up or cancel) */
   else              /* check whether input mandatory and reply in range */
      {
      in_num = atol(buf);     /* convert ASCII input to long integer */

      /* If mandatory and number is zero, this is an error. */
      if (mand && in_num == 0)
         err_warn("Non-zero data mandatory:", "");

      /* Otherwise, verify in_num is inside specified range, provided */
      /*   prompt is mandatory or number entered is non-zero. */
      else if ((in_num < min_val || in_num > max_val) &&
         (mand || in_num != 0))
         {
         sprintf(buf, "%ld to %ld", min_val, max_val);
         err_warn("Enter a number from:", buf);
         buf[0] = '\0';
         }
      else            /* got a good value; done prompting */
         more = NO;
      }
   }
```

*(continued)*

NPROMPT.C *continued*

```
   while (more);
      if (rtn == STEPOK)          /* then echo, right justified */
      {
      *p_num = in_num;            /* pass value back to caller */

      /* Echo number right justified in screen field. */
      ntput(row, col, in_num, buf, max_len);
      }
   return (rtn);
   }
```

The *nprompt()* function expects seven arguments: *address_of_long,
match_str, minimum_num, maximum_num, mandatory_flag, cursor_row,*
and *cursor_column.* The return from *nprompt(),* like that from *prompt(),*
is a value with our synonym type *stepcode* to indicate whether any data
was entered (*STEPOK*) or not (*STEPBACK* or *STEPCANC*). The *ord_itm()*
function calls *nprompt()* as follows:

```
step_rtn = nprompt(&quantities[ipart], "#", 0L, H_QUANTITY,
   MAND, row, 59);
```

The & *(address of)* operator you see with *quantities[ipart]* in this example
must be present for *nprompt()* to assign a value to an element in the array. (See Chapter 15.)

## The *ship_pay()* function

Next, the user must enter the shipping carrier, sales tax, and payment
terms. The *ship_pay()* function does those jobs by prompting for those
fields of the order after all part numbers and quantities are input.

```
/***********************************************************************
 * ship_pay() prompts for shipping carrier, shipping charges, sales-tax
 *   rate, and payment terms. Input these data after items are entered.
 ***********************************************************************
 */

stepcode ship_pay(
   stepcode step_rtn)      /* if screen is backed into, step_rtn == STEPBACK; */
                           /*   otherwise step_rtn == STEPOK */
```

*(continued)*

*ship_pay()* *continued*

```
{
IMPORT char office[], user[], cust_name[], company[],
   ship_car[], pay_terms[], comment[], scrn_title[];
IMPORT money part_total, tax_amt, ship_amt;
IMPORT double inp_ship_amt, tax_pcnt;
IMPORT char is_resale[];                /* yes means no sales tax */
IMPORT byte last_part;
IMPORT long quantities[];
IMPORT short ship_weights[];
IMPORT short tot_weight;
char dbuf[14];
byte ipart;
enum prompts {SHIP_CAR, SHIP_AMT, TAX, PAY_TERMS, COMMENT, ENDSTEPS};
enum prompts step;

/* Verify that something has been ordered; else return STEPBACK. */
if (quantities[0] == 0 !! parts[0][0] == '\0')
   {
   err_warn("Nothing ordered:", "");  /* give diagnostic */
   return (STEPBACK);                 /* back up to previous screen */
   }

/* Begin new screen. */
beg_scrn(user, scrn_title, office, "SHIP, TAX, PAY");
pnt_ship_pay();                        /* paint screen */
tput(4, 30, cust_name);
tput(6, 30, company);

/* Sum ship weights and show total (weights in ounces). */
for (ipart = 0, tot_weight = 0; ipart <=last_part; ++ipart)
   tot_weight += (short)(ship_weights[ipart] * quantities[ipart]);
ntput(9, 30, (long) tot_weight, dbuf, 10);    /* show total weight */

/* Begin at last prompt if screen backed into. */
step = (step_rtn == STEPOK) ? 0 : ENDSTEPS - 1;
for (step_rtn = STEPOK; step_rtn != STEPCANC &&
   (step < ENDSTEPS) && step >= 0; )
   {
   switch (step)
      {
      case SHIP_CAR:            /* get shipping carrier */
         step_rtn = prompt(ship_car, "L", 1, L_SHIP_CAR, OPT, 11, 30);
         break;
```

*(continued)*

*ship_pay()* continued

```
            case SHIP_AMT:                  /* get shipping charges, if */
                if (ship_car[0] != '\0')      /*   a carrier was entered */
                    step_rtn = fprompt(&inp_ship_amt, "F", 0.20,
                        H_SHIP_AMT, 11, 2, OPT, 11, 65);
                    ship_amt = (money) (inp_ship_amt * 100.0 + 0.5);
                break;
            case TAX:                       /* get sales-tax percentage */

                /* If sale is for resale, then don't add sales tax. */
                if (strchr("Yy1", is_resale[0]))
                    tax_pcnt = 0.0;
                else                        /* prompt for local tax rate, if any */
                    step_rtn = fprompt(&tax_pcnt, "F", 0.0,
                        H_TAX_PCNT, 4, 2, OPT, 14, 30);
                tax_amt = (money)((tax_pcnt * (double)part_total) / 100.0);
                tput(14, 64, "$");
                ftput(14, 65, (double) tax_amt / 100.0, 2, dbuf, L_TAX_AMT);
                ftput(18, 65, (double) part_total / 100.0, 2, dbuf, L_PRICES);
                ftput(20, 65, (double) (part_total + tax_amt + ship_amt) / 100.0,
                    2, dbuf, L_PRICES);
                break;
            case PAY_TERMS:             /* get payment terms code */
                step_rtn = prompt(pay_terms, "L", 1, L_PAY_TERMS, MAND, 17, 30);
                break;
            case COMMENT:               /* get order comment (if any) */
                step_rtn = prompt(comment, "L", 1, L_COMMENT, OPT, 22, 11);
                break;
        }

        /* Determine next step based on return from last one. */
        if (step_rtn == STEPOK)             /* last was successful? */
            ++step;                         /* yes; go on to next step */
        else if (step_rtn == STEPBACK)
            --step;                         /* no; back up to last step */
    }
    return (step_rtn);
}
```

Processing in this module begins with a check to ascertain whether something has indeed been ordered: Obviously, it would be a waste of time to ask for shipping, tax, and payment information for an empty order. If nothing has been ordered, *ship_pay()* forces the user back to the last field in *ord_itms()* by returning *STEPBACK*. If something has been ordered, *ship_pay()* begins prompting for the shipping data.

The name of the shipping carrier is optional; however, if one is supplied, the program will prompt for the shipping-charge entry. The program prompts for sales-tax percentage only if this order is not for resale. (Goods for resale are not subject to sales tax, at least according to most tax laws at the time of this writing.)

## fprompt()

The *ship_pay()* function calls *fprompt()* to input both the tax percentage and the shipping charge. Just as *ftput()* is the double-precision floating-point equivalent of *ntput()*, *fprompt()* is the alternative to *nprompt()*. Once again, the floating-point function requires additional arguments to handle the decimal point. These arguments specify the width and decimal precision of the number being input.

```
/* SOURCE FILE: FPROMPT.C
 **************************************************************************
 * fprompt() inputs a double-precision floating-point number from standard
 *    input. It behaves the same as nprompt(), except that the arguments
 *    width and precision must be passed to fprompt() to indicate the width
 *    of the field and the number of digits to prompt for on the right of the
 *    decimal point.
 **************************************************************************
 */

#include <stdio.h>
#include <string.h>
#include <stdlib.h>
#include "syntypes.h"
#include "ansiscrn.h"
#include "projutil.h"

stepcode fprompt(
    double *d_num,          /* default passed in, input data returned */
    char match_str[],       /* pattern describing input format */
    double min_dval,        /* minimum input value */
    double max_dval,        /* maximum input value */
    short width,            /* input field width */
    short precision,        /* number of decimal places */
    flag mand,              /* if yes, data cannot be zero on return */
    short row,              /* cursor row to begin input */
    short col)              /* cursor column to begin input */

{
    char buf[80];           /* prompt input buffer */
    bflag more = YES;
```

*(continued)*

FPROMPT.C *continued*

```
    double in_dnum;         /* ASCII input number converted to double */
    short min_len = 1;
    stepcode rtn;

    /* Supply the double d_num points to as the default if it is non-zero. */
    if (*d_num == 0.0)      /* zero value passed in? */
        buf[0] = '\0';      /* no default */
    else
        ftput(row, col, *d_num, precision, buf, width);    /* display default */

    do
        {
        rtn = prompt(buf, match_str, min_len, width, mand, row, col);
        if (rtn != STEPOK)
            more = NO;
        else
            {
            in_dnum = atof(buf);    /* convert ASCII to double */
            if (mand && in_dnum == 0.0)
                err_warn("Non-zero data mandatory:", "");
            else if ((in_dnum < min_dval || in_dnum > max_dval) &&
                (mand || in_dnum != 0.0))
                {

                /* Create string to pass to err_warn(). */
                sprintf(buf, "%.*f to %.*f", precision, min_dval,
                    precision, max_dval);
                err_warn("Enter a number from:", buf);
                buf[0] = '\0';
                CUR_MV(row, col);
                }
            else
                more = NO;
            }
        }
    while (more);

    if (rtn == STEPOK)              /* then echo, right justified */
        {
        *d_num = in_dnum;           /* pass value back to caller */
        ftput(row, col, *d_num, precision, buf, width);
        }
    return (rtn);
    }
```

## Saving the entered data: *wrt_ord()*

The order-entry program now holds all the data entered by the sales-person, in *SEMIGLOBAL* variables shared by the middle-level functions in the source file *ordbuild.c.* But if the program were to terminate right now, the order would be lost because the data are in electronic memory, which can be clobbered by the next program run or erased when the power is turned off. We must write the data to permanent storage before we exit the program. But before we decide how to do this, let's step back a minute and look at the larger picture.

```
/**************************************************************************
 * wrt_ord() writes an order to standard output after asking if all is OK.
 * The order number is assigned from a counter.
 **************************************************************************
 */

/*  File data to be output are written to the standard output file (stdout).
 *     This permits data to be redirected at the command line. For example:
 *       ORDENTRY > SS891225.ORD        Creates new file;
 *                                        note date encoded in name.
 *       ORDENTRY >> NEWORDS.DAT        Appends data to file.
 *       ORDENTRY : ORDSAVE : ORDPRINT  Serves as source for a pipeline.
 *
 *  This standard file use scheme gives flexibility in the way the program
 *     may be used. Text and control characters are output to the standard
 *     error file (stderr), so they won't appear in the redirected output.
 */

stepcode wrt_ord(void)
   {

   /* IMPORT all the fields of the order. */
   IMPORT char office[], user[], cust_name[], company[], ship_name[],
      ship_cmpy[], ship_strt[], ship_strt2[], ship_city[], ship_state[],
      ship_zip[], bill_name[], bill_cmpy[], bill_strt[], bill_strt2[],
      bill_city[], bill_state[], bill_zip[], adv_ref[], resale_id[];
   IMPORT char is_resale[];                /* yes means no sales tax */
   IMPORT char parts[][L_PARTS + 1];
   IMPORT long quantities[];
   IMPORT money prices[];
   IMPORT byte last_part;
   IMPORT short tot_weight;
   IMPORT char ship_car[], pay_terms[], comment[];
   IMPORT money part_total, tax_amt, ship_amt;
```

*(continued)*

*wrt_ord()* *continued*

```
        long order_id;                 /* order number, from order_num() */
        long long_time;                /* time of day, from time() */
        byte ipart;
        char is_ok[2];                 /* are data OK? message buffer */
        char log_buf[80];              /* buffer for logentry() string */
        stepcode step_rtn;

        /* Ask if order is OK. */
        tput(23, 2, "Is order OK? <y/n>  _ ");
        strcpy(is_ok, "y");                    /* default is yes */
        step_rtn = prompt(is_ok, "Q", 1, 1, MAND, 23, 22);
        if (step_rtn != STEPOK)
      ' return (step_rtn);
        else if (0 != strchr("NnO", is_ok[0]))
            return (STEPBACK);

        /* Write order data to standard output. Each line begins with
         *   two uppercase characters or numbers that indicate the
         *   meaning of that data item.
         */
        order_id = order_num();
        sprintf(log_buf, "ORD %ld, SL %s, TL %ld", order_id, user, part_total);
        logentry(log_buf);             /* record order in log file as an audit */
                                       /*    trail for sales and commissions */
        printf("\nBEGIN ORDER %ld\n", order_id);
        time(&long_time);              /* get time of day as a long */
        printf("TM %s", ctime(&long_time));   /* save time of day */

        printf("OF %s\nSL %s\nCN %s\nCO %s\n", office, user, cust_name, company);
        printf("SN %s\nSC %s\nST %s\n", ship_name, ship_cmpy, ship_strt);
        if (ship_strt2[0] != '\0')
            printf("S2 %s\n", ship_strt2);
        printf("SY %s\nSS %s\nSZ %s\n", ship_city, ship_state, ship_zip);

        if (bill_name[0] != '\0')    /* save billing address if different */
            {
            printf("BN %s\nBC %s\nBT %s\n", bill_name, bill_cmpy, bill_strt);
            if (bill_strt2[0] != '\0')
                printf("B2 %s\n", bill_strt2);
            printf("BY %s\nBS %s\nBZ %s\n", bill_city, bill_state, bill_zip);
            }

        if (strchr("Yy1", is_resale[0]))       /* is order for resale? */
            printf("RS %s\n", resale_id);      /* yes; save resale_id */
```

*(continued)*

*wrt_ord()* *continued*

```
/* List each part, quantity, and price. */
for (ipart = 0; ipart <= last_part && quantities[ipart]; ++ipart)
   printf("PN %s\nQY %ld\nPR %ld\n", parts[ipart],
      quantities[ipart], prices[ipart]);
printf("TL %ld\nTX %ld\nSH %s\nSA %ld\nWT %d\n", part_total,
   tax_amt, ship_car, ship_amt, tot_weight);
if (adv_ref[0] != '\0')
   printf("AD %s\n", adv_ref);
printf("PA %s\n", pay_terms);
if (comment[0] != '\0')
   printf("CM %s\n", comment);
printf("END ORDER %ld\n", order_id);
return (STEPOK);
}
```

## Storage format

We now have a completed order. Our goal is to forward that order to the company's central office, from which we ship all our products. The central office receives orders from several remote computers (via modem) and from floppy disks delivered overnight, so we want to choose a format that will work for both these media, as well as for any new media we may add later.

We decide on ASCII rather than binary format for the data because ASCII has both portability and communication advantages. The portability advantage is simply that ASCII format is the same on all systems, whereas binary format is not. The communication advantage is that ASCII uses only 7 of the 8 bits in a byte, whereas binary uses all 8 bits, and the 7-bit data format can be handled by more communications software than machine-specific binary format.

There are 50 fields in our order, although some may be empty. We'll output each field on its own line, each line beginning with a two-character code that identifies the kind of data it contains (*TM* for time, *OF* for office, and so on). This code is followed by a space and then the value of the associated data field. If the value is numeric, it is converted to an ASCII string by the library function *printf()*.

The following segment of code from *wrt_ord()* shows how *printf()*'s format specifiers are used to output different data types in ASCII format. The variables *part_total*, *tax_amt*, and *ship_amt* are output using the *%ld* format specifier; *%s* is used for the string *ship_car* and *%d* for the *short* integer *tot_weight*. The optional advertising reference ("How did you hear about us?") is included only if the salesperson got a response from the customer.

```
printf("TL %ld\nTX %ld\nSH %s\nSA %ld\nWT %d\n", part_total,
    tax_amt, ship_car, ship_amt, tot_weight);
if (adv_ref[0] != '\0')
    printf("AD %s\n", adv_ref);
```

The *printf()* output is the first in the order-entry program to use the standard output file, *stdout*; all previous output has been directed to the user's screen, using the standard error output file, *stderr*. (See Chapter 12.) We use *stdout* so that the command-line file-redirection commands >, >>, and ¦ (pipe symbol) will control only the order data, as in these examples from *wrt_ord()*'s initial comment:

```
*       ORDENTRY > SS891225.ORD        Creates new file;
*                                        note date encoded in name.
*       ORDENTRY >> NEWORDS.DAT        Appends data to file.
*       ORDENTRY ¦ ORDSAVE ¦ ORDPRINT  Serves as source for a pipeline.
```

### The order log

It is good business practice to log every new order. The function that performs this task for the order-entry application is named *logentry()*.

```
/**************************************************************************
 * logentry() appends message text to the end of the log file, typically for
 *    audit, error detection, and security purposes.
 **************************************************************************
 */

void logentry(char msg[])
    {
    }
```

Here's how the process works: The call to *sprintf()* in *wrt_ord()* converts its arguments to ASCII using the C format specifiers; the resulting string is saved in the variable *log_buf*, which is passed to *logentry()*. Then *logentry()* records the string passed, by adding a new entry at the end of the log file. The *logentry()* function is a stub at this point, as is the *order_num()* function called to obtain *order_id*.

```
/***********************************************************************
 * order_num() returns the order number to use for the next order. The order
 *   number is a counter that increases by one with each order.
 ***********************************************************************
 */

long order_num(void)
  {
  return (10001L);
  }
```

## Time and date functions

Getting the time and date for each order may seem a confusing job at first because of the variety of time- and date-associated functions in C's standard library, but we can limit ourselves to only two of them.

The two library time functions we use in the *wrt_ord()* function are *time()* and *ctime()*. The *time()* function saves the order-entry time (obtained from the system in seconds elapsed since midnight January 1, 1970 GMT) in the *long* variable whose address is passed to it. Then *ctime()* converts that *long* value to a readable date-and-time format and returns the converted value to *printf()* for output with the order:

```
time(&long_time);                /* get time of day as a long */
printf("TM %s", ctime(&long_time));   /* save time of day */
```

## The last word

It is good practice to inform the user when the program is about to save the order and to offer an opportunity to change data or cancel the transaction. This should be the very last step, after all data are entered but before the order is recorded. Consistently "asking before updating" makes a program easier and safer to use.

The code for this task simply asks the user a yes-or-no question and obtains a reply by calling the *prompt()* function. The default value of the response variable *is_ok* (entered when the user simply presses Return) is set to 'y'. In this call to the *prompt()* function, the match character is "Q". "Q" matches only responses acceptable to a yes-or-no question: 'Y', 'y', or '1' for yes; 'N', 'n', or '0' for no. If the user says that things are not OK, the program will back up to the shipping, tax, and pay terms screen. Otherwise, *wrt_ord()* sends the order to *stdout*.

Now that we've analyzed the mechanics of the top and middle levels of our order-entry application, let's move on to Chapter 12, where we'll take a closer look at the bottom-level functions that control screen output.

C H A P T E R **12**

# Painting the Screen

So far we've worked our way from the upper levels of the order-entry program downward, getting a top-down view. Now let's reverse our perspective for a while and see how things look from the bottom up. The techniques for outputting text to the user's screen will be the object of our bottom-up scrutiny.

## Screen Management and Application Portability

Programmers writing for the family of MS-DOS–compatible personal computers have three choices for outputting text to the user's screen, listed here in order of decreasing portability and increasing speed:

- Standard C library I/O functions
- Calls to the operating system's ROM BIOS
- Video RAM access for memory-mapped display

As you can see, the fastest display technique is unfortunately the least portable. (You probably would have guessed that anyway.)

# Standard Library I/O Functions

Our first option is to use output functions from the C compiler's standard library. The standard error file, *stderr*, is normally directed to the user's display. However, if command-line output redirection is not applied, output from the standard output file *stdout* will also appear on the screen. The standard I/O functions *printf()*, *puts()*, and *putchar()* output only to *stdout*, but you can use the standard functions *fprintf()*, *fputs()*, and *fputc()* to output to *stdout*, *stderr*, or any other file. All of these functions output by calling the low-level library function *write()*.

The order-entry program sends only order-detail information to the standard output file (by calling *printf()*), where it can be redirected to a file or through a pipe to another program. Other information sent to the screen, such as prompts for information and strings for cursor movement (discussed in this section), would be "clutter" in the middle of valuable order data, so they are kept separate by calling *fprintf()* to write them to *stderr*.

The function *fprintf()* accepts the same string of format specifiers and literal text as does *printf()*, but *fprintf()* takes the format string as its second argument, unlike *printf()*. The first argument to *fprintf()* is called a *stream* (see Chapter 17), and the stream *stderr* is declared in *stdio.h*. So be sure to include *<stdio.h>* along with your *#include "ansiscrn.h"*. (The order of the two does not matter.) The arguments after the *fprintf()* and *printf()* format strings depend on the contents of the format string.

Strings of ordinary printable ASCII characters sent to the screen by the standard I/O functions are displayed as you would expect: What you send is what you see. However, special strings of ASCII characters known as *escape sequences* are interpreted as screen-control commands: They move the cursor, erase a line or the entire screen, and control highlighting. These escape sequences all begin with the escape character '\33' (or the hexadecimal or decimal equivalent '\x1b' or 27, respectively).

In our order-entry application, the header file *ansiscrn.h* gives us control of the screen through macros that output escape sequences for various screen-control commands. One of these is the *CUR_MV* macro, which outputs a cursor-movement command to the standard error file by calling *fprintf()*. For example, *CUR_MV(8, 15)* moves the cursor to line 8, column 15, by sending the string "\33[8;15H" to the screen, and *CUR_UP(1)* moves the cursor up a line by sending the string "\33[1A".

The following macro definitions are those found in *ansiscrn.h*:

```
#define CUR_MV(row, col) fprintf(stderr, "\33[%d;%dH", row, col)
#define CUR_UP(num) fprintf(stderr, "\33[%dA", num)
#define CUR_DN(num) fprintf(stderr, "\33[%dB", num)
#define CUR_RT(num) fprintf(stderr, "\33[%dC", num)
#define CUR_LT(num) fprintf(stderr, "\33[%dD", num)
#define CUR_SKIP fprintf(stderr, "\n")
#define CUR_SAVE fprintf(stderr, "\33[s")
#define CUR_REST fprintf(stderr, "\33[u")
#define CLR_SCRN fprintf(stderr, "\33[2J")
#define CLR_LINE fprintf(stderr, "\33[K")
#define CLR_EOS(r, c) {byte i_; CUR_MV(r,c); \
    for (i_=r; i_<=25; ++i_) CLR_LINE, CUR_DN(1); CUR_MV(r,c); }
#define BELL fprintf(stderr,"\a")
```

I have not included the five commands used to control highlighting in *ansiscrn.h* since highlighting is hard on the eyes and in any case is not portable to some types of display. If you want to use highlighting, you will need to add the following definitions:

```
#define HLT_OFF fprintf(stderr, "\33[0m")    /* normal mode */
#define HLT_BOLD fprintf(stderr, "\33[1m")    /* bold display */
#define HLT_UNDR fprintf(stderr, "\33[4m")    /* underscored display on */
                                              /* a monochrome display */
#define HLT_BLNK fprintf(stderr, "\33[5m")    /* blinking display */
#define HLT_RVRS fprintf(stderr, "\33[7m")    /* reverse video display */
```

On most MS-DOS systems, these macros and definitions require that the *CONFIG.SYS* file on the boot disk contain the statement *DEVICE=ANSI.SYS*. To determine whether this is the case for your system, compile and execute this short C program:

```
/* Test screen commands: Clear screen and say "Hi" in center. */

#include <stdio.h>
#include "ansiscrn.h"

void main(void)
    {
    CLR_SCRN;
    CUR_MV(12, 40);
    puts("Hi");
    }
```

If the program outputs something like *[2J[12;40HHi* instead of *Hi*, add *DEVICE=ANSI.SYS* to your *CONFIG.SYS* file, reboot the system, and run the program again. This time it should execute properly.

The escape sequences used for display commands in the *ansiscrn.h* definitions and macros are by no means universal. They work on MS-DOS systems, but not for some CRT terminals. If you require portability to multiuser systems, you will have to deal with the tremendous variety of escape sequences used by different CRTs. In that case, you might want to consider using the UNIX operating system, with its *termcap* database of hundreds of encoded descriptions for terminal control. The functions necessary to access and use *termcap* data are supplied with UNIX. A higher-level UNIX package called *curses* is also available for more advanced screen-control functions.

Except in unusual circumstances, C's standard-library I/O functions are the best choice for screen output. Their portability is excellent, and they offer a wide range of display features. However, you should at least be aware of the alternatives, so we'll take a minute to discuss each of them.

## ROM BIOS

The IBM PC–compatible class of personal computers comes with a ROM (read-only memory) chip that holds functions used by the operating system to perform basic input/output services (BIOS) for itself and for your programs. These service programs are known as *firmware* because they can be changed only by replacing the existing ROM chip with one that is programmed differently.

Calls to C's standard-library I/O functions for screen output actually execute code that interfaces with the ROM-BIOS routines, so the only reason to call ROM BIOS directly would be the need to use a feature not supported by the library. Figure 12-1 lists a few of the ROM input/output services. (Notice that the services are numbered.)

| NUMBER | ROM SERVICE |
|--------|-------------|
| 0 | Set video mode (text/graphics, color/monochrome, resolution) |
| 1 | Set cursor size |
| 6 | Scroll up |
| 7 | Scroll down |
| 15 | Read current video mode |

FIGURE 12-1
*Commonly used ROM-BIOS services*

To call a ROM-BIOS routine, you must use either assembly language or one of the C library's three DOS interface functions: *bdos*, *intdos*, and *intdosx*. (These particular functions are specific to Microsoft's C library, but other C vendors supply similar DOS interface functions for various operating systems.) C programs that make use of these DOS interface functions will not be portable to other operating systems because of software incompatibilities. But when maximum display performance is needed, portability concerns sometimes have to go out the window!

## Video RAM access for direct display

*Memory mapping* is a display technique that ties what is displayed on the screen directly to the contents of a specific block of memory. To change what is displayed, you must change the specific bytes of memory to which the display is mapped. In effect, the screen is a slave of that special area of memory. The IBM PC and PC-compatible microcomputers all have memory-mapped displays, as does the Apple II.

The reason for storing directly into video memory is, quite simply, speed: It is obviously much faster to store a byte directly than to ask a C library output function to ask a ROM-BIOS routine to store that same byte. You go right to the heart of the matter when you play with video RAM, and such breakneck speed can be important in selected applications, such as animation and special effects.

The thought of accessing video memory directly sends tingles up the spines of many application programmers. Just think of it: direct control of hardware that you can watch! So why should something that sounds like so much fun be regarded as bad programming practice? Well, mainly because memory-mapping schemes vary greatly among systems. Code that directly manipulates screen memory is portable to only a small class of ''clone'' systems, and converting code from one display scheme to another can be time-consuming. In addition, future upgrades in display hardware may render your programs inoperative because they depend on the now-obsolete memory-mapping scheme. However, it is possible to manipulate screen memory directly using C's pointers. We'll discuss this in detail in Chapter 14.

To summarize the bottom-level view of screen output: You call *printf("Hi")* to print *Hi*; *printf()* calls the low-level library function *write()*; *write()* calls ROM BIOS for screen output; ROM BIOS saves *Hi* in screen memory; and finally you see *Hi* on your monitor.

# Displaying Information for the User

Now let's move up one level and take a look at how we want our order-entry application to display information to the user. We need to look more closely at the library functions *ltoa()*, *fcvt()*, and *sprintf()* and the order-entry functions *tput()*, *strrjust()*, *ntput()*, and *ftput()*, all of which are associated with screen output of character strings and numeric values.

## Displaying a string of text

The *tput()* function moves the cursor to a designated position on the screen and then prints a string of text. More specifically, the *CUR_MV* macro moves the cursor, and then *fputs()* prints the text on the screen.

```
/* SOURCE FILE: TPUT.C
 ************************************************************************
 * tput() displays a string at a specified row and column.
 ************************************************************************
 */

#include <stdio.h>
#include "ansiscrn.h"
#include "projutil.h"

void tput(
    short row,          /* cursor row */
    short col,          /* cursor column */
    char text[])        /* text to display */

    {
    CUR_MV(row, col);
    fputs(text, stderr);
    }
```

To call *tput()*, you must supply three arguments: a row, a column, and the text to display, like this:

```
tput(12, 20, "Salesperson");
```

## Displaying a number

Lists of integers are almost always displayed and printed right aligned, with spaces for padding on the left. Floating-point numbers, on the other hand, are aligned on the decimal point and then padded on the left with spaces and on the right with zeros to a specified number of decimal places. In C, we can use formatted output to display numbers in a much more flexible way than we have seen so far by storing the field width and precision in variables. For instance, to display the *long* integer *quantities[ipart]* on line 14, column 65, in a field whose width is calculated to be the *short* variable *max_len*, you would enter the following commands:

```
CUR_MV(14, 65);
fprintf(stderr, "%*ld", max_len, quantities[ipart]);
```

The * in the format specifier means that the width of the field is passed as an argument. Since *max_len* is calculated to be the length of the largest allowable value of *quantities* (which is 999, so the length is 3), the preceding *fprintf()* statement produces the same output as:

```
fprintf(stderr, "%3ld", quantities[ipart]);
```

Both forms of *fprintf()* print the value of *quantities[ipart]* right justified in a field three characters wide.

When formatting floating-point numbers for output, you must additionally consider the number of decimal places to be displayed. In the following example, the *double* variable *inp_ship_amt* is displayed in a field *width* number of characters wide and with *precision* digits to the right of the decimal point:

```
fprintf(stderr, "%*.*f", width, precision, inp_ship_amt);
```

We can simplify things considerably for our order-entry application by writing a few new functions that consolidate several of these standard operations. First we'll create a function *ntput()* that produces the same output as the two steps in the first example with one call:

```
ntput(14, 65, quantities[ipart], buf, max_len);
```

and then we'll create a companion function *ftput()* to do the same for double-precision floating-point variables.

```
ftput(14, 65, inp_ship_amt, precision, buf, width);
```

Note that *ftput()* works for both single- and double-precision floating-point values. Recall that single-precision arguments to a function will be promoted to double as they are passed. In both of these examples, *buf* is a string that will contain the formatted number to be output by *ntput()* or *ftput()*. We'll use the order-entry function *strrjust()* in the functions *ntput()* and *ftput()* to right justify the string in *buf* for the appropriate field width.

```
/* SOURCE FILE: STRRJUST.C
  ***************************************************************************
  * strrjust() takes a string and a length and right justifies the string in
  *   a field of that length. If the string is longer than the field, no
  *   action is taken.
  ***************************************************************************
  */

#include <stdio.h>
#include <string.h>
#include "projutil.h"

void strrjust(
    char str[],    /* text to be right justified (padded on left with spaces) */
    short fld_len) /* length of field to format text in */

    {
    short end_char, ichar, move;

    /* Find index of last non-space in str and back up from there */
    /*   toward beginning; then fill left end of str with blanks. */
    for (end_char = strlen(str) - 1;
        str[end_char] == ' ' && end_char > 0; --end_char)
        ;
    move = fld_len - end_char - 1;          /* number of positions */
    if (move > 0 && end_char >= 0)          /* need to move anything? */
        {

        /* Copy characters. */
        for (ichar = end_char; ichar >= 0; --ichar)
            str[ichar + move] = str[ichar];

        /* Fill left end with blanks. */
        for (ichar = move - 1; ichar >= 0; --ichar)
            str[ichar] = ' ';
        str[fld_len] = '\0';                /* null terminator */
        }
    }
#if defined(DBGMAIN)
#define TEST(cond, msg) printf((cond) ? "" : \
    "!!! TEST FAILED !!! %s\7\n", (msg))
```

*(continued)*

STRRJUST.C *continued*

```
/* Test driver main() for strrjust(). */
main()
    {
    char str[81];

    strcpy(str, "abc");
    strrjust(str, 5);
    TEST(0 == strcmp(str, "  abc"), "strjust #1");
    strcpy(str, "ABCDE");
    strrjust(str, 5);
    TEST(0 == strcmp(str, "ABCDE"), "strjust #2");
    strcpy(str, "");
    strrjust(str, 5);
    TEST(0 == strcmp(str, ""), "strjust #3");
    printf("strrjust tests complete\n");
    }
#endif
```

The data we'll output with these new functions are in the computer's internal binary format, not in human-readable ASCII format, so we'll need to call library functions to convert the binary values to their ASCII representations. We'll use *ltoa()* to convert the *long* values, using a *radix* (also known as *modulo* or *base*) of 10. The radix can be any number from 2 to 36. We'll use *fcvt()* to convert the floating-point numbers (*fcvt()* does not use a radix).

```
/* SOURCE FILE: NTPUT.C
 ************************************************************************
 * ntput() converts a long integer to ASCII and displays it right justified
 *   in field of specified width. The left side is padded with blanks.
 ************************************************************************
 */

#include <stdlib.h>
#include "projutil.h"

void ntput(
    short row,              /* row to output text on */
    short col,              /* column to output text in */
    long long_val,          /* value to be displayed */
    char buf[],             /* output buffer */
    short field_len)        /* length of field to right justify in */
```

*(continued)*

NTPUT.C *continued*

```
{
ltoa(long_val, buf, 10);        /* convert long to ASCII string */
strrjust(buf, field_len);       /* right justify field */
tput(row, col, buf);            /* display on screen for user */
}
```

Now, like *printf()*, the library function *sprintf()* performs formatted output conversions, but without producing any output on the screen. The data produced for output are saved in a string that is passed as *sprintf()*'s first argument, so this next call to *sprintf()* produces the same results as the calls to *ltoa()* and *strrjust()* in the preceding *ntput()* example:

```
sprintf(buf, "%*ld", field_len, long_val);
```

In this example, the value of the *long* variable *long_val* is converted to a string of ASCII characters and placed in *buf*, right justified in a field *field_len* characters wide.

# C O M M E N T

*The object code for* printf(), fprintf(), *and* sprintf() *is large, but if your program never actually calls these functions, their object code won't be linked into your program at all.*

If we can do the same job with one function call, why would we want to use *ntput()* instead of *sprintf()*? Quite simply, because *sprintf()* consumes about 5,000 bytes of object code, so replacing it with the smaller *ntput()* saves both disk space and program memory.

Since *fcvt()* does essentially the same task as *ltoa()*, you would expect it to operate in much the same manner; however, that is not the case. The *fcvt()* function has a couple of quirks you need to be aware of. First, you do not pass to *fcvt()* a string that will be given a value. Instead, *fcvt()* creates its own temporary string and returns its address. Since this string is temporary, you must call *strcpy()* to copy its contents to your own string after you call *fcvt()*, or you will lose it at the next *fcvt()* call.

```
/* SOURCE FILE: FTPUT.C
 **************************************************************************
 * ftput() converts a double-precision floating-point number to ASCII and
 *   displays it right justified in field of specified width, with
 *   specified decimal places.
 **************************************************************************
 */

#include <string.h>
#include <stdlib.h>
#include "projutil.h"

void ftput(
   short row,              /* cursor row to display value on */
   short col,              /* cursor column to display value in */
   double double_val,      /* value to be displayed */
   short dec_place,        /* number of decimal places to display */
   char buf[],             /* output buffer for formatting data */
   short field_len)        /* length of field */

   {
   int dec;                /* decimal point position (from fcvt()) */
   int sign;               /* flag (0/1): is minus sign needed?  (from fcvt()) */

   /* Copy contents of temporary string buffer to buf. */
   strcpy(buf, fcvt(double_val, dec_place, &dec, &sign));
   if (sign)                     /* double_val is negative */
      {

      /* memmove needed to copy into overlapping data area. */
      memmove(buf + 1, buf, 1 + strlen(buf));
      buf[0] = '-';              /* insert minus sign prefix */
      }
   if (dec >= 0)                 /* insert decimal point between digits */
      {
      memmove(buf + dec + sign + 1, buf + dec + sign,
         strlen(buf) + 1 - dec - sign);
      buf[dec + sign] = '.';     /* insert the decimal point */
      }
   else                 /* dec is negative, so leading zeros are needed */
      {
      memmove(buf + sign + 1 - dec, buf + sign,
         strlen(buf) + 1 - sign);
      for (; dec; ++dec)         /* count from dec up to zero */
         buf[sign - dec] = '0';  /* insert a leading zero */
      buf[sign] = '.';           /* insert the decimal point */
      }
   strrjust(buf, field_len);
   tput(row, col, buf);
   }
```

Second, *fcvt()* does not put a decimal point in the string it creates. Instead, you must pass it the address of a short variable whose value, on return, will be the element of the string where the decimal point belongs. It is up to you to actually insert the decimal point. (This allows for international variations in the character that represents the decimal point.) The actual call to *fcvt()* from *ftput()* looks like this:

```
strcpy(buf, fcvt(double_val, dec_place, &dec, &sign));
```

Notice that *fcvt()* is also passed another address, *&sign*. The *short* variable *sign* will be set to zero if the sign of the *double* value is positive or to a non-zero value if it is negative. The function *memmove()* is called when a minus sign must be inserted to make room for it:

```
memmove(buf + 1, buf, 1 + strlen(buf));
buf[0] = '-';          /* insert minus sign prefix */
```

The function *memmove()* moves each character in array *buf*, up to and including '\0', to the memory location of the next higher element in *buf*. The order in which data is moved is extremely important. If *buf[0]* is moved into *buf[1]* before *buf[1]* has been moved into *buf[2]*, the old value in *buf[1]* will be clobbered and lost before it can be moved into *buf[2]*. The following table illustrates how *memmove()* moves each character in an array.

|                       | buf[0] | buf[1] | buf[2] | buf[3] |
|-----------------------|--------|--------|--------|--------|
| Before *memmove()*    | 3      | 5      | '\0'   | ?      |
| After *memmove()*     | ?      | 3      | 5      | '\0'   |
| After *buf[0]* = '-'; | -      | 3      | 5      | '\0'   |

You can see that *memmove()* must start at the last byte of the array, the '\0', and move it first, then the *5*, and finally the *3*. This is exactly what *memmove()* does, because *memmove()* guarantees that it will move bytes in overlapping areas nondestructively. The functions *memcpy()*, *strcpy()*, and *strncpy()* make no such guarantee and should never be used with overlapping areas of memory.

To insert the decimal point into the proper position in the string of digits is not a trivial process. The value of *dec* may be negative after returning from *fcvt()*, which means that leading zeros are needed. A positive value for *dec* indicates that the decimal place can be inserted between digits in the converted string returned from *fcvt()*. Making room for leading zeros and decimal points is a job that is handled by *memmove()* in the *ftput()* function.

## Designing the screen

Now that we've created the necessary low-level screen-output tools, let's see how they're used to create a whole screen.

We use the expression *painting a screen* to describe the process by which our program displays the names and values of data fields in an attractive, readable, and efficient format. In the case of our order-entry prompt screens, that means placing fields in the order they are needed, with no extraneous data to confuse or distract the user, and aligning the field titles and the input fields themselves in columns. (Scanning down a column is the easiest motion for the human eye.)

Uniformity among the visible features of a program and among the styles of user interface is important to user productivity. A good place to begin addressing these concerns is at the top of the prompt screen. The heading of the screen should show the name of the user (most users will hesitate to use another's name and password, knowing that a passerby could easily notice), the office identification, the name of the program in use, and the portion of the program currently executing. The order-entry function *id_cust()* calls *beg_scrn()* (see Chapter 11) to clear the screen and display these headings. It passes to *beg_scrn()* the arguments *user*, *scrn_title*, *office*, and *"IDENTIFY"*. Only the last argument, which is a description of the part of the order-entry process currently executing, changes in calls made by other order-entry functions.

Armed with this knowledge of how to manage screen output and paint entire screens, let's move on to management of the user's input through prompts and error messages.

# Prompting for Data

The job of obtaining data from the user is the most important task of our order-entry program. In this chapter, we'll look at the standard library functions used for prompting, as well as some custom functions that perform more strictly controlled prompting. First, let's talk about some of the elements that make prompts "friendlier." Then we'll look at the way our order-entry application handles prompting for data.

## Friendly Prompting

We want our software to be easy for new users to learn to use. We also want experienced users, who know the software well, to be able to work as productively as possible. These two goals can sometimes pull programmers in opposite directions, but it doesn't have to be that way. Here are some suggestions that meet both goals without difficulty.

### Menus and help screens

Menus that give detailed lists of commands and plenty of on-line help messages where needed will help a new user feel at home and become productive sooner. But to experienced users, menus and messages they already know by heart are just clutter that distracts them and slows them down.

One solution is to provide at least two modes of operation and make them user-selectable. In novice mode, the user sees full instructions on order entry and on how to obtain additional help. In expert mode, the more experienced user sees only brief explanations and receives no help messages. If an application is so complex that two user levels are insufficient, it is easy to add more.

On-line help messages should always be presented within the program that they explain, at the step where they are needed, and should make it clear what the user must do next.

## Defaults and abbreviations

Good defaults are helpful to both the novice and the experienced user. They permit the user simply to press Return to enter frequently given responses. User-defined abbreviations for responses are also a helpful feature. We don't use abbreviations in our order-entry software because we don't expect to have many common responses that aren't already included as defaults, but this may not be the case in your next application. You might consider an inventory part number as an abbreviation for the detailed description of the part.

## Screen controls and uniformity

The amount of effort required to correct a typing error after the user has entered subsequent data items can most definitely separate friendly from unfriendly software. What if the customer changes something on the order or the salesperson misunderstands a word and discovers the mistake a few steps later? What about typing errors? It's important that we plan our screen controls so that the user can back up, rather than having to start over from the beginning.

All software users appreciate uniform prompting and option conventions. There is security and efficiency in knowing what to expect. For instance, in our order-entry application, the user always has the same four options at data-entry prompts: type some data; type *Ctrl-R* to back up and retype the response to a previous prompt; type *Ctrl-E* to erase the field; or type *Ctrl-X* to cancel the order.

The computer's "bell" can also be used to make software friendlier. For example, many data-entry operators don't read the screens as they type. They are busy looking at pieces of paper that contain the information they are to enter, and it seriously affects their efficiency to keep looking back and forth between paper and monitor. This makes it important for programs to include a means of attracting the operator's attention when necessary. Ringing the bell is an easy and inoffensive solution.

## Prompt messages

A *prompt message* is text your program displays to inform the user that some kind of response is required. The message should make clear what that requirement is. For instance, if you are asking the user to choose among several actions, list all the options clearly, omitting no possibilities.

Each prompt message is followed by the field on the screen that is to contain the user's response. It is helpful to mark this field by filling it with a repeated character such as the underscore, to create a *prompt mask*. Always move the cursor to the first character of the prompt mask before beginning the user's input. If your program has provided a default response, the prompt mask should display that default value. If a response is mandatory and there is no default reply, the user must enter data.

In this next example of a screen display, adapted from the *id_cust()* function in *ordbuild.c*, you see two prompts for names. The name of the customer making the order is input first. Then the default value for the ship-to name is set to the customer's name, since in our business the order is usually shipped directly to the customer:

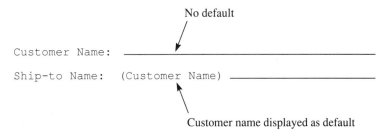

This kind of friendly default often saves the user a considerable number of keystrokes.

## Input control

User productivity (quantity) is a major concern in planning prompts, but correctness of the data entered (quality) is equally important. There are a number of ways we can use prompting to prevent or detect user errors:

- Each character of input can be matched against a list of acceptable characters.

- A character string can be compared with a match-pattern string that defines which characters are acceptable in each position of the input.

- A check can be made for a reasonable response and a message such as "Are you sure? <y/n>" or "Please re-enter the last item" displayed if the program finds the user's entry "unreasonable." (One way to set up a reasonableness check is to require that all item quantities above a certain number, such as 100, be entered twice.)

- More complex diagnostics can be used to actually explain errors to the user and describe remedial actions to be taken.

We'll spend the rest of this chapter looking at these techniques individually, using some of our order-entry functions as examples.

# Input Using Standard Library Functions

Data read from the standard input file can come from a user typing at a keyboard or, if *stdin* is redirected, it can come from a saved file, from a modem, or from another device. Filter tool programs (see Chapter 6) usually obtain their input through these standard input functions:

| FUNCTION | INPUT |
| --- | --- |
| *getchar()* | Character |
| *gets()* | Line |
| *scanf()* | Formatted |

We need to discuss a couple of points before we begin talking about these functions individually. First, Microsoft C buffers input by lines, enabling the user to correct typing errors before the program sees them, since the characters of the input line are not handed over to the program until the user has typed the entire line and pressed Return. This means that, even when the program is calling for single-character input using *getchar()*, it appears to input complete lines at a time rather than individual characters.

Second, remember that standard input can be redirected from the command line so that data are obtained from a disk file. When this is done, end-of-file checking becomes important. When input is not redirected, the user at the keyboard can easily give the standard input functions an end-of-file signal simply by typing *Ctrl-Z* alone on a line (UNIX and some other systems use *Ctrl-D* instead).

## Character-at-a-time: *getchar()*

The macro *getchar()* is defined in the header file *stdio.h*. The returned character is an integer. If a program attempts to read past the end of the file, the value of *stdio.h*'s defined symbol *EOF* is returned. The value of *EOF* in the Microsoft C environment is −1, but use *EOF*, not −*1*, for end-of-file checking, so that your code will operate correctly on other systems where the value of *EOF* may not be −1.

This next filter program copies its standard input to standard output one character at a time:

```
/* Copy standard input to output using getchar() and putchar(). */
#include <stdio.h>

void main(void)
    {
    int input;

    input = getchar();    /* input next character */
    while (input != EOF)  /* end-of-file checking -- loop until no more input */
        {
        putchar(input);    /* output a character */
        input = getchar(); /* input next character */
        }
    }
```

When this copy program is executed interactively, without redirections, it produces this kind of dialogue:

```
Hello there!
Hello there!
Bye!
Bye!
^Z
```

But why does the program echo after each line, rather than after each character? The answer, of course, is that input is buffered a line at a time. The program *would* echo after each character if no input buffering were performed and the program obtained each character immediately after it was typed. (Some operating systems, such as UNIX, permit the C programmer to turn off input buffering and actually input one character at a time with calls to *getchar()*. MS-DOS systems, however, use a separate function, *getch()*, to perform unbuffered input.)

This next filter program counts lines and characters in its standard input file. Notice how we avoid using two separate calls to *getchar()* by embedding the call in the loop test *(input = getchar()) != EOF*.

```c
/* Count the number of lines and characters in stdin(). */
#include <stdio.h>

void main(void)
    {
    int input;                /* input returned from getchar() */
    long chars, lines;        /* counters for lines and characters */

    for (lines = chars = 0; (input = getchar()) != EOF; ++chars)
        if (input == '\n')    /* end of a line? */
            ++lines;          /* yes; increment count of lines */
    printf("%ld lines, %ld characters\n", lines, chars);
    }
```

An important point to remember when working with *getchar()* is that it automatically sends your program the newline character '\n' at the end of each line you input. That's how our program was able to count the lines.

## Line-at-a-time: *gets()*

The standard input function *gets()* is called to obtain an entire line of character input from the standard input file. The newline character

'\n' is stripped off the end of the line and replaced with the null character '\0', making the line a null-terminated string. The value *0* is returned by *gets()* if the program tries to read beyond the end of the standard input file.

To copy a file a line at a time using *gets()*, try this small program:

```
/* Copy file from stdin to stdout one line at a time. */
#include <stdio.h>

void main(void)
    {
    char line[BUFSIZ];    /* BUFSIZ is defined in stdio.h as the size */
                          /* of the stdin buffer, typically 512 */

    /* Loop: For each line of input, output the same line. */
    while (gets(line))
        puts(line);
    }
```

If the user types an input line longer than the dimension of *line* in the preceding program, *gets()* will go ahead and store characters beyond the end of the line, possibly clobbering other data. Any time a program stores array data in locations beyond the end (or before the beginning) of the declared dimension of the array, it is using storage designated for other purposes. The result can be anything from lost data to a hung system that needs rebooting. The only protection we have against this is to write our own functions with built-in input controls.

## Formatted input: *scanf()*

You have already seen the details of inputting data using *scanf()* (Chapters 2 and 3). However, using formatted input with this function is not safe. Here's why: Arbitrary numbers of spaces, newline characters, and tab characters may be typed by the user and completely ignored by *scanf()* if it is waiting for the user to input a number. Since there is no way to prevent the user from typing unacceptable characters, such as a letter in the middle of a number, such errors must be dealt with after the user has finished typing the entire entry. Once again, because we just don't have enough control over the type of input with *scanf()*, we need to develop some alternatives of our own.

# Input of Text Under Strict Control

Given the problems connected with *gets()* and *scanf()*, we naturally prefer to write our own input functions for the order-entry application. I've named the text-input function *prompt()* and placed it in the order-entry source file *prompt.c*.

```c
/* SOURCE FILE: PROMPT.C
 ***********************************************************************
 * prompt() inputs text from standard input to the string "data".
 *    The program matches input against an optional match-string argument
 *    and checks minimum and maximum input lengths. If the Boolean (flag)
 *    argument mand is true, the program will not allow "data" to remain null;
 *    the user must make an entry. The parameter "data" is both passed to
 *    prompt() and returned to the calling function. The value passed in is
 *    treated as a default to be used if input is null. Data are input one
 *    character at a time, without automatic echo.
 * Return value: The outcome of prompt has synonym data type stepcode, which
 *    is used to indicate:
 *       STEPOK    Step complete; go on to next step.
 *       STEPBACK  Back up to closest previous step.
 *       STEPCANC  Cancel order entry (quit).
 *    C_BACK, C_NULL, and C_CANC are defined in projutil.h. The user can
 *       request to back up by entering C_BACK, to cancel by entering C_CANC,
 *       or to erase data by entering C_NULL as any character in the reply.
 ***********************************************************************
 */

#include <stdio.h>
#include <string.h>
#include <conio.h>
#include "syntypes.h"
#include "ansiscrn.h"
#include "projutil.h"

stepcode prompt(
    char data[],          /* default passed in, input data returned */
    char match_str[],     /* match string to verify data against */
    short min_len,        /* minimum input data length */
    short max_len,        /* maximum input data length */
    flag mand,            /* if yes, data cannot be null on return */
    short row,            /* cursor row to begin input */
    short col)            /* cursor column to begin input */

    {
    IMPORT bflag bell_ok; /* global permission to ring bell */
    char buf[PRMTBSIZ];   /* prompt input buffer */
    short ichar;          /* input character counter */
```

*(continued)*

PROMPT.C  *continued*

```
      stepcode rtn = STEPOK;   /* return code */
      bflag more;              /* expect more input? */

      /* Display prompt mask or default value, if any.
       * Copy default to buffer. Fill rest of buffer with prompt mask
       *   characters, to maximum length of field prompted for.
       */
      strcpy(buf, data);
      for (ichar = strlen(buf); ichar < max_len; ++ichar)
         buf[ichar] = C_MASK;
      buf[ichar] = '\0';
      tput(row, col, buf);
      CUR_MV(row, col);

      /* Input each character. */
      strcpy(buf, data);                /* copy default value to buffer */
      for (ichar = 0, more = YES; ichar < max_len && more; )
         {
         buf[ichar] = (char)getch();        /* input a character (no auto echo) */
         buf[ichar + 1] = '\0';
         switch (buf[ichar])
            {
            case C_CANC:            /* cancel command */
               rtn = STEPCANC, more = NO;
               break;
            case C_BACK:            /* back up to previous prompt */
               rtn = STEPBACK, more = NO;
               break;
            case C_NULL:            /* force data to null, restart prompt */

               /* Fill buffer with mask characters to maximum length of field. */
               for (ichar = 0; ichar < max_len; ++ichar)
                  buf[ichar] = C_MASK;
               buf[ichar] = '\0';
               tput(row, col, buf); /* show prompt mask in buf */
               ichar = 0;           /* restart at first character */
               buf[ichar] = data[ichar] = '\0';    /* erase data */
               CUR_MV(row, col);    /* move cursor to beginning of mask */
               break;
            case '\r':              /* end of line */
            case '\n':              /* alternate end of line */
               if (ichar == 0 && data[0] != '\0')

                  /* Pass default back to caller. */
                  strcpy(buf, data), more = NO;
               else if (ichar == 0 && data[0] == '\0' && mand)
                  {                 /* mandatory entry, no default supplied */
                  err_warn("Data must be entered:", "");
```

*(continued)*

PROMPT.C *continued*

```
                CUR_MV(row, col);
                }

            /* Too few characters? Check, unless this is first */
            /*   character of reply and reply is optional. */
            else if (ichar < min_len && !(ichar == 0 && !mand))
                {
                err_warn("Too few characters:", "");
                CUR_MV(row, col + ichar);           /* restore cursor */
                }
            else
                buf[ichar] = '\0', more = NO;      /* end of input */
            break;
        case '\b':                   /* backspace (BS) entered */
            buf[ichar] = '\0';      /* delete backspace */
            if (ichar > 0)
                {
                buf[--ichar] = '\0';       /* wipe character before BS */
                fputc('\b', stderr);       /* fix display to match */
                fputc(C_MASK, stderr);
                fputc(C_MASK, stderr);
                fprintf(stderr, "\b\b");
                }
            break;
        default:                     /* check match and length; echo character */

            /* Echo if character is legal; else ring bell. */
            buf[ichar + 1] = '\0';     /* save character and increment ichar */
            if (match(buf, match_str))
                putc(buf[ichar++], stderr);        /* echo good character */
            else if (bell_ok)    /* bad character entered; ring bell */
                putc('\7', stderr);
            if (ichar > max_len)
                more = NO;
            break;
        }
    }

/* Copy buf to data and erase rest of prompt mask (if any). */
if (rtn == STEPOK)
    strcpy(data, buf);
ichar = strlen(data);
CUR_MV(row, col + ichar);
for (; ichar < max_len; ++ichar)
    fputc(' ', stderr);            /* erase end of mask, using spaces */
return (rtn);
}
```

The goal of the *prompt()* function is to control the type of text data the user is allowed to input in response to a prompt message. Only valid characters are echoed as they are typed. If the user types an invalid character, such as *W*, in response to a yes-or-no question, nothing is displayed, the bell rings, and the cursor remains where it is. Also, if the user tries to press Return before the expected number of characters have been entered, *err_warn()*, a diagnostic project utility function, alerts the user that more characters are required and allows another try.

Here is a pseudocode outline of the processing to be done by our order-entry *prompt()* function:

> Build and display prompt mask, using defaults where available.
> Loop once for each character of response that is input.
>> Switch: Depending upon input character, do one of the following:
>>> Cancel (^*X*) or back-up (^*R*) command? If yes, then done.
>>> Erase (^*E*) command? If yes, print spaces to erase the field's old value, then display new mask.
>>> Newline ('\r' or '\n')? If yes, check for mandatory and null, then check length.
>>> Backspace ('\b')? If yes, delete previous character.
>>> Default: Check match pattern and save character if OK.
> Erase any leftover prompt mask characters after user's data.

Notice the declaration and comment for the character array named *data*, which is the first parameter for *prompt()*:

```
stepcode prompt(
    char data[],        /* default passed in, input data returned */
    char match_str[],   /* match string to verify data against */
    short min_len,      /* minimum input data length */
    short max_len,      /* maximum input data length */
    flag mand,          /* if yes, data cannot be null on return */
    short row,          /* cursor row to begin input on */
    short col)          /* cursor column to begin input in */
```

The *data* parameter does two jobs: It passes a default to *prompt()* and it also passes the user's reply back to the function that called *prompt()*. You must always assign a value to the argument passed to *data* before calling *prompt()*; if you don't want to provide a default, simply pass an empty string.

## Character-type and match-pattern checking

The second parameter for *prompt()* is *match_str*, a match-pattern string that is passed to the order-entry *match()* function (the sole contents of the source file *match.c*). This function verifies a data string passed by *prompt()*, character by character, against a specified match string. The return value is *1* if the data match the pattern, *0* if a character in the data does not match the pattern.

```
/* SOURCE FILE: MATCH.C
 ************************************************************************
 * match() verifies a data string, character by character, against a match
 *    string. If the match string is shorter than the data string, the
 *    last match-string character is used to verify the data string.
 *    The match string may be composed of these match characters:
 *
 *    A    A-Z                            (uppercase letters)
 *    #    0-9 only                       (numbers)
 *    S    0-9 or + or -                  (signs or numbers)
 *    F    0-9 or .                       (floating-point numbers)
 *    L    a-z, A-Z, 0-9, or ;:.,/?*-$#()'! (names, addresses)
 *           and non-leading spaces
 *    U    A-Z, 0-9, or ;:.,/?*-$#()'!    (uppercase names, addresses)
 *           and non-leading spaces
 *    P    0-9 or - or () or space        (phone numbers)
 *    Q    one of "Yy1Nn0"                (question reply)
 *    X    any printable character        (text)
 *
 *    Any other character in the match string is ignored. Spaces are matched
 *    by L, U, and P. Empty match string matches any data.
 * Return value: YES = data string matches; NO = no match.
 ************************************************************************
 */

#include <ctype.h>          /* for isxxx() character-type macro definitions */
#include <string.h>
#include "syntypes.h"
#include "projutil.h"

flag match(
    char data_str[],        /* source string to be verified */
    char match_str[])       /* match pattern text */

    {
    short ichar;            /* input character counter */
    char c_data;            /* character of data string */
    char c_match;           /* character of match string */
```

*(continued)*

MATCH.C  *continued*

```
/* Initialize a variable to a function return. */
short len_match = strlen(match_str);
bflag matches = YES;

for (ichar = 0; data_str[ichar] != '\0' && matches; ++ichar)
   {

   /* Determine match character. */
   if (ichar < len_match)     /* use next match character */
      c_match = match_str[ichar];
   else if (len_match == 0)    /* empty match_str */
      c_match = '\0';
   else                        /* use last character of match string */
      c_match = match_str[len_match - 1];
   c_data = data_str[ichar];
   switch (c_match)            /* check match with data */
      {
      case 'A':                /* A-Z */
         if (!isupper(c_data))
            matches = NO;
         break;
      case '#':                /* 0-9 only */
         if (!isdigit(c_data))
            matches = NO;
         break;
      case 'S':                /* 0-9 or + or - only */
         if (!isdigit(c_data) && !strchr("+-", c_data))
            matches = NO;
         break;
      case 'L':                /* a-z, A-Z, 0-9, or ;:.,/?*-$#()'! or space */
         if (!isalnum(c_data) && !strchr(";:.,/?*-$#()'! ",
             c_data))
            matches = NO;
         if (ichar == 0 && c_data == ' ')     /* no leading blanks */
            matches = NO;
         break;
      case 'U':                /* A-Z, 0-9, or ;:.,/?*-$#()'! or space */
         if (!isupper(c_data) && !isdigit(c_data) &&
             !strchr(";:.,/?*-$#()'! ", c_data))
            matches = NO;
         if (ichar == 0 && c_data == ' ')     /* no leading blanks */
            matches = NO;
         break;
      case 'P':                /* 0-9 or - or () or space */
         if (!isdigit(c_data) && !strchr("-() ", c_data))
            matches = NO;
         break;
```

*(continued)*

MATCH.C *continued*

```
        case 'F':                /* 0-9 or . */
            if (!isdigit(c_data) && !strchr(".", c_data))
                matches = NO;
            break;
        case 'Q':                /* Yy1Nn0 as reply to yes/no question */
            if (!strchr("Yy1Nn0", c_data))
                matches = NO;
            break;
        case 'X':                /* must be printable (' 'through '~') */
            if (!isprint(c_data))
                matches = NO;
            break;
        }
    }
    return (matches);
}
```

Figure 13-1 shows those match characters used with the prompts in the order-entry application. Notice that none of the match characters listed permits the user to enter leading spaces, although non-leading spaces are accepted by *L* and *U* (something *scanf()* can't control). The other match characters included in *match.c* are for general use. Feel free to add new ones of your own to suit your own applications.

Nearly all C compilers come with a header file named *ctype.h*, which contains macros for classifying a character by type. Figure 13-2 shows the *ctype* macros we use in our order-entry *match()* function.

| MATCH CHARACTER | DATA ALLOWED | USE |
|---|---|---|
| # | 0–9 only | Numbers |
| *F* | 0–9 or . | Tax and dollar amounts |
| *L* | a–z, A–Z, 0–9, or ;:.,/?*-$#()'! and non-leading spaces | Names, addresses |
| *U* | A–Z, 0–9, or ;:.,/?*-$#()'! and non-leading spaces | Uppercase names, addresses |
| *P* | 0–9 or - or () | Phone numbers |
| *Q* | Y y 1 N n 0 (one only) | Yes/no question responses |

FIGURE 13-1
*Match characters for order-entry prompts*

| MACRO | RETURN VALUE |
|-------|--------------|
| *isupper(c)* | 1 if *c* is an uppercase letter, else 0 |
| *isdigit(c)* | 1 if *c* is a numeric digit 0 through 9, else 0 |
| *isalnum(c)* | 1 if *c* is a letter or number, else 0 |
| *isprint(c)* | 1 if *c* is a printable ASCII character, else 0 |

**FIGURE 13-2**
*Macros from* ctype.h *used in the order-entry application*

This next code segment for the *L* match character uses both the macro *isalnum()* and the library string function *strchr()* (called *index()* in some other C libraries). The *strchr()* function searches within the string passed as its first argument ( *";:.,/?*-$#()'! "* ) for the character passed as its second argument (*c_data*), and returns 0 if the character is not found.

```
case 'L':                 /* a-z, A-Z, 0-9, or ;:.,/?*-$#()'! or space */
      if (!isalnum(c_data) && !strchr(";:.,/?*-$#()'! ",
         c_data))
         matches = NO;
      if (ichar == 0 && c_data == ' ')       /* no leading blanks */
         matches = NO;
      break;
```

The *match()* function performs one iteration of a *for* loop for each character in the data string being tested. The character is compared with a match character from within a large switch statement that holds case actions for several match characters, all similar to the one in the preceding example. The loop ends when all of the characters have been checked or a nonmatching character is found.

# Input of Numbers Under Strict Control

The # and *S* match characters offer us some interesting possibilities for controlling numeric input. (The string *"#"* will match a string of digits; the string *"S#"* will match a string of digits that begins with a plus or minus sign.)

The kinds of numbers that we want to input in our order-entry application are money, quantities, and percentages. (We don't consider phone numbers and zip codes numeric input because we keep them in string form and do not perform arithmetic on them.) The *nprompt()* function in our order-entry program enables integers to be input, so it is used to input quantities and sometimes money.

```
/* SOURCE FILE: NPROMPT.C
 ***************************************************************************
 * nprompt() inputs a long integer from standard input. The program matches
 *   input against an optional match-string argument and checks minimum and
 *   maximum input values. If the Boolean (flag) argument mand is true,
 *   then the program will not permit data to remain zero; data must be
 *   entered. The parameter *p_num is both passed to nprompt() and returned
 *   to the calling function. The value passed in is treated as a default to
 *   be used if input is null.
 * Return value: The outcome of nprompt() has synonym data type stepcode,
 *   which is used to indicate:
 *     STEPOK    Step complete; valid number obtained.
 *     STEPBACK  Back up to the previous step.
 *     STEPCANC  Cancel order entry (quit).
 *   The user can request to back up by entering C_BACK, to cancel by
 *   entering C_CANC, or to set *p_num to zero by entering C_NULL as any
 *   character in the reply.
 ***************************************************************************
 */

#include <stdio.h>
#include <stdlib.h>
#include <string.h>
#include "syntypes.h"
#include "projutil.h"

stepcode nprompt(
    long *p_num,          /* default passed in, input data returned */
    char match_str[],     /* match string to verify data against */
    long min_val,         /* minimum input value */
    long max_val,         /* maximum input value */
    flag mand,            /* if yes, data cannot be zero on return */
    short row,            /* cursor row to begin input */
    short col)            /* cursor column to begin input */

    {
    char buf[14];         /* prompt input buffer */
    bflag more = YES;     /* prompt again? */
    long in_num;          /* ASCII input number converted to binary */
    short max_len = strlen(ltoa(max_val, buf, 10));
    short min_len = strlen(ltoa(min_val, buf, 10));
    stepcode rtn;         /* return code */

    /* Supply as default if p_num points to a non-zero long. */
    if (*p_num)           /* non-zero value passed in? */
        {
        ntput(row, col, *p_num, buf, max_len);     /* display default */
        }
```

*(continued)*

NPROMPT.C *continued*

```
else                     /* no default */
   buf[0] = '\0';

/* Loop: Prompt for number in string form, until value */
/*   entered is in range, or cancel or back up is requested. */
do
   {
   rtn = prompt(buf, match_str, min_len, max_len, mand, row, col);
   if (rtn != STEPOK)
      more = NO;       /* done prompting (back up or cancel) */
   else                     /* check whether input mandatory and reply in range */
      {
      in_num = atol(buf);      /* convert ASCII input to long integer */

      /* If mandatory and number is zero, this is an error. */
      if (mand && in_num == 0)
         err_warn("Non-zero data mandatory:", "");

      /* Otherwise, verify in_num is inside specified range, provided */
      /*   prompt is mandatory or number entered is non-zero. */
      else if ((in_num < min_val || in_num > max_val) &&
         (mand || in_num != 0))
         {
         sprintf(buf, "%ld to %ld", min_val, max_val);
         err_warn("Enter a number from:", buf);
         buf[0] = '\0';
         }
      else             /* got a good value; done prompting */
         more = NO;
      }
   }
while (more);
   if (rtn == STEPOK)           /* then echo, right justified */
      {
      *p_num = in_num;          /* pass value back to caller */

      /* Echo number right justified in screen field. */
      ntput(row, col, in_num, buf, max_len);
      }
return (rtn);
}
```

The data type you use to hold amounts of money depends, quite simply, upon the size of the largest possible amount to be handled and whether decimal values are expected. (Remember to allow for the effects of arithmetic operations such as addition and multiplication.)

In the order-entry application, we will use *long* variables to hold amounts of money in cents (giving us a range of ±$21,474,836.47), since *float* and *double* can cause rounding errors that drop or add pennies and drive accountants crazy. However, we will convert money values to *double* before *displaying* them so that they will appear on the screen (or printer) in familiar decimal format. The *fprompt()* function works with floating-point numbers, so it is used to input amounts of money specified by the user and tax percentages.

```
/* SOURCE FILE: FPROMPT.C
 ************************************************************************
 * fprompt() inputs a double-precision floating-point number from standard
 *   input. It behaves the same as nprompt(), except that the arguments
 *   width and precision must be passed to fprompt() to indicate the width
 *   of the field and the number of digits to prompt for on the right of the
 *   decimal point.
 ************************************************************************
 */

#include <stdio.h>
#include <string.h>
#include <stdlib.h>
#include "syntypes.h"
#include "ansiscrn.h"
#include "projutil.h"

stepcode fprompt(
    double *d_num,          /* default passed in, input data returned */
    char match_str[],       /* pattern describing input format */
    double min_dval,        /* minimum input value */
    double max_dval,        /* maximum input value */
    short width,            /* input field width */
    short precision,        /* number of decimal places */
    flag mand,              /* if yes, data cannot be zero on return */
    short row,              /* cursor row to begin input */
    short col)              /* cursor column to begin input */

    {
    char buf[80];           /* prompt input buffer */
    bflag more = YES;
    double in_dnum;         /* ASCII input number converted to double */
    short min_len = 1;
    stepcode rtn;

    /* Supply the double d_num points to as the default if it is non-zero. */
    if (*d_num == 0.0)      /* zero value passed in? */
        buf[0] = '\0';      /* no default */
```

*(continued)*

**FPROMPT.C** *continued*

```
    else
        ftput(row, col, *d_num, precision, buf, width);    /* display default */

    do
        {
        rtn = prompt(buf, match_str, min_len, width, mand, row, col);
        if (rtn != STEPOK)
            more = NO;
        else
            {
            in_dnum = atof(buf);    /* convert ASCII to double */
            if (mand && in_dnum == 0.0)
                err_warn("Non-zero data mandatory:", "");
            else if ((in_dnum < min_dval || in_dnum > max_dval) &&
                (mand || in_dnum != 0.0))
                {

                /* Create string to pass to err_warn(). */
                sprintf(buf, "%.*f to %.*f", precision, min_dval,
                    precision, max_dval);
                err_warn("Enter a number from:", buf);
                buf[0] = '\0';
                CUR_MV(row, col);
                }
            else
                more = NO;
            }
        }
    while (more);

    if (rtn == STEPOK)              /* then echo, right justified */
        {
        *d_num = in_dnum;           /* pass value back to caller */
        ftput(row, col, *d_num, precision, buf, width);
        }
    return (rtn);
    }
```

The *nprompt()* and *fprompt()* functions begin by obtaining a
numeric value and converting it to a string to be passed to *prompt()* as
a default response. The *prompt()* function is called to input a string of
digits, which is then converted from ASCII to either *long* or *double* by
the library functions *atol()* and *atof()*, respectively. If the number is
within the acceptable range of values, it is right justified and echoed by
*ntput()* or *ftput()*. (We echo numbers right justified to align columns of
numbers on the decimal point.)

The functions *atol()* and *atof()* are from a small family of library functions used to convert ASCII strings of digits to binary numbers:

| FUNCTION | ACTION |
| --- | --- |
| *atof()* | ASCII to *double* |
| *atoi()* | ASCII to *int* |
| *atol()* | ASCII to *long* |

## Diagnostic Messages

Even with all these safeguards, at times the user will enter something unacceptable. The most help we as programmers can provide at such times is a diagnostic message explaining the problem. For example, in *nprompt()* and *fprompt()* we would alert the user about a zero at a mandatory prompt or a value too high or too low for the range of the prompt field. These messages are sent to the user by the order-entry function *err_warn()*. (The diagnostic-message functions *err_warn()* and *err_exit()* are part of the project utility library.)

```
/* SOURCE FILE: ERR_WARN.C
 *************************************************************************
 * err_warn() displays a two-string diagnostic message on line 24, waits
 *    for the user to press ESC, and then erases the diagnostic message.
 *************************************************************************
 */

#include <stdio.h>
#include <string.h>
#include <stdlib.h>
#include <conio.h>
#include "syntypes.h"
#include "ansiscrn.h"
#include "projutil.h"
#define ESC '\x1b'

void err_warn(
   char first[],               /* first part of diagnostic message */
   char second[])              /* part two of diagnostic message */

   {
   IMPORT bflag bell_ok;
   short first_len = strlen(first);
   short second_len = strlen(second);
```

*(continued)*

ERR_WARN.C *continued*

```
    CUR_MV(24, 1);
    CLR_LINE;
    tput(24, 1, first);
    tput(24, 2 + first_len, second);
    tput(24, 3 + first_len + second_len,
        "_ (press ESC)\b\b\b\b\b\b\b\b\b\b\b");
    if (bell_ok)
        BELL;
    while (getch() != ESC)        /* loop until ESC entered */
        if (bell_ok)
            BELL;
    CUR_MV(24, 1);
    CLR_LINE;
    }


/***************************************************************************
 * err_exit() displays a diagnostic message through err_warn() and calls
 *   exit() to terminate execution. The two-part message is displayed on
 *   line 24. When the user presses ESC, the message is erased.
 ***************************************************************************
 */

void err_exit(
    char first[],                 /* first part of diagnostic message */
    char second[])                /* part two of diagnostic message */


    {
    char log_buf[512];

    strcpy(log_buf, first);
    strcat(log_buf, " ");
    strcat(log_buf, second);
    logentry(log_buf);            /* record the message in the log */
    err_warn(first, second);      /* display the message */
    exit(FAIL);                   /* terminate program: FAIL status */
    }
```

A uniform format for error-message displays is helpful to the user: It makes it obvious what is happening whenever that type of message appears. Both of our application's error-message functions take two string arguments, and since *err_exit()* actually calls *err_warn()* to display the warning message, we need to change only one function to modify the message format. The *err_warn()* function does not return a value, and *err_exit()* never returns at all, because it calls the library function *exit()*, which terminates program execution and returns control to the operating system. Which to use? Well, call *err_warn()* for warning messages to the user about problems that can be fixed, and call *err_exit()* for serious or fatal error conditions that require that the program be terminated.

You'll notice two calls to *logentry()* in the *err_exit()* source code. These are used to preserve the serious warning messages in the log file so that we can trace the actions that led to the disaster and help the user avoid them in the future.

## The Batch Job: *exit()* interface

The *exit()* function terminates a program. It takes an argument, such as *SUCCEED* or *FAIL*, which is defined in the header file *syntypes.h*. Have you wondered where the value you pass to *exit()* goes or how you can write code that takes advantage of it?

The solution lies in batch jobs that make use of the *ERRORLEVEL* test. Let's try a little experiment. Here is a C program called *exittest.c* that prompts for an integer to pass to *exit()*:

```
/* exittest.c:  Pass integer entered by user to exit(). */
#include <stdio.h>
#include <stdlib.h>

void main(void)
    {
    int rtn;

    printf("Enter integer to pass to exit():  ");
    scanf("%d", &rtn);
    exit(rtn);
    }
```

Compile and link *exittest.c*, and then we can proceed with the *exit()* experiment by calling *exittest* in this batch job called TEST.BAT:

```
ECHO OFF
EXITTEST
IF ERRORLEVEL 0 ECHO ERROR LEVEL 0
IF ERRORLEVEL 1 ECHO ERROR LEVEL 1
IF ERRORLEVEL 2 ECHO ERROR LEVEL 2
IF ERRORLEVEL 3 ECHO ERROR LEVEL 3
ECHO ON
```

These next two interactions using the TEST batch file demonstrate how the DOS *ERRORLEVEL* test works. It will pass for any error level less than or equal to the integer passed to the *exit()* function.

```
C>TEST
Enter Integer to pass to exit():  0
ERROR LEVEL 0

C>TEST
Enter Integer to pass to exit():  2
ERROR LEVEL 0
ERROR LEVEL 1
ERROR LEVEL 2
```

The *ERRORLEVEL* mechanism has applications beyond examining the success or type of failure of a program. The DOS batch language lacks a mechanism for interacting with a user, say for obtaining a "Yes" or "No" reply and conditionally executing DOS commands based on that reply. A short C program could ask the user for a "Yes" or "No" reply and pass an integer to *exit* to indicate the reply:

```
/* getreply.c:  Get a Yes or No reply.  exit(1) for No, exit(0) for Yes */
/*  exit(2) is called if getreply is unable to read standard input. */

#include <stdio.h>
#include <stdlib.h>
#include <string.h>

void main(void)
    {
    char reply[80];

    do                      /* loop until valid reply is input or gets() fails */
        {
        if (NULL == gets(reply))
            exit(2);
        if (!reply[0] || NULL == strchr("YyNn", reply[0]))
            printf("Enter Yes or No only, please: ");
        }
    while (!reply[0] || NULL == strchr("YyNn", reply[0]));
    exit(reply[0] == 'N' || reply[0] == 'n');
    }
```

The *getreply* program could be used in a batch file, such as the one on the following page, called *SAFEDEL.BAT*, which uses *DIR* to list files and then gives the user the option of typing *Yes* to delete them or *No* not to.

```
REM SAFEDEL.BAT:  (SAFE DEL) SHOW FILE NAMES, ASK USER BEFORE DELETE
ECHO OFF
DIR %1
ECHO DO YOU WISH TO DELETE FILES LISTED?
GETREPLY
IF ERRORLEVEL 1 GOTO DONE
DEL %1
:DONE
ECHO ON
```

To use SAFEDEL to safely delete all *.BAK files, type:

SAFEDEL *.BAK

One last thing before we leave the subject of prompting. You may have noticed the declaration *long *p_num;* in the code for *nprompt()*. The * operator is used before the variable *p_num* to refer to the *long* integer whose address the variable holds. Such variables are called *pointer variables,* and we'll spend the next few chapters learning how, when, and why to use them.

# S E C T I O N

# IV

Section IV presents a pragmatic discussion of some of the features that give C greater power and flexibility than other high-level languages. **Chapter 14** deals with pointers, a low-level C data type that holds the address of another variable or value in memory. **Chapter 15** explores multidimensional arrays, including pointer arrays that pass command-line arguments to a C program's *main()* function. **Chapter 16** discusses the declaration and manipulation of structures, C's most powerful and flexible data type.

# 14

# Pointers: Variations on Data Access

We've talked about the fact that C has features for system programmers usually not available in higher-level languages—features powerful enough to allow the C programmer to write operating systems or hardware interfaces (machine-level programming). Now that you know enough C to produce entire applications, we'll begin looking at some of these special features to see how they can help streamline our programs and extend their capabilities.

Let's begin with the *pointer* data type, which holds the *address* of a variable in memory rather than the value of the variable. Pointers make it easy for system programmers to perform operations that used to require tedious assembly-language routines. Moreover, the close relationship between expressions using pointers and the underlying CPU instructions they compile to makes for very efficient programs.

Your first exposure to pointers was in Chapter 2, where the *address-of* operator (&) appeared in our discussion about inputting numbers with the library function *scanf()*:

```
scanf("%ld", &long_to_be_input);
```

You heard about them again in Chapter 3, when we discussed one-dimensional arrays. In this chapter and in Chapters 15 and 19, we'll look at pointers in detail. First, however, I want to explain my approach to the topic.

Rather than overwhelm you with the full depth of this subject in one dose, I'll introduce pointers a little at a time. In this chapter, you will learn as much about pointers as you need to know in order to use them for their most important application: returning more than one value from a function to its caller. Then, in Chapter 15, I'll expand on the use of pointers for string manipulation. I've saved such advanced pointer topics as dynamic allocation of memory and linked lists until Chapter 19, when we will have covered some other advanced techniques involved in those applications.

## Declaring Pointers

A pointer variable has two important attributes: the *data type* it is declared to point to and the *address* it is assigned to point to. We'll begin by seeing how to declare pointer variables.

The syntax you use to declare a variable as a pointer to any data type is like the syntax of an ordinary declaration, except that you place an asterisk (*) before the name of the variable being declared. Let's look at some examples.

The following statements declare the variables *p_long*, *p_short*, and *p_char* as pointers to types *long*, *short*, and *char*, respectively:

```
long *p_long;     /* p_long is type pointer to long */
short *p_short;   /* p_short is type pointer to short */
char *p_char;     /* p_char is type pointer to char */
```

Every variable declared in a program consumes memory to hold its value: 1 byte for type *char*, 2 bytes for *short*, and 4 bytes for *long*. Pointers are no exception: They consume 2 or 4 bytes, depending on the compiler, memory model, and CPU chip being used. Thus, the declarations in the preceding example use a total of either 6 or 12 bytes of memory, depending upon the system. The important point to remember here is that at this stage, no memory has been allocated for any *long*, *short*, or *char* variables—only for the three *pointer* variables. Also, since the pointers in our example have not been initialized, their values are undefined, and they cannot safely be used. Let's take care of that problem right now.

## Initializing Pointers

Like other data types, *pointers* can contain an initializer in their declaration. The syntax of the initializing declaration uses the & and * operators, like this:

```
long long_val;
long *p_long = &long_val;
```

You can use the unary operator address-of *(&)* only on *lvalues.* (See Chapter 3.) You will recall that the compiler is free to assign any available location in memory (except 0) to hold an *lvalue*; you have no control over this allocation. Let's suppose the compiler has allocated 1 byte at location 1006 to the *char* variable *char_val*. The following pointer declaration obtains that address and assigns it to the pointer *p_char*:

```
char *p_char = &char_val; /* assign address of char_val to pointer p_char */
```

The variable *p_char* is now said to be "pointing to" *char_val,* like this:

You can see that the value of *p_char* is the address of *char_val*, not the contents (*'S'*). Diagrams like this can be helpful, both in learning about pointers and in designing *pointer* data structures.

A double-quoted string constant may be used to initialize a *pointer to type char* variable, just as it is used to initialize a *static, SEMIGLOBAL,* or *GLOBAL* array of characters. The following diagram illustrates the difference in how the initializer is stored in memory in these two cases.

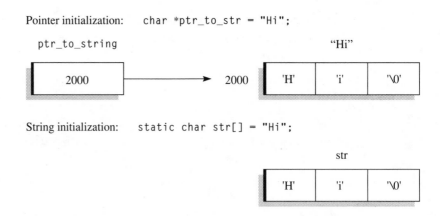

Pointer initialization:   `char *ptr_to_str = "Hi";`

String initialization:   `static char str[] = "Hi";`

In this example, the initialization of *ptr_to_string* simply assigns the address value of the string to that pointer, whereas the initialization of the string *str* actually copies the bytes of the initializer into the bytes reserved for the character string *str*. In C, you can use a string constant such as *"Hi"* as an initializer to assign either the address of the string to a pointer or a constant array of characters to a character string. The type of initialization is determined by the data type of the identifier being declared. (Addresses are assigned to pointers, and characters are copied into arrays.)

## Assignment to Pointers

Initializers are only one way to assign values to pointers. We can also use assignment expressions to assign values to pointer variables *after* they have been declared.

We've already seen the & operator used to obtain the address of a scalar or an element of an array (Chapters 2 and 3). Well, we can assign the resulting *pointer expression* to a variable that has been declared to point to the data type of that scalar or element, as in this example:

```
long long_val, *p_long;
char buffer[80], *p_buffer;

p_long = &long_val;      /* p_long now points to long_val */
p_buffer = &buffer[2];   /* p_buffer points to third byte of buffer */
```

The value of a pointer can even be assigned to another pointer of the same type, like this:

```
double discount;
double *p_discount = &discount, *p_perc_off;      /* declare pointers */

p_perc_off = p_discount;          /* assign a pointer to a pointer */
```

Now both *pointers to type double*, *p_discount* and *p_perc_off*, point to the same location: the address of *discount*.

Once again, we need to keep in mind a couple of DON'Ts:

- Don't assign a pointer declared for one data type to a pointer variable that has been declared for a different data type. Your CPU's memory-alignment requirements may cause the address you are assigning to be rounded to a boundary suitable for the data type pointed to (for example, an address divisible by 4 for type *long* data), and the pointer variable might therefore receive an address other than the one you intended.

- Don't assign a pointer value to a non-pointer variable. It's senseless, it makes your code confusing to read, and it can also cause alignment problems. (It will also generate a warning message from the compiler!)

## Accessing Data Indirectly

Let's look more closely at how we go about accessing the data a pointer is pointing to, so that we can begin to use pointers in real programs.

The familiar *PEEK* and *POKE* functions from BASIC permit you to examine and change a specific byte in memory if you know the address of that byte. C has an analogous and more powerful feature known as indirection. The unary *indirection operator* (*) is used on a pointer to obtain or alter the value it points to, so the expression *p_var* could be read as "the contents of the location *p_var* points to." The operator is called *indirection* because it uses the pointer's value (an address) to obtain the value of the variable the pointer points to, rather than using the direct route, the variable itself.

Let's look at some examples of indirection. Observe how the pointer *p_credit_code* is used to indirectly examine and modify the value of *credit_code* in the program on the next page.

```
/* View and change a variable through a pointer to it. */
#include <stdio.h>

void main(void)
    {
    char credit_code = 'B', old_credit_code;
    char *p_credit_code = &credit_code;

    old_credit_code = *p_credit_code;      /* PEEK at credit code */
    *p_credit_code = 'A';                  /* POKE new credit code */
    printf("Credit Code is now %c. Credit Code formerly was %c.\n",
        credit_code, old_credit_code);
    }
```

Notice that the line of output from *printf()* reflects the changes made to *credit_code* through the pointer variable *p_credit_code*:

```
Credit Code is now A. Credit Code formerly was B.
```

Once a pointer is assigned the address of a variable, all indirect references using that pointer ( *\*p_credit_code*, in our example) refer to the variable itself, not to a copy of the variable's value, so the original value of *credit_code* stored in memory ('B') is actually *replaced* with the new value ('A'). Now you can understand why C requires that pointers be declared to point to a specific data type: The data type that a pointer is declared to point to and that of the expression made up of the unary indirection operator (\*) acting on that pointer variable will always be the same.

Here's another example, using the same pointer in a conditional application. (Since A has the lowest ASCII value of the alphabet, we have to decrement, not increment, to raise the credit rating.)

```
if (*p_credit_code > 'A')   /* If not at top credit level, raise credit */
    --(*p_credit_code);     /*   code one grade. (A has lowest ASCII */
                            /*   value of the alphabet.) */
```

Remember: What is decremented in this example is the contents of the *char* variable, *not* the pointer address. (The parentheses in the second line are for readability only. They have no effect because unary operators like -- and \* group from right to left.)

Now to see what we can actually *do* with pointers. We'll take only a quick peek here and then devote the next few chapters to the details.

## Passing Pointer Arguments

The value of a pointer variable is an expression and therefore may be passed as an argument to a function—a fact that explains how *array* arguments are passed to functions. Let's look at how this works.

Arrays and pointers are closely related in C. In fact, whenever you use the name of an array in any expression, the value of the array name is taken to be the starting address of the array, which is in effect a pointer to its zeroth element. Thus, if *str* is an array of characters and *p_str* is a pointer to type *char*, these two statements are equivalent:

```
p_str = str;
p_str = &str[0];
```

Here's another example of this equivalence. The following three calls to the library function *strcpy()* all cause the text *This is it.* to be assigned to *str*.

```
char str[80];
char *p_str = str;        /* same as: char *p_str = &str[0]; */

strcpy(str, "This is it.");
strcpy(&str[0], "This is it.");
strcpy(p_str, "This is it.");
```

## Returning Pointer Values

Functions can also *return* a pointer value. Library string functions often take advantage of this capability by returning a pointer to one of their arguments, which then can be passed to other library functions to be used in constructing larger, more complex expressions. For example, in this next statement, *strcpy()* returns the starting address of the string it copies to, which is its first argument. This means that you can copy *"This is it."* to *str* and then print *str*, all with one statement:

```
printf("str = %s\n", strcpy(str, "This is it."));
```

### C A U T I O N

*You can easily write tricky, hard-to-read, hard-to-debug code using pointers, so good style and readability are especially important here.*

Here's what actually happens in this example: The starting address of *str* is passed to *strcpy()*, which copies the message *"This is it."* to *str* and returns *str*'s starting address to the calling function. This value is then passed to *printf()* as the starting address of the string it should print. Pointers allowed us to get a lot of mileage out of that one line of code!

## Returning more than one value

Regardless of the number of arguments passed to a function, C's return-value mechanism permits the function to return only a single value. Scalar (non-array) arguments to a C subfunction are passed as copies of their individual values. Changes the subfunction makes to its *copy* of a passed value have no effect on the original value owned and passed by the caller.

But there are times when we need to be able to return more than one value from a function. For example, we might need to keep a tally of the function's main activity, in the same manner as the library function *scanf()*, which returns a count of the number of legal values that were input, as well as the values themselves. How can we handle such a situation? Well, fortunately, C's pointer data type provides a neat solution to the problem. We'll use an example from our order-entry application to see how a subfunction can actually save a value in a calling function's variable if the calling function passes the *address* of its variable rather than the value itself.

The function *inv_find()* from the *stubs.c* source file is passed a part number to find. If it is successful, it passes back a description, price, and shipping weight, as well as a verification that a valid part was found in the inventory list:

```
flag inv_find(
    char part[],        /* part number to look up (passed in) */
    char part_desc[],   /* description of part (returned) */
    money *p_price,     /* pointer to unit price of part (returned) */
    short *p_ship_wt)   /* pointer to shipping weight in ounces (returned) */

    {

    /* Return typical data to test inv_find()'s callers. */
    strcpy(part_desc, "Order-Entry Software Package");
    *p_price = 12345L;
    *p_ship_wt = 123;
    return (part[0] == 'S');      /* YES if 'S' first, else NO */
    }
```

The four lines relevant to this discussion are the declarations and assignments for the pointers *p_price* and *p_ship_wt*. The variable *p_price* is declared as *pointer to type money* (that is, *pointer to type long*). It is used to pass the "typical" price *12345L* back to the calling function. The *pointer to type short, p_ship_wt*, is used to pass *123* back to the *short* integer *ship_weights[ipart]* whose address was passed to *inv_find()* in the following expression from *ord_itms()*:

```
part_found = (bflag)((step_rtn == STEPOK) &&
   inv_find(parts[ipart], part_descs[ipart],
   &prices[ipart], &ship_weights[ipart]));
```

The third argument to *inv_find()*, *&prices[ipart]*, is the address of a *long* integer in the array *prices*, an expression of type *pointer to long*; and the third parameter of *inv_find()*, *p_price*, is declared as type *pointer to long* (since *money* is defined in *ordentry.h* as *long*). Thus argument and associated parameter are both of the same type. This is true for all of *inv_find()*'s other arguments as well.

The declaration of the argument and return types for *inv_find()* in the header file *ordentry.h* reads:

```
extern  int inv_find(char *part, char *part_desc, long *p_price,
   short *p_ship_wt);
```

This prototype declaration permits the compiler to verify that you have passed the right number of arguments of the right data types to *inv_find()* and that you have used *inv_find()*'s return value correctly.

Now here's what happens to one of the variables when the program is executed. The address of a *long*, *prices[ipart]*, is passed to the third parameter, *p_price*. Then *p_price* is used in the statement *\*p_price=12345L;* to assign *12345L* to the *long* whose address was passed, namely *prices[ipart]*. The following diagram that describes memory just after the *\*p_price=12345L;* statement assigns *12345L* to *prices[ipart]* may make this clearer:

Memory owned
by *ord_itms()*,
the caller function:

prices[ipart]

1006        12345L

Memory owned
by *inv_find()*,
the called function:

2400        1600    1006

p_price

So that's how the interaction between the calling function that passes an address argument and the called function's pointer parameter enables the called function to assign data back to the calling function's variable. Actually, you've already used this technique with one-dimensional arrays, perhaps without realizing it.

Now let's look at some more powerful applications of the array and pointer constructs: multidimensional arrays and arrays of pointers.

# Advanced Arrays

C's implementation of arrays is far more flexible than the examples you've seen so far. For instance, you can declare arrays of as many dimensions as you like (although more than two or three dimensions are hard for most of us to visualize), and you can create arrays of pointers to data.

When would you use such advanced arrays? Well, here's one very practical example from the business world.

Suppose you open a small business to sell custom software. You decide to hire a salesperson to take care of marketing so that you can concentrate on application development. After a year, you want to get a picture of how the business is going and whether there are any seasonal fluctuations in sales. To help you analyze the monthly sales record, you could use a one-dimensional array of 12 *long* integers, each of which is one month's total sales. (If you use a defined constant for the dimension in the array's declaration, your code will be more flexible.)

```
#define MONTHS 12
/* ... */
long sales_total[MONTHS];
```

But as your business grows and you hire new salespeople, you'll probably want to compare their sales records. Now there are two dimensions to your analysis, so you'll need an array with a row for each salesperson and a column for each month. Your modified array declaration will look like this:

```
#define SALESPEOPLE 4
#define MONTHS 12
/* ... */
long sales_total[SALESPEOPLE][MONTHS];
```

As business continues to increase and data accumulate, you can continue to add new dimensions to your array, to broaden your sales analysis. For instance, if you also want to analyze sales for each product over a period of years, your declaration might become:

```
#define SALESPEOPLE 4
#define YEARS 5
#define MONTHS 12
#define PRODUCTS 3
/* ... */
long sales_total[SALESPEOPLE][YEARS][MONTHS][PRODUCTS];
```

What we've actually been doing in these examples is using multi-dimensional arrays as in-memory databases to store and access tables of numbers and characters.

## Declaring Multidimensional Arrays

You probably noticed that the array declarations from our scenario look a little different from those you are used to. C does not use a comma-separated list of indices, as many other languages do, to declare the dimensions of an array or to access one of its elements. Instead, C requires that you supply a pair of square brackets (*[]*) for each dimension. Let's look at some examples.

The following code segment declares the identifier *matrix* to be a two-row, three-column array of *short* integers and assigns the numbers 0 through 5 to its elements:

```
short matrix[2][3], row, col;

for (row = 0; row < 2; ++row)
    for (col = 0; col < 3; ++col)
        matrix[row][col] = row * 3 + col;
```

This is how the data for *matrix* would be stored:

| | Column 0 | Column 1 | Column 2 |
|---|---|---|---|
| Row 0 | *0* | *1* | *2* |
| Row 1 | *3* | *4* | *5* |

The diagram shows that *matrix[1][2]* (read as *matrix sub one sub two*) is equal to 5. (Remember that the first row and column have index 0, not 1.)

Now suppose we want to display the elements of *matrix* in an actual matrix format. This next code segment does that for us:

```
for (row = 0; row < 2; ++row)        /* loop through each row */
  {
  for (col = 0; col < 3; ++col)            /* for each column, */
    printf("%d  ", matrix[row][col]);   /* print the element */
  putchar('\n');                       /* skip a line at the end of the row */
  }
```

The output from our routine will look like this:

```
0 1 2
3 4 5
```

Like their one-dimensional counterparts, multidimensional arrays with *auto* storage class cannot be initialized. However, in this next example, *matrix* has *static* storage class, so the same values could be assigned by an initializer:

```
static short matrix[2][3] = {0, 1, 2,
                             3, 4, 5};
```

Note that, as with one-dimensional arrays, the elements of each row can be grouped in curly braces. If you choose to do that and you have more than one row, you must separate the groups of rows with commas and surround the entire initialization with curly braces. And here too, if you supply fewer initializers than elements, the remaining elements are automatically initialized to zero. The following is a two-dimensional array that is initialized with the rows grouped in braces:

```
static short matrix[2][3] = {{0,1,2},{3,4,5}};
```

The syntax for declaring explicitly initialized *static* or *extern* multidimensional arrays allows us to omit the size of the first dimension.

In that case, the number of initializers will determine the size of the array. But empty brackets *must* be included in the declaration, to mark the place of the omitted dimension:

```
static short matrix[][3] = {0, 1, 2,
                            3, 4, 5}
```

There are two other instances where empty brackets are permitted in array declarations. One is when you import an array (using *IMPORT*) that was declared with *SEMIGLOBAL* or *GLOBAL* storage class:

```
SEMIGLOBAL short matrix[][3] = {0, 1, 2,      /* outside all functions */
                                3, 4, 5};
/* ... */
IMPORT short matrix[][3];
```

and the other is when you declare an array parameter within a function, as in this next program that sums each row of a two-dimensional array of *short integers*. (C does require us to decide how many elements are in each row—that is, how many columns our array will have. We'll use three columns for this example.) Remember that the *IMPORT*, *SEMIGLOBAL*, and *GLOBAL* storage classes are terms that we have defined in the *syntypes.h* header file. See Chapter 7 for more information.

```
#include <stdio.h>
#define NCOLS 3

/* Sum rows of an n-row, 3-column array of short integers. */
void main(void)
    {
    static short matrix[][NCOLS] = {0, 1, 2,
                                    3, 4, 5};
    short nrows = 2;
    show_sums(matrix, nrows);
    }
show_sums(
    short matrix[][NCOLS],    /* array of rows to sum */
    short nrows)              /* number of rows to sum */

    {
    short irow, icol, sum;

    for (irow = 0; irow < nrows; ++irow)
        {
        for (sum = icol = 0; icol < NCOLS; ++icol)
            sum += matrix[irow][icol];
        printf("Sum of row %d is %d.\n", irow, sum);
        }
    }
```

This two-function program outputs these two lines of text:

```
Sum of row 0 is 3.
Sum of row 1 is 12.
```

Each row of a two-dimensional (2D) array of any data type is actually a one-dimensional array and therefore may be used in any expression where a one-dimensional array would be legal. (The fact that 2D arrays are actually stored in memory as two 1D row arrays explains why it is impossible to treat a *column* of a 2D array as an array.) This ability to manipulate array cross-sections greatly increases the flexibility of string arrays in C programs. In this chapter, we'll see how to use this technique to create a list of salespeople by storing one name in each row of the array.

## Multidimensional Arrays of Characters

Our previous version of the *pw_find()* function from *stubs.c* merely checked to be sure that the first letters of the user name and password were equal to 'S'. Now that we know how to work with multidimensional arrays, we can modify *pw_find()* so that it will search a list of names for the complete user name we want to validate and then compare the password entered by the user with the correct password for that name. Here's how it's done:

```
static char user_names[][20] = {"Dan", "Mary", "Greg", ""};
static char passwords[][10] = {"tuna", "piano", "fish"};
short iname;

for (iname = 0; iname < 20 && user_names[iname][0]; ++iname)
   if (0 == strcmp(user, user_names[iname]))   /* name found? */
      return (0 == strcmp(password, passwords[iname]));
return (NO);
```

The array *user_names* in this example has four rows, each 20 bytes wide. The empty brackets set the number of initializers to the number of rows—in this case, four. Each row's initializer (the name) has fewer than 20 bytes; any unused bytes in the row are filled with null characters. The last row, *user_names[3]*, is completely filled with null characters to mark the end of the list. During program execution, the *for* loop test checks the first byte of each name for the null character to see if the final name has been reached.

Both calls to *strcmp()* in the addition to *pw_find()* pass two strings: the string to check and a row from one of the 2D arrays to compare it with. The second call to *strcmp()* (within the *return* statement) compares the password entered with the password for the user whose name is known from the first call. Then *pw_find()* compares the return from *strcmp()* with 0 (remember, *strcmp()* returns a negative value if the first string sorts lower in the ASCII scale than the second, it returns a positive value if it sorts higher, or it returns zero if both strings are identical), and returns either 1 (true) or 0 (false). If *pw_find()* couldn't match the string to check with a name from the array of user names, it returns NO (which is defined as 0).

The order-entry application uses two other 2D arrays of characters, *parts* and *part_descs*, for holding part numbers and part descriptions, respectively. Their declarations in *ordbuild.c* read:

```
SEMIGLOBAL char parts[MAX_ITEMS][L_PARTS + 1] = {""};
SEMIGLOBAL char part_descs[MAX_ITEMS][L_PART_DESC + 1] = {""};
```

The function *ord_itms()* (also in *ordbuild.c*) calls the function *inv_find()* to pass rows of these arrays, like this:

```
part_found = (bflag)((step_rtn == STEPOK) &&
    inv_find(parts[ipart], part_descs[ipart],
    &prices[ipart], &ship_weights[ipart]));
```

# Arrays of Pointers

Now let's look at a different kind of array: the *array of pointers*. This structure gives C programmers another means of storing a collection of strings under a single name. Since each row in a conventional 2D array of characters has enough storage allocated to it to hold the longest string and all rows must be the same length, this construct wastes space if the strings in each row do not completely fill the row. When a set of strings is pointed to by the elements of an array of pointers, however, we don't have this problem. Let's see how this approach works.

# Pointers to strings

We've already modified *pw_find()* to work with two-dimensional arrays of characters. Now we're going to modify it again, this time declaring *user_names* and *passwords* as arrays of *pointers to type char*. The following is the new body for *pw_find()*.

```
static char *user_names[] = {"Dan", "Mary", "Greg", NULL};
static char *passwords[] = {"tuna", "piano", "fish"};
short iname;
for (iname = 0; iname < 20 && user_names[iname] != NULL; ++iname)
   if (0 == strcmp(user, user_names[iname]))    /* name found? */
      return (0 == strcmp(password, passwords[iname]));
return (NO);
```

Notice that although the declarations have been modified, the two calls to *strcmp()* use the same arguments in both versions. The difference is that now *user_names* is a one-dimensional array of *pointers*, whereas before it was a two-dimensional array of characters, and the expression *user_names[iname]* now has the data type *pointer to type char*. Let's look at a diagram of the new *user_names* data structure:

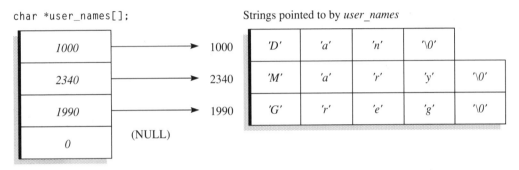

You'll have noticed that the last initializer for *user_names* is now *NULL*, rather than empty quotation marks. The symbol *NULL* is defined in the library header file *stdio.h* as the integer 0 and is often used to mark the end of an array of pointers so that the number of elements need not be saved in a separate variable. It is perfectly safe to end a list of pointers with *NULL* because the compiler ensures that no variable or string constant in your program is assigned *NULL* as its address.

## C A U T I O N

*Do not confuse the NULL pointer with the null character. Both are used by convention to end an array and both have the numeric value zero, but the NULL pointer 0 is an integer used to end an array of pointers, whereas the null character '\0' is a single byte used to end an array of characters.*

You've already seen how you can change the value of a string in a 2D character array by using the library functions *strcpy()* and *strncpy()* (Chapter 14) or by using the assignment operator on one character at a time (Chapter 3). But this isn't always the best way to change a string pointed to from an array of pointers. Let's look at an example.

The strings pointed to by elements of *user_names* in the following line of code cannot be changed because they are constants:

```
static char *user_names[] = {"Dan", "Mary", "Greg", NULL};
```

If you want to make the second element of *user_names* point to *Marie* instead of *Mary*, you can't copy the *ie* from *Marie* over the *y* in *Mary*; instead, you assign a new value to *user_names[1]*, like this:

```
user_names[1] = "Marie";
```

Had the elements of *user_names* been made to *point to* string variables instead of string constants, we could have assigned new values to those strings through the individual elements of *user_names*. But because *user_names* points to string constants, the whole string must be replaced in order to change any characters.

When you need to examine a character from the middle of a string pointed to from an array, you can access the character by using the one-dimensional array of *pointers to type char* as though it were in a two-dimensional array of characters. For example, to obtain the *r* in *Marie* from the *user_names* array, you use the following expression, which yields a value of type *char* (not an array or a string):

```
user_names[1][2]
```

If you need to use the address of a character from within *user_names* in a larger expression, the syntax should by now be no surprise. The next two code fragments test for *"ie"* after the *'r'* in *"Marie"*:

```
if (0 == strcmp(&user_names[1][3], "ie"))
```

or

```
if (0 == strcmp(strchr(user_names[1], 'r'), "ie"))
```

Now that you understand the basics of the *array of pointers* data structure, let's look at a common application: obtaining command-line arguments passed to *main()*.

# Command-line arguments

The command line is the line of text you type to direct the operating system to execute your compiled and linked C program. (The command line also may come from a DOS batch file or a UNIX shell script rather than from keyboard input.) The first word on the command line is the name of the executable file (for DOS, omit the *.EXE* extension). The name of the executable file and any additional strings of text on the command line, except file-redirection commands, are gathered and passed as arguments to *main()*. Thus command-line arguments are simply strings passed from the command line to your *main()* function. (Your *main()* function may choose to ignore these arguments if they aren't appropriate to the environment, thus helping to preserve the portability of your programs.)

The processing of the command line, before it is passed to *main()*, involves placing the words that are separated by white space (spaces and tab characters) into individual strings. (This process of character checking and string isolating is known as *parsing* the command line for its arguments.) Wildcard characters that appear in file-name arguments will (if you link with *\LIB\SETARGV*, which we'll discuss shortly) be expanded to the file names they match. The new data structure that is built from the command line and passed is actually an array of *pointers to type char*. (If you want to pass an argument that contains white space, you must surround that argument with double quotes.) Let's see how we can use this new structure to obtain command-line arguments.

## Declaring command-line parameters

The changes you must make to your *main()* to obtain command-line data are minor, and no additional compiler options need to be specified. The declaration of the parameters for *main()* is no different than for any other function: *main()*'s parameters, and only its parameters, must be declared before its opening curly brace. A typical *main()* function definition would look like this:

```
void main(
    unsigned ac, /* Argument count. 1 if no arguments were given, because */
              /*   the command (program) name counts as the first argument. */
    char *av[]) /* Argument vector. av[0] points to the command name, av[1] */
              /*   points to the first argument, av[2] the second, ... */
    {
```

The data passed to *main()* are in string form and so can be copied and compared using the standard library string functions. For example, if you want to allow the first argument to *main()* to be the switch *-s*, you would instruct your program to copy the second command-line argument to a string variable. This is shown in the following example, which uses the string variable *arg*.

```
if (ac < 2 && 0 == strcmp(av[1], "-s"))      /* test first argument */
    strcpy(arg, av[2]);   /* copy second argument to arg */
```

## Obtaining numeric data

Let's take these concepts one step further and use them in a real program that uses numeric data from the command line. The example we'll use is a reindenting program that changes the number of spaces used for each level of indenting from some previous number to a new one. This program can be used to reformat C source files that are indented with spaces (but not with tab characters).

Numbers you get from the command line will be in string form and must be converted to internal binary format before they can be used for counting. The library functions *sscanf()* (for *scanf()* strings) and *atoi()* (ASCII to integer) both can do this for us. We'll use *atoi()* because it is simpler and smaller than *sscanf()*, so we can save some space and end up with less code. Here is the source file *rein.c*:

```
/***************************************************************************
 * REIN reindents C programs, converting from one number of spaces per
 *   indent to another. REIN is a filter. The following call converts from 5
 *   spaces per indent to 3:
 *     REIN 5 3 < OLDPGM.C > NEWPGM.C
 ***************************************************************************
 */

#include <stdio.h>

main(                  /* main() is passed two parameters */
    unsigned ac,       /* command line argument count; 1 if no arguments */
    char *av[])        /* array of pointers to strings from command line */
                       /* av[0] is program name REIN, av[1] is first arg */
    {
    char buf[BUFSIZ];
    short old_indent, new_indent, indent, new_spc;
```

*(continued)*

282

REIN.C *continued*

```
    if (ac != 3)
        {
        printf("\aUsage: REIN #_old_indent #_new_indent\n");
        exit(0);   /* terminate the program */
        }

    old_indent = atoi(av[1]);     /* convert command-line numbers */
    new_indent = atoi(av[2]);     /* from string to binary */
    if (old_indent < 1 !! new_indent < 1)
        {
        printf("\aREIN: Pass two numbers, both > 0\n");
        exit(0);   /* terminate the program */
        }
    while (gets(buf))   /* loop for each input line */
        {

        /* Count leading spaces. */
        for (indent = 0; buf[indent] == ' '; ++indent)
            ;
        new_spc = indent * new_indent / old_indent;
        while (new_spc--)               /* print new leading spaces */
            putchar(' ');
        puts(&buf[indent]);             /* print rest of line after spaces */
        }
    }
```

To use this program to reindent the source file *oldpgm.c* from five spaces per level to three and direct the output to the file *newpgm.c*, simply enter this command line:

```
REIN 5 3 < OLDPGM.C > NEWPGM.C
```

The following diagram illustrates the way the data will be passed to the reindenting program's *main()* function.

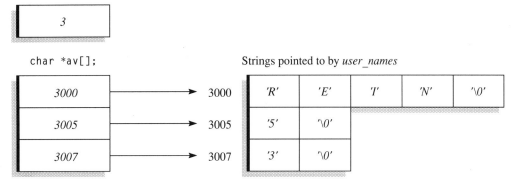

---

# C O M M E N T

*If you are using MS-DOS version 3.0 or later, the first argument on any command line is the drive specification and the program's full path name. For example, each time you execute the* rein *program from the root directory of the C: drive,* av[0] *equals* ''C:\rein.''

---

## Wildcard characters in file names

The characters *∗* and *?* are wildcards in DOS—that is, they represent any other character when used in a file name or extension. The *∗* represents any series of (zero or more) characters in the file's first name or extension, but not the period between them. The *?* represents any single character.

The following program, *wildcard.c*, outputs each of its command-line arguments by calling *printf()*. It is similar to the *ECHO* command in DOS, unless we link the object code from *wildcard.c* with a special object file named *\setargv.obj*, which can be found in the LIB directory.

The object code in *\setargv.obj* does additional processing on the command line; it expands the *∗* and *?* wildcards in file names.

```
/* wildcard.c:  Expand wildcards on command line and show file names. */
#include <stdio.h>

void main(unsigned ac, char *av[])
    {
    short ifile;

    for (ifile = 1; ifile < ac; ++ifile)
        printf("%s\n", av[ifile]);
    }
```

Because the *CL* command accepts object files and C source files as arguments, you would expect this *CL* command to compile *wildcard.c* and link it with *setargv.obj*:

```
CL WILDCARD.C \LIB\SETARGV.OBJ
```

But it does not succeed. Instead, the linker gives this error:

```
C:\LIB\SLIBCE.LIB(dos\stdargv.asm) : error L2044: __setargv :
    symbol multiply defined, use /NOE
```

The linker maintains an internal extended dictionary (a list of the locations of library functions) that it uses to speed up library searches. This internal list already contains an entry for a dummy *setargv()* function that does not expand wildcards, so when you give an additional *setargv()* function, the linker reports that it has multiple definitions of *setargv()*. The solution is to instruct the linker not to search its extended dictionary by supplying the */NOEXTDICTIONARY* switch (abbreviated */NOE*). The */link* switch for *CL* is the means for giving linker options, such as */NOE* or additional library names:

```
CL WILDCARD.C \LIB\SETARGV.OBJ /link /NOE
```

You can use the properly linked *wildcard* program to list the names of all files with the extension *.h* in the directory *\include\sys* on drive C:

```
C>wildcard \include\sys\*.h
\include\sys\LOCKING.H
\include\sys\STAT.H
\include\sys\TIMEB.H
\include\sys\TYPES.H
\include\sys\UTIME.H

C>
```

## Variations in command-line mechanisms

Some C environments differ in their handling of command-line arguments. For instance, the name of the program is not always passed as the first vector argument, *av[0]*. And some programmers use the name *argc*, instead of *ac*, for the argument count, and *argv*, instead of *av*, for the argument-vector array. Except for readability, it makes absolutely no difference what you name *ac* and *av*; it is their data types that are important to the compiler.

Many, but not all, C compilers pass a third argument called the *environment vector*. (Microsoft's C under MS-DOS and C under UNIX both support environment variables and pass an environment pointer as the third argument to the *main()* function.) The argument strings passed are the definitions for operating-system environment variables—data that come from outside your program.

Environment variables are maintained by the operating system from the time they are created in *AUTOEXEC.BAT* onward: They are not erased at the termination of a program. These variables actually represent another source of input data for your program. The programs that compose the Microsoft compiler use environment variables to hold file-directory paths and options.

We've already discussed use of the MS-DOS *SET* command to assign a value to an environment variable (Chapter 8). You can also use the C library function *putenv()* to do this within your program, and you can call the library function *getenv()* to find out an environment variable's present value (or to find out if that variable exists at all). See your compiler manual for the proper use of these functions.

Environment data take the same structure as the command-line argument vector: an *array of pointers to type char*. To include the environment vector, simply declare a third parameter to *main()* with the same type as the second parameter. The program *env.c* lists all environment variables:

```
/* env.c:  Show list of environment variables. */
#include <stdio.h>

void main(unsigned ac, char *av[], char *ev[])
    {
    short ienv;

    for (ienv = 0; ev[ienv] != NULL; ++ienv)
        printf("%s\n", ev[ienv]);
    }
```

Earlier I stated that all programs after Chapter 5 compile with strict checking and give no errors or warnings but that *env.c* is an exception. I know of no way to avoid the following two warnings in *env.c*, since you can't write a function definition that ignores its first two parameters without getting two warnings when you compile with the highest warning level:

```
env.c(9) : warning C4100: 'ac' : unreferenced formal parameter
env.c(9) : warning C4100: 'av' : unreferenced formal parameter
```

Here are my results from the execution of *env*. Your output may differ.

```
C>env
PROMPT=[$p]
PATH=E:\;C:\UTIL;C:\DOS;C:\BIN;C:\
LIB=C:\LIB
INCLUDE=C:\INCLUDE
TMP=E:\
CL=/W3
C>
```

The multidimensional array and array-of-pointers structures we studied in this chapter permit you to build large lists of data in memory, provided all the elements in any array are of the same data type. Powerful as these constructs are, they still impose some limitations on data management, so C has also provided for structures that allow you to combine data elements of *different* types. We'll discuss those next.

# Structures: The Unifying Data Type

C's *structure* data type allows us to combine scalar and array data of many data types under a single name. In addition, C allows us to simplify management of structures with large numbers of elements by organizing them into substructures, much as we organize files into directories. Let's see how structures can be used to manipulate complex combinations of data in an understandable fashion.

First of all, just what are structures? Are they like records in a file, with fields of different types of data? Well, yes and no. Structures do resemble records, but they are actually better suited to in-memory data manipulation than to holding data being read from or written to files by library functions. The reasons for this distinction will become clearer as we go along.

To learn how to create and use structures, we'll write a screen-painting function that combines a cursor location (row and column numbers) with the text of a message to be displayed beginning at that location, and then we'll declare, initialize, and pass an array of such messages.

# Declaring Structures

As you can see from the following example, there are usually two steps to declaring a structure:

```
struct term_msg        /* declare structure tag term_msg */
   {
   short row, col;      /* screen location */
   char *msg;           /* message to display */
   };
```

The first step declares the *structure tag*, which is simply a name that can be used as a new data type. This step in the declaration process consumes no program memory and is optional. Its sole purpose is to give meaning to the name. Once a structure tag is declared, you can use it whenever you want to declare a structure of that type.

## C O M M E N T

*It is good style to always declare a structure tag, even though doing so is optional. It contributes greatly to the clarity of your source code.*

The *tag declaration* defines the actual structure by declaring the elements, or *members*, of the structure inside a set of braces. Notice the position of the structure tag *outside* the opening brace that marks the declaration of the members of the structure, and the required semicolon following the closing brace of the declaration.

From now on, we can use the tag *term_msg* (for terminal message) to declare structures exactly as though *struct term_msg* were a new data type, as in this example of declaring a structure named *form*:

```
struct term_msg form;
```

You should place structure-tag declarations used in more than one source file in a header file that is included everywhere the structure type is used. This method makes it possible for functions in many different source files to use the declarations without making additional copies of them and also significantly reduces the effort involved in adding a new member to a structure.

## Accessing Members of Structures

The *dot operator* (.) is used to access members of a structure. The name of the structure is the left operand, and the name of the member of that structure is the right operand. The dot operator is a primary operator: None has higher precedence. Both as a matter of style and as a reminder of their precedence, we don't use spaces around primary operators:

```
form.row += 2;
form.col = 18;
form.msg = "Street";
```

## Assignment to Structures

Structure declarations can have initializers, provided the structures are not declared as *auto* storage class. The syntax is the same as for array initializers, and here again, if fewer initializers are provided than there are structure members, the remaining members are automatically initialized to zero.

The following example is a *static* version of our structure *form*, declared with an initializer:

```
static struct term_msg form = {4, 10, "Customer Name"};
```

Memory would typically be allocated to the members of the *form* structure from left to right, like this:

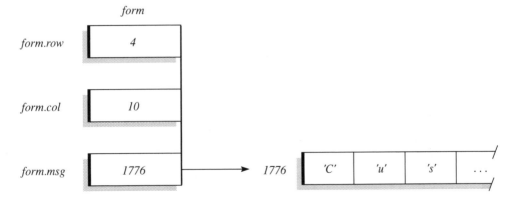

The Microsoft C compiler also permits us to assign an entire structure to another. For example, we could declare two instances of our *form* structure, initialize one, and assign the values of its members to the uninitialized version, like this:

```
static struct term_msg form_one = {6, 10, "Company Name"};
struct term_msg form_buf;

form_buf = form_one;    /* structure assignment, equivalent to: */
                        /*    form_buf.row = form_one.row; */
                        /*    form_buf.col = form_one.col; */
                        /*    form_buf.msg = form_one.msg; */
```

# C O M M E N T

*Assigning one structure to another is a new feature that comes by way of ANSI; however, its use limits the portability of your code to only those compilers that support structure assignment.*

## Nesting Structures

As I mentioned earlier, a member of a structure can itself be a structure, making it possible for us to simplify large or complex structures by grouping related members into substructures that can then be declared within other structures.

Let's change our *term_msg* structure to include such a nested structure for the cursor row and column locations, just to see how this construct works:

```
struct cur_loc        /* declare structure tag cur_loc for cursor position */
   {
   short row, col;    /* screen location */
   };

struct term_msg       /* declare structure tag term_msg for display */
   {
   struct cur_loc cursor;
   char *msg;         /* message to display */
   };
```

If we now were to write a program containing the structure declaration *struct term_msg hello;* we could make assignments to its members using the following member-name syntax.

```
hello.cursor.row = 12;
hello.cursor.col = 30;
hello.msg = "WELCOME TO THE PROGRAM!";
```

It looks as though our *term_msg* structure is becoming useful enough to be placed in a header file. But let's wait a bit: There's more.

# Arrays of Structures

The usefulness of the *term_msg* structure is still somewhat limited in its present form. However, if we used an *array* of *term_msg* structures, we could paint an entire screen. Here's how it's done.

As with ordinary arrays, *static* or *external* arrays of structures can be dimensioned by their initializers: That is, if they are declared with empty brackets, they simply take their dimensions from the number of initializers. The following example that uses data from the source file *pnt_ship.c* shows a declaration (which could have been used in the *pnt_ship_pay()* order-entry function) for some of the field titles painted on the screen.

```
static struct term_msg form_names[] =
    {
    4, 10, "Customer Name",
    6, 10, "Company Name",
    9, 10, "Shipping Weight",

    /* ... */
    0, 0, NULL
    };
```

The 0 row and column numbers plus the *NULL* pointer mark the end of the list of messages in the *form_names* array of *term_msg* structures.

To access specific members in the elements of an array of structures, we use a slightly different form of array subscript:

```
form_names[imsg].row
form_names[imsg].msg
```

The square brackets used to obtain the structure array element with index *imsg* are applied directly to *form_names*, because it is the *structure* that is declared as an array, not its members. Therefore, the entire structure is repeated in memory for each array element as shown by the following diagram.

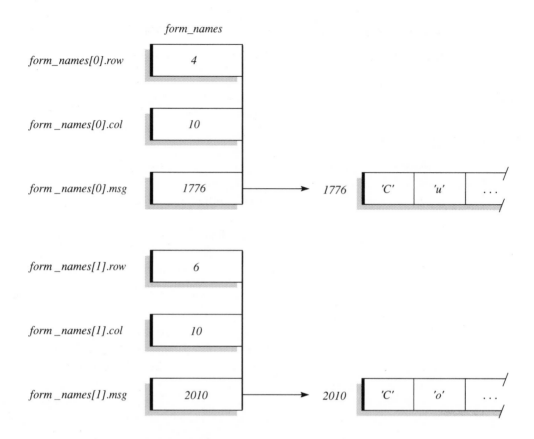

## Structures as Arguments

Another new ANSI feature supported by Microsoft C is the ability to pass structure arguments to a function. Normally, when you pass a structure argument, a complete copy of that structure is made. (You would need to use a copy of a structure if you wanted to make temporary changes to the values of its members without altering the original structure.) However, if a copy is not needed, you can pass only the address of the structure instead.

To see how this works, let's look closely at an example of the *scrn_pnt()* function, which does not return a value and which takes an array of *term_msg* structures as its single argument.

```
struct term_msg          /* declare structure tag term_msg */
   {
   short row, col;       /* screen location to display message */
   char *msg;            /* message to display at the location */
   };

extern void s_tput(struct term_msg *);   /* structure version of tput() */

/* Paint the screen with an array of field names. */
void scrn_pnt(struct term_msg form[])
   {
   short imsg;
   for (imsg = 0; form.msg != NULL; ++imsg)
      s_tput(&form[imsg]);   /* pass structure address to s_tput() */

/* The structure version of tput() prints a message on the screen by */
/*   calling the order-entry project utility library function tput(). */
void s_tput(
   struct term_msg *p_form)  /* p_form is a pointer to a term_msg structure */
   {
   tput(p_form->row, p_form->col, p_form->msg);
   }
```

The processing performed by *scrn_pnt()* consists of looping to obtain each *term_msg* until one with a NULL pointer is encountered. Each *term_msg* in the array *form* is passed to the function *s_tput()*, which is declared right after *scrn_pnt()* in the previous listing. The *primary structure operator* (–>) used with *tput()* in *s_tput()* allows the program to directly access a member whose address is known, without using the structure name with the dot operator.

The arrow operator (a minus sign immediately followed by a greater-than symbol) is provided as a *convenience*: Its job can also be done (if less elegantly) by the dot and indirection (∗) operators. Thus, the following two expressions are equivalent:

```
p_form->row   ◄─────────►   (*p_form).row
```

The values being passed to *tput()* are the row, column, and message in the *term_msg* structure pointed to by *p_form*.

That winds up our discussion of C's special data types. In the next section, we'll look at the compiler library's I/O functions and the role of structures in manipulating data in files, and then we'll move on to the C tools formerly available primarily to assembly-language programmers.

# V

Section V deals with the C compiler's library functions for input and output control. (These are quite standard from one C compiler to another.) By combining library functions with one another, C programmers can implement a wide range of file-access options and data formats. **Chapter 17** deals with normal buffered access and stream file functions. **Chapter 18** discusses direct access to data files, including the use of keys, variable-length ASCII records, and low-level unbuffered file access.

# 17

# Stream File Input and Output

We've already seen that the C language lacks functions for performing file input and output—that, in fact, it has no built-in functions at all. These features must be obtained from a vendor-supplied library, such as the standard library that comes with your C compiler. This library contains functions for file access, math, string manipulation, dynamic memory allocation, searching and sorting, process control, and much more. The library is not built into the compiler, so you do not *have* to use its functions (you can write your own similar functions or purchase additional libraries), but you should at least become familiar with the kinds of file accesses made possible by standard library functions, if only to avoid reinventing the wheel.

You may have heard experienced C programmers refer to files as streams and wondered about that. Are they talking about streams of bytes? Well, yes, sort of. Data saved in C files are treated as large arrays of bytes. The concept of records and fields is not built into the structure of a C file: Your program superimposes the structure you desire. A series of records made up of fields of data is only one possibility for the contents of a file.

The standard library provides low-level file-access functions that you can work with directly or use to implement higher-level file schemes. File-access methods like indexes and binary trees, as well as a variety of database-management systems, are currently available to supplement the standard library. These vendor libraries enhance your programming capabilities but may become a portability problem, depending upon the number of environments the vendor intends to support.

## Normal Buffered Access

Buffered access is a technique that increases the efficiency of file input and output by reducing the *number* of inputs and outputs—that is, by making each access to a file handle more data. A buffer is an area of memory—an array used as an intermediate holding place for file data. Buffers are normally 512 bytes, the value of the symbol BUFSIZ, defined in the header file *stdio.h*.

Here is how input buffering works. You call a function to input a character from a file. However, instead of reading only one character, the function inputs enough characters to fill the entire buffer. Then the first character in the buffer is handed to your program. The next time you ask to input a byte, no actual input is performed; instead, the next character from the buffer is handed to your program. This loop repeats until the buffer is emptied. Then, when you ask for another character, the buffer is completely refreshed (filled again) with new file data. I've used input of a single character only as an example. You may have asked to input a whole line or some other amount of data, depending upon the exact function called to do the input: The principle is still the same. All input functions eventually call the low-level library function *read()*.

Buffering of output is similar to buffering of input. Your program outputs bytes, and the bytes are held in the output buffer instead of being written directly to the device receiving the file. Each output from your program adds data to the output buffer, until it becomes full and is automatically flushed (written to the file) or until you *force* a flush with the library function *fflush()*, *flushall()*, *fclose()*, or *fcloseall()*.

## Opening a file

The buffering of data going to and from a file is accomplished by using a *FILE* type structure. The *FILE* structure is defined in the header file *stdio.h*, which must be included in your program (using *#include*) to open a file for buffered access. The *FILE* structure is allocated and initialized by a call to the library function *fopen()*. The structure contains a buffer, its associated pointers and counters, and a flag that indicates the kind of access permitted on the file being opened (read, write, or both).

The function *fopen()* itself expects two string arguments: the name of the file to open and the mode of access. The return value from *fopen()* is a pointer to a *FILE* structure, or *NULL* if the file could not be opened. The following code segment opens a file named *ordernum.dat*, or else calls *err_exit()*:

```
#include <stdio.h>

FILE *p_file;
static char file_name[] = "ORDERNUM.DAT";

p_file = fopen(file_name, "r");  /* open file for reading */
if (p_file == NULL)
   err_exit("No file:", file_name);
```

Actually, you will often want to obtain the name of the file to open as a command-line argument, for greater program flexibility. The call to *fopen()* to open a file whose name is passed as the first command-line argument can be made in an embedded assignment expression, like this:

```
if (NULL == (p_file = fopen(av[1], "r")))
   err_exit("No file:", av[1]);
```

You can use drive names and directory path names in a command-line file name. (Don't forget to use ''\\'' to make a single backslash in a string constant.)

```
"C:\\DIRNAME\\FILENAME.EXT"
```

Be aware, though, that file names that include drive names and directory paths can lead to portability difficulties. The UNIX and XENIX operating systems use a regular slash (/) in directory paths, rather than the backslash used by MS-DOS, and UNIX and XENIX directory paths point to a specific device, so these systems do not recognize drive names. A better approach is to use MS-DOS environment variables to supply drive-name and directory-path text to be used as prefixes to a file name. These environment variables have UNIX and XENIX counterparts, so your program will remain more portable.

The *fopen()* function expects a *mode* as its second argument. A mode is a string of one to three characters that defines how the file will be accessed. The first letter can be any one of the following:

| MODE | ACTION |
| --- | --- |
| *r* | Read mode; file positioned at start for input |
| *w* | Write mode; file positioned at start for output (existing data overwritten) |
| *a* | Append mode; file positioned at end for output of new data to follow existing data |

Both output modes, write and append, will create a new file if the file does not already exist.

The plus sign (+) is a second mode character, designating these update modes:

| MODE | ACTION |
| --- | --- |
| *r+* | Update mode; both read and write permitted |
| *w+* | Write update mode; empty file created for write and read access |
| *a+* | Append update mode; both read and write permitted, with all writes at the end of file |

However, for maximum portability, it is best to restrict your mode to *r*, *w*, or *a* alone. Also, since reads and writes may not follow each other freely in update mode, they must have an *fseek()* or *rewind()* function call between them to specify where the read or write should begin.

The last mode option character, *t* for text or *b* for binary, is used to distinguish between text and binary files. The difference between opening a file for text mode and opening a file for binary mode is in how the end of a line is handled. In text mode (which is the default), input of the string *"\r\n"* sends your program only *'\n'*, and output of the string *'\n'* by your program actually sends *"\r\n"*. (You may know *"\r\n"* as CR/LF, or carriage return/linefeed.) In binary mode, no translations are made; all characters are treated the same. The following is a list of the access modes that you can use with *fopen()*.

read:    r, rb, rt, rb+, r+b, rt+, r+t

write:   w, wb, wt, wb+, w+b, wt+, w+t

update:  a, ab, at, ab+, a+b, at+, a+t

## C A U T I O N

*The mode option characters* t *and* b *(for text and binary) are specific to MS-DOS and a few other non-UNIX operating systems. The binary option* b *is part of the ANSI standard, so it will be added to systems that are conforming to the standard.*

There are two other ways you can control *fopen()*'s selection of text or binary mode: You can import and set the external *int* variable *_fmode* to *O_BINARY* (from *fcntl.h*), or you can link *binmode.obj* with your object files to make binary mode the default.

The three standard I/O files, *stdin*, *stdout*, and *stderr*, are automatically opened for your program. (These names are actually pointers to *FILE* structures declared in *stdio.h*.)

Once all the necessary files are open, we need to learn how to move data in and out of them.

## File I/O library functions

ASCII data are portable to many different systems, whereas binary data, because of variations in byte ordering and data format, usually need to be converted to suit each CPU's specific requirements. In this chapter, we'll concentrate on saving data in the more portable ASCII text format, to become familiar with file I/O in C. Then in Chapter 18, we'll discuss the more restrictive binary file formats.

The standard library's file input and output functions are actually a family of functions with uniform, easy-to-remember names. The functions used to access stream files that have been opened with *fopen()* strongly resemble the character, line, and formatted I/O functions *printf()*, *scanf()*, *puts()*, *gets()*, *putchar()*, and *getchar()*. Figure 17-1 shows the file versions of these familiar input and output functions.

| FUNCTION | ACTION |
|---|---|
| *int fprintf(p_file, fmt, arg1, arg2, … )* | Converts *arg1, arg2,…* according to the format string *fmt* and outputs the resulting ASCII text to the file *p_file*. Returns the number of characters printed. |
| *int fscanf(p_file, fmt, p-arg1, p-arg2, … )* | Inputs text from *p_file*, converts it according to the format string *fmt*, and stores the results where *p_arg1*, *p_arg2*, … point. Returns the number of values converted and assigned or the integer defined as *EOF* if the program attempts to read beyond the end of the file. |
| *char *fgets(string, n, p_file)* | Inputs a line (including the *'\n'*) of up to *n–1* bytes from *p_file* to the character string *string* and appends a *'\0'*. If the input line is longer than *n–1* bytes, the next call to *fgets()* will get the rest of the line. Returns a pointer to *string* or the zero pointer, *NULL*, if the program attempts to read beyond the end of the file. |
| *int fputs(string, p_file)* | Copies string to *p_file*. Microsoft C returns *0* if the function is successful or a nonzero value if not. (Other versions of *fputs()* don't return anything, so avoid using the return value if portability counts.) |
| *int getc(p_file)* <br> *int fgetc(p_file)* | Macro *getc()* and related function *fgetc()* both input a character from *p_file*. Both return the input character as an *int* or *EOF* if not successful. |
| *int putc(c, p_file)* <br> *int fputc(c, p_file)* | Macro *putc()* and related function *fputc()* both output a character to *p_file*. Both return the output character as an *int* or *EOF* if not successful. |
| *int fclose(p_file)* | Closes the file associated with *p_file*. Completes any output, flushing all buffered data first. Returns *0* or *EOF* if not successful. |

FIGURE 17-1
*Standard library file input and output functions*

## Stream File Functions in Use

Now that we've learned how to access text files, we can complete some of the order-entry functions stored in *stubs.c*. The three functions we will rewrite in this chapter are shown in the following table.

| FUNCTION | ACTION |
|----------|--------|
| *pw_find()* | Reads and scans for records sequentially. Each record is a text line of fields delimited by ' ¦ '. |
| *logentry()* | Appends diagnostic messages to the log file, which holds lines of text with no special format. |
| *order_num()* | Updates an order-number counter by reading the old value, adding 1, and writing over the old value. |

## Delimiting records

Earlier, I said that a C file is not made up of records and that each file should be thought of as a stream of bytes. The first file operations we discussed used the standard input and output files to interact with the user, so we didn't have to think much about how data were organized for storage and retrieval, but now we need to take the time to discuss the management of that stream of bytes in detail.

We have already worked with records to a certain extent in the *wrt_ord()* function in the order-entry application. We can consider each order output by our order-entry program as a record made up of a group of lines of data. Further, we can consider each output line *within* the record as a field that begins with a two-character label identifying the kind of data saved on the rest of that line. The kind of record we will be using with the function that handles the password is a variable-length line of ASCII characters that ends with a *newline* ( '\n' ) delimiter; fields are separated by a vertical-bar ( ' ¦ ' ) delimiter. (It is important that the field itself never contain the delimiter, to prevent its being treated as two fields.) The symbol *DELIM* will make code easier to read and modify:

```
#define DELIM '¦'
```

(As an enhancement, you may choose to allow fields to be further divided into subfields delimited by a different delimiter, such as '^'.)

The benefits of using files made up of delimited records or labeled lines of ASCII text are threefold:

- All records and fields can be of variable length, thus saving storage space.

- Every record need not contain the same number of fields, and no memory is allocated to trailing empty fields.

- All data files are portable, because they are ASCII text.

## Reading and scanning sequentially

Now let's rewrite the stub *pw_find()* so that it reads a file named *passfile.dat* to validate our user's identification. (Be sure to remove *pw_find()* from *stubs.c* now, and place it in its own source file.) The file *passfile.dat* should hold lines of text, each considered a record. Each record has three or four fields, separated by the symbol *DELIM*, which is defined in *pw_find.c* as a ' ¦ ':

```
/* SOURCE FILE: PW_FIND.C
 *************************************************************************
 * pw_find() looks up a user's name and password and returns YES if the user
 *    is found, NO if not. If the user is found, office ID is also checked.
 *    User data contain indication of whether to ring bell.
 *************************************************************************
 */

#include <stdio.h>
#include <string.h>
#include "syntypes.h"
#include "ordentry.h"
#include "projutil.h"
#define DELIM '¦'        /* delimiter to separate fields of a record */

flag pw_find(
    char office[],       /* description of user's office (returned) */
    char user[],         /* name, initials, or abbreviation of user to find */
    char password[])     /* password to look up */

    {
    IMPORT bflag bell_ok;

    /* Use static so file will be opened only in the first call to pw_find(). */
    static FILE *p_passfile = NULL;
    char rec[L_OFFICE + L_USER + L_PASSWORD + 6];
    char find_rec[L_OFFICE + L_USER + L_PASSWORD + 4];
    short len_find;
    flag found = NO;     /* have not found the user yet */

    /* Open passfile if it isn't already open from a previous call. */
    if (!p_passfile && !(p_passfile = fopen("PASSFILE.DAT", "r")))
        err_exit("No file:", "passfile.dat");
    len_find = sprintf(find_rec, "%s%c%s%c%s", office,
        DELIM, user, DELIM, password);     /* first three fields to search for */
```

*(continued)*

306

```
    /* Loop for each record until user found, or EOF. */
    while (!found && fgets(rec, sizeof rec, p_passfile))
        if (0 == strncmp(rec, find_rec, len_find))
            found = YES;
    if (found && rec[len_find] != '\n')      /* fourth field in record? */
        bell_ok = NO;                        /* yes; turn off bell */
    return (found);
    }
```

The string *find_rec* is set to a string containing the office, user, and password (separated by the delimiter). This is the string that we check for validity by comparing it to the records in the *passfile.dat* file. Then record lines from the file are input and compared to *find_rec* one by one until the end of the file is reached or a match is found. Such a sequential pass through a file is an acceptable way to search for a record if the file is fairly short.

## Appending error messages to a log

Users are rarely able to give a complete error report when something goes wrong with their entries—which can present difficulties for the programmer maintaining the software. To avoid this problem, we can append all error messages to a permanent log file so that our programmers need no longer depend upon the users for accurate error reports. (The same function can also be used to provide an audit trail, to verify commissions, and for other similar activities.)

We'll expand the *logentry()* stub to perform these record-keeping tasks, and store the completed function in its own source file, *logentry.c*:

```
/* SOURCE FILE: LOGENTRY.C
 ************************************************************************
 * logentry() appends message text to the end of the log file, typically for
 *   audit, error detection, and security purposes.
 ************************************************************************
 */

#include <stdio.h>
#include <stdlib.h>
#include <time.h>
#include "projutil.h"
```

*(continued)*

LOGENTRY.C *continued*

```
void logentry(
    char msg[])              /* text of message to place in log file */

    {
    static FILE *p_logfile = NULL;
    long long_time;

    /* Open logfile, if it isn't already open. */
    if (!p_logfile && !(p_logfile = fopen("LOGFILE.DAT", "a")))
        {

        /* We can't call err_exit() because it tries to update log. */
        err_warn("No file:", "logfile.dat");
        abort();
        }
    time(&long_time);
    fprintf(p_logfile, "%s %s\n", ctime(&long_time), msg);
    }
```

The *a* option of the *fopen()* call in *logentry()* requests append mode, which means that *logfile.dat* can continue to grow indefinitely. To prevent it from consuming too much disk space, you should periodically print an archival hard copy and delete the file. See Chapter 11 for a discussion of the *time()* and *ctime()* library functions.

## Updating a counter

The file *ordernum.dat* is actually only one line with a single number on it: the last order number used in our order-entry application. This order number is read and incremented by *order_num()*, saved in the file, and then returned to the calling function. Let's look at the rewritten code:

```
/* SOURCE FILE: ORDERNUM.C
 ****************************************************************************
 * order_num() returns the order number to use for the next order. The order
 *    number is a counter that increases by one with each order. It is
 *    stored in the file ordernum.dat.
 ****************************************************************************
 */
```

*(continued)*

ORDERNUM.C *continued*

```
#include <stdio.h>
#include "projutil.h"
#include "ordentry.h"
#define FRSTONUM 10001
#define LASTONUM 99999

long order_num()
    {
    static FILE *p_ordernum = NULL;
    long order_cnt;

    /* Open ordernum, if it isn't already open.*/
    if (!p_ordernum && !(p_ordernum = fopen("ORDERNUM.DAT", "r+")))
        err_exit("No file:", "ordernum.dat");
    rewind(p_ordernum);            /* before switching from writing to reading */
    fscanf(p_ordernum, "%ld", &order_cnt);   /* input old number */
    rewind(p_ordernum);            /* before switching from reading to writing */
    if (order_cnt >= LASTONUM)     /* highest order number? */
        order_cnt = FRSTONUM;      /* yes; start over again */
    else
        ++order_cnt;               /* increment order number */
    fprintf(p_ordernum, "%ld\n", order_cnt); /* save new number */
    return (order_cnt);
    }
```

Note the calls to *rewind()* (which repositions the file pointer to the beginning of the file) following *fscanf()* and *fprintf()*. These calls are required by *fopen()*'s update mode, to switch between reading and writing to the data file.

# File-related Operations

The standard library also contains file functions that don't read and write data but are used in conjunction with the I/O functions we've just discussed to handle such operations as run-time diagnostic messages, break-key control, and file and directory control. Let's take a very quick look at the most useful of these.

## Run-time errors

Many library functions return a value to let you know an error has occurred, without informing you of the *type* of error. Fortunately, the global *int* variable *errno* is set by some of these functions to record the type of error that has occurred. So when debugging or troubleshooting, you should first check the function's return value to see if there was an error. Then, if there was, you can import *errno* and examine its value. A simpler approach, however, is to call the library function *perror()*, which checks *errno* for you and prints to *stderr* the error message, if any, that is associated with the integer value of *errno*. You can also pass *perror()* a string to print with the error message to identify the program and the circumstances of the error. You could use *perror()* in the *ordernum()* function. But since *perror()* does not write to our log file, a separate call to *logentry()* to record the error is also a good idea:

```
IMPORT int errno;
char log_buf[81];

if (!(p_ordernum = fopen("ORDERNUM.DAT", "r+")))
    {
    perror("order_num() can't open ordernum.dat");
    sprintf(log_buf, "order_num() fopen() error: %d", errno);
    logentry(log_buf);
    }
```

The combination of *perror()* and *errno*'s value will help you to identify errors from a variety of library functions, but these next three functions handle only I/O errors associated with open stream files whose file pointers are passed to them:

| FUNCTION | ACTION |
| --- | --- |
| *int ferror(p_file)* | Returns *0* if no read or write errors found |
| *int feof(p_file)* | Returns *0* if end of file not yet reached |
| *void clearerr(p_file)* | Clears the file's error indication |

## Disarming the break key

You can improve data integrity by disabling the action of the break key during such noninterruptible operations as a series of file updates that must run to completion. To do this, you first need to include the header file *signal.h* in your program. Then call the *signal()* function, like this:

```
/* ... */
signal(SIGINT, SIG_IGN);      /* turn break key off */

/* ...critical processing ... */
signal(SIGINT, SIG_DFL);      /* turn break key back on */
```

## File and directory control

The Microsoft C, UNIX, and XENIX standard libraries also supply functions for three important file-management tasks that many other C compilers do not address. These functions are among those declared in the *io.h* header file in Microsoft C:

| FUNCTION | ACTION |
| --- | --- |
| *mktemp()* | Makes up a unique name to use for a temporary file |
| *unlink()* | Deletes a file |
| *rename()* | Renames a file |

Since the grouping of files into directories is being implemented in more and more operating systems as an organizing tool, they also supply the following functions (declared in the *direct.h* header file in Microsoft C) for directory management:

| FUNCTION | ACTION |
| --- | --- |
| *chdir()* | Changes directory to a new directory |
| *getcwd()* | Gets the name of the current working directory |
| *mkdir()* | Makes a new empty directory |
| *rmdir()* | Removes an empty directory |

Since most of these functions will be at least generally familiar to you, we won't spend any more time on them here. See your compiler's standard library manual for details.

Now that you are comfortable with the concepts and standard library functions related to sequential processing of stream files, let's move on to direct access of file data.

# CHAPTER 18

# Direct Access and Keyed Record Retrieval

To purchase a file-access method or database-management system, or to implement one—that is the question: to buy, to build, or to work with stream functions and their fixed style of output. In this chapter, we'll look at one possibility: using combinations of the standard library functions to access records by matching a key field that identifies the record. This approach is often used for business programs.

The low-level, flexible file structure generated by the standard library functions makes it possible for the programmer to use these functions to create a variety of other file structures for accessing and managing data. The two we'll discuss in this chapter are variable-length ASCII text records and fixed-length binary records.

# Variable-Length ASCII Text Records

The records we are about to examine are text lines with fields separated by the '┊' delimiter, as discussed in Chapter 17. Here are a couple of typical lines from *passfile.dat* that are used in our order-entry program:

```
San Diego┊Steve┊tuna
Hoboken┊Bob┊sturgeon┊n
```

The first field is an office name, the second a user name, and the third a password. The optional fourth field seen in the second record is used to set the global variable *bell_ok*, which controls use of the bell in functions like *err_warn()* and *prompt()*. (The standard library functions do not use *bell_ok*.)

## Record string manipulation

The library function *sprintf()* makes record construction easy. (The function *sprintf()* does formatted output conversion and places the result in a string, rather than printing it.) We used an example of this in the rewritten version of *pw_find()* in Chapter 17:

```
#define DELIM '┊'          /* delimiter to separate fields of a record */
    /* ... */
  len_find = sprintf(find_rec, "%s%c%s%c%s", office,
      DELIM, user, DELIM, password);  /* first three fields to search for */
```

However, the standard library does not have a function for *extracting* a field from a record string. The closest it comes is the function *strchr()* (sometimes called *index* by other vendors), which searches a string for a single character. The recent addition of *strtok()* to the standard library (guided by ANSI) also comes close to meeting our needs here, but it is not exactly right either because we need to be able to identify a null string between a pair of adjacent delimiters as a field in a record. What we have been calling a field closely resembles what writers of parsers and compilers call *tokens*. The function *strtok()* returns the next token (field) in its first argument string that is delimited by any of the characters in its second argument string. Neither of these functions is exactly what we need, so we'll have to write our own field-extractor function. We'll call the function *strfld()*, and for now we'll code it in the following way.

```
#define DELIM ';'        /* delimiter to separate fields of a record */

/***********************************************************************
 * strfld() copies a field from a record to a separate string and returns
 *   the starting address of the target, to_str.
 ***********************************************************************
 */

char *strfld(
    char to_str[],        /* target string to copy field to */
    char from_rec[],      /* record string to copy field from */
    short fld_num)        /* field number to copy (first is 1, not 0) */

    {
    short ifrom, ito;     /* indices into from_rec and to_str */

    /* Skip over (fld_num - 1) delimiters to the field to copy. */
    for (ifrom = 0; --fld_num && from_rec[ifrom] != '\0';)
        {
        while (from_rec[ifrom] != '\0' && from_rec[ifrom] != DELIM)
            ++ifrom;
        if (from_rec[ifrom] == DELIM)
            ++ifrom;
        }

    /* Copy field from from_rec to to_str. */
    for (ito = 0; from_rec[ifrom] != '\0' && from_rec[ifrom] != '\n'
      && from_rec[ifrom] != DELIM; ++ifrom, ++ito)
        to_str[ito] = from_rec[ifrom];      /* copy a character to to_str */
    to_str[ito] = '\0';
    return (&to_str[0]);
    }
```

We'll refine this function further in Chapter 21, when we discuss incrementing pointer variables stored in registers to speed access to array data.

## Variations on Direct Access

Ultimately, all direct accesses to disk files made through standard library functions are by byte number. If we think of the file as a large array of bytes, the byte number is, in effect, the *index* of the byte within the file.

## Direct access by byte number

The standard library functions *fseek()* and *ftell()* are used as a team for direct access of a stream file by byte number. As stream data are read or written, the system keeps a byte count that indicates the present position in the file. You can obtain the value of this index by calling the library function *ftell()* and passing it a pointer to the open *FILE* structure. As your program continues to read and write to this stream, the byte number changes. If you want the program to jump to the location returned earlier by *ftell()* or to any other byte in the file, you call the library function *fseek()*. The next input or output to the open file will begin at the byte you specified with the call to *fseek()*. The long integer 0L is used as an offset by *fseek()* and *ftell()* to refer to the first byte of a file. Here is the syntax for these two functions, with details of their behavior:

| FUNCTION | ACTION |
|---|---|
| *long ftell(stream)* | Returns the current byte number (file-pointer position) in the stream, which is a pointer to a *FILE* structure for an open file. |
| *int fseek(stream, offset, origin)* | Moves the file-pointer position in the stream to the byte specified by the offset (a *long* integer) and origin arguments. The origin can take these values that are defined in *stdio.h*: |

| | | |
|---|---|---|
| | SEEK_SET | Offset is the number of bytes to move the file pointer beyond the beginning of the file. |
| | SEEK_CUR | Offset is the number of bytes to move the pointer relative to the present byte number. |
| | SEEK_END | Offset is the number of bytes to move the pointer relative to the end of the file. |

The current pointer position in a file is not always what you might expect it to be, especially in a file opened for text, rather than binary, mode. This is because the text-mode byte number is thrown off by the translations between $"\backslash r\backslash n"$ and $'\backslash n'$ on both input and output. So don't rely on your own estimation of location in a file opened as a text file; instead, let *ftell()* be your guide.

## Direct access through an index

In a file that uses keys, a specific field (typically, the first field of each record) is designated as the key field that identifies the record it is part of. You can use a key value in a program to obtain a specific record by matching the value to the record's key field.

We'll use a data file consisting of a series of text lines made up of delimited fields to demonstrate the use of keys. Our goal is to read one specific line from anywhere in the data file without first having to read all the lines preceding it (the definition of direct access). The index and data in our file represent the inventory for our software business:

| *invntory.ndx* | *invntory.dat* |
| --- | --- |
| S1:0 | S1:System One: Integrated Business Pkg:69500:230 |
| 6GL:52 | 6GL:Sixth-Generation Language:99500:190 |
| DBMS:92 | DBMS:Database-Management System:59500:200 |

Each index record in *invntory.ndx* has two fields: a key and a file offset. The file offset is passed to *fseek()* to locate the *invntory.dat* record (line) for the part identified by the key (the first field of our database).

The index file for the *invntory.dat* data file was built with a program called *bldindex*, which combines our custom *strfld()* function and several library functions to do its job. This program loops through a data file, calling *ftell()* to obtain the byte numbers for the keys by inputting each line of the data file and extracting its key field. Each key field and offset returned from *ftell()* is written to output as a line of text with two fields, separated by the ' : ' delimiter. Here is *bldindex.c*:

```
/* SOURCE FILE: BLDINDEX.C
 ************************************************************************
 * bldindex() constructs an index file for direct access to a data file.
 *   Each output line has two fields: key and offset. The output is written
 *   to stdout, so it can be redirected.
 *   The function takes one or two command-line arguments:
 *       BLDINDEX datafile [key_field_number]
 ************************************************************************
*/
```

*(continued)*

BLDINDEX.C *continued*

```
#include <stdio.h>
#include <stdlib.h>
#include <string.h>
#include "syntypes.h"
#include "projutil.h"
#define DELIM ';'

IMPORT char *strfld(char[], char[], short);

void main(unsigned ac, char  *av[])
   {
   char buf[BUFSIZ];           /* buffer for data record */
   char key[BUFSIZ];           /* key field of data record */
   FILE *p_infile;             /* input file stream */
   long file_pos;              /* return from ftell(): offset */
   short key_field_num = 1;    /* field number that holds key */
   char *end_pos;              /* end-of-record position */

   if (ac < 2 || ac > 3)
      err_exit("Use: BLDINDEX datafile [key_field_number]", "");
   if (NULL == (p_infile = fopen(av[1], "r")))
      err_exit("Can't open file: ", av[1]);
   if (ac >= 3)                    /* key field command-line argument? */
      key_field_num = atoi(av[2]);          /* yes; get field number */

   /* Loop for each record (line) of input file. */
   file_pos = ftell(p_infile);
   while (fgets(buf, BUFSIZ, p_infile))
      if ((end_pos = strchr(buf, "\n")))    /* is there a newline symbol? */
         {
         *end_pos = '\0';        /* strip it */
         strfld(key, buf, key_field_num);
         if (key[0] != '\0')  /* is there any key? */
            printf("%s%c%ld\n", key, DELIM, file_pos);
         file_pos = ftell(p_infile);
         }
   }
```

To compile and link the *bldindex* program, you must first separately compile the *bldindex.c* source file and the file that holds the *strfld()* function (using the */c* switch on the *CL* command line). Next, link these two files and the *projutil.lib* library file, which holds the object code for the *err_exit()* function. When you link to create the *bldindex* program, you must include the */STACK* switch on the

*LINK* command line to increase the size of the stack that your program uses. This is necessary because *bldindex* uses more than the default allocation of stack space when it manipulates strings that are declared to hold the maximum number of characters. The default size of the stack is 2 KB, which isn't big enough for this program. A stack size of 3 KB (3072 bytes) is sufficient for this program, so use the switch */STACK:3072* with the *LINK* command.

The *bldindex* program also permits us to create more than one index file for a single data file, with each of the index files using a different key field. However, keep in mind that adding, changing, or deleting information in a data file will usually cause some of the offsets in its index file to become incorrect, and the problem can be greatly compounded when the data file has more than one index. (Fixed-length fields simplify things somewhat, since the offsets may not change when the file is updated, but this is a trade-off on space.)

Access to data-file information through an index can be facilitated by a function that searches the index for the key and, if it is found, reads and passes back the associated data-file record. Such a function, which we'll call *get_rec()*, could begin like this:

```
flag get_rec(        /* read a keyed record using an index */
    char *rec,       /* record to pass back to caller */
    char *key,       /* key for record to read */
    FILE *pf_data,   /* data file stream */
    FILE *pf_index)  /* index file stream */

{
/* Look up key in index file to obtain offset of record in data file. */
/*    Then call fseek() for data file, using offset. Read data file */
/*    record into rec and return 1 if successful. */
```

As I stated earlier, there are no easy answers to the direct-access question. Variable-length ASCII text files are only one approach. Let's look at another possibility, using a binary file format.

## Binary File Format

Numeric data in binary format are more compact and therefore faster to access than the same data in ASCII. For instance, a 4-digit number takes up 2 bytes in a *short* integer but 4 bytes as ASCII text, and a 10-digit *long* integer needs only 4 bytes in binary format versus 10 bytes as a string of digits. And numeric data read from an ASCII text file must first be converted to binary before you can perform arithmetic on the values, whereas numeric data read from a binary file are ready for use in arithmetic expressions, without conversion. However, when you must choose between ASCII and binary data formats, keep in mind that although binary data formats offer better performance and use less space, they are unfortunately less portable. Also, data in a text file are human-readable and can easily be modified with a text editor, whereas data in binary format often contain bytes with unprintable bit patterns and must be converted to ASCII before they can be viewed or edited.

---

## C A U T I O N

*Modification of data files with a text editor can be very hazardous to the data they contain, and therefore should be done carefully.*

---

Data in binary format can be accessed using some of the standard stream functions we have seen so far. Alternatively, the standard library has a pair of functions, *fread()* and *fwrite()*, that are specifically intended for buffered input and output of binary data. (See Chapter 22.) But right now we are going to pursue a different avenue: *unbuffered* access to binary data.

## Low-level unbuffered access functions

Input buffering improves program performance when a file's records are read one after another, in sequential order, since the record is often waiting in the buffer before you ask for it. However, buffering of input can *impair* performance if access to the file is fairly random, since the program must still read the entire buffer, even though it needs only one record from it. So when random access is the dominant mode for your program, consider using unbuffered input and output.

---

## C A U T I O N

*All of the stream functions we discuss in this section are implemented using calls to the low-level unbuffered functions. To avoid bugs, never mix the two types of functions for the same open file.*

---

The standard library's functions for unbuffered input and output allow you to read and write blocks of data of any size. (Strangely enough, you may even choose to use the unbuffered routines because you desire to work *with* buffers, if the buffers are larger than the standard 512 bytes.) The data structures used by the standard library's low-level unbuffered file functions are simpler than their stream-file counterparts. Instead of using a *FILE* structure holding a buffer, the unbuffered functions use a single integer, known as a *file handle* or *file descriptor number*. These file handles are assigned by calling either *open()* or *creat()*. The first three file handles in a program are always assigned to the standard files, as in our *syntypes.h* header file:

```
/* File handles (descriptor numbers) for standard files to be  */
/*    used with the low-level I/O functions read() and write(). */
#ifndef STDIN
#define STDIN 0
#define STDOUT 1
#define STDERR 2
#endif
```

Here is a summary of the low-level library functions for unbuffered input and output:

| FUNCTION | ACTION |
|---|---|
| *int open(pathname, oflag[, pmode])* | Opens file for type of access described by *oflag*. Returns a file handle to use to access that file, or −1 to indicate an error. Third argument is used to specify the type of access only if a new file is requested. Specific values of *oflag* and *pmode* are portable among MS-DOS, XENIX, and recent UNIX versions of C (less so to UNIX System III and earlier). |
| *int close(handle)* | Closes the file opened to the handle named |
| *int creat(pathname, pmode)* | Creates a new file or, if file exists, deletes its data. Then opens the file for type of access described by *pmode* (read, write, or both). |
| *int read(handle, buffer, count)*<br>*int write(handle, buffer, count)* | Work as a team and are used by all other input and output functions. *read()* inputs a maximum of *count* bytes into *buffer*. Returns the number of bytes input. *write()* outputs count bytes of data from *buffer* to the file associated with *handle*. Returns the number of bytes output. |

*(continued)*

*continued*

| FUNCTION | ACTION |
|---|---|
| long *lseek(handle, offset, origin)*<br>long *tell(handle)* | Work as a team, much like the stream functions *fseek()* and *ftell()*. They provide direct access by byte number to a file opened for low-level access. *lseek()* returns the file-pointer location *after* the seek is performed on the file associated with *handle*. *tell()* returns the present file-pointer location for *handle*'s file. |

## Structures and record-oriented access

*Structures* (see Chapter 16) can be used to hold the binary data from a record in a file. Structures work best with fixed-length fields (especially for arrays of characters). We'll use our inventory data file again to learn how we can use structures to read and write fixed-length records of binary data, and how to update data in place.

---

### C O M M E N T

*The* invmaint *program uses unbuffered binary access to show how to call* read() *and* write(). *Buffered access with* fread() *and* fwrite() *would work just as well, and could be faster.*

---

We'll create a program called *invmaint* to build and maintain the inventory-file data. We'll use the low-level unbuffered functions *read()* and *write()* for all file accesses, including standard file/user interactions, and we'll change the part-numbering scheme so that you assign each part in the inventory an integer as its part number. Since each new part gets the next higher unused part number, this approach eliminates the need to store part numbers: The position of the record in the file *is* actually the part number.

---

### C A U T I O N

*If you construct an inventory file using* invmaint, *be sure to start with part number 0, 1, or some very low number so that the file doesn't use more space than necessary. The* invmaint *program reserves space for all the fixed-length (37-byte) records from the part number 0 to the highest part number. So if your highest part number is 1000, then space for 1000 records is reserved.*

---

```
/* SOURCE FILE:  INVMAINT.C
   ***************************************************************************
   * Inventory file maintenance: lists and adds parts to inventory.
   ***************************************************************************
   */

#include <stdlib.h>
#include <stdio.h>
#include <string.h>
#include <fcntl.h>
#include <sys\types.h>
#include <sys\stat.h>
#include <io.h>
#include "syntypes.h"

/* Macros PROMPT and ERR_EXIT use read() and write() to perform user I/O */
#define PROMPT(msg, mlen, ans, alen) write(STDOUT, msg, mlen), \
ans[read(STDIN, ans, alen) - 1] = '\0'

#define ERR_EXIT(s1) write(STDERR, s1, strlen(s1)), \
write(STDERR, "\a\n", 2), exit(FAIL)

void main(void)
    {
    int fh_inv;          /* INVNTORY.DAT file handle */
    long part_num;       /* integer part number */
    char cmd;            /* command to add or list part */
    char reply[81];      /* user input buffer to hold replies */
    char buf[20];        /* buffer for binary-to-ASCII conversions */
    struct s_inv_rec     /* declare structure type; define tag */
        {
        long price;      /* price to charge for part, in cents */
        short weight;    /* shipping weight, in ounces */
        char desc[31];   /* description of part */
        };
    struct s_inv_rec inv_rec;    /* declare record struct inv_rec */

    /* Open inventory file INVNTORY.DAT for reading and writing. Create */
    /*  the file if it does not exist, and open it in binary mode.     */
    if (-1 == (fh_inv = open("INVNTORY.DAT", O_RDWR | O_CREAT | O_BINARY)))
        ERR_EXIT("No file: INVNTORY.DAT");

    while (1)            /* infinite loop; exit is in loop body */
        {

        /* Prompt for command: Add or List? <a/l> */
        PROMPT("\nInventory Maint: Add or List? <a/l> ", 37, reply, 80);
        cmd = reply[0];
```

*(continued)*

INVMAINT.C *continued*

```
      /* No cmd, so we're done. */
      if (cmd != 'a' && cmd != 'l')
         close(fh_inv), exit(SUCCEED);

      /* Prompt for part number to add or list. */
      PROMPT("\nPart #: ", 9, reply, 80);
      part_num = atol(reply);     /* convert from ASCII to binary */

      /* Position file pointer at start of record for part. */
      lseek(fh_inv, (long) part_num * sizeof inv_rec, 0);
      if (cmd == 'a')             /* add a part */
         {

         /* Prompt for part_desc, price, and ship_weight. */
         PROMPT("\nDesc: ", 7, inv_rec.desc, 30);
         PROMPT("\nPrice: ", 8, reply, 80);
         inv_rec.price = atol(reply);     /* convert ASCII to binary */
         PROMPT("\nWeight (oz.): ", 14, reply, 80);
         inv_rec.weight = atoi(reply);   /* convert ASCII to binary */

         /* Output record from structure inv_rec. */
         write(fh_inv, (char *) &inv_rec, sizeof inv_rec);
         }
      else if (cmd == 'l')        /* read record and list part */
         {

         /* Got whole record? Then list part_desc, price, and ship_weight. */
         if (read(fh_inv, (char *) &inv_rec, sizeof inv_rec) == sizeof inv_rec)
            {
            write(STDOUT, "\nDesc: ", 7);
            write(STDOUT, inv_rec.desc, strlen(inv_rec.desc));
            write(STDOUT, "\nPrice: ", 8);
            ltoa(inv_rec.price, buf, 10);   /* convert price and output */
            write(STDOUT, buf, strlen(buf));
            write(STDOUT, "\nWeight: ", 9);
            itoa(inv_rec.weight, buf, 10); /* convert weight and output */
            write(STDOUT, buf, strlen(buf));
            write(STDOUT, "\n\n", 2);        /* skip two lines */
            }
         }
      }
   }
```

Now that you're familiar with the standard library's file I/O functions (both their virtues and their limitations), let's descend a step further, into the realm of bits and bytes. In Section VI, we'll look at tools that were available primarily to assembly-language programmers—until C was developed.

# VI

And now, the advanced C topics: Section VI gives you information about tools formerly available primarily to assembly-language programmers and about OS/2, the operating system developed jointly by Microsoft and IBM. **Chapter 19** covers dynamic allocation of memory, with emphasis on the linked list that can grow and shrink as the program executes. **Chapter 20** discusses C's easy-to-read bitwise operators that give the C programmer access to and control over every bit of each byte of data. **Chapter 21** presents advanced options for handling array data, discusses sophisticated coding and library techniques for optimizing program performance, and takes a hard look at the pros and cons of various kinds of performance tuning. **Chapter 22** discusses two data types that can be used to decrease the amount of memory your programs use: bit maps and unions. **Chapter 23** introduces the main concepts of OS/2 and discusses how using OS/2 will affect your C programs.

# CHAPTER 19

# Efficient Use of Memory

The amount of installed memory varies from system to system, and you'll always want to take advantage of all the memory you have available: Your programs will perform better, and your users will love you for it. But how can you ensure that your programs will adapt themselves to the memory available on different systems, or that when your user upgrades, your programs will do likewise? It's frustrating to invest in 512 KB of memory only to discover that your favorite program still behaves as if it were on a 64 KB system!

The solution is dynamic allocation of memory: obtaining additional memory for data *while the program is executing*. This is in contrast to the use of ordinary arrays, which must be dimensioned with constant expressions prior to execution. Once again, the C language provides no statements to handle this kind of allocation, so we will have to turn to functions from the standard library.

# Dynamic Allocation Functions

Let's begin with the simplest form of dynamic allocation: duplicating the contents of a string. Suppose that you want to write a function *strprint()* that is passed a string whose non-ASCII characters must be converted to question marks before the string is returned. You do not want to modify the original string that was passed, so you need to copy its contents to a new string. One approach would be to declare a new string the size of the largest possible string that might be passed. However, if the new array had the *auto* storage class, a bug known as a *dangling pointer reference* would result, since the allocated storage would be freed for reuse when the subfunction completes its execution, but the address of the freed memory would still be returned to the calling function.

---

## C A U T I O N

*An error known as a* dangling pointer reference *can result when a function refers to data at an address returned from a subfunction's own* auto *storage. To avoid a dangling pointer reference, have the subfunction return the address of either a* static *storage class variable or a dynamically allocated memory block.*

---

A better alternative is to use the library function *strdup()*, which obtains new storage, equal in size to the length of the string (including the null) passed to it, *before* copying the string to the new storage:

```
/* Copy a string, convert non-ASCII characters to '?', return its address. */
#include <ctype.h>

char *strprint(register char *in_str)
    {
    register char *p_char;
    char *out_str = strdup(in_str);    /* duplicate in_str */

    for (p_char = out_str; *p_char; ++p_char, ++in_str)
        *p_char = isprint(*in_str) ? *in_str : '?';
    return (out_str);
    }
```

The new memory to which *strdup()* returns a pointer is actually obtained by a call to the library function *malloc()* and remains allocated either for the life of the program or until it is explicitly freed.

The standard library functions *malloc()* and *free()* are used to dynamically allocate and free memory. The memory allocator, *malloc()*, takes a single *unsigned int* argument: the number of bytes to be allocated. The return value is a pointer to type *void* that points to the beginning of the block of newly allocated memory. If the program requests more memory than is available, *malloc()* returns *NULL*.

The *sizeof* unary operator is often used with *malloc()*. You can apply it to any variable or to a data type in parentheses. The resulting value is the number of bytes allocated to that variable or needed to hold a value of the parenthesized type.

The following code segment uses *malloc()* and *free()* to dynamically allocate a large temporary array of *long* integers to exist for the duration of this code segment and no longer:

```
long *temp_data, *p_temp, *p_end, total = 0;

temp_data = (long *) malloc(100 * sizeof (long));

get_data(temp_data);              /* input 100 longs to temp_data */
p_temp = temp_data;               /* temp_data points to first long */
p_end = temp_data + 100;          /* p_end points after last long */

/* Add value of a long int to total and point to next long. */
while (p_temp < p_end)            /* loop for each long in array */
   total += *p_temp++;
printf("Total = %ld\n", total);
free(temp_data);                  /* release memory for temp_data */
```

The cast operator (*long* *) before the call to *malloc()* converts *malloc()*'s return value from type *pointer to type void* to *temp_data*'s type, *pointer to type long*. The header files *stdlib.h* and *malloc.h* declare *malloc()* to return type *pointer to void*. This is a way of avoiding designating a specific return type. The return type (*void* *) will be superseded by a caste operator such as the *pointer to type long* (*long* *) that we used. Note that the value of *p_temp* (*pointer to type long*) is actually incremented by four in the shorthand assignment statement, because the size of a *long* is four bytes:

```
/* Add the value of a long int to total and point to next long. */
/* ... */
total += *p_temp++;
```

You can write the *get_data()* function as if it were passed an ordinary array of 100 *long* integers—it doesn't care how the memory for *temp_data* was allocated.

# Linked Lists

A *linked list* is a variable-length chain of structures. One of the elements in each structure is a pointer to the corresponding element in the next structure. Linked lists can become very complex indeed, but you can relax: The application we're going to use is a straightforward one that will make some applications execute faster by eliminating file inputs and outputs. We want to read our inventory file into memory in the form of a linked list so that when the order-entry function *inv_find()* needs to look up a part, it can simply scan the list instead of reading the disk.

Our *inv_find()* function performs two kinds of processing. The first time it is called, it inputs the inventory data file (built with the *invmaint* program from Chapter 18) and builds the linked list. Every time it is called after that, it begins at the head of the list and chains along, link by link, to the link for the part it is looking for and then returns its data. Since dynamically allocated storage remains allocated until explicitly freed, the list will not be lost between calls to *inv_find()* (provided that *inv_find()*'s pointers into the list have *static* storage class so that they don't forget where the list is).

## Building the list

The first call to *inv_find()* has to create the linked list from the data in the inventory file. The following three diagrams show you how the memory used by the list changes as it grows from an empty list with *NULL* head and tail pointers to a one-link and then to a two-link list of inventory data.

The one-element linked list is like a one-person business, in that the link is both the head and the tail.

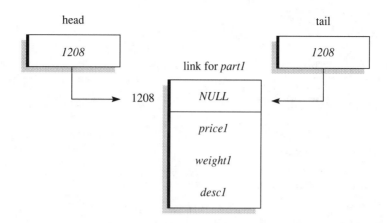

With the addition of a second link, our list finally displays all the attributes of a true linked list. Notice the first member of the link structure in the links for *part1* and *part2*. The pointer in *part1*'s link points to *part2*'s link, like a short chain.

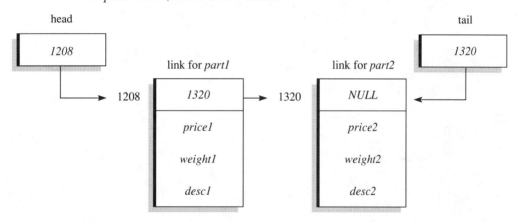

We can insert new links anywhere in a list by using a straightforward splicing process: To insert a link between links 1 and 2, we make a temporary pointer point to link 2, then make link 1 point to the new link, and finally make the new link point to link 2 (which we can access through the temporary pointer). To remove a link from a list, we simply reverse the process: To remove link 1 from our two-link list, we make the head point to link 2, and the job is done. (You can free the storage for link 1 if you like. Otherwise, it remains allocated until the program ends.)

## Searching the list

Now *inv_find()* can begin the job of searching the list. This is a looping process that begins at the head and moves down the chain, link by link, until the desired link is found or the tail is reached. In most applications, the test for whether the link sought has been found involves comparing two values. However, that is not the case in our example. Since the inventory file's data structure stores the part record's index in the file (see Chapter 18), rather than the part number, the program will know in advance how many links to move down the chain: The part number is the link number.

```c
/* SOURCE FILE:  INV_FIND.C
 ***************************************************************************
 * inv_find() looks up part's data in inventory and returns YES if the part
 *    is found, NO if not. Description, price, and weight are passed back.
 ***************************************************************************
 */

#include <stdio.h>
#include <stdlib.h>
#include <string.h>
#include <fcntl.h>
#include <sys\types.h>
#include <sys\stat.h>
#include <io.h>
#include "syntypes.h"
#include "ordentry.h"

struct s_inv_rec          /* declare structure type and define tag */
   {
   money price;           /* price to charge for part, in cents */
   short weight;          /* shipping weight, in ounces */
   char desc[31];         /* description of part */
   };
struct s_inv_link
   {
   struct s_inv_link *p_next;  /* next link in list pointer */
   struct s_inv_rec rec;       /* inventory record, nested structure in link */
   };
flag inv_find(
   char part[],           /* part number to look up (pass in) */
   char part_desc[],      /* description of part (returned) */
   money *p_price,        /* pointer to unit price of part (returned) */
   short *p_ship_wt)      /* pointer to shipping weight (returned) */

   {
```

*(continued)*

INV_FIND.C *continued*

```c
        static struct s_inv_link *head = NULL, *tail = NULL;  /* list start, end */
        static long num_links = 0;  /* number of links in linked list */
        struct s_inv_link *temp;    /* temporary pointer to link in list */
        static int fh_inv;          /* inventory file handle */
        long part_num = atol(part); /* numeric part number -- 0 for first part */

        if (!fh_inv)            /* this is the first call, so build the */
            {                   /* linked list of inventory data now */

            /* Open inventory file for binary reading. */
            if (-1 == (fh_inv = open("INVNTORY.DAT", O_RDONLY | O_BINARY)))
                perror("No file: invntory.dat"), abort();
            head = tail = temp =     /* initialize list pointers */
                (struct s_inv_link *) malloc(sizeof (struct s_inv_link));
            head->p_next = NULL;     /* no next link yet */
            for (num_links = 0L; read(fh_inv, (char *) &(temp->rec), sizeof (temp->rec))
                == sizeof (temp->rec); ++num_links)     /* loop for each inventory record */
                {
                tail = temp;
                temp = (struct s_inv_link *) malloc(sizeof (struct s_inv_link));
                tail->p_next = temp;  /* make previous link point to new */
                temp->p_next = NULL;  /* no next link from new yet */
                }
            if (num_links == 0L)    /* if no list, then no */
                head = tail = NULL;  /* head or tail */
            }

        /* Look up data for part whose number was passed in */
        /* by moving part_num-1 links down the chain. */
        if (part_num >= num_links)
            return (NO);
        for (temp = head; part_num--; temp = temp->p_next)
            ;

        /* Return part data to calling function. */
        strcpy(part_desc, temp->rec.desc);
        *p_price = temp->rec.price;
        *p_ship_wt = temp->rec.weight;
        return (YES);
        }

/***************************************************************************
 * Test driver for the inv_find() inventory-lookup function.
 *   Data for invntory.dat were entered using the invmaint program from the
 *   previous chapter.
 ***************************************************************************
 */
```

*(continued)*

INV_FIND.C *continued*

```
#if defined(DBGMAIN)
#define TEST(msg, cond) if (!(cond)) \
fprintf(stderr, "TEST FAILED: %s\a\n", msg)

main()
    {
    short weight;
    money price;
    char desc[31];

    TEST("#1", !inv_find("99", desc, &price, &weight));
    TEST("#2", inv_find("0", desc, &price, &weight));
    TEST("#3", 0 == strcmp(desc, "DBMS"));
    TEST("#4", price == 59500L && weight == 175);
    printf("inv_find() tests complete\n");
    }
#endif
```

Linked lists may or may not have advantages over ordinary arrays, depending on your needs. For instance, a linked list does not need to be dimensioned before compilation; an array does. And inserting and deleting new links is fast; the analogous changes to arrays are slower to implement. But access to a link requires chaining through other links, whereas array elements are accessed directly. An array of pointers into a linked list brings some array benefits, for the price of consuming some additional memory. As always, there are trade-offs to consider.

Linked lists can become far more complex than the one we've just discussed. For instance, elements of a doubly linked list have both forward and backward pointers. And elements (known as *nodes*) in lists called *trees* may have two or more descendant elements, forming a structure like a family tree. And these are only some of the linked-list data structures available to C programmers!

Now let's narrow our focus one final level. In the next chapter, we will discuss the lowest-level C data structure of all, the bit.

# Bit-Level Operations

Bits are the "atoms" of computer memory: They are the smallest possible amount of data and are indivisible. Since the narrowest C data type is the 1-byte-wide type *char*, C programs usually access individual bits through a *pointer to type char*.

There aren't too many uses for bit-level programming in applications development, but bit-level operations are occasionally used with some standard library functions or to compress data for more efficient use of memory, so we need to spend a few minutes discussing them. First, though, let's quickly review hexadecimal and octal notation for numeric data.

## Non-Decimal Views of Data

Computers store data as arrays of bits that are analogous to the 1s and 0s of a binary (base 2) number, but humans often find these long strings of 1s and 0s difficult to comprehend and manage. We seem to be more comfortable with the familiar digits 0 through 9 and the letters of our alphabet, so we find octal (base 8, using 0 through 7) or hexadecimal (base 16, using 0 through 9 and A through F) notation preferable when we want to see the pattern of bits used to express the internal binary value of a variable.

Hexadecimal notation is more natural than octal for viewing binary values, since a hex digit from 0 through F translates directly into 4 bits ranging in value from 0000 through 1111, and therefore an 8-bit byte can easily be expressed using two hex digits. Octal works nearly as well, but an octal digit represents only 3 bits of data, so three octal digits are needed to display an 8-bit byte.

Characters whose values are not printable can be expressed in a string or character constant using either octal or hex. For instance, in Chapter 2 we saw the escape and paragraph characters expressed these ways:

| CHARACTER | HEX CHARACTER | OCTAL CHARACTER |
|-----------|---------------|-----------------|
| escape    | '\x1b'        | '\033'          |
| paragraph | '\x14'        | '\024'          |

The compiler interprets an *integer* constant with a leading 0x as hexadecimal. If only the leading 0 is present, it interprets the constant as octal.

The data type of hex and octal constants depends on their values. As shown in the following table, larger values require wider data types.

| HEX RANGE | OCTAL RANGE | TYPE |
|-----------|-------------|------|
| 0x0–0x7FFF | 0–077777 | *int* |
| 0x8000–0xFFFF | 0100000–0177777 | *unsigned int* |
| 0x10000–0x7FFFFFFF | 0200000–017777777777 | *long* |
| 0x80000000–0xFFFFFFFF | 020000000000–037777777777 | *unsigned long* |

Hex and octal constants narrower than type *long* can be forced to type *long* with a trailing "*L*" or "*l*", as is the case with decimal integer constants. The following three constants are equivalent:

    0x1bL        033L        27L

## Non-decimal data and library functions

You'll recall that the members of the family of library functions *itoa()*, *ltoa()*, and *ultoa()* convert *int*, *long*, and *unsigned long* values (respectively) to ASCII representation. For the third argument to all three functions, we can supply any radix from 2 through 36, giving us a great deal of flexibility for numeric conversions.

You'll also recall that the *printf()* family of formatted output functions uses format-string arguments to specify how subsequent argument data should be converted (Chapter 2). These functions can also output octal and hexadecimal data, using the following specifiers:

| FORMAT SPECIFIER | ACTION |
|---|---|
| %x | Prints a *short* or *int* value in hex form |
| %lx | Prints a *long* value in hex form |
| %o | Prints a *short* or *int* value in octal form |
| %lo | Prints a *long* value in octal form |

This next, rather unusual-looking, code segment shows how the hexadecimal and octal format specifiers are used:

```
char chr;

for (chr = 'A'; chr <= 'C'; ++chr)
  printf("%c in Hex: %x, Octal: %o, Decimal: %d\n",
    chr, chr, chr, chr);
```

You could use this code to print a table for the entire alphabet if you have reason to make frequent conversions. However, the segment in our example prints only the following output:

```
A in Hex: 41, Octal: 101, Decimal: 65
B in Hex: 42, Octal: 102, Decimal: 66
C in Hex: 43, Octal: 103, Decimal: 67
```

It is interesting to note that the call

```
sscanf(buf, "%o %x", &octnum, &hexnum);
```

converts an octal and a hex number to integer values *octnum* and *hexnum.*

# Operating a Bit

C's bitwise operators act on their operands as if they were arrays of bits, rather than single values. Although the names of the bitwise operators—*AND*, *OR*, and *NOT*—resemble the names of the logical operators, there is a great difference in their behavior, so we'll discuss each of them separately. They are listed in Figure 20-1 on the following page, in descending order of precedence. These operators are for use only in integer expressions—not *float* or *double* expressions.

| PRECEDENCE LEVEL | OPERATOR | ACTION | EXAMPLE |
|---|---|---|---|
| 14 | ~ | Bitwise NOT (one's complement) | ~3 == 0xfffc |
| 11 | >> | Shift right | 0x7f >> 2 == 0x1f |
| 11 | << | Shift left | 0x1f << 2 == 0x7c |
| 8 | & | Bitwise AND | 0x8a & 0x7f == 0x0a |
| 7 | ^ | Bitwise (exclusive) XOR | 0xff ^ 0xc3 == 0x3c |
| 6 | ¦ | Bitwise OR | 0x42 ¦ 0x36 == 0x76 |

Figure 20-1
*C's bitwise operators, in descending order of precedence*

## Turning bits on

The single vertical bar ( ¦ ) is the bitwise *OR* operator. It pairs corresponding bits from its two operands and evaluates them, producing a single bit in that position as the result. This process repeats, bit by bit, until every pair has been evaluated. The binary result has a 1 bit in every position where either operand had a 1 bit; all other bits are 0.

Let's look at an example of the *OR* process using the decimal integers 96 and 9. We'll express both numbers in hex and in binary to get a better idea of what's happening:

| DECIMAL | HEXADECIMAL | BINARY |
|---|---|---|
| 96 | 0x60 | 01100000 |
| ¦ 9 | ¦ 0x09 | ¦ 00001001 |
| --- | ------ | ---------- |
| 105 | 0x69 | 01101001 |

Bitwise *OR* is used with certain library functions, such as *open()*, to express combinations of a number of options in a single integer value. The technique uses separate bits to hold specific options and combines them using the ¦ operator, as in this code segment from *inv-maint.c*:

```
/* Open inventory file INVNTORY.DAT for reading and writing. Create */
/*    the file if it does not exist, and open it in binary mode. */
if (-1 == (fh_inv = open("INVNTORY.DAT", O_RDWR ¦ O_CREAT ¦ O_BINARY)))
    ERR_EXIT("No file: INVNTORY.DAT");
```

All of the options we used in *invmaint.c* are defined in the header file *fcntl.h.* (See your manual for the complete list.)

| | |
|---|---|
| O_RDWR | 0x0002 |
| O_CREAT | 0x0100 |
| O_BINARY | 0x8000 |

The program evaluates the bitwise expression in our example as *0x8102* and passes that value to *open()* as an integer.

## Isolating bits

The bitwise *AND* operator (&) behaves like the bitwise *OR*, except that bits in the result are 1 only if both corresponding operand bits are 1. Bitwise *AND* is often used to isolate the value of a single bit in a byte. The value of the expression *num* & 1 will be 0 if the lowest order bit of *num* is 0 (if *num* is even), or 1 if the lowest-order bit is 1. The expression *num* & 0xf will be 0 only if all four of the low-order bits of *num* are 0.

## Reversing bits

The unary bitwise *NOT* (~) produces an *int* or a *long* that is the complement of its single argument. In effect, each bit's value is reversed. The value of *~1* is *0xfffe.* A 32-bit CPU and compiler will evaluate *~1* as *0xfffffffe.* This evaluation demonstrates that some uses of bitwise *NOT* will make code non-portable.

The bitwise exclusive *OR* (^) produces a 1 bit in its result if *either one but not both* of the corresponding operand bits is 1. (In other words, 1 is the result if the corresponding operand bits are not equal.) Exclusive *OR* can be used to reverse selected bits in an integer. The value of *0xfc* ^ *0xf* is *0xf3.* The *0xf* causes the values of the low-order 4 bits of *0xfc* to be reversed and the high-order bits of *0xf* to remain unchanged.

## Shifting bits

The right- and left-shift operators copy the left operand and slide its bits the number of positions designated by the right operand. The result of a right shift is similar to dividing by 2 raised to the power of the number in the second operand; the result of a left shift is similar to multiplying by that value. Bits that slide off either end are discarded. The vacated bit positions are filled with 0 bits, with one exception: Microsoft's right shift of a negative value will produce a negative result—that is, a 1 bit will be used to fill each vacated bit position on the left. The ANSI standard indicates that the result of a right shift on a negative integer is implementation defined (which means a potential portability problem). So to ensure portable code, use the right shift only on unsigned data types. Since the left shift always fills with 0 bits, you needn't be concerned about portability there.

## Mapping to bits

I'd like to thank one of my former students from the Boston area for asking me how to write this little program, which I've named *bitmap.c*. In a 10-character array, there are 80 bits, which we will number 0 through 79. The initial values of the array named *bitmap* are all '\0'. The program prompts for a number from 0 through 79, turns on the bit with that index in the bitmap, and then displays the modified bitmap in hex. To turn on the correct bit, the program creates a byte with all bits off except for a single bit corresponding to the bit position to be turned on. It does this by right-shifting a byte with only the high bit on by the remainder of the input number after being divided by 8. This special byte is called a *mask* because it masks off some bits and operates on others, like masking tape used by a housepainter. Next, the index of the byte containing the bit corresponding to the input number is found by dividing the input number by 8 (*bit_num / 8*), since there are 8 bits in each byte. The bit in the selected byte is turned on using the shorthand assignment form of the bitwise OR operator ( ¦ =). Finally the program prints the bitmap in hex. Each 2-digit hexadecimal number holds eight bits, so 10 numbers hold the entire bitmap. The process of reading an input number, turning on a bit, and printing the bitmap repeats until you ask to quit.

```
/* SOURCE FILE: BITMAP.C
 ********************************************************************************
 * The bitmap program demonstrates bit-mapping techniques. It prompts for an
 * integer from 0 to 79, maps it to a bit in a 10-character array called
 * bitmap, and turns that bit on. The resulting bitmap is displayed in hex.
 ********************************************************************************
 */

#include <stdio.h>
#include "syntypes.h" /* to get typedef for unchar */
```

*(continued)*

BITMAP.C *continued*

```
#define MAPBYTES 10
void main(void)
    {
    static unchar bitmap[MAPBYTES] = {'\0'};
    unchar byte_mask;
    short bit_num, ibyte;

    printf("Enter bit number (0-79) or q to quit: ");
    while (1 == scanf("%hd", &bit_num))
        {
        byte_mask = (unchar)(0x80 >> (bit_num % 8)); /* select bit in byte */
        bitmap[bit_num / 8] |= byte_mask;                /* turn bit on in byte */
        for (ibyte = 0; ibyte < MAPBYTES; ++ibyte)
            printf("%02x ", bitmap[ibyte]);
        printf("\nEnter bit number (0-79) or q to quit: ");
        }
    }
```

Observe how the input is reflected in the bitmap in these interactions:

```
Enter bit number (0-79) or q to quit: 0
80 00 00 00 00 00 00 00 00 00
Enter bit number (0-79) or q to quit: 15
80 01 00 00 00 00 00 00 00 00
Enter bit number (0-79) or q to quit: 16
80 01 80 00 00 00 00 00 00 00
Enter bit number (0-79) or q to quit: 79
80 01 80 00 00 00 00 00 00 01
Enter bit number (0-79) or q to quit: 78
80 01 80 00 00 00 00 00 00 03
Enter bit number (0-79) or q to quit: q
```

Now you know how to use C right down to machine level. You can write clear, readable code to manage complex operations, and you can manage your files to take maximum advantage of available memory. You're ready to fly! But before you go, let me pass along some handy techniques for optimizing program performance—techniques for writing even more efficient C.

**21**

# More Efficient C

The style rules, tips, and debugging techniques that we have looked at so far have all focused on a single goal: maximizing your efficiency as a C programmer. But there's more—the icing on the cake. Although C programs are small and fast to begin with, there are sophisticated coding techniques and library functions that you can employ to achieve even greater performance. In this chapter, we'll look at ways to squeeze every bit of work possible out of the computer.

## Performance-tuning Philosophy

Once a program is coded, compiled, and debugged, programmers naturally begin looking for ways to streamline it. This is good programming practice, but a word of caution:

> Don't be bit wise and byte foolish.

Those words express a philosophy of program optimization that has produced impressive results. I have seen so much effort wasted on tuning pieces of code that are rarely executed!

However, with code that is executed frequently or is central to the rest of the program, don't be afraid to experiment. If you have a choice of two approaches, take the time to write both, and measure to see which implementation runs faster or uses less memory. Expressed more succinctly, your performance-tuning philosophy now becomes:

Measure before you modify.

The little test driver you write to compare two ways of doing a job might uncover CPU power you never dreamed you had! Or perhaps you will discover that you've saved only a few milliseconds. That's why benchmarks are fun.

## Performance Measurement

The close relationship between C's pointers and arrays has led programmers to write some pretty unreadable code in the name of efficiency. For instance, let's explore the way these next two expressions obtain the same element of an array so that we can compare their performance:

```
array[index]
*(array + index)
```

This little program will do the job for us:

```
/* Compare integer array indexing using [] and using pointer access. */
/* Obtain the number of trials from the command line (default is 1). */

#include <stdio.h>
#include <stdlib.h>
#include <time.h>
#define LDIM 5000

void main(unsigned ac, char *av[])
    {
    long longs[LDIM], sum;     /* increase stack size: use CL flag /F 9000 */
    long beg_time, mid_time, end_time;
    long *p_long = longs, *p_long2 = longs;
    short ilong, itrial, ntrials = ((ac > 1) ? atoi(av[1]) : 1);

    time(&beg_time);           /* array index timing */
    for (itrial = 0; itrial < ntrials; ++itrial)
```

*(continued)*

*continued*

```
   {
   for (ilong = 0; ilong < LDIM; ++ilong)
      longs[ilong] = ilong;
   for (sum = ilong = 0; ilong < LDIM; ++ilong)
      sum += longs[ilong];
   }
time(&mid_time);              /* pointer-arithmetic timing */
for (itrial = 0; itrial < ntrials; ++itrial)
   {
   for (ilong = 0; ilong < LDIM; ++ilong)
      *(p_long + ilong) = ilong;
   for (sum = ilong = 0; ilong < LDIM; ++ilong)
      sum += *(p_long2 + ilong);
   }
time(&end_time);
printf("Array-Subscript Time:    %4ld\n", mid_time - beg_time);
printf("Pointer-Arithmetic Time: %4ld\n", end_time - mid_time);
}
```

This program accepts a single optional command-line argument: the number of trials (repetitions) of the test to perform. The program uses the *time()* function from the standard library, which returns the time in seconds, so we must make enough trials to get significant results. Here are the results of a single trial:

```
Array-Subscript Time:       0
Pointer-Arithmetic Time:    0
```

As you can see, this is not sufficient to get reasonable or useful results. (Bear in mind that I achieved the test results described in this chapter on my Mega Comm Technologies PRO-386 computer with a 16 MHz Intel 80386 CPU chip. Your results will depend on the speed of your CPU and other factors.)

Now let's look at the results in seconds for 10,000 trials:

```
Array-Subscript Time:     521
Pointer-Arithmetic Time:  553
```

Surprised? It is true that pointers can be used to achieve faster access to array elements, but not by simply converting *array[index]* to *\*(array + index)*. We'll see how to use this technique properly a little later in the chapter, when we discuss pointers in registers.

# CPU- or Disk-bound?

The coding techniques you use to improve the performance of a program will, of course, depend on how that program is spending its time. To tune a program successfully, you must begin by watching and listening to your computer as it executes that program. Is the program waiting for the CPU to finish some long array operation or numeric computation? Or could those incessantly blinking busy lights on the disk drive be an indication that the disk is overworked?

When interactive applications run too slowly, it is rarely the speed of the CPU that is the problem. The bottleneck is almost always the disk. If you can reduce the number of disk accesses, the program will speed up. The proper selection of buffered or unbuffered file access and the dynamic allocation of memory (Chapters 18 and 19) are the keys to reducing disk activity.

Your compiler can help, too. Once you have debugged a program and are ready to put it to use, you should recompile it using one of the compiler's optimization switches, all of which begin with */O* (upper-case letter "oh"). Microsoft's compiler offers many optimization switches. For example, you can select optimization for speed (*/Ot*), optimization for program size (*/Os*), or maximum optimization (*/Ox*). The */Od* option disables optimization. The default optimization is */Ot* for speed. You should not use maximum optimization until you debug the code because the optimization prevents some error checking.

Most tuning techniques are a trade-off between program size and program speed. However, there's one technique that can improve both: *register* storage.

## The *register* Storage Class

If you use *register* storage for frequently used *int*-sized (or smaller) variables, your functions will be both smaller and faster. In this next example, you'll see how *register* storage has significantly improved the speed of some simple calculations:

```
#define LOOPS 5000
    /* ... */
    register short ireg, ireg2;
    short iauto, iauto2;
    /* ... */
```

*(continued)*

*continued*

```
ireg = ireg2 = 0;
for (iloop = 0; iloop < LOOPS; ++iloop)
   {
   ireg = ireg * ireg - 2 * ireg + 456;
   ireg2 += ireg * 2 - 2500;
   }
/* ... */
iauto = iauto2 = 0;
for (iloop = 0; iloop < LOOPS; ++iloop)
   {
   iauto = iauto * iauto - 2 * iauto + 456;
   iauto2 += iauto * 2 - 2500;
   }
```

I compiled and ran a program that contains this test four times, compiling with a different optimization switch each time. The results of 1,000,000 iterations of the test were:

|  | /Od | /Os | /Ot | /Ox |
|---|---|---|---|---|
| Register Time | 16 | 14 | 14 | 7 |
| Auto Time | 20 | 17 | 17 | 11 |

We can conclude that maximum optimization produced the most dramatic improvement in speed and that use of *register* storage class does make functions run faster.

# Macros and Functions

In Chapter 6, we discussed the fact that the improved speed a macro offers over an equivalent function may be offset by its increased memory demands: the speed-versus-memory trade-off again. Do we save *enough* time to justify the added memory? In the following macro/function comparison, we are really measuring the overhead of calling a function with three arguments and obtaining a return value:

```
#define AVG3(a, b, c) (((a) + (b) + (c)) / 3)
/* ... */
long avg_3_longs(long a, long b, long c)
   {
   return ((a + b + c) / 3);
   }
```

I created a program that made 1,000,000 calls each to the macro and function in this example. The results are sufficient to demonstrate the greater speed of the macro:

Function Time:  68
Macro Time:     45

## Library Awareness

The linker that comes with your C compiler will combine your object files with only those library functions that are called by the functions in your object files. That is, if your code doesn't call a particular library function and no function that your program *does* call calls it either, that library function will not be linked with your program. But if you *do* call a library function in even one place, you might as well call it everywhere it's useful because it will be included by the linker.

Why do I bring this up? Space again. Since most library functions are small, their size is of little concern, but there are a few functions with multiple capabilities that occupy more memory. For instance, the family of formatted input and output functions—*printf()*, *scanf()*, *fprintf()*, *fscanf()*, *sprintf()*, and *sscanf()*—are all large library functions. If you have a program that uses these functions, rewriting its calls into conversion programs could save 4000 or more bytes of memory. Let's look at an example.

The following test compares *write()*, the lowest-level output function from the standard library, and *printf()*, which ultimately calls *write()*. I compiled this program twice with maximum optimization, once calling *write()* and again calling *printf()*:

```
/* Compare printf() with write(). First compile with PRINTF defined so */
/* printf() is called. Then undefine PRINTF so write() is called. */

#include <stdio.h>
#include <stdlib.h>
#include <io.h>
#include <time.h>
#include <string.h>
#define LOOPS 4000
```

*(continued)*

*continued*

```
void main(void)
    {
    long begin, end;
    short iloop;
    char out[20];

    time(&begin);
    for (iloop = 0; iloop < LOOPS; ++iloop)
#ifdef PRINTF
printf("****************************************\n");
#else
write(1, "****************************************\n", 41);
#endif
    time(&end);
    ltoa(end - begin, out, 10);
    write(1, out, strlen(out));
    }
```

The difference in execution time between displaying text using *write()* and using *printf()* was small, but the code grew by 4344 bytes when *printf()* was called.

|           | TIME | CODE SIZE |
| --------- | ---- | --------- |
| printf()  | 114  | 8837      |
| write()   | 109  | 4493      |

## Pointer Arithmetic

We've discussed several times the extremely close relationship between pointers and arrays in C. To see just how close, let's look at the way C adds (and subtracts) integers and pointers.

When an integer is added to or subtracted from a pointer, the integer is first multiplied (for scaling purposes) by the size of the data type the pointer was declared to point to. For instance, if you increment a *pointer to type short*, 2 is added to the pointer. However, if you decrement a *pointer to type double*, 8 is subtracted from the pointer, and if you add 3 to a *pointer to type long*, 12 is added to the pointer's value because three *long* integers take up 12 bytes of memory. (No scaling takes place when an integer is added to a *pointer to type char* because the size of a *char* variable is 1 byte.) A pointer variable sees memory simply as a large array of values of its underlying data type:

```
static long long_array[] = {4444L, 12L};
long *p_long = &long_array[0];
```

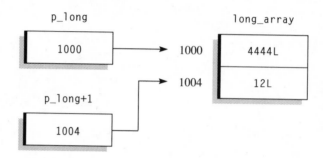

That's all pretty straightforward, but when and how would we use pointer arithmetic in our programs? Let's look at the most important application: faster array accessing.

## Pointers in registers

Pointers in registers can speed array accessing dramatically. The following code segment, excerpted from a timing program, compares various techniques for copying 40 characters from one string to another:

```
char from[41], to[41];
register char *p_from = from;    /* pointer in a register */
register char *p_to = to;        /* pointer in a register */

memcpy(to, from, MOVELEN);       /* memcpy() */

/* ... */
strcpy(to, from);                /* strcpy() */

/* ... */
while (*p_from)                  /* register pointer */
    *p_to++ = *p_from++;         /* copy character and increment pointers */
*p_to = '\0';                    /* end the "to" string */
```

The *while* segment in this example shows how pointers in registers can be used to copy text from the string variable *from* to the string variable *to*. The loop body statement ( *\*p_to++ = \*p_from++;* ) copies the character that *p_from* points to into the location *p_to* is pointing to and then increments both pointers by 1 so that they remain in unison. These next three statements would produce the same result, but far less elegantly:

```
*p_to = *p_from;
++p_from;
++p_to;
```

When I used the timing program (with various optimization switches) to measure a 40-character copy from one string to another for 100,000 trials, these were the results:

| COPY METHOD | /Ox | /Ot | /Od | STRING COPY CODE SEGMENT |
|---|---|---|---|---|
| *strcpy* | 9 | 9 | 9 | *strcpy(to, from);* |
| *memcpy* | 2 | 5 | 5 | *memcpy(to, from, MOVELEN);* |
| Array Index | 29 | 43 | 48 | *to[ichar] = from[ichar];* |
| Pointer | 42 | 42 | 49 | *\*p_to++ = \*p_from++;* |
| Register Pointer | 17 | 19 | 29 | *\*preg_to++ = \*preg_from++;* |

Typically pointer operations are faster than array indexing. However, with this version of the compiler, the optimization is a more important factor. The use of *register* storage class for the pointers made a significant difference, but surprisingly, *none* of the coding techniques was as fast as the standard library functions *strcpy()* and *memcpy()*.

## Bringing It All Together

Benchmarks may be fun, but a real-world example of a string function written for speed is also helpful. Here is the *strfld()* function we developed in Chapter 18, streamlined to give maximum copying performance:

```
#define DELIM '!'

/************************************************************************
 * strfld() copies a field from a record string to a separate string and
 *   returns the starting address of the target, to_str. (A record here is a
 *   string containing fields separated by DELIM.)
 ************************************************************************
 */
```

*(continued)*

*continued*

```
char *strfld(
    register char *to_str      /* target string to copy field to */
    register char *from_rec,   /* record string to copy field from */
    short fld_num)             /* field number to copy (first is 1, not 0) */

    {
    char *p_to_str = to_str;   /* hold initial value for return */

    /* Skip to field to copy.*/
    while (--fld_num && *from_rec != '\0')
        {
        while (*from_rec != '\0' && *from_rec != DELIM)
            ++from_rec;
        if (*from_rec == DELIM)
            ++from_rec;
        }

    /* Copy field from from_rec to to_str. */
    while (*from_rec != '\0' && *from_rec != DELIM)
        {

        /* Copy a character to to_str and increment pointers. */
        *to_str++ = *from_rec++;
        }
    *to_str = '\0';
    return (p_to_str);
    }
```

As a last resort, for those rare instances when C just isn't quick or compact enough...

## How About Assembly Language?

There may come a time in your programming experience when you need the absolute maximum in efficiency. You've implemented the application in C, but the response time simply isn't fast enough or the code is very large and takes up too much disk space. These are good reasons for coding assembly-language subfunctions to do certain frequently needed low-level data manipulations.

The interface between assembly-language and C programs is clean: Data may be passed and returned with no great difficulty. In fact, the only problem with using assembly-language subfunctions in your applications is that your programs become less portable and more difficult to maintain.

Thanks to John Socha for the following example of the kind of assembly-language subroutine that can save your C applications valuable processing time. This small routine calculates the average of three numbers passed to it from the C calling function:

```
                ASSUME  CS:_TEXT
_TEXT           SEGMENT PUBLIC BYTE 'CODE'
                PUBLIC  _AVG_3_LONGS
;-------------------------------------------------------------;
; This C-callable procedure returns the average of three long ;
;       integers as a long integer: (long1 + long2 + long3) / 3 ;
;                                                             ;
; Bugs:          The instruction IDIV divides a long by an int ;
;                to return an int, so if the average is larger ;
;                than 65535, you get a divide-by-zero error.  ;
; Written by John Socha.                                      ;
;-------------------------------------------------------------;
STACK_FRAME     STRUC
OLD_BP          DW      ?
RETURN_ADDR     DW      ?
LONG1           DD      ?
LONG2           DD      ?
LONG3           DD      ?
STACK_FRAME     ENDS
_AVG_3_LONGS    PROC    NEAR
                PUSH    BP
                MOV     BP,SP
                MOV     AX,Word Ptr [BP].LONG1    ;LONG1 into DX:AX pair.
                MOV     DX,Word Ptr [BP].LONG1[2]
                ADD     AX,Word Ptr [BP].LONG2   ;Add LONG2.
                ADC     DX,Word Ptr [BP].LONG2[2]
                ADD     AX,Word Ptr [BP].LONG3   ;Add LONG3.
                ADC     DX,Word Ptr [BP].LONG3[2]
                MOV     BX,3                     ;Divide total by 3.
                IDIV    BX
                CWD                              ;Extend sign into DX.
                POP     BP
                RET
_AVG_3_LONGS    ENDP
_TEXT           ENDS
                END
```

After you use an assembler to create an object file of the assembly-language function, you can use the test driver shown on the following page, as I did, to verify that the function really works.

```
/* Test assembly-language function avg_3_longs. */
#include <io.h>

long avg_3_longs(long, long, long);

void main(void)
    {
    write(1, (35L == avg_3_longs(12L, 37L, 56L)) ?
        "OK\n      " : "BUG!!!\7\n", 8);
    }
```

Now let's slow down from this high-performance pace and dig into some advanced data structures that you can use to make more efficient use of memory.

# Advanced Structures and Unions

Chapter 16 presented an extensive background in the structure data type. In this chapter we'll explore two additional data types: *bit field* and *union*. The bit field data type can only be used as a member of a structure. The bit field is unusual in that the size of a bit field is measured in bits, not bytes. The union is valuable because all members of a union begin at the same location in memory, giving a number of views of a single area of memory, through the "eyes" of differing data types.

Certain uses of bit fields and unions can undermine the portability of your C code. However, properly restricted, neither of these powerful C data types presents a portability penalty.

## Bit Fields

The bit field is a space-saving data type that provides a way of declaring a variable that is as small as a single bit or as large as 16 bits in width. A single *unsigned int* can contain 16 independent one-bit field variables, each of which can be assigned either the value 1 or the value 0. Many of the arithmetic and logical operators that are used on ordinary integers also operate on fields, but some do not. Keep in mind that bit fields can be a hazard to your program's portability because they let you write code that depends on the byte ordering of allocation of bits.

---

# C A U T I O N

*Microsoft C supports bit fields based on* char *and* long *type variables. This ability is not in compliance with the ANSI standard, and use of those types should be avoided. Bit fields should be based on* unsigned int *type to maximize portability. A bit field based on* signed int *behaves like a field based on* unsigned int *in Microsoft C, but the ANSI standard states that other compilers are free to differ in making that distinction.*

---

Bit fields can be declared only as members of structures or unions (discussed later in this chapter). To declare a member so that it is a bit field, insert a colon after the type and member name and follow it with the field width (in bits) of that member. You can access bit fields in the same way you access members of a structure:

```
struct bit_fields
    {
    char string[30];
    unsigned first : 1;        /* 1 bit wide: range 0 through 1 */
    unsigned second : 2;       /* 2 bits wide: range 0 through 3 */
    unsigned third : 3;        /* 3 bits wide: range 0 through 7 */
    unsigned fourth : 4;       /* 4 bits wide: range 0 through 15 */
    unsigned fifth : 5;        /* 5 bits wide: range 0 through 31 */
    unsigned sixth : 6;        /* 6 bits wide: range 0 through 63 */
    unsigned seventh : 7;      /* 7 bits wide: range 0 through 127 */
    unsigned eighth : 8;       /* 8 bits wide: range 0 through 255 */
    unsigned ninth : 9;        /* 9 bits wide: range 0 through 511 */
    long number;
    };

/* ... */
    struct bit_fields bits;    /* bits is a bit_fields type struct */

/* ... */
    if (bits.first)            /* is bit-field first equal to one? */
        ++bits.second;         /* if yes, then increment bit-field second */
    else                       /* otherwise, OR the low order 4 bits of */
        bits.eighth |= (bits.fifth & 0x0f); /* field fifth with field eighth */
```

The *++bits.second;* statement in our example might raise a question in your mind as to what would happen if *bits.second* happened to be 3 before it was incremented (so that both bits are 1). Would the overflow from the addition carry over into adjacent fields? The answer is "no." Bit fields are independent of each other. Any overflow takes place "silently" (unreported to you), as is the case with any other integer overflow, without affecting any other variable.

---

# C A U T I O N

*A bit field (in Microsoft C 5.1) might not reside in consecutive, adjacent bits in memory. This behavior differs from ANSI specifications and may change in the future. (See the end of this chapter.)*

---

Bit fields will never overlap a boundary of the base type, which is typically an *unsigned int*. This means that a bit field cannot be declared to be wider than the number of bits in an element of the underlying type, since that would mean straddling a boundary. The base-type boundary affects the way bit fields are stored in memory. For example, the first five fields in the *struct bit_fields* declaration occupy 15 bits (1 + 2 + 3 + 4 + 5) and will fit in a 16-bit integer. The next field (*sixth*) is six bits wide, so it is too wide to fit in the one remaining bit. Instead, *sixth* will begin in the next integer, which means that the last bit of the first integer will be unused.

## Bit fields and memory alignment

There might be a time when you need to align bit fields in a certain manner in memory. C offers several ways to set the alignment. We've just seen how a field that is too wide to fit in the remaining space in the base type (usually *unsigned int*) will start in a new element of that type. If you want to begin a field in a new element but still have space available in the preceding one, declare a field of width 0. This will force the next bit field to a new element. You should always declare fields of 0 width without any name.

You can also declare unnamed fields that are wider than 0 bits and use them as filler to control alignment (placement with respect to underlying type boundaries) in memory:

```
struct align_on_int
    {
    unsigned color : 4;
    unsigned : 0;       /* force hue alignment to next integer boundary */
    unsigned hue : 4;
    unsigned : 1;       /* unnamed field used to control alignment of shade */
    unsigned shade : 7;
    };
```

Perhaps you are wondering why one might care about how a field is aligned in memory—that is, whether it starts at an address that is even or odd or is divisible by 4. Memory alignment is generally the concern of a programmer writing code to control hardware, such as a display screen, communications port, or other device. Coding close to the hardware means dealing with input/output ports, sense bits, and command registers that have exact formats at specific locations in memory. Code for such jobs is by nature machine-dependent and not portable. Later in this chapter, we'll see how to determine exactly which bits a bit field occupies.

## Bit fields for data compression

Programs that use bit fields as a space-saving mechanism, not as a means of direct hardware interfacing, do not depend on positions of bit fields relative to integer boundaries. We'll look at such a program shortly.

The library function *time()* returns the date and time as a long integer (the number of seconds elapsed since Jan. 1, 1970). The function *ctime()* formats that 4-byte binary date into a human-readable 26-byte ASCII text string that gives the day, date, and time. Unfortunately, no library function exists to convert the string returned by *ctime()* to a long integer equivalent, so we can't undo what *ctime()* does.

The function *ct_binary()* in the next program converts a date in string form to a 4-byte binary integer value made up of bit fields. This result is not the same as the result *time()* returns, but it serves as a way of compressing the data so that it uses as little space as the return from *time()* and yet contains information similar to the return from *ctime()*.

The function *show_dates()* performs the reverse operation by processing dates compressed by *ct_binary()* and restoring them to human-readable text.

```
/* Bit fields used to store a compressed array of dates and times.
 * This binary formatting of a date and time differs from the long int
 * returned by the function time().
 */

#include <stdio.h>
#include <string.h>
#include <stdlib.h>
#include <time.h>

#define NDATES 5

struct date_fields_t        /* 4 bytes wide */
    {
    unsigned year : 6;
    unsigned day : 5;
    unsigned hour : 5;
    unsigned month : 4;
    unsigned minute : 6;
    unsigned second : 6;
    };

struct date_fields_alt     /* 6 bytes wide due to alternate ordering of fields */
    {
    unsigned year : 6;
    unsigned month : 4;
    unsigned day : 5;
    unsigned hour : 5;
    unsigned minute : 6;
    unsigned second : 6;
    };

extern  void fill_dates(struct date_fields_t *dates);
extern  void ct_binary(char *ctime_str, struct date_fields_t *p_date);
extern  void show_dates(struct date_fields_t *dates);

void main(void)
    {
    struct date_fields_t *dates;
    dates = (struct date_fields_t *)      /* dynamically allocate */
        calloc(NDATES, sizeof (struct date_fields_t)); /* memory for dates */
```

*(continued)*

*continued*

```
    printf("One date consumes %d bytes, alternate date uses %d bytes\n",
       sizeof (struct date_fields_t),
       sizeof (struct date_fields_alt));
    fill_dates(dates);     /* create date data to operate on and compress data */
    show_dates(dates);
    }

/* Generate data for dates array using time(), ctime(). */
void fill_dates(struct date_fields_t *dates)
    {
    char *ctime_str;
    long tm;
    short idate;

    time(&tm);
    for (idate = 0; idate < NDATES; ++idate)
       {
       ctime_str = ctime(&tm);
       ct_binary(ctime_str, &dates[idate]);
       tm += 7866061;      /* add approx 91 days (in seconds) to the time */
       }
    }

/* Declare names of months (to be used only by functions after declaration). */
char *month_names[12] = {"Jan", "Feb", "Mar", "Apr", "May", "Jun", "Jul",
   "Aug", "Sep", "Oct", "Nov", "Dec"};

/* Convert ASCII date to binary bit fields.
 *
 * bytes:                  012345678901234567890123 4 5
 * ctime():                Sat Mar 04 23:45:43 1989\n\0
 * size of bit fields:        4  5  5  6  6    6
 *     (in p_date)
 */
void ct_binary(
   char *ctime_str,
   struct date_fields_t *p_date)
   {
   short imonth;

   for (imonth = 0; imonth < 12 &&
      strncmp(ctime_str + 4, month_names[imonth], 3); ++imonth)
      ;
   p_date->month = imonth;
   p_date->day = atoi(ctime_str + 8);
   p_date->hour = atoi(ctime_str + 11);
   p_date->minute = atoi(ctime_str + 14);
```

*(continued)*

*continued*

```
   p_date->second = atoi(ctime_str + 17);
   p_date->year = atoi(ctime_str + 20) - 1970;
   }

/* Convert binary bit field date to ASCII format. */
void show_dates(struct date_fields_t *dates)
   {
   short idate;

   for (idate = 0; idate < NDATES; ++idate)
      {
      printf("%s %02d %02d:%02d:%02d %d\n",
         month_names[dates[idate].month],
         dates[idate].day, dates[idate].hour,
         dates[idate].minute, dates[idate].second,
         dates[idate].year + 1970);
      }
   }
```

The output from the program shows the uncompressed dates, as you would expect, but the first line of output is worth a special mention. Using the *sizeof* operator in the *printf* statement in *main()* reveals that a variable of type *struct date_fields_t*, is 4 bytes wide, and an alternate version of the structure, *struct date_fields_alt*, is 6 bytes wide, even though it consists of exactly the same members, but declared in a different order. Can you see why the order of fields could change the size of the structure from 2 integers to 3 integers?

```
One date consumes 4 bytes, alternate date uses 6 bytes
Mar 23 21:34:02 1989
Jun 22 23:35:03 1989
Sep 22 00:36:04 1989
Dec 22 00:37:05 1989
Mar 23 01:38:06 1990
```

The fields of *struct date_fields_t* occupy 4 bytes:

| Field width in bits | 6 5 5   4 6 6 |
|---|---|
| *int* element counter | 1 1 1   2 2 2 |
| Bits used in *int* element | 16        16 |

The fields of *struct date_fields_alt* occupy 6 bytes:

| Field width in bits | 6 4 5   5 6   6 |
|---|---|
| *int* element counter | 1 1 1   2 2   3 |
| Bits used in *int* element | 15      11   6 |

The first structure, *date_fields_t*, is efficient because it uses every single bit of the two integers allocated to it. The second structure, *date_fields_alt*, wastes space because of "holes" created to avoid having any bit field straddle an *int* boundary. This inefficient alternative wastes 16 bits because it uses only 15 out of 16 of the bits in its first *int*, 11 out of 16 of the second *int*, and a mere 6 out of 16 in the third.

The union data structure will allow us to peek inside the implementation of bit fields to see exactly how they operate in our environment (Microsoft C on a PC).

## Unions for Multiple Views of Data

As was mentioned at the beginning of this chapter, the members of a union overlap because they all begin at the same location in memory. A union resembles a structure in that both have one or more members that can have different data types. The syntax of a union declaration is identical to a structure declaration, except that the keyword *union* is substituted for the keyword *struct*. You define a union tag by including it in a declaration that lists the members of the union, and you can subsequently use the union tag to declare instances of the union. The dot (.) and arrow (->) operators access members of unions as well as members of structures.

Unions give a number of views of a single area of memory, through the "eyes" of a variety of data types. A change in the value of one member of a union could change the values of some or all of the other members despite the fact that they are of different types. Members of a union do not necessarily consume equal amounts of memory—each uses only as much memory as its data type requires. The union is always just large enough to satisfy the memory requirement of its largest member.

It's easy to use a union to examine the internal binary format used to store *long* and *short* integers by making a union combining those two integer types with an array of characters. After numbers are assigned to the integer members of the union, the *char* array can be displayed in hex to examine the bit pattern of the integer data in memory.

```
/* Examine the internal binary format used to store long and short
 * integers with a union that combines a long and a short with an
 * array of characters.
 */

#include <stdio.h>

union overlap
    {
    short short_int;
    long long_int;
    char text[5];
    };

void main(void)
    {
    union overlap data_view;

    /* Print the size of the union and each of its members. */
    printf("Sizes of:  union %d, short %d, long %d, text %d\n",
        sizeof data_view, sizeof data_view.short_int,
        sizeof data_view.long_int, sizeof data_view.text);

    /* Assign values to the integer members of the union and print */
    /* the value of each member in hex. */
    data_view.long_int = 0;
    data_view.short_int = 0x1234;
    printf("short: 0x%x, long: 0x%08lx, text[0:3]: %02x %02x  %02x %02x\n",
        data_view.short_int, data_view.long_int, data_view.text[0],
        data_view.text[1], data_view.text[2], data_view.text[3]);

    /* Assign a new value to the long member of the union and print */
    /* the value of each member in hex. */
    data_view.long_int = 0x12345678;
    printf("short: 0x%x, long: 0x%08lx, text[0:3]: %02x %02x  %02x %02x\n",
        data_view.short_int, data_view.long_int, data_view.text[0],
        data_view.text[1], data_view.text[2], data_view.text[3]);
    }
```

# C A U T I O N

*Use of unions can produce code whose results vary, depending on the architecture of the CPU the code was compiled and executed on. This certainly makes your program non-portable.*

As the nearby "Caution" box warns, use of unions can render programs non-portable. This restriction can have a hidden benefit, however, if you learn from its use. If you compare the outputs of the previous program on a variety of CPUs, you can see how the byte ordering of *short* and *long* integers varies from machine to machine. For example, the output of the program on a Mega Comm Technologies PRO-386 PC looks as follows:

```
Sizes of:  union 5, short 2, long 4, text 5
short: 0x1234, long: 0x00001234, text[0:3]: 34 12  00 00
short: 0x5678, long: 0x12345678, text[0:3]: 78 56  34 12
```

The output of the program on a Digital Equipment Corp. VAX 785 looks like this:

```
Sizes of:  union 5, short 2, long 4, text 5
short: 0x1234, long: 0x00001234, text[0:3]: 34 12  00 00
short: 0x5678, long: 0x12345678, text[0:3]: 78 56  34 12
```

The output of the program on a Sun Microcomputers 4/110 looks like this:

```
Sizes of:  union 8, short 2, long 4, text 5
short: 0x1234, long: 0x12340000, text[0:3]: 12 34  00 00
short: 0x1234, long: 0x12345678, text[0:3]: 12 34  56 78
```

Now we see that the *short* and *long* integers are stored the same way on a VAX as on a PC—namely, least-significant bytes first. The byte ordering on the Sun is the reverse—the most-significant bytes are stored first.

## Unions of structures

Unions of structures may be the most flexible and descriptive data type. They offer a variety of views of a data space. The following program writes personnel data in binary format (held in a union) for employees and contractors of a hypothetical company to a single data file. The *rec_personnel* union has two members, a *rec_employee* structure for employee data and a *rec_contractor* structure for contractor data.

Each file entry begins with a 2-byte data length containing the size of the structure in the entry, followed by a data type code of *E* for employees or *C* for contractors and then either a contractor or employee structure, depending on the type code of record. The library functions *fread()* and *fwrite()* are used to handle the binary file access.

```
/* Union of structures used to hold data from records read from a binary */
/* file. Records contain a code indicating their type of record format. */

#include <stdio.h>
#include <stdlib.h>

struct rec_employee
    {
    char name[30];
    long salary;
    };

struct rec_contractor
    {
    char name[30];
    char company[30];
    long rate;
    };

union rec_personnel
    {
    struct rec_employee employee;
    struct rec_contractor contractor;
    };

extern  void bin_put(char code, union rec_personnel *p_personnel,
    short size, struct _iobuf *pers_file);
extern  void bin_list(struct _iobuf *pers_file);

static struct rec_employee employee_data = {"Brad Green", 3223315};
static struct rec_contractor contractor_data = {"Hilda White",
    "HW Consultants", 5000};

void main(void)
    {
    FILE *pers_file;

    if (NULL == (pers_file = fopen("PEOPLE.DAT", "w")))
        abort();

    /* Output sample employee and contractor records to personnel file. */
    bin_put('E', (union rec_personnel *) &employee_data,
        sizeof employee_data, pers_file);
    bin_put('C', (union rec_personnel *) &contractor_data,
        sizeof contractor_data, pers_file);
```

*(continued)*

365

*continued*

```
    /* List contents of personnel file. */
    fclose(pers_file);
    if (NULL == (pers_file = fopen("PEOPLE.DAT", "r")))
        abort();
    bin_list(pers_file);
    }

/* Output a binary record from a union of records. */
void bin_put(
    char code,
    union rec_personnel *p_personnel,
    short size,
    FILE *pers_file)

    {
    fwrite(&size, 2, 1, pers_file);
    fwrite(&code, 1, 1, pers_file);
    fwrite(p_personnel, size, 1, pers_file);
    }

/* Read and list a binary file with different record types. */
void bin_list(FILE *pers_file)
    {
    char code;
    union rec_personnel personnel;
    short size;

    do
        {
        fread(&size, 2, 1, pers_file);
        fread(&code, 1, 1, pers_file);
        fread(&personnel, size, 1, pers_file);
        if (!feof(pers_file))
            {
            if (code == 'E')
                printf("Employee: %s, salary %ld\n",
                    personnel.employee.name, personnel.employee.salary);
            else if (code == 'C')
                printf("Contractor: %s, %s, rate %ld\n",
                    personnel.contractor.name, personnel.contractor.company,
                    personnel.contractor.rate);
            }
        } while (!feof(pers_file));
    }
```

This is the output from the personnel program:

```
Employee: Brad Green, salary 3223315
Contractor: Hilda White, HW Consultants, rate 5000
```

It's time for a final look at bit fields, this time in conjunction with unions so that we see them from an implementation standpoint.

# Internal Storage of Bit Fields

Now that we have some knowledge of unions, we can use that knowledge as we return to bit fields and examine them a little more. Let's throw all portability concerns out the window for a moment, and try to learn how Microsoft C allocates bits within an *unsigned int*. I think you'll find the answer quite surprising!

The *bit_overlay union* type in the following program overlays an *int*, a *char* array, and a structure of bit fields to give three perspectives of a 2-byte data space. Values are assigned to the integer view, and then each of the members of the union are output. Each time through the loop, a different single bit is on in the integer view of the data. This is accomplished by shifting the integer right one bit each time. First the highest-order bit is on, and then subsequently lower-order bits. Bear in mind that the highest-order byte of the integer is the second in memory, not the first, due to the byte ordering of integers that we discussed earlier in this chapter.

```
/* Examine the internal binary format used to store integers, characters, */
/* and bit fields by creating a union that holds all three. */

#include <stdio.h>

struct bits
    {
    unsigned field_0 : 1;
    unsigned field_1 : 1;
    unsigned field_2 : 1;
    unsigned field_3 : 1;
    unsigned field_4 : 1;
    unsigned field_5 : 1;
    unsigned field_6 : 1;
    unsigned field_7 : 1;
    unsigned field_8 : 1;
    unsigned field_9 : 1;
```

*(continued)*

*continued*

```
    unsigned field_10 : 1;
    unsigned field_11 : 1;
    unsigned field_12 : 1;
    unsigned field_13 : 1;
    unsigned field_14 : 1;
    unsigned field_15 : 1;
    };

union bit_overlay
    {
    unsigned integer;
    unsigned char str[2];
    struct bits flds;
    };

void main(void)
    {
    short ibit;
    union bit_overlay view;
    view.integer = 0x8000;

    for (ibit = 0; ibit < 16; ++ibit)
        {
        printf("%2d  int:%04x  str: %02x%02x  "
            "bits: %x%x%x%x %x%x%x%x  %x%x%x%x %x%x%x%x\n",
            ibit, view.integer, view.str[0], view.str[1], view.flds.field_0,
            view.flds.field_1, view.flds.field_2, view.flds.field_3,
            view.flds.field_4, view.flds.field_5, view.flds.field_6,
            view.flds.field_7, view.flds.field_8, view.flds.field_9,
            view.flds.field_10, view.flds.field_11, view.flds.field_12,
            view.flds.field_13, view.flds.field_14, view.flds.field_15);

        /* Shift integer to the right by 1 bit. */
        view.integer >>= 1;
        }
    }
```

Line 15 of the output demonstrates that the first bit field, *field_0*, is stored as the least-significant bit of the integer, which resides in the first byte of the integer, since our implementation of integers stores the least-significant byte first. Line 0 shows that the most-significant bit of the integer occupies the same memory location as the last bit field, *field_15*.

```
 0  int:8000  str: 0080  bits: 0000 0000  0000 0001
 1  int:4000  str: 0040  bits: 0000 0000  0000 0010
 2  int:2000  str: 0020  bits: 0000 0000  0000 0100
 3  int:1000  str: 0010  bits: 0000 0000  0000 1000
 4  int:0800  str: 0008  bits: 0000 0000  0001 0000
 5  int:0400  str: 0004  bits: 0000 0000  0010 0000
 6  int:0200  str: 0002  bits: 0000 0000  0100 0000
 7  int:0100  str: 0001  bits: 0000 0000  1000 0000
 8  int:0080  str: 8000  bits: 0000 0001  0000 0000
 9  int:0040  str: 4000  bits: 0000 0010  0000 0000
10  int:0020  str: 2000  bits: 0000 0100  0000 0000
11  int:0010  str: 1000  bits: 0000 1000  0000 0000
12  int:0008  str: 0800  bits: 0001 0000  0000 0000
13  int:0004  str: 0400  bits: 0010 0000  0000 0000
14  int:0002  str: 0200  bits: 0100 0000  0000 0000
15  int:0001  str: 0100  bits: 1000 0000  0000 0000
```

I promised a surprise and this next program is the source. Let's declare a structure that contains five bit fields, each three bits wide. Then we'll turn on all bits in each bit field, one bit field at a time. The function *show()* is passed the address of the union and uses the arrow (->) operator to access its members.

```c
/* Examine the internal binary format used to store integers, characters, */
/* and 3-bit bit fields by creating a union that holds all three. */

#include <stdio.h>

struct bits
    {
    unsigned first : 3;
    unsigned second : 3;
    unsigned third : 3;
    unsigned fourth : 3;
    unsigned fifth : 3;
    };

union bit_overlay
    {
    unsigned integer;
    unsigned char str[2];
    struct bits flds;
    };

extern void show(union bit_overlay *p_view);
```

*(continued)*

*continued*

```
void main(void)
    {
    union bit_overlay view;

    view.integer = 0;
    view.flds.first = 0x7;   /* remember: 0x7 equals 111 in binary */
    show(&view);

    view.integer = 0;
    view.flds.second = 0x7;
    show(&view);

    view.integer = 0;
    view.flds.third = 0x7;
    show(&view);

    view.integer = 0;
    view.flds.fourth = 0x7;
    show(&view);

    view.integer = 0;
    view.flds.fifth = 0x7;
    show(&view);
    }

/* Print the integer and string members of the union. */
void show(union bit_overlay *p_view)
    {
    static short count = 0;

    printf("%2d  int:%04x  str: %02x%02x\n",
        ++count, p_view->integer, (p_view->str)[0], (p_view->str)[1]);
    }
```

Line 3 of the output demonstrates the fact that Microsoft C does not always store all the bits of a bit field in adjacent bits of memory!

```
1  int:0007  str: 0700
2  int:0038  str: 3800
3  int:01c0  str: c001
4  int:0e00  str: 000e
5  int:7000  str: 0070
```

The *str* view (which gives the bytes in the order they appear in memory) shows that the third field of three bits is split between the high-order two bits of the first byte and the lowest-order bit of the second byte. That is a surprise and also does not conform to the ANSI standard, which states: "If enough space remains, a bit field that immediately follows another bit field in a structure shall be packed into adjacent bits of the same unit." (In this case, the unit is an unsigned integer.)

Microsoft will probably move closer to conformance to the ANSI standard in future releases of its C compiler. Speaking of the future, the relationship between the C language and Microsoft's entry into the world of advanced operating systems bears closer examination and is the subject of the last chapter.

# OS/2 Programming

After you become familiar with C programming under MS-DOS, you might consider making the transition to OS/2. To help you make a decision, this chapter presents general information that will give you a clearer notion of what to expect once you begin writing new software and porting existing C source code to OS/2. Extensive detail on how to build large, interactive applications that use OS/2 libraries and other capabilities is beyond the scope of this book.

For an overview of OS/2, see *Inside OS/2* (Microsoft Press, 1988), by Gordon Letwin. Ray Duncan discusses in detail everything about OS/2 except the Presentation Manager in his book *Advanced OS/2 Programming* (Microsoft Press, 1989). For information about C programming for the Presentation Manager, see *Programming the OS/2 Presentation Manager* (Microsoft Press, 1989), by Charles Petzold.

## The Need for OS/2

OS/2, the new multitasking operating system, goes a long way toward unleashing the power of Intel's 80286 and 80386 chips. Sophisticated applications for business professionals, such as electronic publishing and integrated desktop communications, database, and spreadsheet applications, can be much more functional and easier to use in OS/2's rich development environment.

From a technical standpoint, the features of OS/2 are very desirable. Who could resist a standardized, window-oriented graphical user interface, the end of the 640 KB program-size barrier, virtual memory, multitasking, sophisticated interprocess communication, and increased device independence?

# Key Elements of OS/2

Perhaps you'll decide to convert to OS/2 strictly by a careful weighing of benefits and drawbacks. Or maybe you'll find yourself swept up by an impulse to own a system that's closer to the cutting edge of technology. No matter what is your overriding reason for converting, you should take a look at what OS/2 has to offer. The following are some of the major features of OS/2:

*Virtual memory*
*Dynamic link libraries*
*Multitasking*
*Interprocess communication*
*Background processing*
*Backward compatibility of real mode*
*Memory protection*
*Dual-mode programming*
*Character-based user interface*
*Graphical user interface of Presentation Manager*
*Device independence*

Let's look at each of these features in turn.

## Virtual memory

OS/2 supports the use of virtual memory, which gives the illusion of an unlimited amount of physical memory. If a process requires the use of more memory than is available in physical memory, it will swap data from memory that isn't being used to disk in order to make room for what is needed.

The 80286 and 80386 chips are able to address up to 16 MB of RAM (physical memory). Support for virtual memory means that a program could theoretically contain 1000 megabytes of code and data, excluding data stored in files. With virtual memory, a program's code and data are organized into smaller blocks, called *pages*. Not every page resides in memory at any moment that the program is executing. OS/2 can store pages on disk and retrieve them into memory when needed by performing an operation known as *swapping*. A disk file used for swapping acts as an extension of RAM, making a computer act as if it were configured with much more RAM than is actually present.

Accessing a disk is a time-consuming task, so swapping can slow down your program's performance. If you find that your machine is doing more swapping than working, you should install more RAM.

---

## C O M M E N T

*Support for virtual memory does not mean that you can declare a million-byte string and operate on it with standard library string functions, such as* strlen() *and* strcpy(). *That ability requires full 32-bit addressing and is not available with Microsoft C 5.1.*

---

The 1000 MB theoretical program size is trimmed by the 32 MB limitation on the size of a logical disk drive to allow for file-system compatibility with MS-DOS. Combining the 16 MB of RAM with the 32 MB limitation of disk space yields a 48 MB space for programs—still quite an impressive amount compared with the former 640 KB limit. In time, the support for larger disk-drive partitions will be available and when it is, we will see the program-size limit grow as well.

## Dynamic link libraries

OS/2 uses dynamic linking to access functions or resources outside an executable file during execution. The functions or resources are contained in what is called a dynamic link library, which is loaded into memory the first time an executing program needs to link with it.

Tremendous savings of disk and RAM space are realized because of dynamic linking. Executable programs do not contain copies of dynamic library functions (they just need to get the address of the function in memory), so they are much smaller. A single copy of each dynamic library function is shared in memory by all programs calling it.

The possibility of applications that can have whole interfaces or pieces of functionality replaced without relinking them has become a reality with dynamic linking. This breakthrough in software technology is used extensively within OS/2 and may also be applied to applications developed under it. By facilitating the ability to have plug-in replacements for subsets of applications or for interfaces, the door has been opened to great improvements in the quality of application and system software.

## Multitasking—processes and threads

Multitasking is a facility of OS/2 that allows more than one program to be running at a time. This means that your system can appear to be compiling a program, editing a file, receiving data via a communications port, printing, managing a database, receiving a file from another network user, and more, all at the same time. Multitasking is a means of squeezing more work out of your computer. For example, the time your system spends idle between your keystrokes as you type in new text with an editor can be devoted to doing work for another program.

Each executing program is associated with its own task unit called a *process*. The process is the fundamental unit of ownership of OS/2. Each process owns the memory that it is allocated and may also own opened files, dynamic link libraries, and semaphores (the latter two are discussed later in this chapter). When a process begins execution, it contains a single *thread*. A thread is the mechanism that describes the point of execution of a process. It is the thread that performs each instruction in the program.

Because OS/2 supports multitasking, several threads may execute at once. The management of threads is handled by OS/2. Each thread is given control of the CPU for a short interval, called a *time slice*, during which it does some work. Then control is switched to a different task. If the current thread needs some of its pages of code or data that are not in RAM because they were swapped out, a swapping-in operation is performed during the time slice. Switching between tasks happens quickly and time slices are short enough so that each thread of a program process has the illusion of owning the machine and working alone.

The ability to do concurrent operations within a process is made possible by the use of multiple threads in one process. A program that processes blocks of data from a disk file can start a thread that will read the next block of data into a buffer while the current block is being processed. This operation creates an overlapping of effort and eliminates some or all of the time that the machine would otherwise spend idle, waiting for the next block to be read from the input file after the last one was completely processed.

## Interprocess communication

The IPC (interprocess communication) facilities of OS/2 are quite elegant and complete. The following is a list of the IPC methods of OS/2:

- *Semaphores* are software flags that can be accessed by more than one process so that the processes can synchronize their activities with each other.

- *Pipes* are special memory-resident files that can be written to by one process as they are being read by another process.

- *Shared memory segments* can be used between processes to create a "clipboard" capability so that data from one process can be moved to the shared area and examined by another process very quickly.

- *Queues* can be used to hold several messages in shared memory at the same time.

- *Signals* are mechanisms that temporarily suspend program execution. OS/2 gives processes the ability both to handle the system signals and to send signals to and receive signals from other processes.

## Background processing

Not every user-initiated process interacts with the user and displays information on the screen. Non-interactive programs can be executed in the background by use of the *DETACH* command. Once started, these background programs cannot be stopped by the user; they must terminate themselves. Background processing is nice for large file searches and compilations, among other things. It's quite a thrill to hear your

disk drive doing work for a background process while you initiate
other programs in the foreground.

## Modes of operation: real and protected

The 80286 and 80386 microprocessors have two modes of operation:
real and protected. *Real mode* uses the same memory-addressing method
as MS-DOS. *Protected mode,* on the other hand, uses a new method of
memory addressing that enables memory protection, virtual memory
management, and the other features of OS/2.

An important goal of the designers of OS/2 was to make the transition from MS-DOS as easy as possible. A special window, called the
*3.x box* or the *compatibility box,* operates in real mode, making it possible to run most MS-DOS 2.x and 3.x programs there. The 3.x box fills
the entire screen when it is active. There is only one 3.x box, so you
can have only a single active MS-DOS program. The 80386 chip can support multiple 3.x boxes, but the 80286 cannot.

The compatibility of real mode doesn't come without cost. Because it addresses memory the same way MS-DOS does, program space
is limited to 640 KB, and virtual memory is not available. Real mode
also offers little memory protection, so a program in real mode can
alter memory it doesn't own, which can bring down the entire system.
Some applications won't run in the compatibility box, so you must
boot MS-DOS (probably from a floppy disk) to run them. Reboot OS/2
after you finish so that you can work with results of the program that is
real-mode incompatible.

Any process outside the 3.x box runs in protected mode. Protected mode is where you'll find the new OS/2 functionality. Programs
that execute in protected mode are able to take advantage of multitasking, virtual memory, and the new graphical user interface, and
they benefit from the safety of memory protection. Protected-mode
programs will execute in a full-screen OS/2 window, unless they call
functions compatible with the Presentation Manager (the OS/2 graphical user interface) to operate the display within user-sizable Presentation Manager windows.

C programs that you write or that you have source code for (including all programs in this book) can be compiled and linked to run
in protected mode as long as you don't use any DOS-specific commands in them. Your C compiler comes with two sets of link libraries
in order to support linking for real- and protected-mode execution.

Standard C library functions, such as *printf()* and *scanf()*, are found in both sets of libraries and make it easy to create executable files for either mode of operation, with few (if any) code changes. OS/2 also contains more efficient alternatives to the C standard I/O functions, as we will see shortly.

---

## C O M M E N T

*Protected mode gets its name from its advanced memory protection facilities. If a process misbehaves, others can usually continue to function. A program that tries to examine or clobber memory that it does not own will be stopped from doing so. A memory-protection fault will be reported to the user and the process that is to blame will be terminated.*

---

## System services for C programs in MS-DOS and OS/2

MS-DOS and OS/2 offer vastly different methods for accessing their services from C programs. Many MS-DOS system services can be called from C programs through specialized interface library functions, such as *_dos_creat()*, *_dos_open()*, *_dos_setdrive()*, and *_dos_setvect()*. Other MS-DOS system services are not available from specialized single-purpose interface functions. They can be requested using more general lower-level system call functions, such as *bdos()*, *intdos()*, and *intdosx()*. Higher-level standard library functions perform some additional work and may ultimately call one or more system services for you. The variety of ways of making system calls and obtaining error return codes in MS-DOS can be confusing due to their inconsistency. OS/2 has cleaned up system services by implementing a uniform interface to its system services.

The Application Program Interface (API) is a collection of functions that make OS/2 operating-system services available to C programs. Some examples of these functions are *DosOpen()*, *DosCreateThread()*, *KbdGetCp()*, and *VioSetFont()*. The set of API services is large (about 250) and is a superset of the (100 or so) services available to MS-DOS programs. Some of the API services resemble MS-DOS counterparts, and other API services are unparalleled in MS-DOS because they interface to advanced OS/2 functionality, such as multitasking, interprocess communication, and virtual-memory management.

## The Family API and dual-mode bound programs

Microsoft has taken steps to make it easier to write code that will execute without modification in three worlds: under MS-DOS, in the 3.x box, and in protected mode. A subset of the API functions, called the *Family API*, can be called from all three environments with identical or nearly identical results. The most exciting aspect of this family is that a single executable program can be built to run in all three environments. In fact, many OS/2 utilities are Family API applications.

The *BIND* utility converts a protected-mode executable program, enabling it to run in protected mode or real mode under OS/2 or on MS-DOS 2.x and 3.x machines. If you want to bind a program, you must restrict the API library function calls to bind to Family API functions, a subset of all API library functions. The executable program that you bind is said to be a *bound executable*. The Family API function *DosGetMachineMode()* can be called to determine which mode a program is running in, so calls to any restricted protected-mode functions can be avoided in real mode.

## User interfaces

The character-based user-interface functions give a character-oriented, rather than a graphics-oriented, view of the screen world. This interface is reminiscent of bygone days of teletype computing and may ultimately serve as a means of easing your transition to the superior graphical user interface offered by the Presentation Manager. The functions that OS/2 offers for managing the screen, the keyboard, and the mouse in the character-based interface are very fast for character-oriented screen output and offer much more flexibility than their MS-DOS predecessors. Many will operate within OS/2 Presentation Manager windows, and most belong to the Family API, so they can be called in bound executables.

The following is a screen-saver program that calls Family API functions and therefore can be bound to execute under MS-DOS and the 3.x box, in addition to OS/2 protected mode. The definition of the constant *INCL_SUB* before the *#include* for *os2.h* restricts the code included from *os2.h* to what is needed.

```
/* A screen-saver that clears the screen and makes the cursor invisible. */
#define INCL_SUB
#include <os2.h>

void main(void)
    {
    KBDKEYINFO keyin;   /* keyboard information structure for KbdCharIn() */
    VIOCURSORINFO cursor;  /* cursor information structure */

    VioGetCurType(&cursor, 0);       /* obtain cursor characteristics */
    cursor.attr = -1;                /* set hidden cursor attribute */
    VioSetCurType(&cursor, 0);       /* make the cursor invisible */
    VioWrtTTY("\033[2J", 4, 0);      /* clear the screen (requires ANSI ON) */
    KbdCharIn(&keyin, 0, 0);         /* wait for any keyboard input */
    cursor.attr = 0;                 /* set visible cursor attribute */
    VioSetCurType(&cursor, 0);       /* restore prior cursor characteristics */
    }
```

How fast is screen output using OS/2 video I/O (VIO) functions? Nearly as fast as direct video memory accesses under MS-DOS (and far more portable). It was no wonder that many MS-DOS programs that needed fast, sophisticated display output "cheated" by accessing video RAM directly—it was far faster than doing the job "legally" through system calls or the C library. This program will let us make a performance comparison by displaying alternating screenfuls of Zs and periods:

```
/* A program that times how long it takes to display alternating */
/* screenfuls of Zs and periods */
#define INCL_SUB
#include <os2.h>
#include <time.h>
#include <stdlib.h>
#include <stdio.h>
#include <string.h>

#define SCRNLEN (24 * 80)

void main(void)
    {
    char *buf1 = malloc(SCRNLEN), *buf2 = malloc(SCRNLEN);
    short iscreen, ichar;
    long begin, end;
```

*(continued)*

*continued*

```
   for (ichar = 0; ichar < SCRNLEN; ++ichar)    /* fill both output buffers */
      {
      buf1[ichar] = '.';
      buf2[ichar] = 'Z';
      }
   time(&begin);   /* save time at the start of output */
   for (iscreen = 0; iscreen < 100; ++iscreen)    /* screen output loop */
      {
      VioSetCurPos(0, 0, 0);   /* move cursor to home */
      VioWrtTTY((iscreen % 2) ? buf1 : buf2, SCRNLEN, 0);   /* fill screen */
      }
   time(&end);
   sprintf(buf1, "\r\nElapsed time (seconds): %ld\r\n", end - begin);
   VioWrtTTY(buf1, strlen(buf1), 0);   /* output the results */
   }
```

These are the results of my timings for output of 100 full screens:

| TEST ENVIRONMENT | TIME IN SECONDS |
|---|---|
| Protected mode under OS/2 | 17 |
| 3.x box under OS/2 (*BIND* used) | 66 |
| MS-DOS (*BIND* used) | 85 |
| MS-DOS with equivalent calls to *write()* | 85 |
| 3.x box with equivalent calls to *write()* | 67 |

The times in the preceding table indicate that VIO screen output in protected mode is four or five times faster (on my 80386 machine) than standard I/O under MS-DOS. The *VioWrtTTY()* function can fill the entire screen in a sixth of a second, which should be fast enough for just about anyone. We also see that the bound executable with calls to *VioWrtTTY()* is faster in the 3.x box than the same program modified to call *write()*. The bound executable is slower under MS-DOS than the *write()* equivalent and is also larger.

VIO functions enable you to create your own graphic output in the character-based interface, as long as you observe some restrictions. Graphics output functions are not supplied, but you are free to write your own. Their portability is up to you, so proceed carefully. If you want to combine text and graphics with device independence inside an elegant window environment, you need to learn to work with the Presentation Manager.

# The Presentation Manager

The Presentation Manager is the direction in which future OS/2 applications are heading. A uniform graphical user interface of icons, windows, and window parts (such as scroll bars, pull-down menus, title bars, and more) makes it possible for different applications to share a common look and feel. This similar nature means that users will find Presentation Manager programs easy to learn to use.

The number of Presentation Manager window options and controls is quite large. It's good to know that one can start slowly and learn the features a few at a time, instead of having to learn a great deal before being able to produce any working Presentation Manager applications. Graphics output within windows is created by making calls to Graphics Programming Interface (GPI) functions. Although the GPI includes functions for handling text in windows, you can also use the same VIO functions you used in the character-based interface. Using the familiar VIO functions will give you a base from which to begin learning how to program in the Presentation Manager.

The richness of the GPI for developing graphics is impressive. There are far more functions that give much greater control than the graphics functions that come with the MS-DOS C compiler. Once you've learned the GPI functions, you won't need to learn a new set to output to different screen or printer devices, because the GPI functions are device independent.

Among the many Presentation Manager functions is a set that enables programs to make use of the *clipboard*. The clipboard is a mechanism that makes it possible to transfer graphics and text between applications running in different windows. Cut, copy, paste, and clear operations are supplied. OS/2 uses shared memory as the medium for the transfer of clipboard data.

Let's look at an example of a Presentation Manager program so that you can get an idea of what's involved. The program that we'll examine simply reports the location of the mouse pointer. Every movement of the mouse is reflected by a change in the coordinates displayed in the red rectangle that appears in the lower-left corner of the window. A single click of the left mouse button causes the mouse-pointer coordinates to be displayed at the mouse-pointer location. Two notes are played for that mouse click, and the pitches of the notes are based on the horizontal and vertical coordinate values. The window is

cleared each time the left mouse button is double-clicked (pressed
twice in rapid succession) or the window size is changed by the user.

```
/* OS/2 Presentation Manager Demonstration */
#define INCL_WIN
#define INCL_GPI
#include <os2.h>
#include <string.h>
#include <stdlib.h>

MRESULT EXPENTRY pmdemo(HWND, unsigned short, MPARAM, MPARAM);

int main(void)
   {
   static char class[] = "PM Demo";
   static unsigned long frame_flags = FCF_TITLEBAR : FCF_SYSMENU :
      FCF_SIZEBORDER : FCF_MINMAX : FCF_SHELLPOSITION : FCF_TASKLIST;

   HAB hab;                          /* handle to anchor block */
   HMQ hmq;                          /* handle to message queue */
   HWND hwnd_frame;                  /* handle to window frame */
   HWND hwnd_client;                 /* handle to client window */
   QMSG qmsg;                        /* message queue identifier */

   hab = WinInitialize(0);           /* initialize system for PM function calls */
   hmq = WinCreateMsgQueue(hab, 0); /* create a message queue */

   /* Register class of this window. */
   WinRegisterClass(hab, class, pmdemo, 0L, 0);

   /* Create the main window */
   hwnd_frame = WinCreateStdWindow(HWND_DESKTOP, WS_VISIBLE,
      &frame_flags, class, NULL, 0L, NULL, 0, &hwnd_client);

   /* Let PM know icon to use to display this window when it is minimized. */
   WinSendMsg(hwnd_frame, WM_SETICON, WinQuerySysPointer(HWND_DESKTOP,
      SPTR_APPICON, FALSE), NULL);

   while (WinGetMsg(hab, &qmsg, NULL, 0, 0))    /* loop for each message */
      WinDispatchMsg(hab, &qmsg); /* dispatch message to pmdemo() */

   WinDestroyWindow(hwnd_frame);  /* delete the window */
   WinDestroyMsgQueue(hmq);       /* delete the message queue */
   WinTerminate(hab);             /* release pmdemo resources */
   return (0);
   }
```

*(continued)*

*continued*

```
/* pmdemo() fields all messages dispatched to window. */
MRESULT EXPENTRY pmdemo(HWND hwnd, unsigned short msg, MPARAM mp1, MPARAM mp2)
  {
  static POINTL mouse_pos;        /* x and y mouse position coordinates */
  HPS hps;                        /* handle to presentation space */
  static char buf[20];            /* text buffer to display coordinates */
  static POINTL point = {10L, 10L};   /* screen location for text output */
  static RECTL pos_rect = {0L, 0L, 75L, 28L};  /* rectangle around text */
  static long move_count = 0;     /* counter for mouse movements */

  switch(msg)         /* message processing depends on type of message */
    {
    case WM_MOUSEMOVE:            /* mouse has moved */
      hps = WinGetPS(hwnd);       /* get handle to presentation space */
      if (!move_count++)          /* if this is the first mouse movement */
      GpiErase(hps);              /* then clear the screen */
      mouse_pos.x = MOUSEMSG(&msg)->x;   /* get x (horizontal) position */
      mouse_pos.y = MOUSEMSG(&msg)->y;   /* get y (vertical) position */

      /* Convert mouse position and display in a red rectangle. */
      ltoa(mouse_pos.x, buf, 10);
      strcat(buf, ", ");
      ltoa(mouse_pos.y, buf + strlen(buf), 10);
      WinFillRect(hps, &pos_rect, CLR_RED);
      GpiCharStringAt(hps, &point, (long) strlen(buf), buf);

      WinReleasePS(hps);          /* release handle to presentation space */
      break;
    case WM_SIZE:                 /* window size has changed */
    case WM_BUTTON1DBLCLK:        /* left mouse button was double-clicked */
      hps = WinGetPS(hwnd);       /* get handle to presentation space */
      GpiErase(hps);              /* clear the presentation-space screen */
      WinReleasePS(hps);          /* release handle to presentation space */
      break;
    case WM_BUTTON1DOWN:          /* left mouse button was pressed */
      hps = WinGetPS(hwnd);       /* get handle to presentation space */
      GpiCharStringAt(hps, &mouse_pos, (long) strlen(buf), buf);
      DosBeep((short)mouse_pos.x + 37, 250); /* tone for horizontal pos */
      DosBeep((short)mouse_pos.y + 37, 250); /* tone for vertical pos */
      WinReleasePS(hps);          /* release handle to presentation space */
      break;
    case WM_PAINT:                /* window needs to be repainted */
      hps = WinBeginPaint(hwnd, NULL, NULL);   /* prepare to paint */
      WinEndPaint(hps);                        /* finished painting */
      return (0);
    }
  return (WinDefWindowProc(hwnd, msg, mp1, mp2)); /* default processing */
  }
```

The appearance of the main function is typical of many Presentation Manager programs. It creates a standard window and the means for managing and communicating with that window. The central loop, in which *WinGetMsg()* and *WinDispatchMsg()* are repeatedly called, passes messages from the Presentation Manager to the message-handling procedure, *pmdemo()*. The message-handling procedure you supply can choose to process these messages, ignore them, or permit default Presentation Manager processing of them, depending on the requirements of the application.

The *pmdemo()* procedure is the heart and personality of the application because it describes how to handle program events, such as window creation, keyboard input, mouse activity, the need for window repainting, and window termination. The mouse-movement message will probably be the most common message sent to the procedure since every movement of the mouse, no matter how small, generates one.

These descriptions of writing new applications in OS/2 might make the process sound inviting, but you also need to consider support for converting existing MS-DOS C code.

# Porting from MS-DOS to OS/2

How much effort are you willing to expend to modify your code to make it work under OS/2? A range of choices exists for porting MS-DOS applications, from doing virtually nothing at all to total commitment by making use of the advanced features found in the Presentation Manager.

The 3.x box is the means for the OS/2 user to achieve the greatest backward compatibility to MS-DOS versions 2.x and 3.x. Porting code from MS-DOS to the 3.x box requires the least effort when you enter the OS/2 universe. Differences between running in the 3.x box and MS-DOS do exist, so some MS-DOS software will not perform in that OS/2 window exactly as it did under MS-DOS. Programs that violate the software restrictions of the 3.x box can crash OS/2, necessitating a reboot. All programs found in this book will perform no differently in the 3.x box and will not need any modification.

The use of extended memory is one restriction to programs running in the 3.x box, which means some print spoolers and RAM-disk programs can't be used there. Expanded-memory programs that adhere to the Lotus/Intel/Microsoft specifications will continue to operate. Programs that are unable to tolerate suspension of their execution momentarily, such as some communications software, may also have difficulties. The majority of other restrictions center around interrupt handling and hardware control and are outside the scope of this book.

The functions for the character-based interface are an excellent middle route to take from MS-DOS to OS/2. They offer substantial improvements in speed and capability yet are not radically different from older standard library functions. The added performance and functionality derived from a move to character-based programs, combined with retaining the ability to execute under MS-DOS (using the BIND utility), make this porting option very attractive.

The Presentation Manager is at the opposite end of the spectrum from the 3.x box. Programs that use its features have made the full transition to the new operating system. These programs call library functions to create and manage graphics windows and their contents. The amount of work for this kind of port can be large. You may want to consider writing new applications for the Presentation Manager and porting existing ones to the character-based interface as an initial strategy.

## A Happy Note

I like to end discussions on a happy note, so let me present a character-based random music program that can play more than 30,000 different tunes. Each tune is selected by supplying an integer as the first and only command line argument. If you omit the optional seed argument, which is the melody-selection mechanism, the time of day will be passed to *srand()* to set the random seed.

```
/* TUNE.C: Play a random tune. The random number seed from the command line  */
/*   is optional. For example:   TUNE 1010 */
#define INCL_SUB
#include <os2.h>
#include <stdlib.h>
#include <time.h>
```

*(continued)*

TUNE.C *continued*

```
void main(unsigned ac, char *av[])
    {
    short itone;
    short seed;
    long tm;

    if (ac > 1)
        seed = atoi(av[1]);   /* accept optional random seed */
    else
        {
        time(&tm);
        seed = (short)tm;     /* generate seed "randomly" from the time of day */
        }
    srand(seed);              /* pass the seed to the random-number generator */

    for (itone = 0; itone < 1000; ++itone)
        DosBeep(rand() % 1000 + 40, rand() % 1000);
    }
```

# S E C T I O N

# VII

Section VII contains six useful appendixes for quick reference. **Appendix A** lists C's standard reserved keywords. **Appendix B** lists all of C's operators, with precedence and grouping. **Appendix C** provides a summary of preprocessor commands by type of action. **Appendix D** summarizes the standard library I/O functions. **Appendix E** summarizes standard C formatted I/O and conversions. **Appendix F** lists the ASCII codes for both printable and nonprintable characters.

# A

# Standard Keywords

These are C's standard keywords, with brief descriptions of their uses. They are reserved and cannot be used as identifier names.

| KEYWORD | USE | DESCRIPTION |
| --- | --- | --- |
| *auto* | Storage class | For life of function only; the default |
| *break* | Control flow | Command to exit closest enclosing loop or block |
| *case* | Control flow | Choice in the case-like *switch* statement |
| *char* | Data type | 1-byte signed integer |
| *const* | Data type | For variables that cannot change |
| *continue* | Control flow | Command to jump to start of next loop iteration |
| *default* | Control flow | Fall-through case label for *switch* statement |
| *do* | Control flow | Command to begin test at bottom of *do...while* loop |
| *double* | Data type | 8-byte double-precision floating-point value |
| *else* | Control flow | Optional second half of *if* statement |
| *enum* | Data type | Enumerated list of integer-constant names |
| *extern* | Storage class | For import declarations of global variables |
| *float* | Data type | 4-byte single-precision floating-point value |

*(continued)*

*continued*

| KEYWORD | USE | DESCRIPTION |
|---------|-----|-------------|
| *for* | Control flow | Loop with initializer, test, and step |
| *goto* | Control flow | Anachronism and major cause of unreadable code |
| *if* | Control flow | Conditional execution of a statement |
| *int* | Data type | 2- or 4-byte integer (depends on CPU) |
| *long* | Data type | 4-byte long integer |
| *register* | Storage class | For faster memory (request only) |
| *return* | Control flow | Command to jump back to caller function (after call) |
| *short* | Data type | 2-byte short integer |
| *signed* | Data type | For *char, short, int*, and *long* variables that may be negative |
| *sizeof* | Operator | Number of bytes in expression or type |
| *static* | Storage class | For life of program; can be shared |
| *struct* | Data type | For combining elements of different data types |
| *switch* | Control flow | Command to choose one from any number of listed actions |
| *typedef* | Data type | For definition of a synonym data type |
| *union* | Data type | Like *struct*, but members are at same address |
| *unsigned* | Data type | Modifier in declarations; never negative |
| *void* | Data type | For function declarations and definitions |
| *volatile* | Not used | |
| *while* | Control flow | Conditional execution of statements in *while* and *do...while* loops |

# Table of Operators

These are C's operators, in descending order of precedence. The L (for left to right) or R (for right to left) after the precedence number indicates the grouping order of the operator.

| PRECEDENCE | TYPE | OPERATOR | NAME | EXAMPLE |
|---|---|---|---|---|
| 15L | Primary | () | Parentheses | *len = (end−beg) * len;* |
| | | [] | Subscript | *elem = array[index_val];* |
| | | −> | Arrow | *val = struct_ptr −> member;* |
| | | . | Dot | *val = structure.member;* |
| 14R | Unary | ! | Logical not | *more = !done;* |
| | | ~ | Bitwise NOT | *all_bits_on = ~0;* |
| | | ++ | Increment | *++count;* |
| | | −− | Decrement | *while (count_down−−)* |
| | | − | Negative | *minus =−pos;* |
| | | (type) | Cast | *r2 = sqrt((double) area);* |
| | | * | Indirection | *obj = *ptr_to_type;* |
| | | & | Address of | *ptr_to_type = & obj;* |
| | | sizeof | Size of | *int_size = sizeof (int);* *arr_size = sizeof array;* |

*(continued)*

*continued*

| PRECEDENCE | TYPE | OPERATOR | NAME | EXAMPLE |
|---|---|---|---|---|
| 13L | Arith-metic | * | Multiplication | *product = first * last;* |
| | | / | Division | *div = top / bottom;* |
| | | % | Remainder (modulus) | *is_odd = num % 2;* |
| 12L | Arith-metic | + | Addition | *sum = prev + next;* |
| | | − | Subtraction | *diff = current − prev;* |
| 11L | Bitwise | << | Left shift | *lsb_to_msb = val << 8;* |
| | | >> | Right shift | *high_byte = val >> 8;* |
| 10L | Relational | > | Greater than | *if (curr > prev)* |
| | | >= | Greater than or equal to | *positive = (num >= 0);* |
| | | < | Less than | *for (i = 0; i < hi; ++i)* |
| | | <= | Less than or equal to | *for (i = 1; i <= hi; ++i)* |
| 9L | Relational | == | Equal to | *if (cur == 5 ¦¦ prv == 1)* |
| | | != | Not equal to | *while (state != DONE)* |
| 8L | Bitwise | & | Bitwise AND | *mst_sig_bit = chr & 0x80;* |
| 7L | Bitwise | ^ | Exclusive OR (XOR) | *ms_bit_rev = chr ^ 0x80;* |
| 6L | Bitwise | ¦ | Bitwise OR | *low_bit_set = chr ¦ 0x1;* |
| 5L | Logical | && | Logical and | *if (x > low && x < hi)* |
| 4L | Logical | ¦¦ | Logical or | *if (c < ' ' ¦¦ c > '~')* |
| 3R | Condi-tional | ?: | Then, else | *max_ab = a > b ? a : b;* |
| 2R | Assign-ment | = | Assign-ment | *variable = value;* |
| 2R | Assign-ment | +=, /= (see next table) | Shorthand assignment | *total += amount;* *reading /= SCALE;* |
| 1L | Sequence | , | Comma | *++right, ++score;* |

This is the complete list of assignment shorthand operators.

| TYPE | OPERATOR |
|---|---|
| Arithmetic | +=, −=, *=, /=, %= |
| Bitwise | <<=, >>=, &=, ^=, ¦= |

# Preprocessor Summary

All preprocessor commands are executed one per line. They begin with a pound sign (#) and can be continued on the following line by using a backslash (\). The conditional compilation commands are used to control a combination of one or more C statements and other preprocessor statements. This list groups the preprocessor commands by application.

Commands to add, replace, or remove definitions of identifiers:

| COMMAND | ACTION |
| --- | --- |
| *#define IDENTIFIER definition* | Replaces all subsequent uses of the name *IDENTIFIER* by the definition text |
| *#define MACRO(x, y) (expansion statement using (x) and (y))* | Replaces all subsequent uses of *MACRO* (plus its two arguments) with the expansion (with arguments substituted in it) |
| *#undef IDENTIFIER* | Removes the definition of the symbol or macro named *IDENTIFIER* |

Commands to insert the contents of another file:

| COMMAND | ACTION |
| --- | --- |
| *#include <pathname>* | Replaces itself with the contents of the file *pathname.* The file is searched for in all the "standard" places |
| *#include "pathname"* | Replaces itself with the contents of the file *pathname.* The file is searched for only in the current directory |

Conditional compilation of preprocessor commands or C statements:

| COMMAND | ACTION |
| --- | --- |
| *#if restricted_const_expr* | Compiles lines that follow only if *restricted_const_expr* is non-zero |
| *#ifdef ID* | Compiles lines that follow if *ID* is a defined symbol or the name of a macro |
| *#ifndef ID* | Compiles lines that follow if *ID* is not defined as a symbol or the name of a macro |
| *#else* | Ends one of the above *#if*-type commands and compiles lines that follow if the condition tested for did not hold |
| *#endif* | Ends the closest unclosed group of lines beginning with an *#if*-type command or an *#else* |

Microsoft and ANSI extensions to conditional compilation:

| COMMAND | ACTION |
| --- | --- |
| *#if defined(ID)* | Compiles lines that follow if *ID* is defined as a symbol or as the name of a macro. Is equivalent to *#ifdef ID* |
| *#elif restricted_const_expr* | Compiles lines that follow if the condition in the *#if*-type or *#elif* command before it was zero and the condition here is non-zero. Can be chained to a single *#if*-type or *#elif* command |
| *#elif defined(ID2)* | Like *#elif,* but tests whether *ID2* is a defined symbol or a macro name |

# APPENDIX D

# Standard I/O Library Functions

These standard library functions perform stream-oriented input and output. The first two groups of functions output to the standard output stream, *stdout*, and input from the standard input stream, *stdin*. The rest can be used with any stream, once it has been opened using *fopen()*.

Functions that send output to *stdout*:

| COMMAND | ACTION |
|---------|--------|
| *int putchar(c)* | Outputs a character |
| *char puts(str)* | Outputs a string, appends '\n' |
| *int printf(fmt, ...)* | Outputs formatted data |

Functions that obtain input from *stdin*:

| COMMAND | ACTION |
| --- | --- |
| *int getchar()* | Inputs a character and returns it as an integer. Returns *EOF* for attempts to read beyond end of data |
| *char \*gets(str)* | Inputs a line, replaces *'\n'* with *'\0'*. Returns *NULL* for attempts to read beyond end of data |
| *int scanf( fmt, ...)* | Inputs formatted data |

Functions that open or close a stream:

| COMMAND | ACTION |
| --- | --- |
| *FILE \*fopen(path, mode)* | Opens a stream for the file *path*, in specified mode (*"r"* for read, *"w"* for write, or *"a"* for append, with optional + for update and *b* for binary mode) |
| *int fclose(stream)* | Closes a stream and flushes its buffer |

Functions that send output to a stream:

| COMMAND | ACTION |
| --- | --- |
| *int fputc(c, stream)* | Outputs a character *c* to a stream |
| *int fputs(str, stream)* | Outputs a string *str* to a stream |
| *int fprintf(stream, fmt, ...)* | Outputs formatted data to a stream |

Functions that obtain input from a stream:

| COMMAND | ACTION |
| --- | --- |
| *int fgetc(stream)* | Inputs a character from a stream |
| *char \*fgets(str, n, stream)* | Inputs at most *n−1* characters from a stream into the string *str* |
| *int fscanf(stream, fmt, ...)* | Inputs formatted data from a stream |

# Formatted I/O and Conversions

The formatted I/O functions *printf()*, *fprintf()*, *sprintf()*, *scanf()*, *fscanf()*, and *sscanf()* convert and input or output data according to the literal text and format specifiers contained in the format string.

## Formatted Output or Output Conversions

All three of the output functions convert their arguments from internal binary format to an ASCII string.

| FUNCTION | ACTION |
|---|---|
| *printf( fmt, …)* | Sends formatted output to *stdout* |
| *fprintf(stream, fmt, …)* | Sends formatted output to *stream* |
| *sprintf(str, fmt, …)* | Converts data to specified format and returns it in string *str* |

The *fmt* argument specifies the number and types of arguments that follow it, as well as how they should be formatted for output. If the type width is too narrow to display the data, it is ignored. The format string holds literal text and 0 or more format specifiers that use this syntax:

%[-][w][.p][m]t

These option symbols have the following meanings:

| | |
|---|---|
| *[-]* | Left justification (default is right justification) |
| *[w]* | Width of field, or * to obtain width in next argument (width with leading zero gives output with leading zero) |
| *[.p]* | Precision (places to right of decimal point), or maximum output width if used for string output |
| *[m]* | Modifier; *l* stands for long, *h* for short, *N* for near pointer, *F* for far pointer (N and P are Microsoft extensions) |
| *t* | Data type: *d* for decimal, *u* for unsigned decimal, *o* for octal, *x* for hex, *f* for floating-point decimal, *e* for floating-point scientific, *c* for character, or *s* for string |

Here are some examples of the formatted output functions:

| FUNCTION CALL | RESULT |
|---|---|
| *printf("%09ld", x)* | Outputs the *long x* as a 9-digit decimal number with leading zeros |
| *printf("%*d", w, n)* | Outputs *n* as a decimal integer, right justified in a field *w* characters wide |
| *printf("%.2f", dbl)* | Outputs the double *dbl* with two decimal places |
| *printf("%-30.25s", t)* | Outputs up to 25 characters of string *t*, left justified in a field 30 characters wide |
| *printf("%-*.*s", w, p, t)* | Outputs at most *p* characters of string *t*, left justified in a field *w* characters wide |

# Formatted Input or Input Conversions

All of the input functions use the format passed to them to determine how to input and store data. Scalar parameters must be passed by address.

| FUNCTION | ACTION |
| --- | --- |
| *int scanf( fmt, ... )* | Inputs formatted data from *stdin* |
| *int fscanf(stream, fmt, ...)* | Inputs formatted data from *stream* |
| *int sscanf(str, fmt, ...)* | Converts data from string *str* to specified format |

The format specifiers for input differ slightly from those for output. With *scanf()*, formats must distinguish between *float* and *double*, and between *short* and *int*. The return value from *scanf()* is the number of successfully converted and assigned fields, or *EOF* for attempts to read beyond the end of the file. The syntax for an input format specifier is:

%[w][m]t

These option symbols have the following meanings:

| | |
| --- | --- |
| *[w]* | Width of field |
| *[m]* | Modifier; *l* stands for *long*, *h* for *short*, *N* for near pointer, *F* for far pointer (N and P are Microsoft extensions) |
| *t* | Data type: *d* for decimal, *u* for unsigned decimal, *o* for octal, *x* for hex, *f* for floating-point decimal, *e* for floating-point scientific, *c* for character, *s* for string, or *p* for *far* pointer to *void* |

Here are some examples of the formatted input functions:

| FUNCTION CALL | RESULT |
| --- | --- |
| *scanf(" %hd %ld", &x, &y)* | Inputs a *short* for *x* and a *long* for *y* |
| *scanf(" %9lu", &lng)* | Inputs up to 9 digits, unsigned *long*, to *lng* |
| *scanf(" %c %s", &ch, str)* | Inputs first character to *ch* and next string of non-white space to *str* |

Note: The *%c* format specifier does not cause *scanf()* to skip leading spaces; instead, it inputs the next character, no matter what it is. If you want to input a single character, skipping any leading spaces, use *%1s*.

# Table of ASCII Codes

ASCII is a set of values that represent printable characters and characters used to control output devices such as printers and terminals. These characters can be represented using 7 bits, which means that there are 128 different ASCII characters, with decimal values from 0 through 127. The characters from 32 (space) through 126 (~) are printable; the other 33 characters are not.

## Nonprinting ASCII Characters

This table lists the nonprinting characters, including the keyboard keys used to produce each character (^ means control: ^G stands for control-G).

| DECIMAL | KEY | HEX | OCTAL | ESCAPE SEQUENCE | NAME |
|---|---|---|---|---|---|
| 0 | ^@ | '\x00' | '\000' | | NULL |
| 1 | ^A | '\x01' | '\001' | | SOH |
| 2 | ^B | '\x02' | '\002' | | STX |
| 3 | ^C | '\x03' | '\003' | | ETX |
| 4 | ^D | '\x04' | '\004' | | EOT |
| 5 | ^E | '\x05' | '\005' | | ENQ |
| 6 | ^F | '\x06' | '\006' | | ACK |
| 7 | ^G | '\x07' | '\007' | '\a' | BELL |
| 8 | ^H | 'x08' | '010' | '\b' | BKSPC |
| 9 | ^I | 'x09' | '011' | '\t' | HZTAB |
| 10 | ^J | 'x0a' | '012' | '\n' | NEWLN |
| 11 | ^K | 'x0b' | '013' | '\v' | VTAB |
| 12 | ^L | 'x0c' | '014' | '\f' | FF |
| 13 | ^M | 'x0d' | '015' | '\r' | CR |
| 14 | ^N | '\x0e' | '\016' | | SO |
| 15 | ^O | '\x0f' | '\017' | | SI |
| 16 | ^P | '\x10' | '\020' | | DLE |
| 17 | ^Q | '\x11' | '\021' | | DC1 |
| 18 | ^R | '\x12' | '\022' | | DC2 |
| 19 | ^S | '\x13' | '\023' | | DC3 |
| 20 | ^T | '\x14' | '\024' | | DC4 |
| 21 | ^U | '\x15' | '\025' | | NAK |
| 22 | ^V | '\x16' | '\026' | | SYN |
| 23 | ^W | '\x17' | '\027' | | ETB |
| 24 | ^X | '\x18' | '\030' | | CAN |
| 25 | ^Y | '\x19' | '\031' | | EM |
| 26 | ^Z | '\x1a' | '\032' | | SUB |
| 27 | ESC | '\x1b' | '\033' | | ESC |
| 28 | | '\x1c' | '\034' | | FS |
| 29 | | '\x1d' | '\035' | | GS |
| 30 | | '\x1e' | '\036' | | RS |
| 31 | | '\x1f' | '\037' | | US |
| 127 | DEL | '\x7f' | '\177' | | DEL |

# Printable ASCII Characters

This table lists the characters that output the familiar uppercase and lowercase letters of the alphabet, numeric digits, and punctuation that combine to form the set of printable ASCII characters.

| DECIMAL | KEY | HEXADECIMAL | OCTAL |
|---|---|---|---|
| 32 | (spacebar) | '\x20' | '\040' |
| 33 | ! | '\x21' | '\041' |
| 34 | " | '\x22' | '\042' |
| 35 | # | '\x23' | '\043' |
| 36 | $ | '\x24' | '\044' |
| 37 | % | '\x25' | '\045' |
| 38 | & | '\x26' | '\046' |
| 39 | ' | '\x27' | '\047' |
| 40 | ( | '\x28' | '\050' |
| 41 | ) | '\x29' | '\051' |
| 42 | * | '\x2a' | '\052' |
| 43 | + | '\x2b' | '\053' |
| 44 | , | '\x2c' | '\054' |
| 45 | − | '\x2d' | '\055' |
| 46 | . | '\x2e' | '\056' |
| 47 | / | '\x2f' | '\057' |
| 48 | 0 | '\x30' | '\060' |
| 49 | 1 | '\x31' | '\061' |
| 50 | 2 | '\x32' | '\062' |
| 51 | 3 | '\x33' | '\063' |
| 52 | 4 | '\x34' | '\064' |
| 53 | 5 | '\x35' | '\065' |
| 54 | 6 | '\x36' | '\066' |
| 55 | 7 | '\x37' | '\067' |
| 56 | 8 | '\x38' | '\070' |
| 57 | 9 | '\x39' | '\071' |
| 58 | : | '\x3a' | '\072' |
| 59 | ; | '\x3b' | '\073' |
| 60 | < | '\x3c' | '\074' |
| 61 | = | '\x3d' | '\075' |
| 62 | > | '\x3e' | '\076' |

*(continued)*

*continued*

| DECIMAL | KEY | HEXADECIMAL | OCTAL |
| --- | --- | --- | --- |
| 63 | ? | '\x3f' | '\077' |
| 64 | @ | '\x40' | '\100' |
| 65 | A | '\x41' | '\101' |
| 66 | B | '\x42' | '\102' |
| 67 | C | '\x43' | '\103' |
| 68 | D | '\x44' | '\104' |
| 69 | E | '\x45' | '\105' |
| 70 | F | '\x46' | '\106' |
| 71 | G | '\x47' | '\107' |
| 72 | H | '\x48' | '\110' |
| 73 | I | '\x49' | '\111' |
| 74 | J | '\x4a' | '\112' |
| 75 | K | '\x4b' | '\113' |
| 76 | L | '\x4c' | '\114' |
| 77 | M | '\x4d' | '\115' |
| 78 | N | '\x4e' | '\116' |
| 79 | O | '\x4f' | '\117' |
| 80 | P | '\x50' | '\120' |
| 81 | Q | '\x51' | '\121' |
| 82 | R | '\x52' | '\122' |
| 83 | S | '\x53' | '\123' |
| 84 | T | '\x54' | '\124' |
| 85 | U | '\x55' | '\125' |
| 86 | V | '\x56' | '\126' |
| 87 | W | '\x57' | '\127' |
| 88 | X | '\x58' | '\130' |
| 89 | Y | '\x59' | '\131' |
| 90 | Z | '\x5a' | '\132' |
| 91 | [ | '\x5b' | '\133' |
| 92 | \ | '\x5c' | '\134' |
| 93 | ] | '\x5d' | '\135' |
| 94 | ^ | '\x5e' | '\136' |
| 95 | _ | '\x5f' | '\137' |
| 96 | ` | '\x60' | '\140' |
| 97 | a | '\x61' | '\141' |

*(continued)*

*continued*

| DECIMAL | KEY | HEXADECIMAL | OCTAL |
|---------|-----|-------------|-------|
| 98 | b | '\x62' | '\142' |
| 99 | c | '\x63' | '\143' |
| 100 | d | '\x64' | '\144' |
| 101 | e | '\x65' | '\145' |
| 102 | f | '\x66' | '\146' |
| 103 | g | '\x67' | '\147' |
| 104 | h | '\x68' | '\150' |
| 105 | i | '\x69' | '\151' |
| 106 | j | '\x6a' | '\152' |
| 107 | k | '\x6b' | '\153' |
| 108 | l | '\x6c' | '\154' |
| 109 | m | '\x6d' | '\155' |
| 110 | n | '\x6e' | '\156' |
| 111 | o | '\x6f' | '\157' |
| 112 | p | '\x70' | '\160' |
| 113 | q | '\x71' | '\161' |
| 114 | r | '\x72' | '\162' |
| 115 | s | '\x73' | '\163' |
| 116 | t | '\x74' | '\164' |
| 117 | u | '\x75' | '\165' |
| 118 | v | '\x76' | '\166' |
| 119 | w | '\x77' | '\167' |
| 120 | x | '\x78' | '\170' |
| 121 | y | '\x79' | '\171' |
| 122 | z | '\x7a' | '\172' |
| 123 | { | '\x7b' | '\173' |
| 124 | ¦ | '\x7c' | '\174' |
| 125 | } | '\x7d' | '\175' |
| 126 | ~ | '\x7e' | '\176' |

# Index

## Special Characters

! logical *NOT* operator 31, 47, 393

!= relational not-equal operator 31, 46

" string constant delimiter 15

*#define* preprocessor command
   defined symbols with 78–79, 80
   definitions to avoid 80–81
   definitions with defined symbols 80
   in header files 93
   macros 81–85
   syntax for 78
   variable names with 81

*#elif* preprocessor command 87

*#error* preprocessor directive 97–98

*#ifdef* preprocessor command 90

*#ifndef* preprocessor command 90

*#if* preprocessor command 85–87

*#include* preprocessor command 70, 92–93, 97

*#pragma* commands 97

# preprocessor commands, beginning of 78, 395

# stringizing operator 84–85

*#undef* preprocessor command 91

## token-pasting operator 85

% arithmetic remainder (modulo) operator 31, 37, 394

% I/O function format specifier 23, 24, 42, 219, 401

%= arithmetic remainder (modulo) assignment operator 394

& bitwise *AND* operator 31, 32, 337, 338, 339, 394

& unary address-of operator 25, 31, 49, 206, 212, 224, 263, 265, 266, 393

&& logical *AND* operator 31, 47, 394

&= bitwise *AND* assignment operator 37, 394

' character constant delimiter 31

() with function-call argument list 66

() with function-definition parameter list 68

() grouping operator in expressions 31, 393

() in macro definitions 82

() unary cast operator 206, 329

∗ arithmetic multiplication operator 31, 264, 394

∗ pointer declaration symbol 31, 264–65

∗ unary indirection operator 267, 268, 295, 393

∗ wildcard 284

∗/ comment end delimiter 12, 15, 40, 41, 46, 47, 49, 68, 86, 106, 109, 264, 301

∗= arithmetic multiplication assignment operator 37, 41, 394

+ arithmetic addition operator 31, 83, 394

+ update mode for *fopen()* 302, 398

++ unary increment operator 31, 39–40, 47, 393

+= arithmetic addition assignment operator 31, 37, 394

, *comma* sequence operator 31, 38, 39, 394

, in enumeration list 185

, in initializer list 105

– arithmetic subtraction operator 31, 394

– unary minus operator 20, 31, 393

–– unary decrement operator 31, 39–40, 42, 47, 268, 393

–= arithmetic subtraction assignment operator 31, 37, 394

–> arrow (structure-member pointer) operator 31, 295, 362, 369, 393

. dot (structure-member) operator 291, 362, 393

/ arithmetic division operator 31, 394

# X

# Z

**STEVE SCHUSTACK**

After completing his bachelor of arts degree in mathematics at the State University of New York at Binghamton, Steve Schustack studied computer science under Gerald Weinberg at SUNY's School of Advanced Technology. Schustack has worked as a systems programmer at Argonne National Laboratory, has written programs for the United States Navy, and has served as a senior designer of electronic publishing software at Xerox Corporation. He has also conducted seminars on professional C programming for major corporations all over the country.

Schustack now conducts corporate seminars that teach the concepts and methods of object-oriented programming. As an independent consultant, he works with clients to design and implement solutions to their problems. For more information, Schustack can be contacted at P.O. Box 99161, San Diego, CA 92109.

The manuscript for this book was prepared and submitted to
Microsoft Press in electronic form. Text files were processed and
formatted using Microsoft Word.

Cover design by Thomas A. Draper
Interior text design by Darcie S. Furlan
Illustrations by Becky Geisler-Johnson
Principal typography by Lisa Iversen
Color separations by Rainier Color

Text composition by Microsoft Press in New Baskerville with
display in Helvetica Condensed, using the Magna composition system
and the Linotronic 300 laser imagesetter.

# *Hardcore Computer Books*

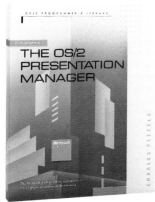
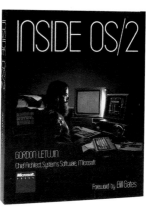

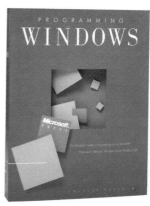

# Solid Technical Information. Expert Advice.

## ADVANCED MS-DOS® PROGRAMMING, 2nd ed.
*Ray Duncan*

The preeminent source of MS-DOS information for assembly-language and C programmers — now completely updated with new data and programming advice covering: ROM BIOS for the IBM PC, PC/AT, PS/2, and related peripherals; MS-DOS through version 4; version 4 of the LIM EMS; and OS/2 compatibility considerations. Duncan addresses key topics, including character devices, mass storage, memory allocation and management, and process management. In addition, there is a healthy assortment of updated assembly-language and C listings that range from code fragments to complete utilities. And the reference section, detailing each MS-DOS function and interrupt, is virtually a book within a book.
**$24.95    [Book Code 86-96668]**

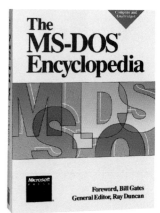

## THE MS-DOS® ENCYCLOPEDIA

The ultimate reference for insight, data, and advice to make your MS-DOS programs reliable, robust, and efficient. 1600 pages packed with version-specific data. Annotations of more than 100 system function calls, 90 user commands, and a host of key programming utilities. Hundreds of hands-on examples, thousands of lines of code, and handy indexes. Plus articles on debugging, writing filters, installable device drivers, TSRs, Windows, memory management, the future of MS-DOS, and much more. Researched and written by a team of MS-DOS experts — many involved in the creation and development of MS-DOS. Covers MS-DOS through version 3.2, with a special section on version 3.3.
**$134.95 (hc)   [Book Code 86-96122]**
**$69.95 (sc)   [Book Code 86-96833]**

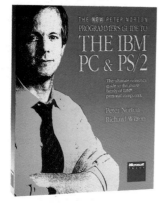

## THE *NEW* PETER NORTON PROGRAMMER'S GUIDE TO THE IBM PC® & PS/2®
*Peter Norton and Richard Wilton*

A must-have classic on mastering the inner workings of IBM microcomputers — now completely updated to include the PS/2 line. Sharpen your programming skills and learn to create simple, clean, portable programs with this successful combination of astute programming advice, proven techniques, and solid technical data. Covers the microprocessors; ROM BIOS basics and ROM BIOS services; video, disk and keyboard basics; DOS basics, interrupts, and functions (through version 4); device drivers and video programming; and programming in C, QuickBasic, and TurboPascal. Accept no substitutes; this is the book to have.
**$22.95    [Book Code 86-96635]**

## MICROSOFT® MOUSE PROGRAMMER'S REFERENCE
*Microsoft Press*

The MICROSOFT MOUSE PROGRAMMER'S REFERENCE — from the hardware experts at Microsoft — is a complete guide to providing mouse support in all your MS-DOS® programs. Both an essential reference to the mouse programming interface and a handbook for writing functional Mouse menus, this one-of-a-kind guide includes: ■ ready-to-run Mouse Menu programs ■ a complete reference to the mouse function calls ■ specifics on writing mouse programs for IBM EGA modes ■ the Microsoft InPort® technical specification. Two 5.25-inch companion disks include sample Mouse menus, MOUSE.LIB and EGA.LIB, and a collection of valuable programming examples in Microsoft QuickBASIC, interpreted BASIC, Microsoft QuickC, Microsoft C, Pascal, Microsoft Macro Assembler, and FORTRAN.
**$29.95    [Book Code 86-97005]**

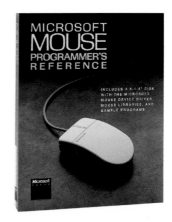

*Available wherever books and software are sold. Or order directly from Microsoft Press.*

# Unbeatable Programmers' References

## THE PROGRAMMER'S PC SOURCEBOOK
*Thom Hogan*

Here is important factual information — previously published in scores of other sources — organized into one convenient reference. Focusing on IBM PCs and compatibles, PS/2s and MS-DOS, the hundreds of charts and tables cover: ■ numeric conversions and character sets ■ DOS commands and utilities ■ DOS function calls and support tables ■ DOS BIOS calls and support tables ■ other interrupts, mouse, and EMS support ■ keyboards, video adapters, and peripherals ■ chips, jumpers, switches, and registers ■ and more. **$24.95   [Book Code 86-96296]**

## PROGRAMMER'S GUIDE TO PC® & PS/2® VIDEO SYSTEMS
*Richard Wilton*

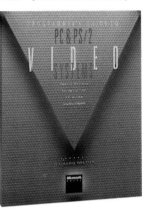

No matter what your hardware configuration, here is all the information you need to create fast, professional, even stunning video graphics on IBM PCs, compatibles, and PS/2s. No other book offers such detailed, specialized programming data, techniques, and advice to help you program directly to the hardware. And no other book offers such invaluable source code examples. Whatever graphic output you want — text, circles, region fill, alphanumeric character sets, bit blocks, animation — the info is here.   **$24.95  [Book Code 86-96163]**

## THE MICROSOFT® QUICKBASIC PROGRAMMER'S TOOLBOX
*John Clark Craig*

This essential library of subprograms, functions, and utilities designed to supercharge your QuickBASIC programs addresses common *and* unusual programming tasks: ANSI.SYS screen control ■ mouse support ■ pop-up windows ■ graphics ■ string manipulations ■ bit manipulation ■ editing routines ■ game programming ■ interlanguage calling ■ and more. You're guaranteed to turn to this superb collection again and again   **$22.95  [Book Code 86-96403]**

*Available wherever books and software are sold.*
*Or order directly from Microsoft Press.*

# Programmer's Quick References

At last! Now you can have instant access key programming information. Whet you're an assembly-language or C progra mer, you'll find these books exceptionally u ful. The guides include overviews of each s vice along with a list of the parameters arguments the service requires, the results returns, version dependencies, and valuable program-ming notes and warnings. All at your fingertips!

## IBM® ROM BIOS
*Ray Duncan*
All the core information on each
of the ROM BIOS services.
**$5.95   [Book Code 86-96478]**

## MS-DOS FUNCTIONS
*Ray Duncan*
Covers DOS through version 3.3.
**$5.95   [Book Code 86-96411]**

## ESSENTIAL OS/2 FUNCTIONS
*Ray Duncan*
Great for anyone involved in OS/2
application programming! Here is the
most accurate, up-to-date information
on the OS/2 1.0 Kernel functions calls
within the applications
program interface (API).
**$9.95   [Book Code 86-96866]**